AMAZING NORTHEAST

ASSAM

AMAZING NORTHEAST

ASSAM

Edited & Compiled by
Aribam Indubala Devi

Vij Books India Pvt. Ltd.
(Publishers, Dustributors & Importers)

4675-A, 21, Ansari Road, Darya Ganj,
New Delhi-110002

Published by
Vij Books India Pvt. Ltd.
(Publishers, Distributors & Importers)
4675-A, 21, Ansari Road, Darya Ganj,
New Delhi-110002
Phone: 91-11-65449971, 91-11-43596460
Fax: 91-11-47340674
E-mail: vijbooks@rediffmail.com

First Edition: 2010

ISBN: 978-93-80177-24-3

Contents

Preface

In India, the Northeastern region is quite charming and interesting enough to be known about. Among the eight Northeastern States, Assam is the scout of the area and gateway to the eight States. The State is close to India's international borders, with Bangladesh and Bhutan. Assam is surrounded by Bhutan and Arunachal Pradesh on north, Manipur, Nagaland and Arunachal Pradesh on east and Meghalaya, Tripura and Mizoram on south.

The word 'Assam' as interpreted by some scholars, is derived from the Sanskrit word *Asoma*, meaning peerless or unparalleled. But the widely accepted opinion of the academic circles is that the term has come from the original name of the *Ahoms*, who ruled the land for several hundred years, prior to its annexation by the British. The races like Austric, Mongolian, Dravidian and Aryan that came to this land long ago, have contributed to its composite culture. Thus, Assam has a rich legacy of culture and civilization. Assam was known as Pragjyotisha or the place of eastern astronomy, during the epic period and later named as Kamrupa. The earliest epigraphic reference to the kingdom of Kamrupa is found in the Allahabad pillar inscription of king Samudragupta. Kamrupa is mentioned as a *Pratyanta* or frontier state outside the Gupta empire but with friendly subordinate relations with it.

Hiuen Sang, the Chinese scholar-pilgrim, who visited Kamrupa in about 743 AD on an invitation of its monarch, Kumar Bhaskar Varman, left a record of the kingdom, he called Kamolupa. Kamrupa also figured in the writings of the Arabian historian Alberuni in eleventh century. Thus, from the epic period down to the twelfth century AD, the eastern frontier kingdom was known as Pragjyotisha and Kamrupa and kings called themselves 'Lords of Pragjyotisha'. The advent of the Ahoms across the eastern hills in 1228 AD was the turning point in Assam's history. They ruled Assam for nearly six centuries. The Burmese entered through the eastern borders and overran the territory at a time, when court intrigues and dissensions were sapping the vitality of the Ahom royalty. It became a British protectorate in 1826, when the Burmese ceded Assam to the British under the provision of the Treaty of Yandabo.

This small but comprehensive and compact book on this northeastern state, offers all information, within one cover. Hopefully, it would serve all those working on or interested in knowing about northeastern India, be they scholars, researchers, journalists, students or general readers. This is in fact, 'Knowledge in Nutshell'.

— *Editor*

Assam

An Overview

Governor	:	Janaki Ballav Pattanaik
Chief Minister	:	Tarun Gogoi
Speaker	:	Tanka Bahadur Rai
Chief Secretary	:	P.C. Sharma
Capital	:	Dispur
High Court	:	Guwahati

Brief Description

Assam is the gateway to the Northeastern States and has been aptly described as the sentinel of Northeast India. Seven Indian states and two countries, Bhutan and Bangladesh, surround Assam that lies between 89.5° to 96.1° East longitude and 24.3° to 28.0° North latitude. The State is also strategically close to India's international borders with China and Myanmar. Assam is contiguously surrounded by Bhutan and Arunachal Pradesh on the north, Manipur, Nagaland and Arunachal Pradesh on the east and Bangladesh, Meghalaya, Tripura and Mizoram on the south. With Bangladesh, Assam shares a 262- kilometre-long international boundary.

Facts and Figures

- *Area (sq km):* Total: 78,438 (30% of area of North East); Rural: 77,476 (98.7% of total area of Assam); Urban: 962 (1.3% of total area of Assam)

- *Geographical Location:* Longitude: 89.420E to 96.00E, Latitude: 24.50N to 28.00N

- *Capital:* Dispur (Guwahati)

- *Population:* 2,66,55,528 (2001 Census) (68.2% of population of North East) Male: 13,787,799; Female: 12,850,608

- *Density (per sq km):* 340 (National Figure: 324)

Contd...

In olden times Assam was known as *Pragjyotishpura* or the Land of the eastern lights. In medieval times, it became known as Kamrupa. The present name Assam or Asom is the anglicised name for the State. Spread over an area of 78,438 square kilometres, Assam is the second largest State in the Northeastern Region. It represents 2.39 per cent of the Indian landmass and 29.92 percent of the North-East. The State has two distinct natural regions: the Brahmaputra Valley and the Barak Valley (also known as Surma valley). The Brahmaputra Valley comprises a total area of 71,516 square kilometres and the Barak Valley is spread over 6,922 square kilometres. For administration and revenue purposes, Assam is divided into 27 districts.

According to the Census 2001, Assam has a total population of 2,66,55,528, constituting 2.59 percent of India's total population and 68.24 per cent of the entire North-East. Ranked 14th in terms of total population in India, the State has a population density of 340 (persons per square kilometre). There are 16 Scheduled Castes and 23 Scheduled Tribes constituting 7.40 and 12.82 per cent respectively of the State's population. Bodos are the largest plains tribes in the state. The other tribes include the Karbis, Dimasas, Rabhas, etc.

Assamese is the major language of the State. Other recognised Indian languages spoken in the State include Bengali and Hindi. Languages including Oriya, Mundari, Santhal, Tamil and Telegu are mostly spoken mostly by the five million workers in

- *Hindu:* 1,72,96,455
- *Muslim:* 82,40,611
- *Christians:* 9,86,589
- *Sikhs:* 22,519
- *Buddhists:* 51,029
- *Jains:* 23,957
- *Languages:* Assamese, Hindi, Bengali, Bodo, Mising
- *Sex Ratio:* 935 females to 1,000 males (National figure: 933 females to 1,000 males)
- *Literacy Rate (2007):* 76.3% (National Figure: 67.6%)
- *Per Capita Income (in Rs) (2006-07):* 20166 (National Figure: Rs. 29,901)
- *Net State Domestic Product (NSDP) (Rs. in crore) (2007-08):* 62,852 (National Figure: 38,11,441)
- *Per Capita NSDP (2007-08):* Rs. 21,464 (National Figure: Rs. 33,283)
- *Per Capita GSDP (2004-05):* Rs. 15,661 (National Figure: Rs. 25,944)
- *Birth Rate (2006):* 24.6 (National Figure: 23.1) Death Rate (2006): 8.7 (National Figure: 7.4)
- *Infant Mortality Rate (2007):* 66 (National Figure: 55)
- *No. of Villages:* 26,312 (as per 2001 Census)
- *No. of Towns:* 125 (as per 2001 Census)
- *Population below Poverty Line (2004-05):* 19.7 percent (National Figure: 27.5%)

Contd...

the 800 odd tea gardens spread across the length and breadth of the state, bracketed as the tea tribes. The literacy rate of Assam is 64.28 and it holds the 24th position in this regard among the Indian States. According to the Human Development Report 2001, Assam ranks 26th in human resource development index and 21st in poverty index in India.

The economy of Assam is overwhelmingly agricultural, providing employment to more than half of the state's working class. Assam produces nearly half of the country's total Tea. According to the Census 2001, 52.65 per cent of the total workforce in the state (58.40 per cent in India) is engaged in agricultural and allied activities. Assam's per capita Gross State Domestic Product (GSDP) in 2004-05 in Rupees 15,661 and the per capita Net State Domestic Product in 1999-2000 is Rupees 9,720.

As per Census 2001, out of total population of 2,66,55,528 in Assam, 70,83,046 were main workers, 24,74,018 were marginal workers and 1,70,81,343 were non-workers. Among the male population 42.35 per cent were main workers, 7.58 per cent were marginal workers and 50.07 per cent were non-workers, while among the female population 9.68 per cent were main workers, 11.12 per cent were marginal workers and 79.20 per cent

- *State Bird:* White-winged Wood Duck
- *State Animal:* One-horned Rhino
- *State Flower:* Fox-tailed Orchid
- *No. of Districts:* (27) Tinsukia, Dibrugarh, Sivasagar, Dhemaji, Jorhat, Lakhimpur, Golaghat, Sonitpur, Karbi Anglong, Nagaon, Marigaon, Darrang, Kamrup Rural, Nalbari, Barpeta, Bongaigaon, Goalpara, Kokrajhar, Dhubri, North Cachar Hills, Cachar, Hailakandi, Karimganj, Kamrup Metropolitan, Baksa, Chirang, Udalguri.
- *Major Towns:* Guwahati, Kokrajhar, Nalbari, Bongaigaon, Barpeta, Goalpara, Nagaon, Tezpur, Diphu, Sivasagar, Jorhat, Dibrugarh, Tinisukia, Lakhimpur
- *Major Crops:* Rice, Maize, Wheat, Jute, Cotton, Sugar Cane, Arecanut, Coconut
- *Major Plantations:* Tea, Rubber, Coffee
- *Major Fruits, Vegetables & Spices:* Banana, Pineapple, Orange, Potato, Sweet Potato, Papaya, Cabbage, Onion, Tapioca
- *Major Minerals:* Coal, Limestone, Petroleum, Granite, Sillimanite, Iron ore, Quartzite, Feldspar, Clay
- *Airports:* Lokapriya Gopinath Bordoloi International Airport, Salnibari, Roroia, Mohanabari, Lilabari, Kumbhirgram

were non-workers. Similarly, out of a total 95,57,064 workers in Assam, 37,41,912 were cultivators, 12,89,902 were agricultural labourers, 328541 worked in household industries and 41,96,709 belonged to the Other Workers category.

Assam is very rich in natural resources such as oil and natural gas, coal, rubber, tea and minerals. Abundant water resources in the State form the potential for irrigation and generation of hydroelectricity. Its forests too are the storehouses for quality timber.

However, the state is a classic case of high potential and low achievement. Underutilisation of the resources has resulted in the underdevelopment of the state and its poor economy. The state, on the other hand, has struggled to equally distribute the available limited resources equitably among the populace of the state. The problem has further contributed to the rise of several insurgency movements in the state based on ethnicity.

Area, Population and Headquarters of Districts

S.No.	District	Area (sq km)	Population (in Lakh)	Headquarters
1.	Barpeta	3,245	1,647,201	Barpeta
2.	Bongaigaon	2,510	904,835	Bongaigaon
3.	Cachar	3,786	1,444,921	Silchar
4.	Darrang	3,481	1,504,320	Mangaldai
5.	Dhemaji	3,237	571,944	Dhemaji
6.	Dhubri	2,798	1,637,344	Dhubur
7.	Dibrugarh	3,381	1,185,072	Dibrugarh
8.	Goalpara	1,824	822,035	Goalpara
9.	Golaghat	3,502	946,279	Golaghat
10.	Hailakandi	1,327	542,872	Hailakandi
11.	Jorhat	2,851	999,221	Jorhat
12.	Kamrup	4,345	2,522,324	Guwahati
13.	Karbi Anglong	10,434	813,311	Diphu
14.	Karimganj	1,809	1,007,976	Karimganj
15.	Kokrajhar	3,169	905,764	Kokrajhar
16.	Lakhimpur	2,277	889,010	Lakhimpur
17.	Marigaon	1,704	776,256	Marigaon
18.	Nagaon	3,831	2,314,629	Nagaon
19.	Nalbari	2,257	1,148,824	Nalbari
20.	North Cachar Hills	4,888	188,079	Haflong
21.	Sivasagar	2,668	1,051,736	Sibsagar
22.	Sonitpur	5,324	1,681,513	Tezpur
23.	Tinsukia	3,790	1,150,062	Tinsukia
24.	Kamrup Metro	1,272	212,635	Guwahati
25.	Udalguri	1,852	760,644	Udalguri
26.	Baksa	2,400	862,552	Mushalpur
27.	Chirang	1,469	454,208	Kajalgaon

[Based on Latest Official Data Available]

Assam

Outline Map

Geographical Map

Tourist Map

Districts of the State

Introduction

Assam is a Northeastern State of India with its capital at Dispur, in the outskirts of the city Guwahati. Located south of the eastern Himalayas, Assam comprises the Brahmaputra and the Barak River valleys and the Karbi Anglong and the North Cachar Hills with an area of 30,285 square 78,438 km.

Assam currently is almost equivalent to the size of Ireland or Austria. It is surrounded by the rest of the *North-East States:* Arunachal Pradesh, Manipur, Mizoram, Meghalaya, Nagaland, Sikkim and Tripura. These states are connected to the rest of India via a narrow strip in West Bengal called the Siliguri Corridor or 'Chicken's Neck'. Assam also shares international borders with Bhutan and Bangladesh; and cultures, peoples and climate with South East Asia — important elements in India's Look East policy. Assam became a part of British India after the British occupied the region following the Treaty of Yandaboo of 1826. Assam is known for Assam tea, petroleum resources, Assam silk and for its rich biodiversity. It has successfully conserved the one-horned Indian rhinoceros from near extinction, tiger, numerous species of birds and provides one of the last wild habitats for the Asian elephant. It is increasingly becoming a popular destination for wildlife tourism and notably Kaziranga and Manas are both World Heritage Sites. Assam was also known for its Sal tree forests and forest products, much depleted now. A land of high rainfall, Assam is endowed with lush greenery and the mighty River Brahmaputra, whose tributaries and oxbow lakes provide the region with a unique hydro-geomorphic and aesthetic environment.

Etymology

Assam was known as Pragjyotisha in the Mahabharata; and Kamarupa in the 1st millennium. Assam gets its name from the Ahom Kingdom (1228-1826), then known as

Kingdom of Assam. The British province after 1838 and the Indian state after 1947 came to be known as *Assam*.

On February 27, 2006, the Government of Assam started a process to change the name of the state to *Asom*, a controversial move that has been opposed by the people and political organisations.

Significance of State

Assam belongs to the Eight Sister Region of Northeast India, which consists of Arunachal Pradesh, Meghalaya, Manipur, Mizoram, Nagaland, Tripura and Sikkim. A part of the rich northeastern legacy of India, the bountiful land of Assam consists of magnificent hills and valleys and mighty rivers like the Brahmaputra and Barak. It is well known for its picturesque beauty, it's rich blend of crops and variety of minerals.

Assam possibly has more folklore and tradition than any other place in India. There are archaeological ruins all over Assam but the ones around Sibsagar simply must be seen. The largest river island of the world, Manjuli, is a must too along with Kaziranga wildlife sanctuary. Crossing the magnificent Brahmaputra so deeply linked to life in Assam, one reaches Guwahati, the capital where the famous Kamakhya Temple is located on a hilltop. Guwahati has evolved into a major business centre and most of the travel linkages pass through it. The state of Assam has been badly affected by armed insurgency over the last one and a half decades with various insurgent groups in action.

Historical Aspects

The history of Assam is the history of a confluence of peoples from the east, west and the north; the confluence of the Indo-Aryan, Austro-Asiatic and Tibeto-Burman cultures. Politically, it has been invaded, but has never served as a vassal or a colony to an external power till the advent of the Burmese in 1821 and subsequently the British in 1826.

The history of Assam is known from many sources. The Ahom Kingdom of medieval Assam maintained chronicles, called *Buranjis*, written in the Ahom and the Assamese languages. History of ancient Assam comes from rock inscriptions and the many copper plates and royal grants the Kamarupa Kings issued during their reign. Protohistory is reconstructed from folklore, epics like Mahabharata, and two medieval texts compiled in the Assam region — the Kalika Purana and the Yogini Tantra.

Pre-historic Period

Assam and adjoining regions have evidences of human settlements from all the periods of the Stone Ages. The hills at the height of 1,500-2,000 feet (460 to 615 m) were popular habitats probably due to availability of exposed doleritic basalt useful for tool-making.

According to Kalika Purana (c.17-18th AD), written in Assam, the earliest ruler was Mahiranga followed by Hatak, Sambar, Ratna and Ghatak; Naraka removed this line of rulers and established his own dynasty. It mentions that the last of the Naraka-Bhauma rulers, Narak, was slain by Krishna. Naraka's son Bhagadatta, mentioned in the Mahabharata, fought for the Kauravas in the battle of Kurukshetra with an army of *kiratas*, *chinas* and *dwellers of the eastern coast*. Later, rulers of Kamarupa frequently drew their lineage from the Naraka rulers. However, there are lots of evidences to say that Mahayana Buddhism was prominent in ancient Assam. After Hiuen Tsang's visit Mahayana Buddhism came to Assam. Relics of Tezpur, Malini Than, Kamakhya, Madan Kam Dev Temple are the evidences of Mahayana Buddhism.

Ancient and Medieval Period

Ancient Assam known as Kamarupa was ruled by powerful dynasties: the Varmanas (c. 350-650 AD), the Salstambhas (*Xalostombho*, c. 655-900 AD) and the Kamarupa Palas (c. 900-1100 AD). In the reign of the Varman King, Bhaskaravarman (c. 600-650 AD), the Chinese traveller Hiuen Tsang visited the region and recorded his travels. Later, after weakening and disintegration (after the Kamarupa Palas), the Kamarupa tradition was somewhat extended till c. 1255 AD by the Lunar I (c. 1120-1185 AD) and Lunar II (c. 1155-1255 AD) dynasties.

Two later dynasties, the Ahoms and the Koch left larger impacts. The Ahoms, originally a Tai group, ruled Assam for nearly 600 years (1228-1826) and the Koch, a Tibeto-Burmese, established sovereignty in c. 1510 AD. The Koch Kingdom in western Assam and present North Bengal was at its zenith in the early reign of Naranarayana (c. 1540-1587 AD). It split into two in c. 1581 AD, the western part as a Mughal vassal and the eastern as an Ahom satellite state. Since c. 13th AD, the nerve centre of Ahom polity was upper Assam; the kingdom was gradually extended till Karatoya River in the c. 17-18th AD. It was at its zenith during the reign of Sukhrungpha or Sworgodeu Rudra Simha (c. 1696-1714 AD).

Among other dynasties, the Chutiyas (Pronounced 'Sutia') ruled the northeastern Assam and parts of present Arunachal Pradesh and the Kacharis ruled from Dikhow River to central and southern Assam. With expansion of Ahom Kingdom, by c. 1520 AD the Chutiya areas were annexed and since c. 1536 AD, Kacharis remained only in Cachar and North Cachar more as an Ahom ally than a competing force. Despite numerous invasions, mostly by the Muslim rulers, no western power ruled Assam until the arrival of the British.

The most successful invader Mir Jumla, a governor of Aurangzeb, briefly occupied Garhgaon (c. 1662-63 AD) the then capital, but found it difficult to control people making guerrilla attacks on his forces, forcing them to leave. The decisive victory of the Assamese led by the great general Lachit Borphukan on the Mughals then under command of Raja Ram Singha at Saraighat (1671) has almost ended Mughal ambitions. Mughals were finally expelled in c. 1682 AD from lower Assam.

Modern Period

Ahom palace intrigue, and political turmoil due to the Moamoria rebellion, aided the expansionist Burmese ruler of Ava to invade Assam and install a puppet King in 1821. With the Burmese having reached the East India Company's borders, the first Anglo-Burmese War ensued. The war ended under the Treaty of Yandaboo in 1826, with the Company taking control of the Lower Assam and installing Purander Singh as a King of Upper Assam in 1833.

The arrangement lasted till 1838 and thereafter British annexed the entire region. Initially, Assam was made a part of the Bengal Presidency, then in 1906 it was a part of Eastern Bengal and Assam province and in 1912 it was reconstituted into a Chief Commissioners' province. In 1913, a Legislative Council and in 1937, the Assam Legislative Assembly was formed in Shillong, the erstwhile capital. The British tea planters imported labour from central India adding to the demographic canvas. After few initial unsuccessful attempts to free Assam during 1850s, the Assamese since early-20th century joined and actively supported Indian National Congress against the British. In 1947, Assam including present Arunachal Pradesh, Nagaland, Mizoram, Meghalaya became a state of the Union of India (princely states, Manipur and Tripura became Group C provinces) and a district of Assam. Sylhet chose to join Pakistan.

Post British Era

Since 1947, with increasing economic problems in the region, separatist groups began forming along ethnic lines, and demands for autonomy and sovereignty grew, resulting into fragmentation of Assam.

Since the mid-20th century, people from present Bangladesh have been migrating to Assam. In 1961, the Government of Assam passed a legislation making use of Assamese language compulsory. It had to be withdrawn, later under pressure from Bengali speaking people in Cachar. In the 1980s, the Brahmaputra valley saw a six-year Assam agitation triggered by the discovery of a sudden rise in registered voters on electoral rolls. It tried to force the government to identify and deport foreigners illegally migrating from neighbouring Bangladesh and changing the demographics. The agitation ended after an accord between its leaders and the Union Government, which remained unimplemented, causing simmering discontent. On the other hand, political parties neglecting the burning problem have used the Bangladeshi card as a vote bank.

The post-1970s experienced the growth of armed separatist groups like United Liberation Front of Assam (ULFA) and National Democratic Front of Bodoland (NDFB). In November 1990, the Government of India deployed the Indian army, after which low-intensity military conflicts and political homicides have been continuing for more than a decade. In recent times, ethnicity based militant groups (UPDS, DHD, KLO, HPCD, etc.) have also mushroomed. Regional autonomy has been ensured for Bodos in Bodoland

Territorial Council Areas (BTCA) and for the Karbis in Karbi Anglong after agitation of the communities due to sluggish rate of development and aspirations for self-government.

Geographical Aspects

Comprising valleys, hills and the perennial river of Brahmaputra, Assam geography presents a fact file of the locational traits of the state. Assam shares its internal boundaries with West Bengal, Nagaland, Tripura, Mizoram and Arunachal Pradesh, while Bangladesh and China surrounds the international contours of the state.

Physical Geography

Physical Geography of Assam is extremely interesting with its geologic origin, geomorphic characteristics, climate, rich biodiversity, etc. Assam, extending from 89°42' E longitude to 96° E longitude and 24°8' N latitudes to 28°2' N latitudes in the graticule is a Northeastern State of India. Assam is located at the central part of the North-East India and with an area of 78,438 sq km it is almost equivalent to the size of Ireland or Austria.

Geologic and Geomorphic Origin

Geologically, as per the plate tectonics, Assam is in the eastern most projection of the Indian Plate, where it is thrusting underneath the Eurasian Plate creating a subduction zone. It is postulated that due to the northeasterly movement of the Indian Plate, the sediment layers of an ancient geocyncline called *Tethys* (in between Indian and Eurasian Plates) have been pushed upward to form the Himalayas. It is estimated that the height of the Himalayas is increasing by 4 cm each year. Therefore, Assam possesses a unique geomorphic environment, with plain areas, dissected hills of the south Indian plateau system and with the Himalayas all around its north, northeast and east.

Geomorphic studies also conclude that the Brahmaputra is a palaeo-river, older than the Himalayas, which often crosses higher altitudes in the Himalayas eroding at a greater pace than the increase in the height of the mountain range to sustain its flow. The height of the surrounding regions still increasing forming steep gorges in Arunachal.

Physiography

Entering Assam, the Brahmaputra becomes a braided river and along with its tributaries, creates the flood plain of the Brahmaputra valley. The Brahmaputra valley in Assam is approximately 80 to 100-km wide and almost 1,000-km long and the width of the river itself is 16 km at many places within the valley.

The hills of Karbi Anglong and North Cachar and those in and around Guwahati and North Guwahati (along with the Khasi and Garo Hills) are originally parts of the South Indian Plateau system. These are eroded and dissected by the numerous rivers in the region. Average height of these hills in Assam varies from 300 to 400 m.

The southern Barak Valley is separated by the Karbi Anglong and North Cachar Hills from the Brahmaputra Valley in Assam. The Barak originates from the Barail Range in the border areas of Assam, Nagaland and Manipur and flowing through the district of Cachar, it confluences with the Brahmaputra in Bangladesh. Barak Valley in Assam is a small valley with an average width and length of approximately 40 to 50 km.

Mineral Resources

Assam is endowed with petroleum, natural gas, coal, limestone and many other minor minerals such as magnetic quartzite, kaolin, sillimanites, clay and feldspar. A small quantity of iron ore is also available in western parts of Assam.

The Upper Assam districts are the major reserves of oil and gas. Petroleum was discovered in Assam in 1889. It is estimated that Assam and surrounding region possess around 150 million tonnes of petroleum reserves. Presently, Assam is the 3rd largest producer of petroleum (crude) and natural gas in the country accounting for 16 per cent and 8 per cent respectively of the total production of this mineral in the country.

A tertiary coal belt is located in Tinsukia, Dibrugarh, Sivasagar, Karbi Anglong and North Cachar Hills districts with an estimated reserve of 370 million tonnes. Assam coal is friable in nature and has a high sulphur content. It is mainly utilised by local railways, steamers, and hydro power stations. Low moisture, low volatile cooking coal has been discovered in Hallidayganj Singrimari area.

Assam has rich limestone reserves. The major reserves of limestone are in North Cachar Hills and Karbi Anglong districts. A total reserve of 97 million tonnes of limestone is already proved in these two districts and almost half of the reserve is of cement grade. Moreover, there is an estimated reserve of 365 million tonnes of limestone near Umrangshu in the North Cachar Hills District.

Among the minor minerals, there are quartzite reserves in Nagaon District, kaolin reserves in Karbi Anglong and Lakhimpur District and sillimanite bearing rocks in Karbi Anglong District.

Climatic Characteristics

With the 'Tropical Monsoon Rainforest Climate', Assam is a temperate region and experiences heavy rainfall and humidity. Winter lasts from late-October to late-February. The minimum temperature is 6 to 8°C. Nights and early mornings are foggy, and rain is scanty. Summer starts in mid-May, accompanied by high humidity and rainfall. The maximum temperature is 35 to 38°C, but the frequent rain reduces this. The peak of the monsoons is during June. Thunderstorms known as *Bordoicila* are frequent during the afternoons. Spring and Autumn with moderate temperatures and modest rainfall are the most comfortable seasons.

Biodiversity

Assam is one of the richest biodiversity zones in the world. There are a number of tropical rainforests in Assam. Moreover, there are riverine grasslands, bamboo orchards and numerous wetland ecosystems. Many of these areas have been protected by developing national parks and reserved forests. The Kaziranga and Manas are the two World Heritage Sites. The Kaziranga is the home for the rare Indian Rhinoceros, while Manas is a tiger sanctuary.

Apart from the Rhinoceros and the Tiger, the Spotted Deer or Chital/*Futukihorina* (Axix axix), the Swamp Deer or *Dolharina* (Cervus duvauceli duvauceli), the Clouded Leopard (Neofelis nebulosa), the Hoolock Gibbon or *Holoubandor*, Pigmy Hog or *Nolgahori* (Sus salvanis), the Wild Buffalo, the Hispid Hare, the Golden Langur (Chloropsis cochinchinensis), the Golden Cat, the peculiar Giant Civet, the Binturong, the Hog Badgers, the Porcupines, the Civet cats, etc., are found in Assam. Moreover, there are abundant numbers of Gangetic Dolphins, Mongooses, Giant Squirrels and Pythons.

Few of the major birds in Assam are: Bluthroated Barbet or *Hetuluka* (Megalaima asiatica), the White-winged Wood Duck or *Deuhnah* (Cairina scultulata), the Ring-tailed Fishing Eagle or *Kuruwa* (Haliaeetus leucorythus), the Great Pied Hornbill or *Rajdhonesh* (Buceros bicornis homrai), the Himalayan Golden-backed three-toed Woodpecker or *Barhoituka* (Dinopium shorii shorii), and the Migratory Pelicans.

Natural Disasters

The region is also prone to natural disasters. High rainfall, deforestation, and other factors have resulted in annual floods that cause widespread loss of life, livelihood and property. The region is also prone to earthquakes. Mild tremors are familiar, and strong earthquakes are rare. There have been three strong earthquakes: in 1869, the bank of the Barak sank by 15 ft; in 1897, (8.1 on the Richter scale); and in 1950, (8.6).

Rivers

Assam has extensive river system consisting of the Brahmaputra, the Kusiyara and the Barak and their tributaries. All the rivers in Assam are liable to floods, mainly because they receive heavy rainfall within a short time. These rivers are in their early stage of maturity and are very active agents of erosion. The river waters collect a tremendous amount of silt and other debris and raise the level of the river beds. Therefore, it becomes impossible for the main channel to cope with the vast volume of water received during the rains.

Social Aspects

One of the most beautiful states of India, Assam is the gateway to the enchanting and unexploited northeastern part of the country. With the majestic Brahmaputra River, the breath taking hills, rich flora and fauna, it is a tourist paradise. The vibrant life style, the all-smile people, presence of diverse tribes and cultures, are the main points of the wonderful Assam society. The state is located between east longitude 90° to 96° and north latitude 24° to 28°.

The history of Assam dates back to the time of the Aryans and it has got its mention in the epics, the Tantric, Vedic and Buddhist literature. The land has been ruled by great rulers of many dynasties. The people of the state are friendly and they belong to different tribes and communities.

Several religions are practised in the state, proving its secular outlook. Some of the religions that are followed in the state are Hinduism, Buddhism, Christianity, Islam and Vaishnavism.

Apart from the Assamese, the Bengali speaking population and the Nepalis also form a major portion of the state. The diverse culture of the state has brought a rich treasure of art, craft and music with it. Assam is famous for its wood, cane and bamboo crafts, pottery, handlooms, jewellery and colourful masks. The feet tapping Bihu and Jhumur dances of the state are no more bounded by its borders but they are quite popular in all parts of the country.

Demographics

Total population of Assam was 2,66,55,528 with 4.91 million households in 2001. Higher population concentration was recorded in the districts of Kamrup, Nagaon, Sonitpur, Barpeta, Dhubri, Darrang and Cachar. Assam's population was estimated at 28.67 million in 2006 and at 30.57 million by 2011, 34.18 million by 2021 and 35.60 million by 2026.

In 2001, the census recorded literacy in Assam at 63.30 per cent with male literacy at 71.30 and female at 54.60 per cent. Urbanisation rate was recorded at 12.90 per cent.

Growth of population in Assam has experienced a very high trajectory since the mid-decades of the 20th century. Population grew steadily from 3.29 million in 1901 to 6.70 million in 1941, while it has increased unprecedentedly to 14.63 million in 1971 and 22.41 million in 1991 to reach the present level. The growth in the western and southern districts was of extreme high in nature mostly attributable to rapid influx of population from the then-East Pakistan or Bangladesh.

Assam has many ethnic groups and the people of India project has studied 115 of these. Out of which 79 (69%) identify themselves regionally, 22 (19%) locally, and 3 transnationally. The earliest settlers were Austroasiatic, followed by Tibeto-Burman, Indo-Aryan speakers and Tai-Kadai speakers. Forty-five languages are spoken by different communities, including three major language families: Austroasiatic (5), Sino-Tibetan (24) and Indo-European (12). Three of the spoken languages do not fall in these families. There is a high degree of bilingualism.

Major religions are Hinduism (64.9%) and Islam (30.9 per cent — grown to the second largest proportional population among Indian states after J&K). Others include Christianity (3.7%), Sikhism, Animism, Buddhism (Khamti, Phake, Aito, etc. communities).

People

Keeping in sync with the picturesque landscapes and colourful customs, the Assam people are a perfect example of unity in diversity. Consisting mostly of numerous tribes, the people of Assam practice different religions and customs. There are people from all parts of the country residing in the state with a prominence of Bengali speaking community and the Nepalis. The major tribes of the state are: Bodo, Santhal, Phake, Rabha, Singpho, Dimasa, Karbi, Khamti, Khamyang, Mishing and Nishi.

The Bodos are the most prominent Mongoloid tribe of the state. Some sections of the Bodos have also demanded a separate state for themselves – the Bodoland, which has resulted in insurgency in the state. The Santhals are one of the oldest tribes of east India. They are good soldiers and proud of their race. The Phake or the Phakial tribes are said to be having their origins in Thailand. They live mostly in the Tinsukia and Dibrugarh districts of the state. Another colourful tribe of the state is the Rabhas. The Singphos of Tinsukia District are also found in Arunachal Pradesh. They are divided into several clans. Seen mostly in the North Cachar area of the state, the Dimasa people built their homes in the hill slopes. Inhabiting the Karbi Anglong region, the Karbis are also found in other Northeastern States. A small number of Khamti people, who have their origin in Myanmar also live in Assam. The Khamyang, Mishing and Nishi are also other important tribes of the state.

Music

The music of Assam can be divided into various categories of folk music. In recent times a nascent music industry has emerged that caters to local popular demand too.

A basic characteristic of the ethnic music of Assam is its descending scale which distinguishes it from the raga-based or folk music from the rest of India. This style is shared by ethnic music of the hill people surrounding the state of Assam, and by the music of Thailand, Myanmar and China. Furthermore, the tunes are structured in a pyramid, in contrast to the music of rest of India which is *meend* based. Assam is a state with valleys and hills, and the home of many ethnic tribes. Just as the geography and varied people coexist, the pulsating Bihu songs coexist with languorous music of other forms.

Musical Instruments: There are various types of Assam musical instruments. The Assamese people have made good use of bamboo. There are some of the most exquisite types of flutes made from bamboo available in the land of Assam. The other wind instruments used in this region are pepa, kali, gagana and the singa. The chiphung is used by the Bodos. This is a long wind instrument made of bamboo and resembles the flute in many ways. The chiphung is an important part of the Bodo festival.

The kali is an important part of the Assamese wedding ceremonies. It is played on such occasions and resembles the north Indian shehnai in some ways. The singa is made from the horn of buffaloes. A small bamboo pipe is also used in this. Some of the people of the hilly regions of Assam also use ox horn to make the singa. This musical instrument is an integral part of some of the best folk music of Assam.

The dhol, mridanga, nagara, khol, jaidhol and daba are some of the most important percussion instruments of Assam. These accompany the famous bihu dance. The jaidhol is played on wedding ceremonies. The khol is an essential part of Vaishnava music and is thus played during the religious festivals.

Some of the other musical instruments are tokari, khanjari, serenda and the been. The tal is also an important part of the Assamese folk music.

Dance

Dance culture of Assam also represent another facet rich culture. There are two well-known dance forms namely the Bihu Dance and the Sattriya Dance. Bihu dance is mostly performed during the Bihu festival and Sattriya Dance is a classical form of dance.

Bihu Dance: Bihu is the most popular folk dance of Assam and is enjoyed by all, be they young and old. Bihu is celebrated to mark the beginning of the spring festival, sometime in mid-April. This festival is called the Rongali Bihu. Essentially, a festival meant to celebrate the agricultural season, it is celebrated through Bihu dance accompanied by wild and lusty beats of the dhol (drum), pepa (buffalo hornpipe), gogona (a string reed attached to a bamboo piece at the end), takka (a portion of bamboo split to form a clapper) and Bihu songs woven round the theme of love. The most common formation in this dance is the circle or parallel rows. The Bihu dance demonstrates, through song and dance, the soul of the Assamese at its richest. The festival and the dance continue for about a month.

This dance is performed by young men and girls who gather in the open and dance together in separate groups of men and women. A tourist on a visit to Assam, during the harvest season, can witness the Bihu dance is almost every nook and corner of the Brahmaputra valley.

Cinema

Assamese cinema is cinema in the Assamese language, watched primarily in Assam. The industry was born in 1935 when Jyoti Prashad Agarwal released his movie *Joymoti*. Since, then Assamese cinema has developed a slow-paced sensitive style, especially with the movies of Bhabendra Nath Saikia and Jahnu Barua.

However, despite its long history, and its artistic successes, for a state that has always taken its cinema seriously, Assamese cinema has never really managed to make the breakthrough on the national scene despite its film industry making a mark in the

National Awards over the years. Although, the beginning of the 21st century has seen Bollywood-style Assamese movies have hit the screen, the industry has not been able to compete on the market, significantly overshadowed by the larger industries such as Bollywood.

Economic Aspects

The economy of Assam is mainly agricultural. There is a widespread practice of traditional farming techniques and low practice of modern techniques. About seventy-five per cent of the population depends on agriculture and sixty-nine per cent of the workforce in the state is engaged in agricultural activities. Rice is the staple diet of the people. Most of the people are engaged in the cultivation of rice. Other agricultural products cultivated are pulses, jute, tea and fruits. Sugarcane, potatoes, cotton, oil seeds, coconut and areca nut cultivation is also practised on a substantial scale. One of India's few oil regions, Assam produces more than half of the nation's Tea. There are around eight hundred tea estates in Assam. Sixty-seven per cent of the area is cultivated by rice. The fruit crops cultivated are oranges, bananas, pineapples and mangoes.

Macroeconomy

Economy of Assam today represents a unique juxtaposition of backwardness amidst plenty. Growth rate of Assam's income has not kept pace with that of India's; differences increased rapidly since 1970s. Indian economy grew at 6 per cent per annum over the period of 1981 to 2000, the same of Assam was only 3.3 per cent. In the Sixth Plan period, Assam experienced a negative growth rate of 3.78 per cent when India's was positive at 6 per cent. In the post-liberalised era (after 1991), the differences widened further.

According to recent analysis, Assam's economy is showing signs of improvement. In 2001-02, the economy grew (at 1993-94 constant prices) at 4.5 per cent, to fall to 3.4 per cent in the next financial year. During 2003-04 and 2004-05, the economy grew (at 1993-94 constant prices) more satisfactorily at 5.5 and 5.3 per cent, respectively. The advanced estimates placed the growth rate for 2005-06 at above 6 per cent. Assam's GDP in 2004 was estimated at $13 billion at current prices. Sectoral analysis again exhibits a dismal picture. The average annual growth rate of agriculture, which was only 2.6 per cent per annum over 1980s has unfortunately fallen to 1.6 per cent in the 1990s. Manufacturing sector has shown some improvement in the 1990s with a growth rate of 3.4 per cent per annum in comparison to 2.4 per cent in the 1980s. Since past five decades, the tertiary sector has registered the highest growth rates than the other sectors, which even has slowed down in the 1990s in contrast to 1980s.

Mining

Mainly four industrial minerals — coal, oil and gas, limestone, and sillimanite, are significant in the mining sector of the Assam's economy. Petroleum mining is also an outstanding feature of the economy of state. It is regulated by Oil India Limited and the Assam Oil Company. Along with these major minerals, other minerals like gravel, sand, building stone, and ballast are also produced. Assam's economy gets good rewards from the economic minerals found in different parts of the state like the clay, iron ore, copper, feldspar, gold, and gypsum.

Industry

Apart from tea and petroleum refineries, Assam has few industries of significance. Industrial development is inhibited by its physical and political isolation from neighbouring countries such as Myanmar, China and Bangladesh and from other growing South East Asian economies. The region is landlocked, situated in the eastern periphery of India and is linked to the mainland by a flood and cyclone prone narrow corridor, known as the Siliguri Corridor or Chicken's Neck, with weak transport infrastructure. The international airport in Guwahati is yet to find airlines providing direct international flights. The Brahmaputra suitable for navigation does not possess sufficient infrastructure for international trade and success of such a navigable trade route will be dependent on proper channel maintenance and diplomatic and trade relationships with Bangladesh.

Assam is a major producer of crude oil, exploited by the Assam Oil Company Ltd., and natural gas in India and is at the second place in the world (after Titusville in the United States) where petroleum was discovered. Asia's first successful mechanically drilled oil well was drilled in Makum (Assam) way back in 1867. Most of the oilfields are located in the Upper Assam region. Assam has four oil refineries located in Guwahati, Digboi, Numaligarh and Bongaigaon with a total capacity of 7 million metric tonnes (7.7 million short tons) per annum.

Although having a poor overall industrial performance, several other industries have nevertheless been started, including a chemical fertilizer plan at Namrup, petrochemical industries at Namrup and Bongaigaon, paper mills at Jagiroad, Panchgram and Jogighopa, sugar mills at Barua Bamun Gaon, Chargola, Kampur, cement plant at Bokajan and Badarpur, cosmetics plant (HLL) at Doom Dooma, etc. Moreover, there are other industries such as jute mill, textile and yarn mills, silk mill, etc. Unfortunately, many of these industries are facing loss and closer due to lack of infrastructure and improper management practices.

Agriculture

Accounts for more than a third of Assam's income and employs 69 per cent of workforce. Assam's biggest contribution to the world is tea. It produces some of the finest and expensive teas and has its own variety *Camellia Assamica*. Assam also accounts for fair share of India's production of rice, rapeseed, mustard, jute, potato, sweet potato, banana, papaya, areca nut and turmeric. It is also the home of large varieties of citrus fruits, leaf vegetables, vegetables, useful grasses, herbs, spices, etc.

Assam's agriculture yet to experience modernisation in real sense. With implications to food security, per capita food grain production has declined in past five decades. Productivity has increased marginally; but still lower comparing to highly productive regions. For instance, yield of rice (staple food of Assam) was just 1,531 kg per hectare against India's 1,927 kg per hectare in 2000-01 (which itself is much lower than Egypt's 9,283, USA's 7,279, South Korea's 6,838, Japan's 6,635 and China's 6,131 kg per hectare in 2001). On the other hand, after having strong domestic demand, 1.5 million hectares of inland water bodies, numerous rivers and 165 varieties of fishes, fishing is still in its traditional form and production is not self-sufficient.

Livestock

The population of livestock Assam is not as high as most of the other states of India. The livestock of Assam mainly belong to the indigenous kind. According to the livestock census, the population of livestock in state increased to 134.67 lakh in the year 1997 from 129.23 in 1994. The livestock survey reflected a remarkable rise of 29.03 per cent in the poultry population in the year 1997. Amongst the livestock population of the state cattle are the largest in number. There were 80.30 lakh cattle in the 1997. Next in the list are the Goats with a population of 26.77 lakh. During the same year, there were 10.82 lakh pigs and 7.28 lakh buffaloes in the state.

A development scheme for the Livestock Assam has been planned. The main aim behind this scheme is the socio-economic development of the state.

There are many other schemes planned by the Government of Assam. They are related to the increase in livestock products in the state. According to the data made available by the State Directorate of Animal Husbandry and Veterinary, the production of milk in Assam in 2002-03 was estimated at 773 million litres indicating an increase of 3.06 per cent over the production of the previous year. The production of egg during the year 2002-03 has been estimated at 509 million. The production of meat during the same year was estimated at 20.94 thousand tonnes, against the 19.48 thousand tonnes of the previous year. Thus, a rise in the products of Livestock is one of the major aims of the state.

Forests

Forests form an important part of the Assam's economy, with the forest products like timber and bamboo earning great revenue for the state. A large variety of citrus fruits are grown for the markets as well. However, the main commercial product of the Assam's economy are the tea plantation which offer employment to over a million people. Guwahati is the biggest centre of auction of CTC Tea in the world.

Transport and Communication

Assam being the gateway to the other states of the Northeastern Region of the country, the need for development of transport and communication sector in the state is of vital importantance for speedy economic development of the region. Due to its geographical isolation, transport has been a major bottleneck in the process of economic progress of the state. The existing infrastructures and facilities of transport and communication are hardly adequate enough to meet the requirements. The state is no doubt served by all the modern means of transport, viz., roads, railways, waterways and airways but there is enough scope for further improvement of the facilities.

Political Aspects

The Governor heads the political structure of Assam. He is assisted by a council of ministers headed by the Chief Minister. The legislative structure is unicameral and consists of 126 members. The members are elected for a period of 5 years. The Assembly is presided over by the speaker. The political parties of Assam are: Asom Gana Parishad, Asom Gana Parishad (Progressive), Autonomous State Demand Committee, Bharatiya Janata Party, Bodo Peoples Progressive Front, Communist Party of India, CPI (Marxist), Indian National Congress, Purbanchaliya Loka Parishad, Trinamul Gana Parishad and the United Monitary Front.

Since the Indian Independence, Congress has been in power from 1947 to 1978. After which the Janata Party came to power but this government did not last for two years and again Congress came back to power and ruled till 1985. They were again succeeded by the AGP (Asom Gana Parishad). Since then (1985) the Congress and the AGP had been in power alternatively. Sadly, the state has suffered from political violence since the Untied Liberation Front of Asom (ULFA) began an armed struggle for independence in 1985. In the early-1990s, Assamese nationalism sparked opposition from minorities giving rise to further insurgence. However, though bombings, bandhs and in-fighting still continue, the situation has vastly improved and tourists are not a target. In the 2006 elections, Congress retained power. There are twenty district courts in Assam. District and session judges head these courts. A number of subordinate courts at the district and subordinate levels come under these district courts.

Government

The Government of Assam is the provincial governing authority of the state of Assam. It consists of the Governor as the head of the state, who is nominated by the Government of India. The head of government is the Chief Minister, who is the leader of the group that commands a majority in the 126-membered unicameral Assam Assembly. The Assam Assembly is elected by universal adult suffrage for a period of maximum 5 years. The Chief Minister is assisted by a Council of Ministers that he nominates, the size of which is restricted.

Executive

The Executive, Judiciary and Legislature are the divisions of the Government of India. Democracy without these three branches are unthinkable. Assam Executive has important place in the Indian Government. The Executive bodies of the different states of India form the part of the democracy of the country. The governor is an important person in the Assam Executive besides the Chief Minister of the state.

The Council of Ministers is a significant division in the Assam Executive. The Chief Minister occupies a distinct position in the Council of Ministers. There are nineteen cabinet ministers who have been assigned their respective departments. There is one who has been assigned with independent charge of the state.

Legislature

Legislature of a state is one of the important pillar of democracy. The legislative bodies work in unison for smooth running of the state and to implement the laws that are made by the Executive of the state. Assam Legislature comprises a number of divisions. In a Parliamentary system of Government, the legislative body functions very significantly. The legislature not only can enact the laws but has important role in passing money bills, deal with issues related to tax and budget.

In the year 1937, the Legislative Assembly of Assam came into existence by the Government Act of 1935. Assam Legislative Assembly became a bicameral government. There were 108 members adorning the assembly. The tenure of the assembly is generally 5 years. Lok Sabha and Rajya Sabha form parts of the Assam Legislature. There are fourteen constituencies in the Assam for Lok Sabha. The members representing Assam are affiliated to different political parties like INC, BJP, IND and AGP.

Assembly

The Assam legislative structure is unicameral and consists of the 126-member Assam Assembly. Members are elected for a period of 5 years. The Assembly is presided over by the Speaker, who is generally a member of the ruling party.

In 1990, however, Assam was put under direct central government rule.

Judiciary

The Assam judiciary is divided into the Assam High Court that is situated in the city of Guwahati and the district courts of the state. The judiciary works effectively meeting out laws and maintaining order in the state.

The Guwahati High Court was set up after the Assam Legislative Assembly initiated a law stating the necessity to set up a high court in the state under Article 214 of the Constitution which read that each state will have a high court. The Assam High Court was established on April 5, 1948. The High Court has the strength of 23 judges and additional judges and is presided over by the honourable Chief Justice of Assam. The high court has the powers of legislation over the other subsidiary courts and tribunals. It can issue territorial laws and orders over the encompassing area of its control.

The Chief Justice of the High Court is an important component of the judiciary system. The first Chief Justice of the Guwahati High Court was Sir R. F. Lodge. The position is sacred to the judicial system and is highly respected.

State Commissions

The Assam State Commissions aid the government in the governance of the state. They are statutory bodies that work ensuring the welfare of the citizens of the state. There are various state commissions in the state.

The government is aided by the State Human Rights Commission that ensures that the rights of the citizen of the state are not encroached upon. The commission is headed by the chairman of the commission.

The government also has the Assam Electricity Regulatory Commission. Established in the year 2001, the commission works for the regulation of the tariff for electricity and ensures proper regulation and efficient distribution of electricity in the state.

Some of the other commissions of the state are mentioned below:

- Administrative Reforms Commission.
- State Commission for Women.

The government of Assam desires to set up the state information commission that will be led by the State Chief Information Commissioner and will comprise ten more state commissioners. The powers and functions of the state commission will be to receive complaints and to order enquiries and acquire information. The centre will be established in the place desired by the government. The commissions assist in the governance of the region and are dedicated to the welfare of the people.

Capital of State: Dispur

Dispur is the capital of Assam. This place that existed as a locality on the outskirts of Guwahati, took its place as the capital of Assam in 1973. This was after Shillong, the erstwhile capital became the capital of the state of Meghalaya that was carved out of Assam.

To the south of Dispur is the mythologically important site of Basistha Ashram and the Shankardev Kalakschetra, a cultural centre created in the 1990s. Next to Dispur is the ancient township of Jatia. Assam State Secretariat buildings are also located here.

History

The northern parts of India hold a true and respectful history. The Capital of Assam, Dispur City became the leading city in the year 1973 and since has had a strong historic background.

First, Assam, known geologically as the "Light of the East" (Epic Period) has held humans since 2000 BC. Through the first 1000+ years the city of Dispur was just a normal, small village in the scheme of things for Assam. The local dynasty was believed to be Varman, although the country held many different beliefs and underwent several changes through this time period. It was not until the 18-19th centuries that the Assam Kingdom started falling apart from the inside government, to the outside influence of neighbouring countries. The British began to take control of Assam's 27 districts and began to run the then Capital, Shillong. With Britain controlling the Assam, industrial changes began to take place, such as the breakthrough uses of the natural resources of oil, tea and iron.

The British started educating the people of Dispur City (the literacy rate stands at 63.25 per cent today) and they developed the first central government that Assam ever had. By the 1900s, Dispur City and Assam as a whole, began to pull away from the British control and took full responsibility for the running and the economy of the country. One of India's northern most states became a forceful contributor to India's overall economic situation and started showing signs of prominence it has today.

Culture

The city of Dispur is a known cultural hot spot for the local people and for tourism as a whole. People come from all over to take part in the cultural amenities that Dispur offers.

Dispur City has its own unique form of dancing rituals called *Husari* and *Bihunas*. The two exclusive dancing formats are the backbone of the Dispur culture. In Husari, men and boys go home to home throughout the city and sing carols filled with joy and passing. The songs are soothing and are sung while collecting money that will be spent on city repair and additional feasting for the entire population to enjoy. The dances last barely a few minutes at each home, and the participants are strictly male. In the Bihuna dances, songs of religious theme dominate the words while praise is sung towards the end festival. Drums, bamboo and voices make up the musical treatment of the Bihuna dances. In Dispur City, frequent theatrical performances are held called *Bhawariya's*. These plays are a much anticipated event in the city and all the most prominent people in Dispur are there. The theatrical acts include dancing, loud music and performers wearing various forms of masks and costumes. The different songs used in these plays are called *Zikirs*, which are complete with clapping and circle dancing in the form of ancient godly rituals. The overall culture of Dispur City is wide, and although many of the people hold similar beliefs, the people love the diverse nature of the land.

Climate

If one is thinking about visiting or moving to the city of Dispur, then one should have a good idea of what the climate is like in this city. This may determine when the absolute best time for one to visit Dispur will be.

The temperature in Dispur will vary according to seasons. It may get as low as forty-five degrees Fahrenheit, and as high as one hundred degrees Fahrenheit. The lower temperatures, of course, will occur during winter time. Winter in Dispur is between the end of October and the end of February. During this season, the nights and early mornings are often foggy and it tends to rain a lot less than it usually does. Summer begins in the middle of May. With this season, there also comes a lot of humid weather, as well as a lot of rain.

Monsoon season takes place during the month of June. Thunderstorms also tend to occur a lot in the afternoons during this time. The entire Assam is very prone to earthquakes — however, they do not occur often but when they do infrequently occur, they are very mild.

If one is looking for the best season to visit the city of Dispur, it is probably either spring or autumn. During these two seasons, the temperatures are not too hot or not too cold. It also does not rain too much, nor too little during this time.

Festivals

No matter what religion a citizen of Dispur City is, the festivals of Dispur City are nationally celebrated festivals with people from all over India flocking to Dispur to contribute in the fun. Smaller tribes in Dispur even worship the gods and goddess's of ancient times.

Bihu is a festival mostly celebrated by the Assamese people and is held on the last day of Aswin (A weekly Bihu holiday) and is a feast with great food and drink. The festival comes directly after a great fast.

The Magh is a festival held around the 15th of January every year and marks the beginning of harvest gathering in the city/country. The celebrations include bonfires, where the gods are worshipped and it is believed that a good harvest will be brought in and fertility will be increased among the women.

The Kangali bihu is a festival held between the months September and October. This is the poorest part of the harvest period and food is scarce among all the people (hence the name Kangali bihu, meaning poor festival). This period is where the younger men and women attempt to meet their future spouses. Other festivals that happen in Dispur City are: Deul of Barpeta and Devaddhvani. The two festivals are each held once per year.

Dispur City, the capital of Assam is a great cultural and celebratory city that is encouraged by its many religious based festivals. The festivals are a time of great fun, meaning and hopefulness for the future.

Tourism

As one of the smallest capital cities in the world, Dispur City is a popular place for tourists to visit to see the great way of life of tribal and unconnected people. It is known for its hilly, grassy countryside and is free from pollution that invades other cities. Nature reigns with bushy forests and flowing blue rivers.

The "get-away" as Dispur is called by tourists is overrun during its busy season in the January to July months. With the Eastern Himalaya Mountains off at the outmost skirts of the state and the Naga Ranges bordering on the East, Dispur City has a lot to offer in views and tourism attractions for nature enthusiasts. The largest known natural attraction is the strong Brahmaputra River which flows directly through Assam as a whole. Tourists enjoy the river for its beauty, strength and rapids. Rarely a visitor will leave Dispur without at least a tea bag with classic Dispur City made tea. The tea is renowned in the city and is rare with herbs and spices found only in Dispur. The City seems to attract a wide array of people, just as the city itself tends to contain a diverse group of nations and races. In the outskirts of the city, tourists enjoying sightseeing at the Hindu temples, in Guwahati. The biggest attraction for visitors in Dispur City, however, is the Kaziranga National Park, which showcases India's own one-horned Rhinoceros. The animals are rare in the world and are typically found only spread throughout India.

Dispur City is a huge hit for tourists and despite its small population size proves to show visitors that a store of knowledge is contained among the cities boundaries.

2

Salient Features

Among the states and union territories of Northeastern India, Assam commands a unique and significant place. At one time the state of Assam embraced all these political units barring Manipur and Tripura which were native states of the British India. However, the present union territory of Arunachal Pradesh was constituted in a separate division by the British under the name of NEFA, i.e. Northeastern Frontier Agency. Because of its location on a very sensitive front (surrounded by Bhutan, China and Burma and later on by East Pakistan, i.e. Bangladesh of today) Assam has always enjoyed a unique place in the annals of Indian history. Once a very large political unit, Assam later on came to be vivisected in different segments.

The word Assam is a Sanskrit word and refers to unevenness. If one looks at the political unit that once was known as Assam, one would find each type of landform located in it. Towering snow-covered mountains, forest clad hill ranges, gorges, canyons-valleys of varying dimensions and shapes, plateau surfaces, foothill plains, river valley plains, alluvial flats, river terraces and a variety of other relief features dotted the landscape of the then Assam. Thus it was aptly called as such. Now the state of Assam is by and large confined to the Brahmputra valley, which is on the whole a tract of level stretches and the name seems to be misleading like that of Punjab. But a political unit once named continues to be called as such until and unless strong regional or political considerations warrant a change in the nomenclature as it has happened in the case of Maharashtra, Karnataka, Tamil Nadu, etc.

Some scholars are of the opinion that the word Assam has been derived from the word Ahom. The Ahom dynasty ruled over this region for a long time and it is conjectured that the word Ahom corrupted to Akhom and finally to Asom and Assam. But this derivation does not appear to be correct. The other observation, however, deserves to be examined. The Ahoms are said to have immigrated here from the Shan plateau of Burma.

The word Shan is believed to have become Ashan and ultimately Assam. No wonder the word ahom itself may also be the gradual derivation from the word ashan itself. The word ashan also means unequalled or unrivalled. The Ahom ruller Chukapha commenced his rule in 1228 AD. He is said to have made many splendid conquests and thereby added many territories to his kingdom. His conquests were termed Assam whence some scholars derive etymology of the nomenclature of the state.

Some scholars, on the other hand, are of the opinion that the word Assam means unequal and fearless. They opine that when Chukapha invaded Assam in 1228 AD, the natives called his feat as unequal and fearless. Thus he was named as Assam, the name later on given to his country. This contention is accepted by others with some modification. They assert that this term is the Sanskritised form of Acham. The word Acham in the Tai language means undefeated conqueror. Nonetheless, Assam word is of modern origin. The region in ancient period was called Kamarupa. In Hindu mythology the God of love, Kamadeva, is considered to be the most handsome God. He is said to have lived and ruled here. It was in this region that Lord Mahadeva punished Kamdeva for his acts of omission and commission. Only after this punishment Kamdeva became omnipresent but invisible. Thus the region appears to have been named Kamrupa after the name of Kamdeva.

The Highlights

Physiography: Geographically Assam is a shadow of its former self. It has been reduced to one-third of its original size in thirty years.

In the partition of India (1947) Assam lost Sylhet district, except a major portion of Karimganj subdivision, to East Pakistan, now Bangladesh. Out of the 27 lakh population of Sylhet, Assam retained only 7 lakh, the rest going to East Pakistan (now Bangladesh). Thereafter, Assam continued to lose territory and population step by step as Nagaland, Meghalaya, Mizoram and Arunachal Pradesh were separated from it.

Assam, as it is today, may be divided into two important physical regions — the Barak valley and the Brahmaputra valley.

Assam is dominated by the Brahmaputra river (length: 2,900 km). Its drainage area is roughly 935,500 sq km.

Rainfall, one of the highest in the world (between 178 and 305 cm), is concentrated in 4 months, June to September. The state experiences floods and droughts.

History: An ideal meeting ground for diverse races, Assam gave shelter to streams of human waves carrying with them distinct cultures and trends of civilization. Austro-Asiatics, Negritos, Dravidians, Alpines, Indo-Mongoloids, Tibeto-Burmese and Aryans penetrated into Assam through different routes and contributed in their own way towards the unique fusion of a new community which came to be known in later history as the Assamese.

Assam, however, remained predominantly a land of the Tibeto-Burmese. The vast section of the people of Assam belong either to this stock or owe, their origin to the fusion of this stock with other racial groups.

Assam, known in ancient lore as Kamarupa, originally included in addition to modern Assam, parts of modern Bengal and Bangladesh. Guwahati, the pulsating centre of Assam, is an ancient town whose history goes back to the puranic days. The city, anciently known as Pragjyotishpur, was said to have been founded by King Narakasur, who is mentioned in the puranas and epics. His son Bhagadatta led a large elephant force to the battlefield of Kurukshetra, and fell fighting on the side of the Kauravas.

In the 13th century, the country was conquered by the Ahoms under Sukapha, a Prince of the Shan tribe, in the upper Irravaddy Valley. The advent of the Ahoms changed the course of Assam's history. They appointed Barphukans (Viceroys) to rule Kamarupa and Guwahati became the capital of these Viceroys. The last of the Viceroys was Badanchandra, who in an ill-advised bid for power invited the Burmese to help him. The Burmese dislodged the Ahoms and dismissed their Viceroy, Badanchandra. The Ahoms appealed to the British for help.

The British defeated the Burmese in several battles, in what has since been called the First Burmese War. With the Treaty of Yandabo in 1826, the Burmese vacated Assam, leaving the British in possession.

The conquered territory was placed under the administration of an Agent to the Governor General. In 1832 Cachar was annexed to Assam. In 1835, the Jaintia Hills were made part of Assam. (Upper Assam was annexed to Bengal in 1839). In 1874, a separate province of Assam under a Chief Commissioner was created, with Shillong as capital.

On the partition of Bengal in 1905, Assam was united to the eastern districts of Bengal under a Lt. Governor. From 1912, the Chief Commissionership of Assam was revived, and in 1921 a Governorship was created.

On the partition of India almost the whole of the predominantly Muslim district of Sylhet was merged with East Bengal (present Bangladesh). Dewanagiri in North Kamarupa was ceded to Bhutan in 1951.

In 1948, the North East Frontier Agency was separated from Assam, for security reasons. In 1963, Nagaland was carved out of Assam as a full-fledged state. On 21st Jan. 1972, Meghalaya was cut out of Assam, as a separate state and Mizoram became a Union Territory. In 1987, Mizoram was granted statehood.

The Legislature consists of only one house — the Legislative Assembly (126 members).

Economy: Assam is rich in mineral wealth: oil, coal, limestone, refractory clay, dolomite and natural gas. Tea is a major industry. There are nearly 750 tea plantations in the state. Assam contributes 15.6 per cent of world's tea production and 55 per cent of the country's tea output. Assam is first state in the country where oil was struck in 1889 at Digboi. The state has four oil refineries. There is also a public sector fertilizer factory at Namrup. The Numaligarh refinery (3 m tonnes capacity, cost Rs. 2,350 crore) was commissioned on July 9, 1999. Other industries are sugar, jute, silk, paper, plywood, rice and oil drilling. Important cottage industries are handloom, sericulture, manufacture of cane and bamboo articles, carpentry, smithy and manufacture of brass utensils. Assam is the largest producer in the world of the golden coloured 'muga' silk.

Total length of roads: 33,110 km. Railway network: 3,816 km.

There are six civil airports, at Dibrugarh, Guwahati, Jorhat, Silchar, Lakhimpur and Tezpur. The government has demanded a Rs. 1000-crore central assistance for the construction of a permanent capital at Dispur.

Academic Institutions

* Assam Agricultural University, Jorhat.
* Assam University, Silchar.
* Dibrugarh University, Dibrugarh.
* Guwahati University, Gopinath Bardoloi Nagar, Guwahati.
* Guwahati University, Guwahati.
* Indian Institute of Technology, Guwahati.
* Tezpur University, Tezpur.

Tourist Centres: Guwahati-Kaziranga-Sibsagar and Guwahati-Manas are two travel circuits promoted by the Union Government. Additional circuits proposed by the state: 1. Guwahati-Bhairabkunda-Orang-Bhaluking Tezpur, 2. Guwahati-Diphu-Haflong-Silchar. Kaziranga National Park, famous for one-horned rhinos and elephants and Manas are two important national parks.

Physical Features

The land of a vast green valley and majestic blue hills, Assam is one of the loveliest States of India. The State spreads beneath the foothills of the Eastern Himalaya and covers a total area of 78,438 square kilometres. The two hill districts (North Cachar and Mikir Hills) account for 15,224 sq km (nearly 19.5 per cent of the total area of the state) area. The mighty Brahmputra passes through the middle of the state. Thus by and large the state of Assam covers the Brahmputra valley also termed as the Assam valley. The Valley spreads over a length of 640 km between Dhubri and Sadiya. Its average width hovers around 100 km. The valley lies between the Shillong plateau and the Eastern Himalaya.

The valley in a way is the gift of the Brahmputra and its tributary streams. The sediments brought by these streams have been deposited here to create the valley tract. The streams continue to add to the sedimentary strata of the valley. The Himalayas stand like a steep wall to the north of the Assam valley. Heavy rainfall and a large number of tributaries contribute to the large volume of water in the Brahmputra. Resultantly the mighty river is quite deep throughout its plain stage. Large boats and steamers are thus plied in this stream from its delta to Dibrugarh for a distance of nearly 1,130 km.

The State of Assam enjoys Monsoonal climate which is not very hot. Heavy rainfall, excessive humidity and not very high temperatures are the salient characteristics of the climate of the valley. In fact the temperatures do not rise very high as a result of heavy rainfall. The average summer temperatures on the average hover around 29°C. The rainy season commences here right in the month of April and May. This rainfall is the result of pre-monsoon showers. Besides lowering the summer temperatures, rainfall also curtails the length of the summer season.

The regular southwest monsoons start blowing by the beginning of June and thereby commences the period of excessive and heavy rains. It rains nearly for eight months in a year in Assam. Relative humidity during this period remains between 85 to 94 per cent. The existence of a large number of streams in this region is directly related to the amount and duration of rainfall. Excessive rainfall also leads to floods at some places where the landscape has become marshy. Thus the climate is otherwise not invigorating and is also not very congenial for human health. That is why maximum number of malarial patients are found in Assam every year.

Alluvial soils are found in the valley, whereas the hilly tracts are covered with laterite soils. The new alluvium found in the vicinity of river courses is quite fine and fertile. Their upper layers are renewed every year. This type of soil is termed as Khadar. The alluvium found away from the river courses and relatively on the high ground is less fertile and is popularly known as Bangar. The laterite soils found in the districts of Sibsagar and Nowgong are no doubt rich in humus but lack in phosphorus, potassium and lime. Thus these soils are not very fertile.

Nearly 40 per cent of the total area of the state is reported to be covered with forests. Nonetheless, these forests include even notional forests. The density of forests increases on the hill slopes. The forests of the plain tracts have by and large been cleared to create cultivable land. Along both sides of the Brahmputra course wherever landscape is flooded every year, long reed type grasses grow in abundance. Because of Monsoonal type of climate, forests of different types are found. Evergreen forests, broad leaved deciduous forests, mangrove forests, savana type of grasslands, sal forests and bamboo forests are found in Assam.

Till recently Assam was the only State of India that produced mineral oil and natural gas. Even at present a large share of petroleum and petroleum products are obtained from Assam. A belt measuring nearly 1,200 metres long lying in the state is the petroleum-bearing tract. Digboi, Badarpur and Naharkatiya contain the largest number of oil as well as natural gas wells. Coal of low grade has also been mined in Assam and particularly around Sadiya. The coal mined here is found to contain sulphur. Resultantly on coming into the contact of atmosphere such coal is reduced to small pieces. Deposits of limestone and sillimanite are also reported to occur in Assam.

Lingual and Literary Features

Assamese and Bodo are the major indigenous and official languages while Bengali holds official status in the three districts in the Barak Valley.

Traditionally, Assamese was the language of the commons (of mixed origin — Austroasiatic, Tibeto-Burman, Magadhan Prakrit) in the ancient Kamarupa and in the medieval Kingdoms of Kamatapur, Kachari, Cuteeya, Borahi, Ahom and Koch. Traces of the language is found in many poems by Luipa, Sarahapa, etc., in Charyapada (c. 7-8th AD). Modern dialects Kamrupi, Goalpariya, etc., are the remnant of this language. Moreover, Assamese in its traditional form was used by the ethno-cultural groups in the region as *lingua franca*, which spread during the stronger kingdoms and was required for needed economic integration. Localised forms of the language still exist in Nagaland, Arunachal Pradesh, North Bengal, Cachar, etc. and in the south, languages such as Chatgaia, Siloti, etc. exhibit similarities. The form used in the upper Assam was enriched by the advent of Tai-Shans in the 13th century.

Linguistically modern Assamese traces its roots to the version developed by the American Missionaries based on the local form in practice near Sibsagar (Xiwoxagor) District. Assamese (*Oxomeeya*) is a rich language due to its hybrid nature with its unique characteristics of pronunciation and softness. Assamese literature is one of the richest. Bodo is an ancient language of Assam. Spatial distribution patterns of the ethno-cultural groups, cultural traits and the phenomenon of naming all the major rivers in the North-East Region with Bodo-Kachari words (e.g. Dihing, Dibru, Dihong, D/Tista, Dikrai, etc.) reveal that it was the most important language in the ancient times. Bodo is presently spoken largely in the Lower Assam (Bodo Territorial Council area). After years of neglect, now Bodo language is getting attention and its literature is developing. Other native languages of Tibeto-Burman origin and related to Bodo-Kachari are Mishing, Karbi, Dimaca, Rabha, Tiwa, etc. Rajbongshi also known as kamatapuri/Goalpariya is also widely spoken by the people of western Assam.

There are smaller groups of people speaking Tai-Phake, Tai-Aiton, Tai-Khamti, etc., related to Tai-group of languages. The Tai-Ahom language (brought by Sukaphaa and his followers), which is no more a spoken language today is getting attentions for research after centuries long care and preservation by the Bailungs (traditional priests). There are also small groups of people speaking Manipuri, Nepali, Khasi, Garo, Hmar, Kuki, etc. in different parts. In the past century, migration of Bengalis in the Barak Valley has led to their majority, prompting the Government of Assam to include Bengali as the official language in the area.

Literature

Assamese literature is the entire corpus of poetry, novels, short stories, documents, etc. written in the Assamese language. It also includes such writings and popular ballads in the older forms of the language during its evolution to the contemporary form. The rich literary heritage of the Assamese language can be traced back to the 6th century in the Charyapada, where the earliest elements of the language can be discerned.

Media

The state of Assam is perhaps the most important Northeastern State of the country. It is the most convenient gateway to North-East India and has immense significance in terms of tourism, agriculture and industries. It is also a hot bed of political activities. The steady inflow of visitors and tourists throughout the year keep the state busy. Numerous people of diverse culture and community inhabit Assam. All these factors make the state a favourite with the media. No wonder, the Assam Media with all its forms is working to serve the people with information, education and entertainment.

The print media, the electronic media and the *e*-Media have equally contributed in the mission. The media in Assam can be roughly classified into the following divisions:

- Print Media — newspapers, magazines.
- Electronic Media — television, radio.
- *e*-Media — websites, news portals.

Famous Writers

Assamese is spoken all along the Brahmaputra valley and sounds quite similar to Bengali, except for a few differences. In fact, the old text Charya Padas is claimed by both Old Assamese and Old Bengali.

The oldest Assamese writer was perhaps Hema Saraswati, who wrote his famous Prahlada Charita in the late 13th century AD. Madhava Kandali (14th century) was the next well-known figure, having written a vernacular Ramayana. Prominent among 15th century works were Durgavara's Giti Ramayana, poems and songs from the Puranas by Pitambara and Manakara and the mass of literature called Mantras of unknown authorship.

Educational Features

In the Northeastern Region of India, Assam occupies a distinct place in the field of education. The overall literacy rate of Assam is 76.3 per cent, where the literacy rate of male is 71.93 per cent and female 56.03 per cent. Huge number of educational institutions are established here imparting education to the students of entire Northeastern Region. Formal education starts in schools with elementary, secondary, higher secondary. Then the students move to a college and pursue education in a stream he is interested in. The Directorate of Elementary Education of Assam organises numerous activities to Universalise Elementary Education (UEE). The Elementary education in Assam includes classes from Class I to Class VII, within the age group of 6-14 years of students. Secondary and higher secondary schools covering class tenth and twelfth, respectively, finally prepares the child for higher education.

Assam has set up many educational institutions for higher studies following high standards to impart education in the field of engineering and management. The Government of Assam provides free and compulsory education for children till the age of 14. The requirement for technical education has been increasing gradually as a result the government has paid due attention in this field and set up many esteemed institutions in state. Assam has 6 universities namely Indian Institute of Technology (Guwahati), Assam Agricultural University (Jorhat), Dibrugarh University (Dibrugarh), Guwahati University (Guwahati), Tezpur University (Tezpur) and Assam University.

Schools

Assam schools occupy an important position. Guwahati has become a major destination for education because of its world-class schools. The schools are either affiliated to Indian Certificate of Secondary Education (ICSE) and the Indian School Certificate (ISC) examinations of Delhi, Assam Board of School Education, or Central Board of Secondary Education (CBSE) board.

Most of the schools have very good infrastructure with good school buildings, libraries, playgrounds, laboratories, etc. Some of the schools have residential facilities for outstation students. The different schools are run by different organisations, either they are Government schools or run by private organisations. The medium of instruction in these schools is either Assamese or English.

Some of the schools imparting good education to the children are:

- The Assam Valley School, P.P. and T.O., Balipara, Distt: Sonitpur.
- Kendriya Vidyalaya Narangi, Guwahati.
- Kendriya Vidyalaya Guwahati.
- Kendriya Vidyalaya No.2, Tezpur, Guwahati.

- Gurukul Grammar School Pub., Gita Nagar, Guwahati.
- Kendriya Vidyalaya Maligaon, Guwahati.
- Oil Valley School, Bogapani Colony, P. S. Digboi.
- Maria's Public School, Birkuchi Narangi, Guwahati.
- Delhi Public School, ONGC Nazira.
- Vivekananda Kendra Vidyalaya Post Umrangso N. C. Hills.
- Delhi Public School Oil India Ltd., Dibrugarh.
- Vivekananda Kendra Vidyalaya, Baragolai Post Margherita Tinsukhia.

Colleges and Universities

The education imparted at the colleges and universities is very important as it plays a very significant role in moulding a person's career. In the entire North-East Region of India, Assam enjoys a significant place in the educational scenario of India. Some of the esteemed educational institutions like the Indian Institute of Technology, Guwahati, National Institute of Technology, Silchar and Guwahati University are established in the state that provide quality education to its pupils.

Assam has 6 universities namely Assam Agricultural University (Jorhat), Assam University, Dibrugarh University (Dibrugarh), Guwahati University (Guwahati), Indian Institute of Technology (Guwahati), Tezpur University (Tezpur). In the colleges and universities, many eminent scholarly professors and lecturers impart knowledge to the pupils. Several undergraduate, graduate, post-graduate, medical, engineering, law, polytechnics and ITIs are set up both by the Government of Assam and private organisations. The courses offered by the Assam colleges and universities are B.A. (English, Hindi, Bengali, History, Political Science, etc.), B.Sc. (Physics, Chemistry, Maths, Botany, Zoology, etc.), M.A. (English, Hindi, Economics, Bengali, History, Political Science, etc.), M.Sc. (Maths, Physics, Botany, Zoology, Chemistry, etc.), various technical streams, medicine, etc.

Libraries

Assam is one of the leading states in North-East where literacy and overall education is of a great concern. The educated mass in the state has resulted in increased readership. More and more schools, colleges and technical institutes are coming up in the state. With that, an inflow of students from different states can be observed. All these factors have encouraged in the growth of many libraries in Assam. These libraries help the students, professionals, service holders and book lovers to get hold of their desired books, which may be not available in the market.

The state has a Central Library, which is an important library in the state, has a total of eighty-one thousand volumes of books. These include various kinds of textbooks, reference books, and non-book materials like slides, audiotapes and videotapes. It also subscribes to a total number of about four hundred and eighty-four recent periodicals.

Distance Education

The concept of distance learning has made the journey of acquiring higher education easier for those people who are already working. This helps them to work and study in the same phase by saving a lot of precious time. Assam Distance Education is popular among the people of the state, especially for those who are working or are engaged in the household works and are yet eager to enrol themselves for a course. Distance learning is offered in the different universities. There are other institutes that provide only courses on distance education.

Distance learning courses are also known as Correspondence Courses. In the fast pace of life today, correspondence or distance learning is highly preferred as it saves a lot of valuable time. It gives ample scope for one study along with doing other activities. One can stay at one's own place and study from a university situated far away.

Assam Distance Education is very popular. The distance learning centres and the universities that offer distance or correspondence courses charge much lower amount of fees than the regular study programmes.

The distance education courses or the correspondence courses provide all the necessary materials for study in the distance courses. Guwahati University, one of the leading universities of Assam, conducts some special classes on holidays so that the students are able to attend to the classes. The classes are intentionally held on holidays so that the students, who are working or live far away, can manage to attend to the classes and clarify their doubts.

Scientific Features

Assam, the gateway to Northeast India and the hot seat of ancient Indian culture is also a centre of academic excellence. Science and technology have crossed all borders and placed the state at the zenith of technological excellence.

The Assam Science Technology and Environment Council (ASTEC) opened its doors during the period spanning between 1986 and 1987 as an independent council under the Department of Science Technology and Environment, Government of Assam. The ASETC has eventually turned out to be a central body that is committed to the cause of promoting science and technology amongst the common masses, inculcate a scientific temper, generate awareness and inquisitiveness on environmental issues and the complex phenomenon on the workings of the world.

The Council is divided into the Energy, Science and Technology, Environment, and Remote Sensing departments. The council has to its credit several major achievements and is the proud recipient of a distinguished award from the Ministry of Non-conventional Energy Sources, Government of India for its outstanding work on Solar Lighting in Rural areas of Assam. The Council has also worked diligently for the promotion of science in schools and colleges and also celebrates all major national scientific events.

Apart from the ASTEC, the Indian Institute of Technology (IIT), Guwahati, a torchbearer of Science and Technology is another elite academic institute that ranks with some of the best technical institutes in the world. The institute boasts of an excellent infrastructure and research and development facilities and does its utmost to promote science and technology amongst the masses.

Backdrop of Economy

Agriculture continues to be the mainstay of the people of Assam. Some tribes living in hilly as well as inaccessible areas practice jhuming, i.e. shifting cultivation. In the valley, settled and permanent agriculture is pursued. Rice, maize, sugarcane, potatoes, tobacco, oilseeds and fruits are the major crops grown in Assam. Jute and tea are the principal cash crops of Assam. After the partition of India, when consequent upon the falling of Jute growing belt in erstwhile East Pakistan (now Bangladesh) India faced shortage of raw material jute, cultivation was started in Assam also. Now after West Bengal, Assam is the second-largest jute growing state of India. Nearly 40 per cent of jute production of Assam comes from Goalpara district alone.

The wildly growing tea plants in Assam were first noted by an Englishman Robert Bruce, an officer of the East India Company in 1820. On his recommendation the then Governor General, William Bentick, sent some Englishmen to China to learn the tea growing and processing know-how. Those trained personnel started planting tea plantations on the hill slopes of Assam in 1836. At present more than half of the Indian tea production is supplied by the state of Assam.

Pulses, mustard, castor, meseta, banana, oranges, lemons, papaya, betel leaf and arecanut are also raised in different parts of Assam. The Nepali graziers have helped in the development of livestock breeding farms around important towns and industrial centres.

As far as the industrial development is concerned Assam is a backward state. Oil refinery at Digboi is, however, a big industrial concern that is in operation since 1899. Some factories manufacturing matchstick, plywood and silk are also located in Assam. Assam enjoys a place of pride in India for manufacturing muga silk. A jute mill has also now come into existence at Amingong near Guwahati. In and around Guwahati small industrial concerns making brass utensils, iron wares, furniture, etc. have been sprung up. Among the cottage industries of Assam sericulture and handloom silk fabrics enjoy the top-most position. Beeculture, basket making from bamboos and cane, boat-building, making of mats, oil milling and ivory works are other significant crafts of Assam.

As stated above the Brahmputra or the Assam valley is the nerve centre of the socio-economic canvas of the state of Assam. Nevertheless, one comes across many variations when one travels from one corner of the state to another. Thus it is worthwhile to review the picture in the light of the subdivisions of the valley.

The districts of Lakhimpur and Sibsagar constitute the Upper Assam Plain, the funnel-shaped and of the valley. The sub region enjoys damp and cool (maximum temperature 28°C; minimum temperature 18°C, and average annual rainfall 175 cm), climatic conditions. The soils on the whole are alluvial in nature although the fringes at the foothills are characterised with diluvium mixed with grit and pebbles. Large evergreen, semi-evergreen and wet deciduous forests are found here. The sandy soil patches near river courses support Simul (bombax malabaricum), reed, long grasses and herbs. Rice and tea are abundantly grown. Ideal slopes, suitable climatic conditions and favourable soils have made this part the most important single-tea growing area in the world.

More than 75 per cent of the tea gardens of Assam are found in this subregion alone. Sugarcane is another important crop. All the oilfields and some of the coal mines of Assam are also located here. In terms of industrial development, it is a fairly developed part. Oil refinery (Digboi), fertilizer plant (Namrup), Sugar mill (Dergaon) and the power station (Nahatkatiya) are the major industrial units apart from a number of saw mills and light engineering works; internal as well as external lines of transport and communication are on a sound footing. Thus Upper Assam valley forms a distinct personality of its own and enjoys the reputation of being the most important region of the state.

The bowl-shaped tract of the Central Assam Plain covers the district of Nowgong that once used to be inundated annually by the Kapili floods. The frequent silting as a result of floods rendered this part to be the most fertile area in the state. Although it enjoys similar temperature conditions as those experienced by the Upper Assam Plain, in matters of precipitation it stands out as a distinct unit. Lying on the lee of the Shillong plateau, the region falls under the rain shadow. Annual average rainfall approximates 100 cm. The soils, excepting the alluvial fringe of the Shillong plateau, are fertile everywhere. Rich Sal (Shorea Robusta) abounds in the foothills while tall grasses are common along the river banks. Marshy vegetation consisting of water hyacinth is notoriously common in the low-lying patches. Among the grasses are found reed, cane and long thatch grasses. Rice, jute and tea are the important crops. It is a poor region in the context of industrial development. A jute mill (Silghat), a spun silk mill (Jagiroad) and few rice mills are the only industrial units of the area. However, the subregion enjoys better transport and communication links.

The districts of Kamrup and Goalpara fall in the Lower Assam Plain. Many rainy season torrents lose their courses over the coarse soils and go underground. The rainfall is the lowest in southeast and increases towards north and west. The northern foothill zone is laid with bhabar soils covered with dense forests and tall grasses. The Brahmputra banks and the charlands have swampy forests. However, valuable sal and teak forests are found along the foot of the Shillong plateau. Lumbering and saw milling have recently emerged as important economic activities.

Although with immense forest resources and fertile soils the region can be an agriculturally rich part but the untamed razing lull torrents coming down the Bhutan Himalaya pose a problem in this regard. Once the rivers are tamed, large areas can be fruitfully cultivated to raise rice, jute and vegetable crops. The industrial development of the subregion is confined to Guwahati, a town that enjoys historical significance, as well as central location. An oil refinery, food-processing units and light engineering plants dominate the industrial landscape of Guwahati. Rice and saw mills are other important industrial establishments of the region. Dhubri houses a match factory. Soalkuchi and Palasbari have a name for the weaving of muga and endi silk. Bell-metal work is a traditional craft of a section of the populace of Sarthebari area.

The North Bank Plain of the Brahmputra covers the district of Darrang although a small part of the Kamrup district also falls in it. Similarly the Majauli island of Sibsagar and some part of Western Lakhimpur also come under this sub region. The foothill tract is covered with diluvium, central higher belt is composed of silt while the low-lying belt along the bank of the Brahmputra is filled with alluvium. The average annual rainfall of the sub region nears 200 cm.

The diluvium of the foothill zone is dominated by boulders and pebbles. On this tract are found the three storeyed dense jungles of valuable timbers. The low-lying belt is covered with tall grasses and canes. Though the region exhibits remarkable agricultural potentialities, devastating floods and consequently changing river courses stand in the way of the optimum use of the land resources. Rice and jute are the leading crops. Some tea gardens are also found here. Industrially the region is quite backward. A sugar mill, however, has come to be established at Biswanath Charali. Transport and communication lines are also poorly developed.

The Barak Flain or the Cachar Plain spreading over the Cachar district, is the only plain tract of the state that falls outside the main Brahmputra valley. The headward erosion by streams and subsequent deposition have led to the creation of this plain. On the whole, the plain is dotted with tillas, i.e. sandstone hillocks. The alluvial fringe of the plain is covered with loose talus. The subregion receives an annual rainfall of more than 250 cm. The Barak and its main tributary, the Khushiyara have raised their beds and obviously lead to chronic floods. Even after the rainy season some waterlogged depressions can be seen here and there. The alluvial slopes of the sub region are covered with valuable forests. Tea gardens are found on some slopes and tillas. Low-lying areas are now used for growing jute. Rice is the major food crop of the area. It is an industrially backward area which awaits the removal of transport bottlenecks for its industrial development particularly in the field of agro-based units.

Tradition and Myths

The ancient history of Assam lies in a great degree of obscurity. It is not particular to Assam alone. The chronicle of the entire Northeastern India, similar to the chronicles of many eastern countries, is fabulous and uncertain. With regard to its pre-historic period one has to look towards mythology for getting a peep into the past. According to mythology, mother earth bore a child of Lord Vishnu. This child was found lying in a skull (Kapal) of a human being and was located by Raja Janak, the ruler of Mithila. This King was the same who also fathered Janaki, i.e. Seeta. Since the child was found in the Kapal of a nar (man), he was given the name of Narak. Raja Janak asked one of his maid servants named Katyayani to bring up the child as per royal traditions, without disclosing the parentage to the child. Katyayani spared no effort to prove to the expectations of the ruler. Within sixteen years Narak came of age and emerged as a stout youngman who was unfortunately disposed towards evil designs. Because of this reason this progeny of the gods has been categorised as, asur, i.e. ungodly and Narak thereafter came to be known as Narakasur.

One day while Narakasur was strolling on the banks of the Ganga, Lord Vishnu is believed to have appeared there and disclosed him his past. He was led by Lord Vishnu to Pragjyotishpur (present Guwahati) where in a fierce battle he defeated a Kirat ruler, Ghatak. Thereafter, for sometime he became a favourite of god. The Gods appointed him the guardian of the Kamakhya temple. By virtue of this position he came to preside over the Kingdom of Kamrupa. Narakasur got married to the Princess of Vidharbha, namely Maya. He is also credited to have invited Brahman scholars, artists and craftsmen to settle down in Pragjyotishpur.

It is said that a fairly large number of these personnel migrated from Mithila to Kamrupa. Those of the local chiefs who opposed Narakasur were driven away and this act helped in the expansion of Kamrupa Kingdom. However, he developed intimacy and friendship with Banasur (another asur ruler) of Shonitpur. His (Narakasur) misdeeds and ungodly acts reached a climax when he refused entry in his kingdom to sage Vasishtha who wanted to pay a pilgrimage to the Kamakhya temple. The sage cursed the asur King saying, 'So long as Narakasur is alive the goddess Kamakhya shall remain invisible and she would appear only after his death'. This did not have any effect on Narakasur. Instead, he became more arrogant and aggressive. He is said to have invaded the Devalok (the habitat of gods), humbled some gods and deprived some of their belongings.

Lord Krishna got extremely annoyed with Narakasur, for his acts of oppression and high handedness. He is believed to have slain Narakasur with his weapon, i.e. Sudarshanachakra and Bhagadatta, a son of the deceased was made to succeed. One fails to comprehend as to how does the story of Narakasura suddenly jump from the Ramayana period to that of Mahabharata but Bhagadatta the successor of Narakasur is a character in the Mahabharata epic. When the Mahabharata hero Arjuna visited this region during the Rajsuyayajna victory, he is said to have come into a clash with Bhagadatta, who in return for fear of being defeated by Arjuna sought peace and friendship. However, in the Mahabharata war, Bhagdatta supported the Kauravas. Bhagadatta was very old then but marched and fought at the head of an army consisting of Kirat and Chin soldiers as well as numerous elephants. He fell in the battlefield at the hands of Arjuna. Aine-Akbari mentions that after Bhagadatta, twenty-three rulers of his lineage ruled Kamrupa one after another. Although there is no authenticity of this, fact in Puranas there is a reference that hints towards the possibility of retention of Kamrupa Kingdom by some of the descendants of Bhagdatta for a short period. On the other hand, according to Ramayana resources, the Pragjyotishpur Kingdom was established by one Amurt, a ruler of the solar dynasty.

According to Jogini Tantra resources, it is gathered that after Narakasur it was a Shudra King, Debeswar who came to occupy the throne of Kamrupa. According to another legend a Brahman's cowboy rose to be the ruler of Pragjyotishpur by dint of his luck. He assumed a Hindu name and ruled as King Neeldhwaja and was succeeded by Chakradhwaja. It was however, Nilambor a King of this dynasty who is believed to have left his mark on the history of this region. He paid equal attention towards territorial expansion as well as public welfare activities. He built not only the fort but also roads and temples. But his and was quite tragic. He fell prey to the treachery of his Prime Minister. A unique feature of the history of Assam is that this region was not subjected to any massive Aryan migration or invasion. The caste system and the organised form of Hinduism was carried to Assam during the times of Narakasur. Mythology apart, some historians view Narakasur as a Mongolian proteinate with some articulate Aryan traits and traditions. However, by the time the caste system arrived in the Brahmputra valley, its original virulence and orthodoxies had, to a great extent, relaxed.

The Ahoms who hailed from the Shan plateau of Burma were the original conquerors of Burma. In the early years of the thirteenth century AD the Chinese Empire broke up under the constant thrust of the Mongols Kublai Khan had succeeded to establish himself in China. The Shans under the growing southward intrusion of the Mongols fled to India. It was Chukapha, the first Ahom leader who entered Assam around 1228 AD. He led an army of his followers riding horses and elephants. His march was opposed by the local people but in the struggle that ensued, he achieved many glorious and unparalleled conquests and thereby set up an independent kingdom. It is said that because of his 'unequalled' as well as "unrivalled" conquests, his territories come to be known as Assam. He put up his capital on a hill named as Charaydevi hill.

During the initial years of their rule the Ahoms attempted to propagate their Burmese language but their small numbers stood in their way and they had to take recourse to the local dialects. Resultantly it was ultimately the Assamese language that emerged as *lingua franca* and official language. Moreover, the Ahoms also felt that in order to have their complete control over the territory they had to opt for the religion of the natives, also. Thus they got converted to the Vaishnav cult of Hinduism.

The Chutiyas had by that time established a large kingdom centred around Sadiya. Nevertheless, the Ahoms humbled them and took over Sadiya. The credit for this success goes to Chu Humung who forcefully evicted the Chutiyas, and made them to flee to northern parts. He also helped the inmigration of Ahom families to settle down in Sadiya. It was during the rule of this Ahom King that some useful crafts were developed and expanded so as to provide alternative means of employment to the people. The use of gun-powder based arms was also started during his time.

The Kachharis who are believed to be the crossbreeds of the Tibetans and the Burmese, had a hold over the central and southern parts of Assam. The Kachharis are credited to have established the settlement of Dimapur in the Naga Hills. Their territory spread to the banks of the Dhanisiri river. They too were subjugated by the Ahoms. After their capital was captured, the Kachharis made Khaspur as their capital. Chukhengmung, who occupied the throne in 1539 AD is said to have built the fort of Ghergong on the banks of the Dikho river and shifted his capital there.

It was Chutumla who occupied the throne in 1654 AD and changed his name to a complete Hindu name of Jaidhwaja Singh. The most important event of his time was the Mughal invasion on the Brahmputra valley. Mir Jumala, the Mughal Subedar of Bengal made a daring attempt to overthrow the Ahoms. No doubt the march towards the Ahom capital was tedious, fatiguing and full of privations, but as Mir Jumala shared every privation with his soldiers and often walked on foot with them, the soldiers did not lose heart.

The army succeeded in capturing the Ghergong fort and the Ahom ruler was obliged to seek refuge in the hills. Mir Jumala elated by this success communicated to the Mughal Emperor of Delhi, Aurangzeb, that he had opened the road to China and would shortly hoist the Mughal flag in Peking (now Beijing). But the unusual rains of 1662 aborted all his plans. Not only the floods but even pestilence took a heavy toll on the lives of the Mughal soldiers. The Ahom King cashed in on the opportunity. He came out of the hills and attacked the Mughal fortification and defeated Mir Jumala. This struggle resulted in a treaty which was humiliating for the Mughal Empire.

The Mughal Emperor Aurangzeb who had by that time brought a major part of India under his direct control could not tolerate an independent rule in Assam. Thus, under the generalship of Raja Ram Singh of Amber he despatched a large force to teach a 'befitting lesson to the rats of Assam'. At that time the Ahom forces were commanded by a very capable general Barphukan. He did not allow the Mughal forces even to cross the Brahmputra. After a long and unsuccessful battle the Mughal army retreated and came back. Barphukan is still recalled as one of the greatest and dedicated Ahom generals. He is compared to the Maratha Kesari Shivaji and the Mewar hero Maharana Pratap. Chulekpha, more commonly popular as Lora Raja who was elevated to the throne by Barphukan is notorious in the annals of Assam history for his barbarious acts of tyranny and cruelty.

The Ahoms are said to have followed a tradition as per which any person entitled to become a King forfeited his eligibility to the throne on being handicapped. Afraid of losing his own position in a house where coups were a common feature, the Lora Raja started creating such physical infirmities in all the children who could possibly be named to become a ruler. A heir apparent Prince Gadadhar Singh from the Tung Khung dynasty, however, disappeared from the scene and hid himself in the Naga Hills with a purpose of teaching a lesson to the cruel King. During his days of fugitiveness, the cruel King tortured Gadadhar's wife in many ways so as to obtain the whereabouts of her husband.

Although she was ultimately butchered by the Lora Raja, yet she did not leak out the information. By her such an act of valour, Jayamati the wife of Gadadhar has left an ideal of loyalty to the husband. On the other hand, Gadadhar Singh raised an army in exile and attacked the Lora Raja. In a fierce battle, the cruel King was defeated and put to death. Gadadhar Singh became the new King in 1681. He died in 1695 and was succeeded by his son Chukungpha who sat on the throne under the name of Raja Rudra Singh.

Raja Rudra Singh was undoubtedly the greatest of all the Ahom rulers of Assam. Besides being a capable administrator, he was a worthy and brave general. He expanded his kingdom on all sides and also received the submission of many hill tribes. He commanded such an awful authority that Assam remained free from foreign invasions during his times. He was a great diplomat and through his skill in diplomacy he brought many Hindu rulers under one banner with an objective of putting an and to the Mughal rule in Bengal. Ratna Manikya, his contemporary in Tripura, also supported this cause. Unfortunately his untimely death on the banks of the Brahmputra, opposite Guwahati brought an and to all such plans. The Rudreshwara temple now standing near Guwahati on the bank of the Brahmputra was later on got constructed by his son as a memorial to Rudra Singh. Rudra Singh himself was a great builder. The fort and town of Rangpur owe their existence to Raja Rudra Singh. Jayasagar was built by him in the memory of his mother Jayamati. He also got many shrines built. He was a good poet also.

Rudra Singh was succeeded by his son Chutunpha who assumed kingship under the name of Raja Shib Singh. Phooleshwri, the wife of Shib Singh was a staunch devotee of Shakta sect and even succeeded in dissuading her husband from the Vaishnava sect. The Queen was obstinate in her religious feelings to such an extent that she got some Vaishnavites humiliated on a festive occasion. The enraged Vaishnavites led a revolt against the King who was overthrown and taken as captive. He was slain in 1744. After him three rulers, viz. Parmutta Singh (Chulekpha), Rajeshwar Singh and Lakhmi Singh ruled till 1780. Lakhmi Singh was followed by his son Gaurinath Singh (Chuhitpungpha) and his time witnessed British intervention in Assam for the first time.

Gaurinath Singh had to face many domestic problems right from the beginning of his rule. Tired of uprisings every now and then he appealed to the East India Company to assist him in tiding over the crisis. Resultantly to quell armed insurgencies in Assam,

Captain T. Welsh was sent to Assam with a detachment in 1792. Captain Welsh successfully put down the insurrection and helped the King to stabilise his position. The King however, died of bilious fever soon after. After him Kamleshwar Singh became the ruler who died issueless in 1809. Thus, his brother Chandrakant Singh became the ruler. The foundations of the Ahom rule had already been badly shaken by internal strives and palace intrigues and the edifice built so laboriously by earlier Ahom rulers crumbled down during the time of Chandrakant Singh.

Chandrakant Singh was a minor King and Purananada Buragohain, the Prime Minister was his regent. On some issues Buragohain came to be at loggerheads with Badan Bar Phukan, another minister in the Cabinet. Badan, later on came to know about it. While Burgohain was preparing a plan to exterminate, Badan approached the East India Company for help, but the Company at that time did not favour intervention in the internal affairs of Assam. The Governor General of the Company in this way disappointed Badan who for fear of being exterminated by his powerful foes did not like to come back from Calcutta. Incidentally he came across a Burmese then staying in the city. That Burmese had links with the higher authorities of his country. He wanted to cash in on the situation and thus took Badan to Burma with an assurance that Burmese would help him in his cause.

Badan was introduced to the royal family of Burma. As luck would have it, it was discovered that Badan was distantly related to Hemo, the then Queen of Burma. Now it was rather an obligation on the part of the ruling house of Burma to extend a helping hand towards Badan. Badan was given an armed contingent of four thousand Burmese soldiers for his attack. Badan heading the contingent entered Assam through Patkoi Pass, the entrance which had been used by the Ahoms during the thirteenth century to enter Northeastern India. A bloody battle was fought between the Burmese and the Assamese forces, but, it were the Burmese led by Badan who carried the day. While Purnanada was killed. Chandrakant Singh fled to Guwahati. Badan proceeded towards Guwahati and captured the town. Nonetheless, in his hour of triumph he showed magnanimity towards Chandrakant Singh, whom he helped to become the ruler again. However, somebody slained Badan one day.

The Queen of Burma who had masterminded the plan to attack Assam was greatly shocked by the news pertaining to the killing of Badan. In a bid to wreak vengeance she again sent a Burmese force to set the Assamese house in order and punish the culprits. The Burmese army this time wrought havoc on Assam by perpetrating indiscriminate massacre, torture and terror. Some historians compare the event to the ruthless massacre carried out by Nadir Shah in Delhi. In a way Burmese action surpassed that of Nadir Shah. After about a year Burmese forces, more in numbers this time, attacked Assam. Besides recklessly killing people, the armed personnel burnt standing crops, razed to the ground the dwelling units, shrines and forts.

It is gathered that as a result of this wholesale havoc the populace of Assam was reduced to nearly half. Encouraged by their success after success in Assam the Burmese started trespassing into the territories controlled by the East India Company also. As would be evident, the Burmese and Company forces came into a direct clash. Captain Campell gave a crushing defeat to the Burmese who were thrust back across their frontiers. The Burmese were also forced to sign the Yandaboo Treaty on January 26, 1836. As per terms of this treaty the Burmese had to pay a huge sum as war indemnity and had also to surrender their control over the territories of Arakan and Tanasserim. The British also brought Assam under their direct control.

Gomdhar Konwar was to inherit the throne after Chandrakant Singh. Finding the hopes dashed to the ground consequent upon the British control over Assam, he instigated some Ahom chieftains and tribal leaders to revolt against the East India Company. Before these people could involve the native populace and organise a force their plans leaked out. The British caught hold of the rebel leaders and Gomdhar Konwar was put to gallows for his subversive activities and acts of treason.

On the other hand Pichli Barphukan, the son of Badan Barphukan had been seething with range for the fate meted out to his father. He too came on the war path. He gathered an armed contingent and attacked a British camp Shibsagar, also spelt as Shibsagar. Apart from killing some British soldiers who were caught unaware, Pichli Barphukan set the British arsenal on fire. Nonetheless, the British forces rose to the occasion. They not only reversed the attack but also took Pichli Barphukan and his lieutenant Jieooram Dualiya Barua as captives. With a purpose to terrorise the people the British hanged both these rebels at Sibsagar in 1830.

Nearly after two decades Maniram Barbhandar Barua rose in arms against the British authorities in 1850. To begin with Barua was a British spy in Assam but later on being unsatisfied over a deal Barua turned sides. He was interested in his patron Kandpeshwar Sinha and wished him to be the ruler of North Assam. He went to Calcutta and started negotiating on this issue with the East India Company. The latter on the other hand had tasted the fruit of gaining power over Indian territories. Instead of giving up their control on any areas the British were interested in consolidating their power over the captured areas and also wished to expand their jurisdiction.

Thus the demand of Barua was directly in clash with the company interests in India. Notwithstanding the services rendered by Barua to the Company the British thought of severing their relations with Barua. Thus enraged Barua turned out to be a strong opponent of the British. With the clear-cut aim of overthrowing the British yoke, he started negotiating with other disgruntled rebels. His letters written to one such person Mahesh Chandra Barua, then living at Jorahat were intercepted by the British. The British authorities arrested Maniram Barbhandar Barua at Calcutta and brought him to Jorahat where he and Mahesh Chandra Barua were tried for their subversive activities. Finding them to be guilty of such acts, both of them were hanged in 1858. In the same case Farmud Ali and Bahadur Gaonbara were deported to Black Waters for life.

The next phase of struggle against the British rule initiated in Assam, when Mahatma Gandhi visited Assam for the first time in 1921. He was accompanied by Maulana Muhammad Ali and Shaukat Ali, the two important Muslim rulers who mobilised the mass movement on Khilafat issue. The heaps of foreign, made cloth were put to flames at Guwahati. Thousands of Assamese peacefully participated in the Non-cooperation movement and many went to jails also. After five years, the annual session of the Indian National Congress was held in Assam, for the first time. The historic town of Guwahati hosted the session in 1926, that was presided over by Shrinivas Ayyanagar. This session had a special significance for Assamese. It was only after this session that countless Assamese came attracted towards the Indian National Congress. The Satyagraha movements of 1930 and 1932 received an overwhelming response from Assamese.

The Provincial Autonomy scheme of 1937 was extended to Assam also. The first Provincial Assembly was, however, headed by a Muslim who was by and large a pro-British leader. His government, nonetheless, fell after a year as a result of the acceptance of a no-trust motion against his government by the Assam Legislature. Gopinath Bardoloi, a popular leader, came to the scene. He succeeded as Chief Minister of Assam. This government had to resign consequent upon the decision of the Indian National Congress in 1939. This decision was taken against the British act of forcing India into the Second World' War against the wishes of the representative bodies of the people. Thereafter thousands of Assamese were thrust into jails.

Quit India Movement was welcomed by the Assamese open heartedly. People of all religions, castes, young and old, men and women from different parts of the then Assam struggled for the liberation of the country from the British yoke. People faced the volley of bullets at many places while hoisting the flag of the Indian National Congress atop the administrative buildings. The names of Yogeshwari Phukanani and Kanak Lata shine among the names of those freedom fighters who laid down their lives for the sake of their country while fighting for its freedom. Kamalagiri was another freedom fighter who joined the Quit India Movement while he was ill. He died in the jail itself. Kushal Kunwar was tried in a false and trumped-up case related to subversive activities and this innocent freedom fighter was sent to gallows.

As is well known, the British could not afford to resist the persistent and genuine demands of the Indians. Although they did their best to suppress the freedom movement by all fair and foul means, ultimately they had to yield. The country was granted freedom but unfortunately divided too. While quitting India, the British did the mischief of not treating Assam as a separate province. Assam was tagged to Bengal and given the status of a 'C' state. It was Gopinath Bardoloi who waged a struggle and got a separate statehood for Assam. But the district of Sylhet had already been attached to the erstwhile East

Pakistan. Unfortunately Assam has continued to be a disturbed region right from the Partition days.

The state has witnessed many a worst communal riots and separatist tendencies. In all probability the part played by some foreign missionaries cannot be overruled. Even some political leaders with high ambitions have at times played with the public sentiments. No wonder as a result of all such activities one finds today Assam limited to the Brahmputra valley alone. The States of Meghalaya, Nagaland and the Union Territory of Mizoram were once the parts of Assam State. No doubt from the angle of economic developments the smaller political units, and particularly in a sensitive, strategically located and mountainous region are viable units but it goes without saying that such acts do harm the national interest and give a blow to the sentiments of national integration. Let us hope that this type of vivisection does not leave behind any scars and the coming generations forget all the bickerings their forefathers had and they work unitedly for the nation's progress and national peace.

Cultural Traditions

From ethnological point of view, Assam is a very interesting as well as a fascinating state of India. It is Assam, i.e. uneven not only in the realm of its physiography but also in the field of its human resources. People of different castes, clans and ethnographic groups are found here. People of varying races immigrated to Assam at different periods of history. They fought against and conquered the different native groups and later on settled here. During the process of settlement they assimilated many native traits and at times they intermarried with the natives Resultantly today one finds even the people whose forefathers were a mixed breed.

Australiods, Asiatics, Tibetans, Mongols, Dravidians, Aryans and Burmese, etc. all find representation in Assam of today. The Austro-Asiatics gave the arts of agriculture, music and dancing to Assam. The Dravidians were the aboriginals of India who had come to settle in India even before the Mahabharata period. In the wake of Aryan onslaught over India, some of them reached even the inaccessible parts like Assam. The Mongols came to Assam through Tibet. Their immigration was slow and gradual which led to unopposed assimilation among the natives.

Thereafter followed the Ahoms who have played the major role in the sociocultural stream of the Assamese. Later on, the Santhals entered Assam from Jharkhand. With the gaining of control by the British and the initiation of tea plantations and petroleum mining, people from many parts of India migrated to Assam to seek fortunes. Among them the Biharis, the Bengalis, the Nepalis and the Marwaris have played a significant role in Assam. Their presence in the present context is being resented by the natives and it has led to a very knotty problem. As far as the local culture is concerned it is prudent to discuss it in relation to the Mikirs, the Kachharis and the Santhals.

Mikirs

The Mikirs, locally known as the Arlengs (meaning men), are found in the Mikir Hills, adjacent to the Khasi Hills of Meghalaya, These tall musclemen bear a light yellow brown complexion. A hair knot behind the head is a major characteristic of the personality of a Mikir. They are shifting cultivators and largely pursue jhuming. Weaving is a major allied economic activity of these people. The Mikir males wear dhoti, sleeveless jacket and a cap or turban. Women wear stripped petticoat and an upper garment that tightly laces the breasts. The Mikir women are fond of tattooing. In fact tattooing is the symbol for the attainment of puberty among females.

The Mikirs have rice as their staple diet. They relish meat but are not beef eaters. Nonetheless, the chrysalis of endi silk worm are a delicacy for them. These people are not much fond of music and dances. However, they have dances for funeral occasions. Resultantly they have only flute, drum, one-stringed fiddle and the fife as musical instruments. There is little dancing during harvests but shield dance at funeral sites is very popular.

The Amri, Chenlong and Ronhang are the three major clans of the Mikirs. These clans are exogamous and they intermarry. Their social status depends upon their rank and property. Notwithstanding this segregation they do not mind common feasts. Marriages are normally solemnised after obtaining the consent of the would be partners. Marriage price in kind is paid to the father of the bride. Divorce among the Mikirs is a rare phenomenon. Non-fertility is a cause for divorce. The Mikir girls are on the whole very particular about their chastity. In case a boy seduces a girl, he should marry her. Cases of adultery are also few. With a view to make the punishment exemplary, the indulgent partners are exposed to public jeering.

The property in a Mikir family is inherited by sons alone. The eldest son, however, gets a slightly large share. Women do not have any claim. An issueless widow may retain the property by getting married in her husband's tribal sect. Nonetheless, ornaments and other valuables offered to females at the time of their wedding are treated as their personal assets. The Mikirs continue to be governed by a joint family system. A widowed mother has to be collectively supported by all her sons living together. The Mikirs do not have any custom of adoption. In cases where there are no heirs the property goes to the brothers of the deceased. For want of brothers the nearest agnates in the family inherit the property. Village council is the pivot in a Mikir village. Its members include all male householders. The head of the council is elected. The council arbitrates in all disputes and is also empowered to fine a guilty. All village heads in a region constitute the Greater Village Council, presided over by the Mauzadar who is the senior most village council president. Matters serious in nature are invariably decided by this apex body.

The Mikirs profess animistic faith. They do not follow the concept of an Almighty God, although they believe in a number of gods, whom they worship on a number of occasions. Animal sacrifices are very often offered to appease gods. Abors, i.e. amulets are highly revered. Abors are just pieces of stone or metals found by accident, believed to be importing good luck to the bearer.

Kachharis

The Kachharis are the most widely-spread people of Assam. Before the heyday of the Ahoms it were the Kachharis who held their sway over Assam. The Kachharis are found even outside Assam. The mere stroke of history divided the Kachharis into two distinct groups viz Northern and Southern Kachharis. Strangely enough they do not intermarry and also speak different dialects. The Kachharis are agriculturists who profess cultivation in a cooperative manner. In all important agricultural operations the Kachharis exhibit a remarkable sense of cooperation. Many Kachharis work as labourers in the tea estates also. The Kachharis are a first rate silk worm rearing people. The endi silk of Assam owes its affluence to Kachharis alone.

The Kachharis during their heyday helped the art and culture to attain new heights. No wonder they left a lasting effect on the culture of Assam. They are a powerful and well-built people. Those living in the Brahmputra valley call themselves Bodos or Bodophisa meaning a Bodo son. The Kachharis of the southern Cachar hills name themselves as Dimchha meaning sons of a great river valley. They are a mixture of Chutiya, Lalung, and Moran tribes. They are the same people who are referred to as Malechhas in Puranas. Dimapur at one time housed the headquarters of the Kachhari Kingdom. The ruins around Dimapur speak about a high standard of architecture and art that once flourished there. They built houses of bricks and stones at a time when the Ahoms were completely ignorant about the use of these materials in house-building.

The Kachharis live in thatched bamboo dwellings. All types of meat excepting beef is relished by the Kachharis. Dried fish and pork are their prized delicacies. Zu, i.e. rice beer is consumed lavishly. The Kachharis earlier have been endogamous and a totemistic people. Now with the passage of time many restrictions have been removed. Polyandry is strictly prohibited and monogamy is the general practice. Marriage by capture is also prevalent in a section of the Kachharis. Bride-price has to be paid by the groom. In case he is a poor person he offers to work in the family of the bride for a certain period before marriage. At the termination of this period he gets married and is free to take his wife wherever he likes. Divorce by mutual consent is an easy affair among the Kachharis. But divorce is granted by the village council which may also grant marriage expenses to the groom. The divorcees are at liberty to go for other spouses. Moral standards of the Kachharis are high. Those indulging in adultery are severely punished and in case of pregnancy the offending male is compelled to get married to the grieved girl.

The sons inherit equal shares of the property of their deceased father. Nevertheless, the eldest son enjoys the privilege of getting a slightly more than his normal share. The daughters have no claim in the property of their father. A person dying male-issueless bequeaths property to his eldest living brother who is bound by custom to look after the widow and daughters of the deceased. There are no hard and fast rules related to adoption. Orphans are, however, adopted by and large by their near relations. The Kachharis do not have any shrines but they believe in mother earth, sky, air fire. They think, the spirit modai lives in all these elements and does not act against the interest of the Kachharis. Household gods and village gods are worshipped separately. This society does not have any priestly class and all their religious rituals are performed by the village elders popularly called Deoris.

Santhals

The dark complexioned Santhals, strong in physical built and healthy in appearance originally belong to the Santhal Parganas of Jharkhand. They migrated to Assam in past and settled down at the foot of the Bhutan Hills in the northern part of the Goalpara district. Scantily dressed, and mainly wearing loin cloth (dhoti by females) they are a simple and peace loving-people. They have been a hunting tribe and bow and arrow is sacramental to them. So much is the significance of hunting in their society that when a young Santhal boy attains a certain age, he is ceremonially initiated to hunting. The placenta of a newly-born baby is also cut with the help of an arrow and the same is placed by the side of the baby for five days with a belief that the child is protected from evil spirits. Besides hunting they derive their livelihood by way of working as labourers and pursuing a primitive form of agriculture. They are rice eaters and also brew a liquor out of rice.

The Santhals are divided into twelve gotras and they have only inter-gotra and not intra-gotra marriages. In case of marriage it is the Santhal girl who approves her groom. Only after she has approved her would-be life partner that wedding is ceremonised. Nevertheless, there are instances when the Santhal boy and girl just start living as husband and wife without any ceremony or social sanction. Divorce is permissible on the condition that the aggrieved spouse is compensated in cash. A man who intends to get married to a divorced woman is required to pay a fine.

The village administration of a Santhal settlement is run by the Manjhi, i.e. headman. Assisted by two functionaries, i.e. Paramanik and Jogmanjhi. The headman collects land revenue and supervises other functions. His office is normally hereditary but in case he is survived by no sons and brothers, the Paramanik automatically gets this office. A group of villages are supervised by Parganait assisted by a Dish-Manjhi. The organisation headed by a Manjhi, i.e. Kulidrub decides disputes less important in nature while important and serious matters are decided by the Panchayat presided over by a Parganait.

Faiths and Religion

At present no doubt one finds people professing different faiths and cults in Assam yet it would be worthwhile to briefly review the development of animistic faith tantravad, and Shakta sect of Hinduism two sects that had a hold over the native populace for long and continue to be such with a fairly large section of the people even at present.

There goes a legend that has a relevance here. Goddess Parvati, the consort of Lord Mahadeva once enquired from her husband as to which force controls the human life and which force should be worshipped by man. Lord Mahadeva said that such a force was only woman and also explained the rituals by way of which womanhood be worshipped. This forms the basis of the Shakta cult as well as the tantric faith.

Assam has been a land of tantric practices. In all probability the practice of human sacrifice widely in vogue among the aboriginals has been the sheet anchor of tantric persuasions. The Shakta cult also presents a modified form of tantric faith. The tantric faith in a way Kings upon blood and sacrifice. Besides birds and animals, in Assam human beings used to be sacrificed on certain occasions. On some special occasions only flawless persons in their body could be sacrificed. Some persons used to be selected for the sacrificial altar of the goddess Durga much in advance. Such persons were designated as Bhogis and all worldly pleasures in abundance used to be left at their disposal for their enjoyment. Some of the aboriginals of Assam practised magic and other such rituals. On some occasions, on the completion of pregnancy period of a mother, her newborn child was offered at the altar. Such sacrifice was considered to be of vital significance. Nonetheless, such cruel practices are now losing ground with increased awakening and outside contact.

The spread of the Shakta cult is said to have begun with the establishment of the Kamakhya temple. Kamakhya is considered as a force equivalent to nine Durgas. It is believed that the first Kamakhya temple was got built by King Narakasur, near Guwahati. This temple went to ruins and it was again got constructed by a King named Narnarayan around 1595 AD. It is said that on the completion of this temple a special function was held at which 140 human heads placed on silver plates were offered to the goddess.

It was the saint poet Shankaradeva who brought about a revolution in the field of religion in Assam. Through his compositions and preachings he waged a battle against superstitious beliefs, sacrifices and undesirable rituals. He insisted for the replacement of sacrifices by love, meditation and worship. The form of religion he preached was universal in nature and cosmopolitan in content. He fought tooth and nail against high and low and persuaded people of all shades, categories and ages to sit under one roof and worship the Almighty. He helped people to shun orthodoxy and dogmatism and persuaded them to come under the umbrella of wide awakening and spiritual enlightenment. However, he preached the Vaishnava cult of Hinduism. It does not mean that Shakta cult had been wiped out of Assam. However, the number of followers of this cult had dwindled and decreased. There are Buddhists also in Assam. In a way Buddhism entered Assam at a time when this religion was fast marching towards a period of decay in India. Nonetheless, the Khamtis living close to Bhutan still profess Buddhism. The Shaiv cult of Hinduism also had its impact on Assam. On a river island of the Brahmputra near Guwahati there is the Umananda temple that speaks about it. The Ahom ruler Shib Singh also got two Shiva temples built here.

The Christian missionaries also started entering, particularly the hilly tracts of Northeastern India quite early. The mountainous parts of Assam were no exception. The American Baptist Church has succeeded in converting a fairly large number of tribals to Christianity. Besides the Welsh, Spanish and Italian missionaries have also done work in this regard. These missions have also spread educational facilities among these people.

Traditional Festivals

As already stated the state of Assam today is the home of tribals and non-tribals, Hindus, Muslims and Christians, Vaishnavites and Shaktas and alike. Resultantly people professing different faiths, coming from different clans and shades celebrate different festivals. Nonetheless, one finds the traits of one culture slowly and gradually sneaking unknowingly in that of other, and that is a happy sign. Here it would be useful to make a mention of the important festive occasions.

The new year of the Assamese society starts in April and the occasion is celebrated through the festival of Rangoli Bihu or simply Bihu also termed as Bohag. The festive occasion initiates on the last day of Chaitra (Chaitra Sankranti) month (mid-April to mid-May) of the Vikrami calendar. On the basis of the rituals and specific celebrations, the different parts of the festive period are named differently. The day of initiation is called Goru Bihu. On this day the peasants take their cattle to the nearest water body and they are given a bath.

After the bath, the cattle who directly and indirectly provide them with means of sustenance, are worshipped. As a ritual, a paste made of turmeric and black gram is applied on the hoofs and horns of the cows and oxen. On reaching home the animal sheds are cleansed and insects, etc. are driven away by creating smoke. The old ropes used for tethering these cattle are also replaced by new ones. The agricultural implements and particularly the plough and yoke are also washed on this day. On this day the natives also go for fishing and hunting. The game so obtained becomes a public property and is utilised for the ensuing public feast.

The next six days are covered under the festival of Manhu Bihu. On the first day of the Manhu Bihu the handmade gamchhas (towel-like cloth mostly used by males and placed on the shoulders) are exchanged between near and dear ones. On the following day people start exchanging visits. During these visits people are fed on choicest dishes and local brews (Lao pani, i.e. rice beer) by their hosts. In the Sibsagar-Lakhimpur tract the natives also organise public dancing programmes. Thus, it would be apt to say that the roots of festivals in Assam are embedded in people means of livelihood. People who pursue agriculture and other primary economic activities are, for obvious reasons, likely to base their principal festivals on these activities.

At the time of Bihu, winters have taken leave and a pleasant weather indicative of coming summers sets in. New sprouts decorate the physical environment all around. Flowers start infusing their fragrance in the entire atmosphere. In a way the environment injects mobility in the feet of dames and lads. They seem to be impatient to perform dancing muses to the tunes of Kortal (a fork like instrument of bamboo), drum and Mohor Singa (a blowing instrument made of buffalo horn). The dance apparel used by young girls is their hand made creation. The borders of these costumes are red-lined. Red is a colour that is symbolic for youth and it is the youth who add colour and enthusiasm to the occasion.

The Bilzu Nritya is dominated by the movements of buttocks and hands while feet move only few inches this or that way. In upper Assam, there are mixed dances while in rest of the region no such mixed dances are performed. Nevertheless, at night under the intoxication of laopani, a mixed dance becomes the rule. In Assamese society the art of dancing is a prized gift with a young girl. A girl who does not know the art of dancing and weaving is looked down upon. In fact a girl well versed in these arts is in high demand in the society for matrimony.

In the month of January falls the festival of Bhath Bihu. At this time the autumn-sown paddy is harvested and people feel free. The word bhath in some Indian languages and dialects refers to cooked rice; while in some north Indian languages it is simply bhat. It is an occasion meant for 'eat, drink and be merry'. In the village a huge fire is made in the open at a common place and the fire provides warmth. The common feast is an occasion to partake different non-vegetarian dishes. After the feast the people start dancing under the influence of liquor. In the months of October-November, when poor people fall short of foodgrains, the well to do farmers and other wealthy persons celebrate Kangali Bihu. On this occasion the poor peasants (Kangal stands for abject poverty) and other have-nots of the society are fed during mass feasts hosted by the haves of the Assamese society. Nonetheless, with the advance of heartless materialism and 'cruel' modernism such virtuous gestures are slowly and gradually dying out.

Durga Puja is another important festival of Assam and is an index of the fact that Bengalis in fairly large numbers have made the valley their home. After West Bengal, it is Assam that celebrates Durga Puja with enthusiasm and gusto. Celebrated in autumn the festival also heralds the beginning of winter. After harvesting the summer, sown paddy the people of Bengali origin worship and welcome the goddess Durga. In fact it was Queen Phooleshwri Kunwari the wife of King Rajeshwara Singh who introduced the festival of Durga Puja in Assam during the 18th century.

The mud in water bodies starts drying out and the sprouts of lotus and lilly flowers add to the charm of lakes, tanks and ponds. Such an environment induces a mood of ecstasy among the farmers who are free from the harvests and thus appear to be ready for merry making. The Durga images are prepared of straw, bamboos and mud. The festival spans over five days. On the first day the image of the deity is installed and it is immersed in water on the last day, i.e. day of victory, called *Vijya*. The entire festival is a grand exhibition of cultural functions including musical concerts and dancing muses. This festival continues till Kali Puja which takes piece three weeks later. Animal sacrifices are also made during Kali Puja. The festival of illuminating lamps, i.e. Deepawali is celebrated on the night preceeding Kali Puja. The Muslim population of Assam celebrates Moharram, Prophet Hadrat Muhammad's birthday, Id-ul-Fitar, Id-ul-Adha, etc. The Moharram commemorates the martyrdom of Hassan and Hussain (grandsons of Hadrat Muhammad) in the battle of Karbala in Arabia.

Sport Features

People of Assam are interested in a variety of sports as golf, tennis, football, boxing, and swimming. Golf is played at Dhansiri Polo Club near Bokakhat. Golaghat boxing club is one of the important boxing clubs of Assam, which is situated at the Amolapatty area. In the heart of Golaghat town, there is an indoor stadium having two badminton courts and four table tennis boards. In the field of sports, Golaghat occupies an important place in Assam. The Golaghat tennis club is one of the oldest in state. It has produced several National and International players of repute in athletics, table tennis, boxing and football. There are two lawn courts at Kushal Kunwar Memorial Trust Complex. Next to the indoor stadium of Golaghat town, there is a swimming pool, which is managed by District Sport Office. One of the important stadiums of Assam is the Nehru Stadium, which is a multi-use stadium managed by the board of sports. The stadium holds twenty-five thousand people and was built in 1962. It is used for playing both football and cricket matches.

History

Ancient Times

The ancient history of Assam is shrouded in obscurity. The sources on which the history of Assam has been written are the archaeological sites, published and unpublished documents, memoirs, biographies, writings in journals and periodicals, historical writings in Assamese, Bengalis, and Sanskrit. Some of the writings on which may be termed as the important sources of history of Assam are M'Cosh's Topography of Assam.

This work is of early date and represents the information available from official sources. General works which contain references on the people of the Brahmaputra valley and the people of neighbouring hills are Hobson-Jobson, the Golden Bough, or Perry's Megalithic culture of Indonesia. A number of references to missionary publications, the reports of the Assam Mission Conferences in particular that of 1912, and likewise the reports of the American Baptist Foreign Mission Society, Boston also contain a certain degree of scattered material.

There are references about the history of Assam in the following publications. A Description of Assam by Muhammad Qasim (1792) by H. Vansittart. F. Hamilton's book 'An Account of Assam with some Notices concerning the Neighbouring Territories, Annals of oriental Literature,' T. Fisher's, Memoirs of countries on and Near the E. Frontier of Sylhat (1927).

The Geography and Population of Assam and in Asiatic Researches (1828) by Neufville. Capt. Jenkins account on the Nagas of Assam in the Journal of Asiatic Society (1936). Griffith, Wm: F.L.S. (1837) Report to the Government of India on the journey from Upper Assam towards Hookhoom. W. Robinson (1841), Descriptive Account of Assam, Published by Ostell & Co. London. History of American Baptist Missions (Boston) written by W. Gamell (1849). The North Kachar Hills and their Inhabitants written by G. H. Damant in Calcutta Review, LXI, 1875. The Statistical Account of Assam (1879) by W. W. Hunter and the Assam Gazetteer by W. W. Hunter (1886). Report on the census of Assam (1891) by E. A. Gaite ad A.W. Davis.

Lifestyle: There is interesting information about the mode of life of the Tribes of the plains of Assam in 'Tribes of Brahmaputra Valley in the Journal of Asiatic Society of Bengal, 1901, vol. LXIX. The History of Assam written by E. A. Gait (1906) published from Calcutta. The section about the history of Assam was also consulted from Imperial Gazetteer of India — East Bengal and Assam, published from Oxford. Report on the Administration of Assam (1923) prepared by Lloyd, G. and published from Shillong. The Assam Burma Frontier written by J. P. Mills (1926) and published in the Geographical Journal Assam Mega liths written by J. H. Hutton and published in the Sept. 1929 issue of the Antiquity. The History of Assam Rifles (1929) written by Col. L. W. Shakesphear has also been consulted.

The monumental work of Chaudhry on the history and society of Assam was also consulted.

In addition to these, the secondary sources from the Assame and Bengali historical works were also consulted in the writing of the chapter. The Ahom Buranji (1930) written by G. Barua and published at Guwahati, and S. Basu's Bangalay Nabachetanar Itihas, Calcutta, 1975.

Some of the new works are 'A History of Assam Company' by Antrobus, H. A. Edinburgh, K. L. Barua's 'Studies in the Early History of Assam' published at Jorhat in 1973; H. K. Barpuzari, 1977 'Political History of Assam'; Assam under the Ahoms (1942) by U. N. Gohain; R. M. Lahiri's The Annexation of Assam, Calcutta; W. Robinson's 'A Descriptive Account of Assam, Calcutta 1841, and P. H. Noore's 'General view of Assam' in the Assam Mission Golden Jubilee Volume. Moreover a number of other Historical Journals and Periodicals were consulted to give a precise historical account of Assam.

The ancient history of Assam is involved in a great degree of obscurity. Though we have a few chronicles and works of native composition to refer to, most of the occurrences mentioned in them, especially those relating to more ancient history, are so intimately blended with what is fabulous and uncertain, that we are obliged to receive them with great diffidence.

Mythology: By far the greater portion of the country now known as Assam, was originally included in the ancient Hindu territory of Kamroop (Kamrup); besides which it also included the whole of the modern division of Rungpur (Rangpur), and Rangmati, a portion of Mymensingh district and Sylhet (Silhet) and in all probability also extended over Manipur, Jainia (Jyntia), and Kachar. The earliest tradition concerning the history of Kamrup is, that it was given by Krishna to Norok, the son of Prithibi (Prithvi or the Earth).

This Norok, although an infidel (Osur), was for sometime a favourite of the gods, who appointed him guardian of the temple of Kamakhya, (the giver of pleasure) who naturally presided over Kamroop (Kamrup), the region of desire. This deity is by the Hindus considered a female, and her temple situated near Gowhatti (Guwahati), the place where Norok resided, in still one of great celebrity.

Kamroop is said to have been divided into four Piths, or portions, each of which may naturally be expected to have had an appellation situated to its name, and tutelary deity. They are accordingly called Ram-Pith, Ratno-Pith, Sevarna-Pith, and Choumar-Pith. By the natives the country is considered as the principal seat of amorous delight, a sort of Paphian land; and a great indulgence in promiscuous pleasures in consequently considered as allowable.

Norok did not long merit the favour of Krishna. Being a greater oppressor, and a worshipper of the rival god Sib (Shiva), he was put to death, and was succeeded by his son Bhagadatta. At the time of the wars which are said to have placed Judisthir (Yadhustar) on the throne of India, this Prince engaged in the great contest on the losing side, and followed the fortunes of Durjudhan (Duryodhan). There seems a great probability that this is the same person with Bhagrat of Mr. Gladwin's translation of the Ain-e-Akbari, "who came to assistance of Durjudhan, and gallantly fell in the war of the Mahabharat."

In this great war, Bhagadatta is said to have fallen by the hands of Arjun, brother of Judisthir (Yadhustar); but according to Ain-e-Akbari, twenty three princes of the same family continued to govern after his death. The authority of this work is however, diminished by its supporting that these princes governed the whole of Bengal; which seems entirely without foundation. It is, however, very likely, and is said indeed to be mentioned in the Puranas, that for some time the descendents of Bhagadatta retained the Government of Kamroop (Kamrup).

This account does not agree with that given in the Jogini Tantro, which is considered as the highest authority concerning everything relating to Kamroop (Kamrup). In it there is no mention of Bhagadatta; but it states that the god Sib (Shiva) prophesied, that after the infidel Norok, and at the commencement of the era of Saka, that is, about the end of the first century of our era, these would be Shudra King of Kamroop. The first Raja mentioned is Debeswar, in whose time the worship of Kameswari, or Kamakhya, the knowledge of which had hitherto been confined to the learned, would be published even to the vulgar; and this would happen at the very beginning of the Era of Saka, or AD 76.

The worship of the Linga, according to this prophecy, would begin in the 19th year of Saka. Some indefinite time, after that period, a Brahman, born of the Kerotya river, and named Nagasankar, would be King, and extend the doctrine. After him but at what interval is not mentioned, would be a Raja, named Jolpeswar, who would still further encourage that worship, and who would build the celebrated temple of Jolpis, in Rangpoor (Rangpur). Very considerable ruins are at no great distance from that place, but are ascribed to Prithu Raja, who may have been a person of the same family. This Prithu Raja, from the size of his capital, and the numerous works raised in the vicinity by various dependents and connections of the court, it is supposed must have governed a large extent of country, and for a considerable period of time.

It does not appear that during the dynasty of Adisur any part of Kamroop (Kamrup) was a part of the Kingdom of Bengal. On the contrary, about that time, or not long after, the western parts of the kingdom seem to have been subject to a family princes, the first of whom that has any traces left, was Dharma Pal. Whether or not from his name, we may suppose that he was one of the Pal family, which preceded the dynasty of Adisur, who in the wreak of this family may have saved a portion of their possession, we have not the means to determine. From the works that are attributed to Dharam Pal, he would appear to have been a person of some power, and even the works attributed to relations and dependents of his family possess some degree of magnitude. A few copper grants still in existence would serve to prove, that Dharma Pal's rule extended up the valley as far as Tezpur.

With regard to the next dynasty, there is greater certainty, although as usual the chronology is attended with many difficulties. According to tradition, there was a Brahman whose name in unknown, but who had a servant that tended his cattle, no one knows where. Many complaints were lodged against him, and his master was called one day to come and see him asleep, while his cattle were permitted to destroy the crops of the neighbours.

The Brahmin was advancing with a determination to bestow the merited punishment, when he observed the lines on the naked fact of his servant, and immediately, by his "profound skill in the most noble science of Samudrik Joytish," for saw that the person would become a Prince. On this discovery the Brahma paid him all due respect, rendered it unnecessary for him to perform any low office, and showed him still more kindness by disclosing the certainty of his future greatness. The servant is return promised that when he became a Prince the Brahmin, his master, should be his Chief Minister. Accordingly sometime afterwards, it is not know how, he became the King, and is said to have destroyed the last of the Pal family. It is however, more probable, that on the death or dethronement of the last King, Kamroop had fallen into a state of anarchy favourable for an upstart, and was overrun by a bordering tribe.

The new Raja seems to have been much guided by his minister, the Brahman, assumed a Hindu title. Nilodhoj, and placed himself under the tuition of the sacred order. For this purpose a colony of Brahmins was introduced from Maithilo; and from thence we may perhaps infer the country of the Minister. There is no trace of an earlier colony of

Brahmanas in Kamroop than this from Maithilo. The great merits of the Prince were rewarded by the Brahmans, by elevating his tribe, called *Khyan*, to the dignity of pure Hindus. The Raja having settled his government, built a city called Kamatapur on a branch of Singimari river, in the present district of Rangpur. He had his successors then took the title of Komoteswar, or Lords of Komatu.

The second Prince of his family was Chokrodhoj. During this dynasty the office of Chief Minister seems to have been hereditary, as well as the regal dignity.

Chokrodhoj was succeeded by Nilambor, the third and last Prince of the family. His dominions are said to have extended over the greater part of Kamroop. The upper portion of his Kingdom had however prior to this period, been invaded by a new race of conquerors; who poured in from the northern extremity of the valley, and not long after succeeded in gaining complete possession of the country. Their origin, and progress of their conquests, we shall take not of.

Numerous public works, especially the construction of magnificent roads, and the erection of the fort at Ghoraghat, are attributed to Nilambor, who would seem to have governed-this portion of the country with attention. The circumstances related concerning his overthrow, are accompanied with traits of the most savage barbarity.

Whether from a natural suspiciousness of temper, or from an uncommon accuracy of observing such circumstances, the Raja on entering his seraglo one day, is said to have observed traces which convinced him that a man had been there. He was immediately inflamed with jealousy and having placed some of his people on the look out, a young Brahman, son of Sachi Patro the Prime Minister, was soon caught attempting to enter the royal apartments. He was taken before the King and privately put to death, and part of his body was prepared for food. His father having been invited to a grand entertainment given by the King, is said to have eaten of his son's body. After he had satisfied himself with this monstrous food, the King showed him his son's head, and informed him of the crime, and of what he had been eating.

The minister is said to have acted with a presence of mind well suited for such an occasion. He said that his son no doubt deserved any punishment, but as the King had made him eat such a horrid repast, he could no longer continue in his service, but would retire from the world, and dedicate himself to the duties of a religious mendicant. By this stratagem he was allowed to retire, and having assumed the habit of Sanyasi, immediately left Kamroop. His first object was to procure revenge; and he proceeded without delay to Gour, where he laid before the Mohammadan King information which was followed by an attack on Nilambor. For sometime, however, the invasion did not seem likely to terminate in success; for, after a siege of twelve years, the Muslims had made no impression on the works of Komatapur.

Although the length of the siege is very much exaggerated by tradition, its issue is likely to have long continued doubtful. The place is said to have been at length taken by stratagem, or rather by shameful treachery. The Muslim commander informed the King by message, that having lost all hopes of taking the place, he was desirous of making peace, and of leaving the country on the most friendly terms. This having been accepted, it was proposed that the ladies of the friendly terms.

This having been accepted, it was proposed that the ladies of the Muslim chiefs should pay their respects to the Queen. This also was received as a mark of polite attention, and a number of covered litters were admitted into the Queen's apartments within the citadel. Instead of ladies these litters contained arms, and the bearers were soldiers, who immediately on gaining admission raised their weapons, and secured the person of the Raja.

After the overthrow of Nilambor, two brothers, named Chondon and Madan, established a short government of eight years, at a place about thirty miles north from Komatapur. Their power was not only transient, but seems to have extended to no great distance. It is more than probable, that the paths of Lower Kamroop which were not retained by the Muslims, had fallen into anarchy under the chiefs of adjacent tribes. Among these tribes, by far the most powerful were the Kuchis, who had a number of chiefs at first independent, but who gradually united under the authority of one of themselves named Hajo. He seems to have been a person of great vigour, and is said to have reduced under his government the whole of Rangpur, Ghoraghat expected, together with a large portion of Assam, included in the Government of Kamroop.

He is reported to have had two daughter, Hira and Jira. Hira before the rise of her family had been married to a certain Herya, who is said to have been of the compare tribe called *Mech*. To whom Jira was married is not known, but she had a son named Sisu, while her sister bore a son named Bisu. The latter succeeded to the whole power of his grandfather. As he was not contended with the instruction of the Kolitas, who seem to have been the original priesthood of his tribe, nor with the learning of the Brahmans of Maithilo, who had been formerly introduced, he procured some men of piety, Bandiks from Srihotta (Sylhat) and gave them the title of Kamrupi Brahmans, and these form the second colony of the sacred order that settled here.

To this era, observes Buchnan, may probably be referred the composition or, as the Hindus would say, the publication of many or most of the books called *Tantras*; which are supposed to have been communicated by the god Sib to him wife Parbati about 5,000 years ago. One of the most celebrated of these compositions is the Jogni Tantro, which mentions the Arnows of Hira, and the government of her son; nor is there any doubt that Kamrup is usually considered as the grand source of this system of magic. The period between the time of Bisu, and of his great grand son Prikit, seems to have been the only period when the learning of the Brahmins flourished in this province.

The doctrines contained in these works admit of many indulgences for few convents, and place no restrictions on the Brahmins from sharing in the pleasures of a most sensual people: they inculcate chiefly the worship of the female spirits, which was the original worship of the country, and which has now become very generally diffused among the Brahmins of Bengal, with whom these Tantras are in great repute.

It was now discovered that the Raja was not a son of the poor barbarian Herya; but that his mother, although descended from a Kuch, was not only a celestial origin, but had been the peculiar favourite of the god Sib (Shiva), who was the actual father of the Prince. He then took the name of Biswa Singh, and bestowed on the son of his aunt Jira that of Siba (Shiva) Singh: this latter Prince also claimed for his mother, the honour of the most intimate favour of the god whose name he bore. On this pretended descents the Kuchis, or at least all of them that have adopted the Hindu religion, and have relinquished their impure practices, now assume the title of Rajbasgri, or descendents of princes. All the descendents of Hira, still further elated by their supposed divine origin, assume the title of Deb, or lord, and all the reigning princes of the family claim the title of Naraian, which among the Hindus is one of the names of the Supreme Deity.

Biswas Singh died AD 1528, leaving eighteen sons; the eldest of whom, Nur-Naraiyan, succeeded to the throne. His reign is said to have been very prosperous. He patronised learning, and caused the 12th book of the Bhagabat, and the 18th chapter of the Bharat, together with the Ram Sarasavati to be drawn up under his immediate inspection. In 1565 he rebuilt the temple of Kamakhya, which had been pulled down by Kalapahar, a general of Sulaiman the governor of Bengal, who entered Assam some time between 1550 and 1560, and fearful were the ravages committed by him. He persecuted the Brahmins, destroyed numberless images, and the ruins of many splendid temple scattered throughout the Lower Provinces of Assam, are to this day pointed out, as the work of this terrific general. "He was by birth a Brahmin, but one of the princesses of Gour having become enamoured of him, he turned Muslim, and married her, and then became the most violent persecutor of the Hindus, mentioned in history. Indeed so great was the terror excited by his persecutions, that according to the natives, at the sound of his kettle drum the arms and legs of the idols dropped off for many a cross around."

It was during the reign of Biswas Singh, too, that the great Bund road was constructed, called the Goham Kamul Ali. He died in 1584, after a reign of 56 years, in which he won the affections of all his people.

Prior to his death he had nominated his nephew Ragadeo Nara Naranjan to the succession; but soon after, himself having a son, Ragadeo was laid to suspect that he would be deprived of his promised inheritance. Accordingly on the plea of proceeding on a sporting excursion, he is said to have left the royal palace, to which he never after returned. The old King, in order to appease his nephew, made over part of his possessions to him in AD 1581. The Dikrai formed his eastern boundary, while the Sankos flowed along the western extremity of his dominions. He is reputed, to have founded the city of Ghelabijai in Kamroop, the present temple at Haju, which is said to have been built in 1583, is also ascribed to him.

On the death of Nara Naranjan, his son Lakhi Naranjan succeeded to the other portion of his father's Kingdom which extended from the Sankos on the east, to the Karatuja on the west. From him are said to have descended the subsequent Kings of Kuch Behar (Cooch-Behar).

In 1593 Ragadea dying, was succeeded in his possession by his son Parikhit Naranjan. Here it ends the First Phase of its history. Just after the accession of Parikhit on throne the second period of the History of Assam beings.

Medieval Times

Mughals' Period: Assam like all other states and provinces of India was also affected by the ruling Mughal Dynasty. The King Parikhit was the contemporary of Akbar and was ruling in the province of Assam.

When Abul Fazal composed the Ain-e-Akbari, the subdivision of the Kingdom of Biswas Singh was not known to Delhi, although in all probability it had recently taken place. From prudential motives, perhaps, it had been carefully concealed; and the two branches of the family lived in an amity that was absolutely necessary for their safety. Abul Fazal says, that north from Bengal is the province of Kuch (Cooch), the chief of which commands 1,000 horses, and 1,00,000 foots; which is probably an oriental exaggeration. Kamroop (Kamrup), which is also called *Kamtah*, makes a part of his dominion.

Soon after Parikhit's accession to the throne, he was engaged in hostilities with his neighbour and relative, Lakhi Naranjan. The latter fearing his own safety, is said to have asked the assistance of the Muslim Governor of Dacca; who on discovering the real state of affairs, became very urgent with Parikhit for tribute. The Raja being afraid, did not absolutely refuse to comply, but in order to procure favourable terms, was advised to undertake a journey to Agra, where he was kindly received, and procured an order from the King, directing the governor to take whatever tribute the Raja chose to offer.

On returning to Dacca, the Raja who is said to have been totally ignorant of human affairs, and of the immensity of the sum, offered 20,000,000 of rupees, and returned to his capital highly satisfied with his conduct. When his minister explained to him the nature of the promise he had made, the poor Raja was thrown into consternation, and again set out for Agra, taking his minister with him in order to avoid such mistakes.

Unfortunately he died on the way at Patna (1606 AD), and the Muslims in the meantime took possession of the country, in order to recover the money that had been promised. The minister proceeded to court; where after some trouble, he was appointed Kanungo, or Registrar of the Country, which was divided into four Sirkars.

The brother of Parikhit, Balit Naraiyan, was confirmed in his government of a portion of his brother's dominions, extending from the Dikari on the east, to Monah Nadi on the west; whilst on the unfortunate son of Raja, Bijut Naraiyan, was conferred a large estate extending from the Monah Nadi on the east, to the Sankos on the west.

This territory is still occupied by his descendents, the Raja of Bijut. On the death of Balit Naraiyan, which occurred in 1634, he was succeeded by his son Mohindra Naraiyan. He was a pacific Prince, and employed his time in improving the condition of his subjects, and, among other good deeds, conferred large grants of rent-free lands on the Brahmins. He died in 1653 AD, after a reign of nineteen years. He was succeeded by his son Chandra Naraiyan, who in all general respects trod in the footsteps of his father. On his death, his son Surja Naraiyan succeeded to the throne.

Mazoor Khan's Period: About the year 1662 his territories were invaded by Mazoor Khan, a general of the Emperor of Delhi, when he was himself taken prisoner, and conveyed to the presence of the Emperor. Sometime after, effecting his escape, he returned to his own dominion, but from a sense of shame, is said to have refused resuming the rein of government.

When he had been taken away prisoner, his brother Indra Naraiyan, then only five years of age, was placed on the throne. During his reign the country was distracted with internal convulsions; and the Ahom Kings, taking advantage of these occurrences, made themselves masters of Choumarpith, and Kampith. Durrang alone was all this week Prince found it in his power to retain; and for this portion he was obliged to pay an annual tribute to the Ahom King.

On his death which occurred in 1725, his son Adhitya Naraiyan succeeded but with a small portion of the territories of his ancestors. His boundaries were the Dhansiri on the east, and the Barnadi on the west: the great Burid-road, called the Gohain Kamul Ali, on the north, and the Brahmaputra on the south.

In 1728, his younger brother Mudh Naraiyan seized upon two-thirds of his already very insignificant kingdom, and proclaimed himself King of his newly acquired possessions. Four years after this occurrence, Adhitya Naraiyan died, and was succeeded by another brother, Dhaj Naraiyan, in 1732 AD. About this time the Ahom Kings had become very powerful; and the Durruing family was obliged to acknowledge allegiance to them.

In 1744 Dhir Naraiyan, a son of Surja Naraiyn, usurped the throne of Mudh Naraiyan, but three years afterwards was constrained to give it up, and seek an asylum elsewhere. Mudh Naraiyan died in the year 1778, and was succeeded by his son Mahat Naraiyan. Two years after, his brother Dalab Naraiyn shared the throne with him; and they continued to reign conjointly till 1783, when Dalab Naraiyn died. Mahat Naraiyn also died soon after; and Hangsa Naraiyn, second son of Dalab, succeeded to the throne.

In 1787, the throne was usurped by Kriti Naraiyn, a son of Dhir Naraiyn; but he was not destined long to sway the sceptre, for in the same year he was deposed, and his brother Hangsa Naraiyn assumed the rains of the government.

In 1783, however, Bishtu Naraiyn, the son of Kriti Naraiyn, obtained possession of the throne. A succession of internal commotions followed soon after, which eventually caused the downfall of this once extensive Kingdom.

Evaluation of Ahoms: We turn now to the origin of the Ahoms, a fierce and independent race, who, it is probable, entered the northern extremity of the valley about the beginning of the thirteenth century and gradually extended their conquests till the whole country was brought under their subjection.

Like most eastern nations, willing to derive merit from the splendour of their original, where history is silent, they have made no scruples in having recourse to fable to supply the defect. The Ahoms seem particularly desirous of being thought descended from the gods: from them, therefore, we can gleam no credible memorials relative to their real ancestry.

Their chronicles begin by informing us of a consultation held between Lengdun and Thenkham, Kings of heaven, the result of which was appointment of two brothers, Khunlung and Khanali, to be Kings over the earth. Khuntun, the son of the Moon, and Khunbun, son of the Sun, were at the same time appointed to the office of Gai-Mantri, or Prime Ministers; twelve families of Phokuns and Burunas were also appointed to attend them, together with a body of eight hundred thousand man. These descending from heaven by means of a golden ladder, alighted on the hill Gharai Karang, supposed to be one of the mountains of the Patkoi Range.

Here the brothers divided their ministers and subjects, and took possession of separate sections of the country. At the end of fourteen years, the brothers quarrelled. To put a final termination to their disputes. Khunbung, the more peaceable of the two, returned to heaven, leaving khunlai in possession of undivided sovereignty, below. From him the subsequent Kings of Assam are said to have sprung. Such is the fabulous account given of their descent.

That the Ahoms, or original conquerors of Assam, were of eastern origin, and descended from the Shyans, there can be but little doubt; though the precise period of their emigration it is now impossible to ascertain. As we have already observed, it is probable they may have poured in about the beginning of the 13th century; in which case, the immediate cause of their emigration may be sought for in the breaking up of Chinese Empire by, the Mughals, for at the epoch when Chukapha, the first Ahom King of whom we have any authentic record, had fixed himself in Assam, Kabli Khan had just established himself in China.

Connected with the origin of Ahoms, is a singular fact we may here allude to, namely, that no trace of Buddhism is to be found in their religion. This seems a remarkable deviation from the circumstances of the other Shyan families, the Shyans, Khanti, Laos, etc. whose literature is but a direct translation of Burmese Buddhism, as their alphabets are seem to be but mere modifications of the Burmese, or Pali. From this fact it may be argued, that the emigration of Ahoms from their own country, Siam (Thailand), had taken place prior to the introduction of the Buddhist religion into that quarter. But if this be true, where are we to find the means of reconciling this circumstance with the date of the first emigration.

For traces in proof of the Shyan origin of this people, we return again to their ancient traditions, and comparing them with the old Shyan chronicles discovered by Captain Pemberton during his residence in Munipur (Manipur), we may meet with sufficient evidence to support the above supposition.

The territory of the Shyans, under its ancient limits, was and is still known as the Kingdom of Pong, of which the city called *Mogaung*, or by the Shyans themselves, Mongmaorong, was the capital.

From Khublai, the first King whose name is recorded in the Shyam chronicle, and whose reign is dated as far back as the eighteenth year of the Christian era, to the time of Murgnow, 667 AD, the names of twelve Kings are given. To this period the Pong Kings appear to have been so fully engaged in attempts to consolidate their power at home, as to have had but little leisure to extend their conquest to countries more remotely situated.

In the year 777 Murgnow died, leaving two sons, Sukampha and Samlongpha, or Chukampha and Chambongpha, of whom the elder, Sukampha, succeeded to his father's throne; and in his rein we find the first traces of connection with the more western countries, many of which he is said to have brought under subjection to his authority.

Samlongpha was dispatched by his elder brother at the head of a powerful force, to subdue first the countries to the eastward, including probably the country of Bhumo, which extended from the left bank of the Irawadi to the frontier of Yunan.

On his return from this expedition, which proved successful, he is said to have turned his arms towards the western country of the Basa King, which probably means Banga, the ancient capital of Kachar, where he met with like success. Returning thence he descended into the Munipur (Manipur) valley. The fact of this visit is also recorded in the ancient chronicles of Munipur (Manipur), though the period assigned to it is earlier by thirty years than that given in the Shyam chronicles a discrepancy in dates which it were equally vain and useless to attempt to reconcile.

From Manipur, Samlongpha turned his victorious arms upon Assam, which he also succeeded in placing under his brother's authority. He then dispatched messengers to Mongmaorong, to communicate the intelligence of his success to his brother, and to announce his intended return. The messengers, however, instilled the most serious suspicious into the mind of Sukampha, of the designs of his brother, representing him as determined to assume the sovereignty of the country on his return from Assam. A conspiracy was in consequence entered into, for the purpose of poisoning Samlongpha; who, however, was saved by his mother's having accidentally over-heard the plot, of which she gave him timely notice by letter, and which led to his continuing in Assam. His wife and son were permitted to join him; and from this son, called *Chownakhum*, the subsequent princes of the Assam dynasty are said to be descended.

It this account may be depended upon, we are led to the reasonable conclusion, that the origin of the ancient sovereigns of Assam may be clearly traced to their eastern neighbours the Shyams. In all our researches, however, we meet with a great discrepancy in names, which have no possible means of reconciling.

Since the conversion of the last dynasty to the Brahminical faith, we find a corresponding change in the royal genealogies which have been traced up to India, and the princes of Assam now claim a descent from the King of the gods.

From Indra to Chukapha we have a list of no less than forty-eight names, and nothing but a list. The history of these Kings, if they ever did exist, has long since been lost in the shades of oblivion. This portion of our history then we gladly abandon, whether more or less, to conjecture, and turn to other events, in which we have the light of more modern history to illuminate our path.

Chukapha is said to have commenced his reign AD 1228. He soon after made conquests which had never been equalled at any preceding period; these were termed Asama, whence the Brahmins derive the etymology of the word Assam, "unequalled, unrivalled."

In 1628, he was succeeded by his son Chutuopha, who, bent on following up the conquest of his father, considerably extended the boundaries of his Kingdom. He died in 1281, when his son Chubinpha succeeded to the throne. He was in his turn followed by his son Chukangpha, AD 1293. After a reign of 39 years, his son Chukampha succeeded to the Kingdom, which he continued to govern till 1364. The Ahoms who, as we have already stated, had been hitherto engaged in gradually extending the boundaries of their dominions, had now made considerable progress down the left bank of the Brahmaputra.

Chukampha was succeeded by his brother Chutupha; who anxious to add to the conquest of his predecessors, turned his arms upon the Chutiyas, a tribe occupying the north bank of the river, as far down as Chardwar; and these he succeeded in bringing under his authority. The Chutiyas were probably, like the Ahoms, the descendants of Shyan family; though the period of their emigration it is now in vain to look for. That they had occupied the north bank for a long period prior to this invasion, seems very probable. Certain monuments of their reign are still to be met with in that portion of the country.

The death of Chuthupha, which occurred in 1376 AD, was followed by an inter region of four years; after which the ministers installed Chukemthi, a brother of the late King. He was ruled by his wife, a cruel and tyrannical woman. At her instance he oppressed his subjects, and despoiled them of their property. His ministers seeing that all remonstrance was ineffectual, and being no longer able to endure his tyranny, laid a plot to assassinate him, in which they proved successful in 1389 AD.

His death was followed by another interregnum of nine years; after which his son Chudangpha ascended the throne. After a reign of nine years, he was succeeded by his son Chiyangpha in 1407 AD. He reigned for fifteen years, and in 1422 was succeeded by his son Chuphukpha. On his death which occurred in 1439, his son Chusinghpha succeeded to the throne. He died after a lengthened reign of forty nine years.

His son Chuhangpha now succeeded to the throne. In 1493, he was killed by the spear of a commoner, who, it is said had embezzled the government grain, for which the Raja fined him in the sum of a hundred rupees. A short time after the Raja had desired him to assist in repairing the raised bamboo floor on which the place was built. In this the ruffian managed to secrete a spear, which, watching an opportunity, as the Prince one day unsuspectingly came to the front door of his house, he plunged into his bosom.

The throne now fell into the hand of a ruthless tyrant, who, after a reign of four years, was put to death at the instigation of his ministers. His brother Chu-hum-mung now ascended the throne. His cognomers were Chuhumpha, and Sarga Naraiyn, he also bore the title of the Dihingraja Ram from the locality of his birth. He is said to have made various conquests, but in what part of the country we are not informed. Very probably he was engaged in quelling insurrections, and reducing the refractory chiefs to obedience. He also succeeded in gaining possession of small portion of Kamroop (Kamrup), which about this time had fallen into anarchy. After a reign of forty-two years, he was assassinated by a common manservant, who was instigated to the deed by the heir apparent.

On the death of Sarga Naraiyan, 1539 AD, Chukhenmung succeeded to the throne. He is said to have built the town and for of Gargawn or Ghergong. He reigned thirteen years, and was succeeded by his son Chukampha. Nothing remarkable is recorded of him, except that he enjoyed the throne fifty nine years in comparative peace and comfort.

In 1611, he was succeeded by Chuchengpha, a hot headed youth, who no sooner felt himself established in the supreme power, than he proceeded to execute that vengeance upon those who had offended him, which, he had not previously the power to inflict. He called to mind many frivolous circumstances that occurred during his boyhood, and perpetrated acts of the grossest injustice and tyranny, on those who had given him the slightest offence. At length feeling the pangs of conscience, he professed inability further preside over.

State affairs, alleging as the reason the influenced exercised over his actions by those malignant influences of the destroying spirit which had been sent from heaven to control the government of his body. Acting upon his conviction, and with a view to cast out the spirit within him, he erected a temple on the banks of the river Dikhu. This temple, known by the name of Maheshwar, he consecrated to Mahadeb (Siba), and instituted the worship of that deity by appointing Brahmins to his service, and endowing the temple with a suitable unificence, and the requisite establishment. From this date, Brahmins are said to have taken the lead in the religious institutions of the country, and the Hindu creed was established as the religion of the realm.

Chuchengpha reigned thirty-eight years, and in 1649 was succeeded by his son Churumpha. This Prince grievously oppressed his people, and after a reign of three years was dethroned by his ministers, who installed his brother Chuchingpha. He however, was not destined long to sway the sceptre. He was a weak and imbecile Prince, entirely under the control of his life: after a short reign of two years, AD 1654, he was deposed and cast into prison.

His son Chutumla was then entrusted with the reins of government and soon after his accession to the throne he adopted the Hindoo faith, and introduced Brahmins into his court. He then assumed the Hindu name of Jaiyadhajia Singh.

Mir Jumla's Period: At the latter end of his reign, the valley was invaded by Mir jumla, the Subedar of Bengal. It will be observed that about fifty years prior to this period, the Muslims had obtained possession of the lower part of Kamroop (Kamrup). The usual desire of encroachment, however, induced them to proceed higher up, and to invade the territories of the northern conquerors. The people they were now about to contend with, were far different from those they had hitherto met on the field. They were fierce in their independence, and would not brook submission to a foreign power: they were moreover, 'invigorated' by a nourishing diet and strong drink; and their princes still retained their energy of mind, and hot not then sunk under the enervating and increasing ceremonies of the Hindu doctrines.

Having placed his stores and provisions in his boats, to move up the Brahmaputra, Mir Jumla crossed that river at Rangamati, and marched his army by land. The march was tedious, and on its progress the army was greatly annoyed by the Aassamese. This added to the fatigue of dragging the boats, greatly affected the troops: but as Mir jumla shared every privation with them, and after walked a foot the whole day, there was no murmuring in his camp. The Subedar at length reached the capital, Ghergong; which, after a severe conflict, he succeeded in taking, and the Raja was obliged to take refuge in the mountains.

Mir jumla, elated at his success, wrote to the Emperor Aurangzeb, boasting that he had opened the road to China, and that he would the next year plant the Mohammadan flag on the walls of Peking.

But a sad change was now at hand. The rains of 1662 set in with great violence. The Raja boldly issued to his place of concealment in the mountains, and cut off the provisions to the Mughals. To add to their distress a pestilence also broke out in their camp, which carried off many; whether they returned or remained, they were equally exposed to death. In this miserable state they passed the rains: but no sooner was the country dry, than, according to the historians, they took courage, which Mir Jumla was happy to grant; for he was himself attacked by disease, and his troops were mutinous. The same accounts state, that the Assamese were obliged to give twenty thousand tolas of gold, a hundred thousand of silver, and, forty elephants; and the Raja gave up his daughter to be married to one of the Muslim princes, and agreed to pay an annual tribute.

Jaiyadhajia Singh died in 1663 AD, after a regain of nine years, and was succeeded by Chupungmung, alias Chakradhajia Singh. He reigned for seven years, and leaving no male issue, his brother Sanyatpha, known also by the name of Adayaditya Singh, ascended the throne. There came to his court a Bairagi (religious mendicant), who is said to have been skilled in occult science, and possessed of supernatural powers. The Raja ordered all his subjects to consider this as their spiritual guide; but the injunction greatly incensed the ministers, who immediately invited the younger brother of the King to accept the throne. This ill fated Prince was assassinated after a reign of two years 1672 AD.

Role of Bar Barua: The ministers then installed his younger brother Suklumpha. After a reign of two years he was secretly poisoned, at the instigation of the Bar Baruwa, who installed Suhung, the young Prince of Samaguriya. The Bar Baruwa continued to assume a great degree of authority, which the Queen maintained was an usurpation of her lord's prerogative. At her instigation therefore the King laid a plot for destroying him. His intentions, however, were secretly conveyed to the Bar Baruwa, who lost no time in proceedings to the royal residence. There he found the King and his royal consort in the gardens; the former he dispatched with his own hands, while his myrmidons assassinated the Queen and the members of their council. Thus fell this young King, after a reign of one month and fifteen days.

The self constituted Bar Baruwa next raised Teen Kungiya to the Supreme dignity; but he was not permitted to usurp his arbitrary power much longer. The officers of Guwahati, with a band of armed men, proceeded to the metropolis, and soon succeeded in securing the Bar Baruwa. Him they beheaded; and they ordered the newly raised Raja to be strangled, after a reign of twenty days.

On the destruction of his predecessors, the lord raised Dehingiya Chuhungpha, or Chujinpha, to the throne. It was once intimated to him by his Queen, that these individuals were usurping the powers which ought alone to attach to his prerogative. His pride being thereby aroused, he determined upon assassinating them. His Prime Minister, the Bur Gohain, however, being secretly informed of his intentions, ordered the unfortunate Raja's eyes to be plucked out. The agonised King in despair, and burning with indignation, put an end to his own existence, after a reign of a little more than two years, 1677 AD. He was succeeded by Chudinph, the son-in-law of the Bura-Gohain, by whom he was installed. This minister, however, not long after, laid a plot for his life. He was assassinated in 1679, after a reign of two years.

In the same year Chulekpha, more commonly known as the Lora Raja, the Stirling King, was raised to the throne by Bar Phukan, who himself assumed the office of regent. He practised deeds of the most barbarous tyranny, without regard even to the sacred person of royalty. This caused Gadhadhar Singh, a near relative, with a few others, to conspire his destruction. Having assassinated him, they proceeded to seize the person of the Prince, whom they abused and degraded; when Gadhadhar, who had previously received homage as his successor, discharged a javelin at him as the *coup de grace*, in payment of a debt he had contracted with him when they played together as boys, and thus terminated his career after a reign of sixteen months.

On his death, AD 1681, Ghadhadhar Singh, surnamed Chupatpha, ascended the throne. He died in 1695, after a reign of fourteen years.

He was succeeded by his son Chukungpha, alias Rudru Singh. In 1699, this Prince is said to have founded the fort and city of Rungpoor (Rangpur), where he also caused an extensive tank to be dug, which still bears his name. In the same year he erected a theatre, for the exhibition of sports denominated Tulatuh. In the following year he visited Gowhatti (Guwahati), and died on the side of the river directly opposite the town, on which spot his son afterwards erected a temple in honour of Siba (Shiva), called *Rudreshwar*. And this was the last phase of medieval rulers. After this the Britishers captured Assam for its abundant tea gardens in hope of money making.

Modern Times

Rudra Singh's Period: The modern period of Assamese history begins with ascension of Rudra Singh. Rudra Singh was without doubt the greatest of the all the Assamese princes, he reduced the whole valley to order, and received the submission of all the hill tribes. He also established an extensive trade with Thibbat (Tibbat), which of late years has dwindled down to a mere nothing.

Rudru Singh reigned nineteen years, and was succeeded by his son Chutunpha (Siba Singh). He ordered a new rent role of the revenues of the country to be drawn up, in which was included the settlement of the Durrang country; whence might be, inferred that the Durrung family had acknowledged allegiance to their powerful neighbours the Ahoms. He died in 1744, after a reign of thirty years.

On his death his brother Churempha, alias Prumutta Singh, was raised to the throne. He reigned seven years, and was succeeded by his brother Churenpha, or Rajeshwar Singh. He was afterwards married to a daughter of Juya Singh, the ruling Prince of Manipur, he died in 1769 AD.

Chunguapha, surnamed Lakhmi Singh, next ascended the throne. He was brother to the late King, and youngest son of Rudra Singh. The first act of, note which distinguished the reign of this Prince, was the expulsion of the three sons of Rujirhwar Singh from Court. They were banished to the usual officers. Not after long his accession to the throne the Moamariahs, headed by their, prelate, rose up in rebellion against him. The priest mustering a body of 12,000 men, (his own disciples), led them to capital. He availed himself of a Ruse de guerre by causing the Bar Jona Gohain, the eldest brother of the reigning Prince, to be taken away from his retreat at Kamroop (Karmrup), and carried alongwith his force; and on their approach to the capital he was placed in front of troops.

An army was sent out on the part of the Raja to oppose their progress. The Deka Phukan, their leader, and son-in-law to the Bar Baruwa, on meeting the opponents, and seeing that the Ba Jona Gohain was at their head, dreaded the consequences of the impious act of shedding the blood of royalty. Instead therefore, of withstanding the advance of the insurgents, he and his comrades paid homage to the Prince, and allowed them to pass unmolested.

The Moamariahs soon obtained possession of the citadel; the Bar Baruwa, who it is said had originally incensed the rebellious priest, was put to death, together with every individual member of his family, and the Raja was deposed and placed in confinement. About five months afterwards the adherents of the King raised an insurrection, the Moamariah priest and his partizans were taken by stratagem and put to death, and the deposed King, Lukhmi (Lakhsami) Singh was again placed on the Gaddi (throne). He died in 1780, eleven years after his first accession to the throne.

Chuhitpungpha, alias Gourinath Singh, succeeded his father Lukhmi Singh at the age of fourteen years. Four years after his instalment the Moamariahs again collected the scattered members of their fraternity, and made their appearance in large numbers, to the amount of about 10,000. The Raja hearing of this demonstration of their force, sent a body of 9,000 men to oppose them. A severe battle ensued, in 'Which great number fell on both sides. The insurgents at length prevailed, and the Raja's people were, dispersed.

Another expedition was soon after detached against them, at the head of which were a number of the leading members of the state. The banks of the Gouri Sagar tank formed the point at which it was determined to await the attack of the insurgents. Elated by their late success the Moamariah flew to the assault with the greatest precipitation. They had, however, miscalculated their power; for, after a most arduous and severe struggle, in which the field was disputed for three days, and an immense loss sustained on both sides, the rebels were compelled to give way, and leave the royalists in possession of the field.

The Moamariahs though discomfited were not subdued: they again collected their resources, and took up a strong and well fortified position on the banks of the Jay Sagar. Here they were followed up by the Raja's people, and it is said another arduous battle was fought, which, like the former, also lasted for three days. In this, however, the Moamariahs prevailed, and Gourinath with his courtiers was obliged to effect his escape to Gowhatti (Guwahati). The Moamariahs, elated with their success, installed a successor of their own choice in the person of Bharota Singh.

Nine months elapsed after this event, during which time the Raja and the members of his government were assiduously employed in retrieving their affairs and recollecting the scattered portions of their army.

At the end of that period, AD 1788, an overwhelming force was sent from Guwahati against the Moamariahs; the contest is said to have lasted a number of days, and after many reverses the Raja's people were obliged to retreat. The Raja perceiving the failure of all his resources, at length sent to Mr. Raush (a merchant who had the farm of the Bengal salt in Assam) at Gowlpara, to procure the assistance of the British government.

The history further proceed to say, that seven hundred Burkundaze Sepahees were sent by Mr. Raush, with whom the Raja proceeded to Nowgong, from thence he sent the Burkundazes to the relief of the Bura Gohain at Jorehaut. At a plain about a couple of miles to the north of Jorhaut another action was fought in which the Burkundazes were cut up to a man.

A short time after the veteran Raja of Manipur arrived at Nowgong, according to the invitation of Raja Gourinath, with 500 cavalry and 4,000 infantry, and with this force he proceeded to Jorehaut, where he met the Moamariah. The Manipuirs were however, repulsed with a loss of 1,500 men. The Raja of Manipur was in consequence compelled to retreat with the remnant of his force, and Raja Gourinath was again constrained to take his departure of Guwahati.

New disasters however awaited him. About this time Bistu Naraiyan, the King of Durrung, was deposed, and a relation, Kissen Naraiyan, seized upon the throne. Elated at his success he determined to add the Pergunnahs of Kamroop to his possessions. He took his employ a band of Bengali Burkundazes, with whose assistance he made an attack on Guwahati. Gourinath being thus pressed on all sides, and as he himself expressed it, "representing a laden boat in the act of sinking" again applied to Mr. Raush, who in his behalf wrote to Messrs. Colvin, Bazette and Co. Calcutta, whilst the Raja sent a deputation composed of Bistu Naraiyan, Raja of Durrung, and three influential men, to solicit the assistance of the British government. The result was, that at the close of 1792 a detachment was sent to his assistance, under the command of Captain T. Welsh.

Role of British Government: The grounds on which the British Government interfered in the domestic quarrels of the Assamese were that large bodies of Hindustani Sepoys and Fakeers, subject of the company, were represented by Gourinath to have taken part in the civil wars, and were devastating the province. It was conceived by Lord Cornwallis, that it was incumbent on the British to restrain their own subjects and it was to Assam.

The person who had hired these burkundazes was Kissen Naraiyn, whom Gourinath and his agents, through Mr. Raush, represented as a rebel. Sometimes before Captain Welsh came to Assam the government, at the requisition of Gourinath, endeavoured to stop these armed hands from passing into the province; but they found their way round by the Butan Doars by force or fraud, and it was only when the government found they could not prevent their getting into Assam, that they determined to drive them out.

Captain Welsh left Gowalpara for Guwahati on the 16th November 1792. Three days after he was met by the Raja of Assam, who with a few of his attendants was making his escape from Gowhatti (Guwahati). From, him he learnt that the Moamari chief was in possession of the southern bank of Guwahati, and that Kissen Naraiyan and his rabble had located themselves on the opposite bank. On the morning of 29th, captain Welsh took possession of the southern bank of the river, having completely surprised the Moamariah chief, and on the morning of the 6th December proceeded to the opposite bank, and succeeded in completely routing Kissen Naraiyan from his strong post. Eventually he succeeded in bringing him under an engagement to pay the Assam Raja an annual tribute of fifty-eight thousand rupees.

Having thus satisfactorily, settled the affairs of the Raja as it respected the Durrung family, Captain Welsh next proceeded to quell the insurrections of the Moamariahs.

After Captain Welsh had arrived at Guwahati and made himself acquainted with the state of affairs, he found the Raja a blood thirsty tyrant, and his intellect so totally destroyed by excess, that he was perfectly incapable of restoring the Kingdom to tranquillity, or of governing it when its affairs were restored to order.

He found that Kissen Naraiyan had been driven by injustice to rebellion, and that by our intermeddling so far we had been taking a measure the justice of which was very doubtful, unless we went further. Here on he represented the state of affairs to Lord Cornwallis, and obtained that nobleman's full consent to convene the native chiefs and officers, and, in consultation with them, to take such steps as he found necessary, not only to restore order throughout the Kingdom, but to secure good government to the people, and protection against their imbecile and barbarous Raja.

Captain Welsh successfully put down the Moamariah insurrection, and made arrangements for the permanent rotation of a brigade of British troops in Assam; for the payment of which the revenues of Lower Assam were pledged by the Government, with the full consent of the Bura Gohain, and all the nobles.

But, just as captain Welsh had effected all his arrangements, the great statesman, and excellent man who had sent Captain Welsh to Assam, and who had evinced the liveliest interest in the welfare of this Kingdom, and constantly corresponded directly with Captain Welsh on the measures to be adopted for its complete reorganisation, returned to his native land, leaving the Government of Bengal to Sir John Shore.

With his government commenced a total change of measures towards Assam: and, on the weakest of all pretences — the non-interference system — the whole people of Assam were delivered over to the tender mercies of their fatuous, bloody minded Raja, and again plunged into the miseries of anarchy. Nor would the Bengal government listen to any remonstrances of captain Welsh, who begged to be allowed a short period to prepare the people for his departure, and to leave a small force behind him. But he was ordered instantly to return to Bengal. The miseries of this lamentable policy of the Bengal government inflicted upon Assam may not be dwelt upon.

The British government were in a position to preserve order and good government to a then flourishing and populous Kingdom; but this duty as the paramount power was neglected, and the result was the heaviest blow that British India has sustained the drain of its finances, and the stoppage of all its internal improvements, caused by Burmese war. Captain Welsh returned to Calcutta in July 1794. A few months after, Raja Gourinath was attacked with a bilious fever, of which he died, after a region of nearly fifteen years.

On the death of Raja, the Bura Gohain knowing that he possessed a powerful rival in authority in the person of the Bar Baruwa, and that the present was the time for securing the predominance of his interest, before the succession to before the announcement of the death of the Raja should enable to Bar Baruwa to consolidate his influence. For this purpose, while yet the corpse was warm, he carried into effect a stratagem which soon brought his victim within his grasp. The Bar Baruwa was sent for in the name of the deceased Raja, under pretence of the latter wishing to make to him some particular communications before his death. He unsuspectingly complied with the summons, and the Bura Gohain lying in ambush for his, seized him as soon as he came within the precincts of the Raja's apartments, and caused him to be put to death.

Three days after the foregoing events, Komaleswar Singh was placed on the throne by Purnananda, the Bura Gohain. From this date, this able but violent minister, the Bura Gohain, who as just described had given the first earnest of his disposition, and who was afterwards so notorious for his rigorous tyranny, assumed and reserved to himself all the substantial executive authority of the state, the Raja being in his hands a mere puppet of Convenience. Nothing remarkable is communicated during the reign of this King: he died without issue in 1809, and was succeeded by his brother Chundra Kanto Singh. This Prince upon his accession, countenanced a conspiracy for the destruction of the Bura Gohain; who, on receiving private intimation of it, immediately summoned a state council, and proceeded to put all the conspirators to death. The Bar Phukan, who was implicated in the plot, fled from Assam, and proceeded to Rungpore, whence he took his departure for Calcutta. There, on the part of the Raja, he petitioned the English Government for troops, which, acting upon their lately received notions of non-interference, were refused.

While at Calcutta, the Bar Pukhan gained the friendship of an agent of the Burmese Government, and accompanied him back to the court of Umeerapooru. Thence, he came with 6,000 Burmese troops, to which were added about 8,000 of different tribes, which they collected on their way to Assam. With this force at Bar Phukan entered Assam, and proceeded to Jorehaut to the assistance of the Raja, but the Raja's enemies had made their escape to Guwahati. Chundrekant, however, reimbursed the Burmese army for the trouble and expense of their expedition.

At the instigation of Bura Gohain, the Bar Phukan was put to death; and the former immediately sent to Bura Gohain and his adherents at Gowahatti, to inform them that he had dispatched their enemy, and invited them to join him.

The Bura Gohain however did not accede to this invitation. On the contrary, inheriting his father's resentment against the reigning Raja, he sent his younger brother to Chilmari to invite up Purunder Singh (a Prince of the royal family, and a great-grand son of Rajeshwar Singh, who had resided sometimes in obscurity) to become a competitor for the throne. Purunder Singh was prevented from coming up by the commands of his father Brajanath, who came up himself instead to Guwahati. The Bura Gohain then accompanied him with his army to Jorehaut (Jorhut).

The Raja with his troops fell back in consequence upon Rungpore. He was however soon after inveigled into a consent to visit Jorehaut, where he was been brought up from Chilmari was proclaimed Raja by the Bura Gohain, AD 1816. He succeeded in prejudice to his father Brajanth, who had been previously disqualified from the succession by the mutilation of one of his ears. On the third day after the Raja Chunderkant's disposal, he was visited by the Marangi Khowa Gohain; after the preliminary formula of vilification and abuse, superintended the slitting of his right ear.

The friends of the murdered Bur Phukan fled in fear of their lives to Ava, informed him of the proceedings in Assam. The consequence was, that Keeo Mingee was sent by that court at the head of an army of 30,000 men. The Burmese at first met with considerable opposition, but the Assamese were soon obliged to seek refuge in flight, and in 1818 Keeo Mingee, the Burmese General, reinstated Chunderkant on his throne. A short time after he returned to Ava, leaving zoo troops for the protection of the Raja. A portion of these troops was deputed by the Raja to apprehend Purunder; they accordingly proceeded on their expedition, and Purunder, who was then at Guwahati, fearing that all resistance was vain, took to his boats and fled to Hadira Choke, leaving the Burmese in possession of Guwahati. He was, however, constrained to proceed further down, and take refuge at Chilmari, in the British territories.

In September 1819, Purunder Singh, who had gone to Calcutta, addressed a letter to the British Government, stating that he had been driven from his territories by the Burmese, and soliciting the protection and assistance of the Honourable Company, and offering to become tributary, and to pay the expense of the detachment that would be necessary to effect his restoration to the throne of his ancestors. This application was repeated in the following month, but met with a refusal.

Role by Burmese: Shortly after Mr. Scott, Commissioner of Cooch-Behar, reported to the government that Purunder Singh was employed in collecting troops in the Butan (Bhutan) territory for the purpose of invading Assam. He added, that the reigning Raja Chunderkant was supposed to be very desirous of getting rid of his allies, The Burmese, and was understood to be treating with the Bura Gohain, and other refugees of consequence, for their return, with a view to a combination of the whole means and strength of the country against the Burmese.

On the 30th April 1820, Mr. Scott made known to the British government that the Bur Phokun, who was an adherent of the interests of the Burmese party, had been murdered, as was supposed of the interests of Raja Chunderkant; that the latter had in consequence retired from Jorehaut to Guwahati; and that it was generally believed an army from Ava would — soon invade the country to avenge the death of Bur-Phokun, and to depose the reigning Prince. The above communication was followed immediately by information that the Burmese had set up another Raja in Assam, and that it was supposed Chunderkant would shortly be compelled to flee the country.

In the month of September following Chunderkant was expelled from Assam, and took refuge in the Choke opposite to Gowalpara. At the end of 1821, however, the cause of Chunderkant became again temporarily triumphant; he defeated the Burmese in several skirmishes, and advanced back to Assam nearly as far as Guwahati.

These successes and continued attempts of Purunder Singh and the Bura Gohain from the side of Bhutan and Bijnee to recover their lost dominion, drew forth a letter from the Burmese general, Mengee Maha Silwa (who had arrived some months before to take the command of the troops in Assam), to the address of the Governor General. The object of the letter was apparently to request that assistance might not be afforded to Raja Chunderkant by any persons residing within the British dominions, and to suggest the expediency of his being surrendered, with all other refugees who might seek refuge, or had already taken shelter there; but British government did not think expedient to comply with the wish of the general.

In the month of April, or May 1888: the Burmese party received a considerable reinforcement, commanded by an officer of high rank from the court of Ameerpoora, named Mengee Maha Bandoola. Chunderkant soon gave way, before the new force, and in June was reported to have sustained a decisive defeat at Mowghur, in an action in which he displayed great personnel bravery, and was compelled once more to seek safety in flight.

The continuance of these disturbances in Assam and dread excite by the excesses committed by the Burmese, had now reduced the natives to a most distressing situation; and several thousands of them were compelled to flee the country, and take refuge in the British territory.

The event of Chunderkant's defeat was followed by a representation of rather threatening character on the part of the Burmese officers to Lieutenant Davidson, the officer commanding the post of Gowalpara, stating that their army consisted of 18,000 fighting men, commanded by forty Raja that they had every wish to remain in friendship with company, and to respect cautiously the British territories, but that should protection be given to Raja Chunderkant, they had received positive orders to follow him wherever he might go, and to take him by force out of the Company's dominions. Instructions were accordingly issued to the officer commanding at Dacca, to detach such reinforcement as

Mr. Scott might require, with directions that should the Burmese attempt to carry their threat into execution, they must be instantly repelled by force.

This effectives put a stop to the further progress of the Burmese on the side to Assam; but their encroachments on another point of our frontier, Kachar, led to the force assembled at Gowalpara being ordered to advance into Assam, and the declaration of war against the King of Ava on the 5th March 1824. Before however, proceeding to follow the footsteps of the British army in their conquest of Assam, it will be expedient to notice the state of our relations with Kachar.

From the year 1817 downwards, constant applications had been received from the ancient and legitimate Raja of Kachar, Govind Chunder Narayin praying for the aid and intervention of British Government to settle this affairs, and to protect him against the subjugation with which he was menaced- from the side of Manipur. In 1820, the above chief was entirely dispossess by three brothers, adventures from Manipur, named Chorjit, Manjit, and Gambheer Singh; who had themselves been expelled from their hereditary possessions by the Burmese, and had originally obtained a footing in Kachar by engaging in the Raja's service. Shortly after the expulsion of the legitimate ruler, a struggle for superiority ensued between the brothers; which involving the country in much suffering, disturbed the peace of the frontier, and occasioned renewed appeals for the interference of the British power.

The receipt of an application from Chorijit Singh, in May 1823, offering to cede the sovereignty of Kachar to the British government, and stating his apprehension that designs were entertained against the country by the Burmese, induced the government to take the subject of his proposition into serious consideration.

It did not appear that Kachar had ever been subject or tributary to the Government of Ava. It is true that Manjit when in possession of the Raja of Manipur, which he attained by the aid of the Burmese, and held as their feudatory, did not invade, and for a time possess himself of Kachar: but he was speedily repulsed, and no traces appear of the Burmese having ever laid claim to that country, to any right of interference in its affairs. At the same time there appeared several inducements for the British government to establish its direct authority, or at least a preponderating influence, in the territory of Kachar.

These considerations were not deemed of sufficient strength on former occasions to lead our government to avail itself of the opportunities that presented themselves of effecting this object; nor did they indeed possess the weight that subsequent occurrences and further experience have given them. The position of Kachar, as naturally affording one of the easiest passes from Ava into the company's territories, the recent progress of the Burmese arms, and their occupation of Assam, the force stationed in which country it would also contribute to keep in check, gave the possession of Kachar an importance which did not before belong to it. As the employment of British influence over the country was deemed of importance, and as that could be rendered effectual in no other way than by taking the country openly and decidedly under British protection, it was deemed expedient to extend to Kachar the protection of the government, on the usual conditions of political dependency.

Whilst arrangements and negotiations were in train for defining the terms of our connection with the chief, whom it was determined to reinstate in possession, and who was residing under British protection within the Honourable company's territory, intelligence was received that the Burmes were preparing an army to invade and conquer Kachar. The Governor General's agent on the northeast frontier lost no time in addressing letters to the Burmese governor of Assam briefly apprising him of the nature of our views and measures in regard to the Raj of Kachar, and calling upon him to desist from any project of molesting that country.

Problem of Burmese: It soon appeared that an army had been assembled in the Burmese dependency of Manipur, as well as in Assam, for the execution of the purpose of aggression now distinctly threatened.

Whilst occupying their threatening position in Kachar, the generals of the King of Ava had moreover planned the conquest of Jantiya, another petty chieftainship situated similarly with Kachar in regard to the British frontier but which having formerly been restored as a gift to the Raja's family by the British government, after a temporary convulsion, was more distinctly recognised as a dependency of Bengal.

The Raja of Jamtiya in a letter addressed to him by the Burmese commanders, was called upon to acknowledge submission and allegiance to the King of Ava, and to repair forthwith to the Burman camp. A demonstration was further actually made against Jantiya to enforce the above requisition, when the British troops frustrated the execution of his hostile and men acting encroachment: and simultaneously the advance of the Burmese force both from Manipur and Assam, led to the first collision with the British troops in Kachar, close to the frontier of Sylhet, at the entrance of the Bikrampare pass.

The Governor General in Council was, in consequence of these circumstances, induced to order the advance of the force previously assembled at Gowalpara into the territory of Assam, to dislodge the enemy from the commanding position which they occupied at the head of the Brahmaputra, and to pursue such other measures of offensive warfare as the honour, the interests, and the safety of the British government demanded recourse to.

In obedience to these instructions, Brigadier M'Morin, commanding the force, commenced moving from Gowalpara up the Brahmaputra on the 13th March 1824. On the 28th the force arrived at Guwahati, where the Burmese had erected strong stockades, which were however evacuated on the approach of the British. The necessity of retreat had apparently exasperated them against their unfortunate subjects, and fellow in arms —

the Assamese; the bodies of a great number of whom, barbarously mutilated, were found -upon the road and in the stockade of Guwahati.

Several of the tribes in the eastern portion of Assam, as the Khamtis and Singphos, availed themselves of the unsettled state of affairs to harass the Burmese; but their operations were equally directed against the unfortunate natives of Assam, numbers of whom were carried off by them as slaves.

The Assame displayed the most favourable disposition towards the British; but their unwarlike character, scanty numbers, and reduced means, rendered their cooperation of no value; and the uncertainty of support, and doubt of the capability of the country to maintain a large advancing force, as well as inaccurate information of the state of the roads, induced the commanding officer to pause at Guwahati and at one time to abandon all thoughts of prosecuting the campaign further in the season, notwithstanding the fairest prospect offered of expelling the Burmese altogether from Assam, even by the partial advance of the British force.

Mr. Scott, a Political Agent, having crossed from Sylhet through Jamtiya, arrived at Nowgong, in advance of the Brigadier, on the 15th April, with a party of some strength. Leaving his escort under Capt. Horsburgh to occupy Nowgong, which the Burmese had deserted, he traced a retrograde route to Guwahati to communicate with the head quarters of the invading force. The Burmese had now retreated to their chief stockade at Moramukh; but finding that no steps were taken in pursuit of them, they in the end of April returned to Kohiabar. Colonel Richards, was row therefore detached from Guwahati with five companies of the 23rd N.I. and the flotilla, and having joined the Commissioner's escort at Nowgong, he advanced to Kolibar.

The Burmese now stockaded themselves at Hatbur, on the Kullung, at a short distance from its junction with the main stream: there they pursued their previous system of not waiting for an attack, but deserted it and returned to Ranglighur, a post at the distance of about eight hours' march. A small party however having returned to reoccupy the Hatbur stockade, were surprised by Lieut. Richardson, with a Resalla of horse, and a company of infantry. The surprise was effectual: the enemy is attempting to escape, fell upon the horse by whom a number were killed.

Whilst the main body of the detachment continued at Koliabar, a small party was left under Capt. Horsburgh in the stockade of Hatbur. The Burmese exhibited on this occasion the only proof of enterprise which they had yet displayed in the campaign in Assam; and, advancing from their entrenchment at Ranglighur, they attempted to cut off Captain Horsburgh and his division. Their advance was, however, seasonably ascertained and arrested by the picquet, until the whole detachment could form. Upon Captain Horsburgh's approach with the infantry the Burmese fled; but the irregular horse, which had been sent to their rear, having intercepted the retreat of about two hundred, a great number of them were sabred on the spot, or drowned in crossing the kulling.

After this repulse, they abandoned the Ranglighur stockade, and retrograded to Mara-Mukh, where the chief force of the Burmese, now not exceeding one thousand men, was posted under the governor of Assam. Brigadier M'Morin having died of cholera early in May, Colonel Richards succeeded to the command, and established his headquarters at Kolibar; but finding the rains setting in, he deemed it necessary to retire to Guwahati in order to secure the receipt of supplies. The operations of the first campaign in Assam, were closed by a successful attack upon a stockade on the north bank of the Brahmaputra, by Capt. Wallace; the enemy had time to escape, but the stockade was destroyed. The general result of the operations was decidely favourable; and the British authority was established over a considerable tract of country between Gowalpara and Guwahati.

Upon the return of the British forces in Assam to their cantonment in Guwahati Burmese parties reoccupied the station of Kaliabar, Raha, and Nowgong, levying heavy contributions of the people, and pillaging the country. They even carried their incursions into neighbouring states, and devastated the frontier districts of the British ally and dependent, the Raja of Jamtiya. The renewal of operations in this quarter, therefore, commenced with their expulsion once more from these positions. The force under Lieut. Colonel Richards, who had been continued in the command, consisted altogether of about three thousand men, a crops more then adequate for the purpose it was directed to effect; being fully equal, if not superior, to the aggregate of the Burmese troops in Assam, and infinitely superior in equipment and efficiency.

The force under Lieut. Colonel Richards, who had been continued in the command, consisted altogether of about three thousand men, a corps more than adequate for the purpose it was directed to effect; being fully equal, if not superior, to the aggregate of the Burmese troops in Assam, and infinitely superior in equipment and efficiency. The numbers of the army, and the necessity of recourse to water carriage, preventing the forward movement of the whole body, Colonel Richards detached a body of troops for the purpose of putting a stop to the executions and excesses of the Burmese. His arrangements were attended with complete success: The enemy were compelled to concentrate their forces at Jorehat, leaving the country open for the British advance.

At Jorehat, intestine division contributed to weaken the Burmese still further, and the Chief known by the name of the Bura Raja, who had been considered as the head of the Burmese party is Assam, was killed by the adherents of Sham Phukan, a rival leader, although equally an officer in the Burmese service. Despairing, consequently, of defending the position at Jorehaut, the Burmese Commanders after setting fire to the entrenchment, fell back upon Rungpur, the capital.

The country being thus cleared of the enemy, Colonel Richards proceeded up the Brahmaputra, and on the 25th January, 1825, fixed his headquarters at Gowrisagar, on the Dikko river, about eight miles from Rungpur. On the morning of the 27th the Burmese' garrison of Rungpur made an attack upon the British advanced post, where the thickness of the Jungle rendered it impossible to meat them with advantage; but so soon as they offered a sufficient front, a charge was made, which the Burmese did not wait to sustain; for after delivering their fire, they broke and fled, but were overtaken, and a considerable number put to the sword; the loss of the British was trifling.

On the 29th, Colonel Richards resumed his march towards Rungpur. The approaches to the capital had been fortified by the enemy, and on nearing the defences the assailants faced by- a heavy fire, which brought down half the leading division, and caused a momentary check; but a couple of shells, and a round or two of grape having been thrown in, the column again advanced, and the stockade was escalated and carried.

The result of these two engagements not only dispirited the Burmans, but gave renewed inveteracy to the divisions that prevailed amongst them. The two chiefs, the Sham and Bagli Phukan, were willing to stipulate for terms; but the more numerous party, headed by the subordinate chiefs, were resolutely bent on resistance, and threatened the advocates of Pacific measures with extermination. The latter, however, so far prevailed, as to dispatch a messenger to the British commander to negotiate terms for the surrender of Rungpur; and, through his mediation, they were finally agreed upon. Such of the garrison as continued hostile were allowed to retire into the Burmese territory, on their engaging to abstain from any act of aggression on their retreat, and those who were pacifically inclined, were suffered to remain unmolested; their final destination to await the decision of the Governor General's Agent, but in the event of peace with Ava, they were not be given up to that government.

Colonel Richards was induced to accede to these conditions from a conviction of the impossibility of preventing the escape of the garrison upon the capture of the fort, or of pursuing them in their flight. It was also to have been apprehended, if the evacuation of the province had been much longer delayed, that it might not have been cleared of the enemy during the campaign, as the want of carriage and supplies would have detained the army sometime at Rungpur, and might have delayed its movements till the season was too advanced to admit of its progress far beyond the capital. By the occupation of Rungpur on the terms granted, much time was saved, as well as some loss of lives avoided; and the object of the campaign — the expulsion of the Burmese from Assam, without the fear of their renewing their irruptions with any success, was peaceably and promptly secured.

The persons who surrendered themselves upon these stipulations, were the Sham Phukan and about seven hundred of the garrison: the rest, about nine thousand of both sexes and all ages, including two thousand fighting men, withdrew to the frontiers, but many dropped off on the retreat, and established themselves in Assam.

The surrender of Rungpur, and the dispersion of the Burmans, terminated the regular campaign on the northeastern frontier; but the state of anarchy into which Assam had fallen, and the lawless conduct of the Singphos, and other wild tribes inhabiting its eastern portion, continued to demand the active interference of British detachments throughout the remainder of the season. The Burmese also appeared in some force in May' at Bisa Gam, a Singpha village on the right bank of the Nao Dihing, where they erected a stockade: they also advanced to Duffa Aam, a similar village, a few miles inland from the same river, about ten miles to the -north of the former, where they entrenched themselves. The force at these posts consisted of about 1,000 men, of whom six hundred were Burmese, the rest Singphos, under the command of the governor of Mogaum. From these stations they were dislodged in the middle of June, by a party of troops under the Lieutenants Neufville and Kerr, after a march of great excursion and fatigue.

At Bisa Gam the stockades were five in number, and were carried at the point of the bayonet. The enemy at first formed in front of the stockades, as if determined to offer a resolute resistance; but they retreated precipitately upon the charge of the British detachment, who, following them as quickly as the preservation of order, and the nature of the ground would permit, drove them out of each stockade in rapid succession without firing a shot. On quitting the last entrenchment, the Burmese fled towards their own frontier; but their retreat was pursued by a party under Ensign Bogle, and so closely were they pressed, that they were obliged to abandon several hundred Assamese, who they were carrying off as slaves.

After this defeat no occasion offered for the further prosecution of hostilities against the Burmese in Assam, on the conclusion of the war with Ava, the Burmese government in a treaty concluded on the 24th February 1827, engaged to abstain from all interference with the province, and Assam has ever since continued in the undisturbed possession of the British authorities. That the results of the war, as in respects Assam at least, have not failed to prove highly beneficial, will be evident from a consideration of the present state of the country. Distracted hitherto by incessant feuds, and overrun by hostile armies, a predatory hands, large tracts once inhabited by a happy and numerous population, had been converted into extensive and unwholesome jungles, and ceased not only to be haunts of man, but had become hostile to human life under its new masters. Assam has experienced a tranquillity and security not known for ages, and will again no doubt assume that character of plenty and prosperity which it once wore, and which tradition, and the remains of roads and towns still found in it, indicates it once, enjoyed.

Movement for Independence

Development of Constitution: In 1945, when India's political future was being deliberated and plans were being evolved for ushering into full freedom, the problem of northeastern areas acquired urgency. The Cabinet Mission suggested the formation of an Advisory Committee on the Rights of Citizens, Minorities and Tribal and excluded Areas. Accordingly it was set up on January 24, 1947. The committee appointed a subcommittee known as North-East Frontier (Assam) Tribal and Excluded Areas Committee with Gopinath Bardoloi as its chairman.

The Bordoloi Committee presented a copious report with several recommendations, the main among them being the formation of local Councils for judicial work, the creation of district Councils for legislative purposes such as the use of land, village forests, agriculture, village — and town management, the administration of local and tribal laws and the setting up of regional councils in autonomous districts for the tribes because they had a distinctive culture and civilization of their own. It also recommended that the code of civil and criminal procedure should not apply to these areas which should be administered according to their tribal customs.

Sixth Schedule Presentation: The Bardoloi Committee and the Drafting Committee of the Indian Constitution met together to amend the Sixth Schedule and presented the same before the Constituent Assembly of India. This committee proposed that the hill districts should be classified into autonomous and non-autonomous areas and autonomous districts into autonomous regions in case there are many diverse scheduled tribes in then.

According to it, the autonomous districts were the Khasi, and Jaintia Hills Districts minus the town of Shillong, the North Cachar Subdivision of Cachar district and the Mikir Hills areas of Nowgong and Sibsagar District excepting the Mouzas of Barpathar and Sarupathar. The non-autonomous districts were Sadiya, Balipara, Frontier Tracts, excluding the Lakhimpore Frontier Tract and the Naga Tribal Area.

The Constituent Assembly accepted the proposal. With independence achieved, Assam retained its status as a full fledged state in the Indian Union. It was however, a state full of diversity and heterogeneity in terms of race, religion and language. The different races could not coalesce together to form a cohesive identity and soon Assam underwent a process of phased five section resulting in its areal shrinkage. Large tracts in habitated and dominated by different tribes were amputated to form separate political identities.

Assam's area shrank from 5,79,095 sq km to 78,438 sq km in 1978. Nagaland was carved out of old Assam as a separate state in 1962-63. Meghalaya come into existence in 1971. The Union Territories of Mizoram and Arunachal Pradesh were formed in 1971 and 1972 respectively. The reason for this five section lies in the fact that Assam was polyglot state with several tribal pockets. Assam was left a shadow of her former self.

The average Assamese suffers from a sense of deep hurt that the centre has been primarily responsible for her humiliating reduction to the status of a mini state, one amongst many under shared Governors, and that's too not primus inter pares, but a mere equal. While this was the state of trauma and shock in which the Assamese found themselves, their resentment was exacerbated by yet another sinister fear of being reduced to a minority in their own habitat. The Assamese are faced with the threat of cultural genocide. The steady stream of in-migrants and infiltrators from across the Bangladesh border has assumed menacing proportions. He has a fear of being swamped by the Bengali infiltrators.

Contrary to this the Assamese instead of trying to integrate the minority groups, endeavoured to assimilate them by imposing their own language over them. This was not acceptable to the diverse races of Assam. Consequently Nagaland was the first to go, followed by Mizoram, Meghalaya, and Arunachal Pradesh.

Dangers Ahead: The problem of present-day Assam, stems directly from internal migration. In essence it is linguistic and ethnic, but some people tried to impart it a religious hue also. The rate of earlier migration was small but it soon increased — and what originally a trickling rill of migrants, soon became a torrent and the Assamese developed genuine fear of being swamped by them and eventually reduced to a linguistic minority in their own home land. The Bengali onrush of migrants has upset the demographic and economic balance.

In view of this increasing influx of illegal immigrants, particularly from Bangladesh, the Assamese demanded their deportation. The fact that most immigrants came to Assam after 1947, from East Pakistan (now Bangladesh), have provided a religious dimension to the problem which was basically ethnic and linguistic. Politicians, on account of their vested interests are apt to exploit a situation such as this. By imparting religious hue to a fundamentally ethnic cum linguistic problem, they have complicated the issue. The immigrants are a determining factor in the elections and hence their stay or deportation from Assam has become a political issue. In 1969, B. P. Chalia the then Chief Minister of Assam, established special tribunals for summary tribals to detect and deport foreigners, but the matter was dropped on political grounds.

In 1977, Golap Borbora's Janta Government wanted the detection of names of foreigners from the Mangaldoi Parliamentary Constituency but the matter was protested by other leaders of his party and the programme was dropped. Subsequently, the matter became broad-based. The All Assam Students Union (AASU) and All Assam Gana Sangaram Prishad (AAGSP) spearheaded the movement for the detection and deportation of all foreigners from Assam.

On October 6, 1979 over one lakh people assembled at the judges Field at Guwahati, to demand the immediate settlement of the foreign national issue. This was followed by a week long Gana Satyagrah launched by all Assam students Union on Nov. 12,1978. The movement was followed by Assam Bund in 3rd Dec. 1979, a four day mass picketing of Government officer on December 5,1979 and mourning rallies on December 17,1979. A large number of people protested to prevent oil being pumped' to the Barauni refinery.

On February 4, 1980; the Ganga Satyagraha was launched. On April 21, 1980, all officers remained closed. A there day stoppage of air and rail services was undertaken by AASU and AAGSP. On July 14, 1980, a 14-day mass picketing programme was launched. On Dec. 31, 1981, a 36 hours road blockade programme was launched, followed by a 12 hour road Bund on January 7,1982, a programme of mass hunger strike by all students and college teachers on January 9, 1982, a people's curfew on the Republic Day on January 26, 1982. These were organised by AASU and AAGSP under the leadership of two moderates Prafulla Mohanti and Phrigu Phukan.

What began as a mild political stir has become a mass movement with wide local support. Barring the Cachar valley where the Bengali predominate, in the rest of the Brahmaputra valley the movement received the solid support of Assamese rank and file.

While a long chain of political parleys between the centre and agitation leader, joined at times by the leaders of other political parties began, deadlocked and led to a decision to hold elections on the basis of the 1979 electoral rolls, one may quickly scan the political parleys and proposals emerging there from the parleys centered around one demand — the deportation of foreign infiltrators who illegally sneaked into Assam. The earlier demand of student leaders was to treat 1951 as the cut off line. But after a few rounds of prolonged negotiations the representatives of AASU: and AAGSP agreed to accept all foreigners that entered Assam between 1951 and 1961.

The Government of India, however, agreed to deport only such infiltrators as have entered India after March 25, 1971. Various alternate years were discussed for being treated as cut-off years such as 1961, 1967, 1977, and 1978 but non-consensus could be reached. However, meeting held on May 23, 1981 came to the conclusion that the possible shape of the final agreement becoming clear. In outline it is possible that those who entered Assam between 1951-61 will be absorbed in the state. Those entering after 1971 will be deported.

The movement leaders rejected this proposal. The election became a constitutional necessity. The Assam Assembly was dissolved on March 18, 1982 and hence the Assembly had to be constituted before March 18, 1883, failing which it was feared, the state of Assam would be in a state of Constitutional limbo. The government decided to hold the poll in the teeth of Assamese opposition. The government on its part was not prepared to yield to violence. The agitation was taken over by the extremists as all its liberal leaders were in detention.

4

Geography

The State of Assam located in the northeastern corner of the country has a unique geographical personality and sociocultural milieu. It is well endowed in natural resources. The mighty Brahmaputra; its perennial tributaries, evergreen forests, fertile soil invigorating climate and numerous mineral resources are unparallel in the country.

Stretching over an area of 78,483 sq km and supporting a population of 2,66,55,528 (2001) with a density 340 persons per sq km. It has natural boundaries on three sides. Its northern frontier from the river Sankosh on the west to the entrance of the mighty Brahmaputra into Assam is guarded by the Eastern or Assam Himalayas. To the south of the main Himalayas, there lies a series of sub-Himalayan Hills inhabited by the numerous hill tribes.

Geographical Features

The most dominating feature in the topography of Assam is the course of the river Brahmaputra. It has carved out its gigantic valley between the parallel ranges, i.e. the Assam Himalayas in the north and the Meghalaya Plateau in the south. The river Brahmaputra debouches the plain near Sadiya from where it assumes the name of Brahmaputra, and runs directly westwards for nearly 720 km, traversing every district of the Assam Valley from west to east until it crosses the Garo Hills and turning due south, it enters the plains of Bangladesh.

The valley of Brahmaputra is a monotonous plain, studded with numerous clumps of hills rising abruptly from the general level and surrounded on all sides except the west by mountains and intersected in all directions by many streams and rivulets, which coming out from the neighbouring hills empty themselves into the great channels of the Brahmaputra. To the south and east of the Meghalaya Plateau is the Barak Valley. This valley is also of alluvial origin. Sylhet having gone to Bangladesh Cachar is the only district of this natural unit in the state of Assam.

Thus Assam is naturally a beautiful tract of country, and enjoys all the advantages requisite for rendering it one of the finest under the sun-though at present by far the greater portion of it has been brought under cultivation. Its plains decked with a rich verdant robe and base of a group of beautiful wooded hills, covered to their very summits with trees, interspersed with dark and deep glens, and heaving their swelling ridges into a bright blue sky, constitute altogether a scene of extraordinary magnificence and sublimity, and display a regularity and softness of features that beggars description. On the other hand, there are most rudest and gigantic grand hills in the north, east and southern rims which are hurled together in wild confusion, seem to the spectator like the wrecks of a ruined world.

The geological formation of Assam which ultimately produces the various types of rocks and soils is a gradual process of evolution. The northern, eastern and southeastern hilly and mountainous tract formed a part of the Sea of Tethys which separated the Gondwanaland of the south. During the Tertiary Era, owing to the crystal movements of the earth, the bed of the Tethys Sea began to rise, and was folded into a series of parallel mountain chains. The rising land in Assam was thrown into wrinkles and the whole area contracted in size. The outcrop of the red earth deposited at the end of the Hills may be assumed to be the sediments laid down by the Sea of Teyths several thousand years ago.

The southern part of the state — a part of the Meghalaya Plateau is supposed to be a continuation of the ancient Gondwana land. It is the continuation of the Rajmahal Hills of the Chhotanagpur Plateau. So granite and gneisses are the principal rocks in the Plateau. At the foot of the Hills are frequently found beds of conglomerates.

In between these two ranges lies the narrow Brahmaputra valley, which is alluvial in origin and consists of sand, sandstone, pebbles, clay and sometimes a mixture of sand and clay with decomposed vegetable matter. The tertiary beds include a similarly varied assemblage of rocks — such as hard stone, soft and loose sand, conglomerates, coal seams, shale and sandy clay. The lowest Tertiary beds in some parts of Assam include limestone. Physiographically, the state of Assam is divisible into:

- The Hilly Tract of the North.
- The Brahmaputra Valley.
- The Barak Valley.
- The Hilly Tract of the South.

Physical Features

Assam which is situated in northeast corner of India is surrounded by Bhutan and Arunachal Pradesh on north, Nagaland and Manipur on east, Meghalaya and Mizoram on south and Bangladesh, Tripura and West Bengal on west. Geographical area covered by Assam in 78,438 sq km comprising 27 districts with a population of 266 lakh in 2001 (provisional census record of 2001). Only a narrow strip of submountain region of the Himalayas connects Assam with the Indian mainland. Flat alluvial valley is drained by the mighty Brahmaputra. The great river originates in western Tibet which brings down 6,500 lakh cubic feet of very fertile silt annually which is deposited in the valley between the Himalaya massif and the Meghalaya plateau and thence in the vast tract of Bengal delta. The state's climate is of humid tropical type in the plains and subalpine in the hills.

Hills

Karbi Hills

Karbi Anglong literally means Karbi Hills, lies in the middle of Assam state, sandwiched between the Brahmaputra valley in the North and the Barak valley in the South. Essentially a hill area, its low hills link the Meghalaya state on the western side and the state of Nagaland on the eastern flank.

Bamuni Hills

Located near Tezpur, the sculptural ruins of the Bamuni Hills dates back to the 9th and 10th centuries. It is famous for their excellent creative refinement. A major draw is a cross-shaped bracket lintel ornamented with horned Kirtimukha panels contains the figures of 10 incarnations of Lord Vishnu.

Nilachal Hill

Nilachal Hill stands high at Guwahati, with a height of 562 ft above sea level. The famous Kamakhya Temple is situated on top of it.

The name 'Nilachal' literally means 'blue mountain.' According to legends, Goddess Parvati angered with the disrespect shown by her father, King Daksha, towards her husband Lord Shiva burned herself to ashes. Lord Shiva overcome with grief wandered with his wife's remains.

Water and Drainage

The striking feature in the drainage system of Assam is the dominant control of river Brahmaputra. The people of Assam for generations have watered their fields with the life giving floods and drunk its blessed-water, their whole history and culture being intimately connected with the river Brahmaputra.

The catchment area of Brahmaputra river is 938,000 sq km and on the average it discharges about 425 cm or 15,000 cm. The average annual run-off being 381,000,000,000 cm or 13,463,000,000,000 cu ft.

Throughout the valley of Assam Brahmaputra has a broad course. After flowing about 1,609 km (100 mi) in an easterly direction in Tibet with the name Tsangpo, it cuts the Himalayas and turns south east, making a hair-pin bend at a few miles east of Namcha-Burwa. The bending is well marked near the longitude 94° near Pemkoi Sung, ten miles below Gayala Singdon. The Tsangpo has a vertical drop of 9 metres (30 feet) near this place. There is a waterfall of 46 metres (150 feet) and a lake at the foot of the, fall. The river after crossing the Himalayas takes the name Dishang, and it is met by another stream, Dibong, coming from the north. Another stream Lohit, comes from the east, and joins the two former rivers at Brahmakund — a famous Naligious spot for Hindus and this combined water takes the name of Brahmaputra. The valley of the river in Assam runs between the Himalayas on the north and the Shillong (Meghalaya) Plateau on the south. After crossing the Goro Hills, it makes a smooth turn and meets the Ganga at Goalundo.

During the course of its flow in Assam for about 724 km (450 miles) through almost every district, the river has carved out its own valley running between sandy bands in a wide stretch and forming a divergent channel. The large island as char of Majubi with an area of 1,256 sq km (485 sq mi) is enclosed between such a channel and the main stream.

There are enormous tributaries of Brahmaputra which flow from north as well as from the south. The notable tributaries from the north bank are the Subansiri, the Bharali, the Bornadi, the Pagladia, the Manas with its tributaries Ai, Champamati, Soralbhanga, and Sankosh and from the south are the Buri-Dihing, the Dikhow, the Jhanji, the Dhansiri, the Kulsi, etc. A few miles below the confluence of the Dhansiri and the Brahmaputra, a portion of water runs away from the main stream and flows under the name of Kolong through the district of Nowgong and rejoins the main stream about ten miles (16 km) east of Guwahati. The Kolong is fed by two important tributaries — the Kopili and the Digaru.

The drainage system of Brahmaputra is unique in the world. It provides the only example in the world where the drainage pattern runs is a diametrically opposite direction. Thus, in Tibet, it flows west to east but immediately south of Tibet, it flows from east to west in Assam. Peculiarities of the drainage pattern are again caused by the distribution of the tributaries; for instance, the mighty rivers of Himalayas, except the Brahmaputra, claim to have a tributary at the point where they bend cut through the ranges to meet the plain.

The Himalayas are considered to be younger in age than the Brahmaputra. Due to gradual upliftment of the might range, this old river furnishes a good example of an antecedent drainage system.

Barak or Surma River: The Barak river also known as the Surma river is the most important river on the southern side of the Plateau of Meghalaya (Shillong Plateau). It rises on the escarpment of the Barail Range from the south of Japvo Peavo Peak (Nagaland)

and flows through Manipur, Cachar, and Sylhet and finally empties itself into the old bed of the Brahmaputra near Bhairab Bazar.

Up to Tipaimukh it has a southwesterly journey, and the river is Known as the Barak. It flows through narrow valleys shut in on either side by hills that rise steeply from the river and for a while the river marks the boundary between the Naga Hills and Manipur. At Tipaimukh the river takes a turn to the north and for some distance divides Cahar from Manipur in a line parallel to that taken by the river in its downward sweep, near Lakhimpur, turning to the west, it enters the Cachar District and flows through it in a zigzag course until it passes into the Sylhet District of Bangladesh beyond Badarpur.

A few miles west of this place, the river bifurcates, one branch with the name Surma flow through Sylhet, Chatak and Sunamganj and the other branch known as Kushiara receives the tributary Manu and flows westward.

It again divides it say into two: the northern one Known as Bibyana and afterwards, the Kalni rejoins the Surma river near Ajmirgonj. The southern branch under the old name Barak flows past Nabigonj and meets the Surma little west of Habibganj. The combined outlet is Known as the Dhaleswari which further south becomes Known as the Meghana. The Brahmaputra and the Meghana Coalesce and discharge the water into the Bay of Bengal.

The total length of the Barak river from source to mouth is about 901 km (560 miles). It receives many tributaries, the most important being Jodukata, Jari, Jatinga and Bogapani, Sonai, Langai, Manu and Khowai.

Floods in Assam are a regular feature in the life of the inhabitants of the valley. It has many beneficial effects as well, viz. the silting of agricultural fields and supplying water for pisciculture in the inland bills and tanks, etc. The floods at present are considered as the greatest destroyer of man and property in the state. Now it has become a national problem, the tackling of which must be given top priority.

Like floods in Assam, earthquakes are also a common phenomenon. These may occur several times within a year, but their magnitude and intensity varies. Of all these earthquakes, the two of 1897 and 1950 are the most memorable from the point of view of intensity and the destruction. According to Oldham the zone of epicentre of the 1897 earthquake covered an area of 320 km (200 miles) in length and 80 km (50 miles) in width. This was located in the Shillong Plateau. A total area of 4,142,240 sq km or 1,600,000 sq mi bounded by V and VI isoseismal lines suffered extensive damage.

The earthquake of 1950 occurred on 15th August in the evening. This is considered as the second biggest earthquake of Assam and according to some seismologists it is considered to be one of the five greatest earthquakes in the recorded history of mankind. The epicentre was located at Rema, a small village in Arunanchal Pradesh (NEFA). The area over which minimum destruction was seen, covered about 38,834 sq km (15,000 sq mi). The less damage zone was enclosed by VII isoseismal line and was nearly 194,168 sq km or 75,000 sq mi in area. As a result of the earthquake a number of landslides and rock falls, especially along the foothills of the Himalayas, took place. Fissures of huge dimensions were developed through which sand and silt soaked with water were ejected in many places.

The effect of the earthquake was equally marked in changing the general configuration and drainage of the state. It is the after effect of the shock which brought much more calamity to the people. Some of the tributaries of the Brahmaputra in the mountainous region have changed their sources after this earthquake. Some of the rivers courses were blocked, which when removed, caused serious floods in the valleys below.

Physical Status

In the north the state of Assam lies Bhutan and the state of Arunachal Pradesh in the east it is bounded by the states of Nagaland, and Manipur, while its southern boundary is formed by the states of Meghalaya, Tripura and Mizoram. The western boundary between Assam and Bangladesh is not natural and there lie the districts of Sylhet, Mymensingh and Rangpur of Bangladesh, and Cooch-Behar District of West Bengal. The state is divided into 27 districts, namely, Barpeta, Bongaigoan, Cachar, Darang, Dhemaji, Dhubri, Dibrugarh, Goalpara, Golaghat, Hailakandi, Jorhat, Kamrup, Karbi Anglog, Karimganj, Kokrajhar, Lakhimpur, Marigaon, Nagaon, Nalbari, North Cachar Hills, Sibsagar, Sonitpur, Tinsukia, Kamrup Metro, Udalguri, Baksa, and Chirang. In the past the Assam region was conquered by the Mongolian hordes and Ahoms coming either from China or Buram, through the northeastern frontier passes and finally mixing with the people of the Brahmaputra valley.

The State of Assam was magnificently served before partition by the river of Brahmaputra and its tributaries for trade with Dacca and Calcutta which lie at a distance of about 646 and 1761 km respectively from Guwahati — the main city and trade centre of Assam. After partition in 1947, the lower part of the Brahmaputra beyond Dhubri having gone to East Pakistan (Present Bangladesh), and the main tracks of the Bengal and Assam Railways having gone to East Pakistan, the Brahmaputra valley became completely isolated from the rest of the Union of India. This was partly overcome when the famous link route of the present North-East Frontier Railway from Fikaragram to Siliguri was constructed in 1950. This route with gradual improvement in tract has given Assam a direct connection with Calcutta, Delhi and other parts of Northern India. Air service from Delhi and Calcutta to various towns and cities of Assam have been introduced — and this has saved a lot of time in transit from Assam to any other part of India.

Physical Development

The word Assam is of recent origin. In the past it was Known as 'Kamarupa'. According to some of the experts the word 'Assam' is the outcome of the uneven topography of the country Known in Assamese as 'Asama' in contrast to the plains of the adjacent province of Bengal. According to the former scholar and write Gait, the present name of Assam is derived from the word 'Ahom' the past rulers of Assam. He wrote: "The tradition of the Ahoms themselves is that the present name is derived from Assam in the sense of unequal or "fearless". They say that this was the term applied to them at the time of Sukhaph's invasion of Assam by the local people in token of their admiration of the way in which the Ahom King first conquered and then conciliated them. Dr. Kakati has approved of this interpretation, but he suggests that 'Assam — 'fearless'— may be a latter day Sanskritisation of 'Acham'. In Thai language 'Chain' means to be defeated with the Assamese prefix 'a' 'acham' would mean "undefeated conqueror." If this was the origin of the people, the name was subsequently applied to the region.

Structural Position

The northern Hilly and mountainous tract extends from the river Teasta in Sikkim in the west and the Sadiya Gorage in the east. The rapid rise of the hills from the plains is a characteristic feature and differs from the western portion of the Himalayas in this respect. The foothills of the Assam Himalayas are Known as the Aka, Daffla, Miri, Abor, Mishmi and Khamti ranges. In the northeastern parts of the state there is a big curve round the valley and the range extends south towards the Arakan.

The general appearance of the Northern Hilly region — mostly populated by different tribes of Mongolian origin — is that of a mighty mountain overhanging the plains and grassy expenses which are intersected by river courses, that merge from the strong sunny mountain tracts into sandy alluvial plains, covered with forests and gigantic grasses. Due to great slopes, the rivers are found debouching from higher levels and to spread over the countryside.

The hilly tract has crystalline, metamorphic and sedimentary rocks of which the outermost is the youngest and thickest. The same rocks have been recorded *in situ* in the Daffla Hills, and also in the Upper Dihang Valley. A bed of tertiary bed occurs in the foot hill ranges. In the Dihang valley, excellent exposures of massive lava flows, dark, green and dark reddish in colour, are to be seen.

Valley of Brahmputra: The Brahmaputra valley also Known as the Assam valley is divisible into parts: (i) The Upper Brahmaputra Valley, and (ii) The lower Brahmaputra valley.

The lower Assam Valley consists of the districts of Goalpara, Kamrup, Nowgong and Darrang where the plains are broken by isolated groups of hills, and the Upper Assam valley sprawls over the districts of Sibsagar, Lakhimpur, and Dibrugarh where unbroken plains lie from the Himalayas on the northwest to the Naga Hills on the southeast.

The numerous low hills found scattered near Dhubri, Goalpara, Guwahati, and Tezpur are, in fact, the outlying portions of the Meghalaya Plateau and as such they consist for the greater part of gneisses. The surrounding plains have been formed by the alluvial materials carried down by the mighty Brahmaputra and its numerous tributaries. The Brahmaputra valley is narrowest near the Mikir Hills where the river first encounters the gneissic beds, and above this point upwards the valley in completely free from low hills locally Known as Tillas less than 305 metres (1,000 ft) in elevation.

The Upper Brahmaputra valley lies northeast and southwest, between two fairly parallel ranges. The Sibsagar and Lakhimpur Districts are formed by the alluvial deposits of the Brahmaputra river. There are traces of deposits are different age, the most recent alluvial being within the present level. Undulating plains are found towards the head and side of the valley, an example of which is provided by the one present near Doomdooma. Some river terraces are formed in the Dihang valley near Margheritta, but the best example is provided by the Daffla valley, where three terrace 250,160 and 140 feet (76,49,43 metres) in height, respectively, are formed.

So the surface of the highest and the lowest terrace is, therefore, 100 feet (30.5 metres) above the level of the valley. It is supposed that the Valley is gradually sinking. The depth of the alluvial on the plain is more than seven thousand feet. At the head of the Assam valley, there are a few hills - such as the Tipam Hills of Jaipur and Digboi, which are the outlying portions of the Naga Hills and they consist mostly of sandstone bed.

In general, the Brahmaputra valley is a flat level plain, though surrounded by high mountains. Sadiya (now eroded) near the head of the valley has an altitude of only 440 feet (134 metres) above the mean sea level, Dibrugarh 340 feet (104 metres) and Guwahati only 163 feet (50 metres).

Valley of Barak: The Barak valley consists of its main part largely of swampy flats broken by numerous low isolated hills and ridges. There is a monoceinal fold separating the tertiaries of the Barak Valley from the older rocks of the Meghalaya Plateau. This fold marks the boundary of the north. In the south, the strata have been folded into north and south wave like corrugation which give rise to alternate rows of hills and valleys, but not every row of hills is a line of uplift nor is each valley a line of depression, for the folding has led removing the less resistant beds of clay and shale and leaving parallel ridges where harder strata have more successively and more fully withstood the denuding action of the rains and streams.

The strata of the Barak valley belong entirely to the Never division. The oldest rock found within the valley are the sandstones of the Barial series and even this occupies a small area to the southeast of the Haflong-Disang fault in the north Cachar Hills. The lower beds of the Surma series above the Barail consists of a series of alternation of shale, sandy-shale, mudstone, shaly sandstone and thin conglomerates, having a maximum thickness of about 12,000 feet (3,660 metres) or a fairly high and usually compact group of hills. Such hills are covered by jungles. The Upper beds of the Surma series are mainly soft sandy-shales with thin sandstones. They give rise to a long strip of swampy ground broken by a series of Tillas. Many of the lower and scattered hills are made up of sand clay belonging to the Tipam series.

The lower beds of the Tipam series are harder, and they usually form a valley and a ridge. Most of the tea cultivation in Barak valley is on the Tipam bed. Another interesting feature is the presence of gravel in the plateau deposited by the Barak and its tributaries. In the hoary past, these streams were flowing at a level several hundred feet higher than today. The flat ground is largely occupied by clayey alluvium. Depressions here form bills (marshy places) of different shapes and sizes. The streams follow a tortuous and unstable course in the alluvial ground.

Valley of Mikir and Cachar: The hilly tract of the south includes the undulating and mountainous parts of the Mikir Hills and North Cachar districts and the Kirbi Along districts of Assam. In fact it is the northern fringe of the Meghalaya Plateau. Sandstone and shale form the main group of rocks. On the southeastern part is a broad cynclinal area composed mainly of sandstone. There is little flat ground within the area of the Hilly Tract of the south. The valleys are narrow, steep sided and well-clothed with green vegetation. There are few level stretches of alluvium in the valley bottom. A few accumulations of high level gravels or boulder-beds in several parts of the hilly tracts are also seen.

Mineral Resources

Mineral resources play a vital role in the economic development and social well being of a region. The mineral resources are, however, unequally distributed and they are exhaustible. In fact, the large deposit of a given mineral, continuous mining will exhaust the ores. Minerals are thus finite and exhaustible. The State of Assam is well endowed with petroleum natural gas, coal, limenstone, sillimanite, asbestos, corrundum, fire-clay, china-clay, Fuller's earth, feldspar, gold, iron and copper. The Geological survey of India and the state Department of Geology and Mining are actively busy in exploring and prospecting more minerals in the state.

Coal: Coal, the combustible rock which had its origin in the accumulation and partial decomposition of vegetation is found in the foothills of the Himalayas — running from Alipur Duar to near Sadiya. The Seam of this coal deposit are about two metres in thickness. These coal deposits are of the Gondwana period. Moreover coal deposits of the Cretaceous and Tertiary Formation are found in the Mikir hills, 'and in Upper Assam. According to one estimate the coal reserves in the state are about 450 million tonnes.

In the Upper Valley of the Brahmaputra River Makum Field in Lakhimpur District is well Known for its lignite coal. The deposits of Makum field are about 15 metre in thickness which are mostly composed of grey shale, brownish grey shale, and carbonaceous shale. The reserves in this field are about 25 metres in depth and are estimated at about 20 million tonnes:

> The Jaipur coalfield of the Upper Brahmaputra Valley has a reserve of about ten million tonnes. The dip of its coal seams is very steep and almost vertical towards the east. In the District of Sibsagar in the Catchment Saffrai is another important coalfield of the state which has an estimated reserve of about 12 million tonnes. The Namchik coal-field extends from the Hills of Namphuk to the Namchik river. The dip of the bed is however, very steep. Most of the coal found in Assam is of inferior quality which is consumed in railways, steamships, plantations, domestic purposes and assorted small scale industries established in the various parts of the state.

Oil and Natural Gas: The state of Assam has immense potential of natural gas and petroleum. In fact about 62 per cent of the country's total oil potential and 45 per cent of natural gas reserves are located in the state of Assam. The oil bearing strata in Assam are concentrated in Digboi, Naharkatiya, Hugrijan, DoomDooma, Moran, Rudrasagar, Lakowa, Took, Geleky and between jorhat and Golaghat. Digboi-the first Known oil field in the country has been producing since 1890, but at present it is near depletion. The average annual production is about 65,000,000 gallons. The Naharkatiya-Maran fields also have natural gas reserves of about 850 billion cubic feet.

Limestone: Limestone is a carbonate of calcium. It is found in North Cachar Hills and in the Mikir Hills. In the Mikir Hills, the limestone is well developed in the Lumbha, the Kopili and the Kharkhor river valleys. According to one estimate about 175 million tons of limestone are available in Mikir Hills. It is mainly used in the cement manufacturing industries of the state.

Sillimanite: Sillimanite is a mineral which can be cut into blocks and shapes for use as lining in glass tanks and other furnaces. In fact, the Assam silliminite refectories have a longer furnace life, high resistance to spalling, thermal shock and low productivity. The sillimanite deposits are found in the hilly tracts of the southern rim of the state. Moreover fire-clay is found in association with the coal-bearing horizons in the Mikir Hills, while the alluvial tract of the state contains clay suitable for bricktile manufacture. Various siliva materials in the form of sandstone quartzite occur in the Mikir Hills. Golpara and Kamrup Districts have feldspar deposits. Banded magnetite-quartzite deposits have been located in Golpara and along the Kamrup border. Traces of gold are also found in Lakhimpur, Darang and Sibsagar districts. Copper is found in Goalpara and gypsum is extracted from the Mikir Hills. Enormous quantities of sand, pebbles, and singles are available in the various tributaries of the Brahmaputra and the Barak rivers. Sand stone and other gilding materials are available in the hilly tracts and alluvial plains of the state.

Since the state has limited quantity of power and basic minerals their judicious use is very essential.

Plants and Animals

The State of Assam is well endowed in forest resource. The climate, topography and soils provide ideal conditions for the great diversity of natural vegetation in the region. The forest area in the state covers about 28 per cent of the total area of Assam as compared to 19 per cent for the India as a whole.

So far as the spatial distribution of forests is concerned Lakhimpur and Kamrup districts have over 30 per cent of their reporting areas under forest. In Goalpara, Cachar and Sibsagar the forest area varies between 25 to 30 per cent while in the remaining districts, i.e. Darrang and Nowgong it is less than 20 per cent.

According to Champion and Griffith the forests of Assam may be classified under the following categories: (i) tropical evergreen forests, (ii) mixed deciduous forest, (iii) pine forests, and (iv) Savannah forests. The tropical evergreen forests are found in the Sibsagar, and Lakhimpur, districts and in the sub-Himalayan tract. The dominant species of the evergreen forests found in Assam are Nahar (Mesua Ferrea), Makai (Shorea Assamica), Hollong (Dipterocarpus Macrocarpus) and the famous iron-wood used for constructional purposes. As the two main species, Hollong and Nahar, regenerate luxuriously under natural conditions, their management is very easy.

In the Upper Brahmaputra valley, there are still some large tracts of evergreen forests. In the Cachar District the evergreen forests are confined to the north eastern aspects of the lower slopes. Gurjon (Dipteracarpus), Sundi (Turbinatus), Rata, Titasopa, Champa are some of the important varieties of the evergreen forest in the Cachar region of Assam. The forest areas of Kamrup and Goalpara districts have substantial tracts of Sal forests. Sal is also found in small tracts of Nowgong and Darrang Districts.

Other Creatures

The mixed deciduous forests generally occur in the Lower Brahmaputra Valley. The deciduous forests are found mainly on relatively drier slopes, and ridges of the hills not occupied by the stunted sal. The main species of the deciduous forests 'are Sterculia villosa, Bombax Malabaricu, Dellenia, Pentagyana, Careya Arborea, Lagerstroemia, Paruiflora, Schima, Wallichii, etc. The ground is often covered with thatches, grass and reeds.

Other species of deciduous forests are Sishoo (Dalbergia Sisso and Khair (Accacia Catechu) trees which are found in the Lower Brahmaputra Valley, especially to the north of the Brahmaputra River on the southern slopes of the hills. These valuable forests are also found in Golpara, Kamrup and Darrang. Kadam, Simul, Koroi are found in the alluvial flats and river terraces of the rivers and streams. The pine forests are confined in zones having heights between 750 metres to 1,900 metres in the state. Pine forests in many cases remain mixed up with broad leaved species. The pine trees are exploited mainly for timber and gum.

The Savannah type of forests are found in the highlands in the vicinity of those villages where Jhuming (shifting cultivation) is being carried out for generations. The species found in these areas are Gayera, Arborea, Wrightia, Tomentosa, Zizyphus, and Randia. 'Bata' a Kind of Imperata Arundinacea is found extensively in these areas. Lowland Savannah contains Saccharum Spontanium as the main grass and is located on the banks of rivers and streams which are flooded during the rains.

In addition to timber, the Assam forest is also rich in minor forest products. Reed, cane, bamboos fetch handsome revenue to the State Government and provide employment to the people. Cane is found in abundance in Lakhimpur, Sibsagar, Nowgong, and Cachar Districts. The forests of Assam contain the large reserves of bamboos in India. As discussed in the preceding paras Assam abounds extensive tracts of forests and uncultivated lands. Consequently the native fauna has splendour, and great variety of fauna. Flourishing beneath a genial climate, and nourished by dense vapours and frequent showers, in a soil naturally humid, vegetation here attains a luxuriance inconceivably magnificent. Animal life equally partakes in this exuberance and exhibits under every form, the most singular shapes, and the most brilliant combinations of colours.

Elephants, Tigers, leopards, hyaena rhinoceros, vivaria mongos, wild bovina or bisons, monkeys, foxes bears, Bos-tarus, ox, wild buffaloes, antelopes, goats, sheep, peacocks, tortoise, turtle, testudo, crocodiles, serpents, numerous birds and insects are the main species of animals found in the state of Assam. The one horned rhinoceros of the valley is an important foreign exchange earner, being a rare species and almost extinct elsewhere. The elephants are also important particularly as means of transport in different terrains and as draught animal in the lumbering industry. The richness and variety of wildlife of the region in the reed jungles provide the most ideal location of the game sanctuaries at Kaziranga in Upper Assam and at Manas in Lower Assam. The Kaziranga Game Sanctuary has been developed as a National Park which enjoys internal status as a tourist centre.

The Environment

The state of Assam is situated in subtropical latitudes, but awing to orographic features, the climate of the valley is humid-monsonic. There are, however, micro-level variations in the general prevailing weather and climatic conditions of the state. In the climatic classification advocated by Koppen the Brahmaputra valley has "humid meso-thermal Brahmputra Gangetic type (CWG)." The most distinctive feature of the Valley is, however, the rainfall and the trend and range of temperature which is directly affected by the precipitation and shows spectacular departure from the normal humid mesa-thermal type. In general the climate and weather of the state of Assam are controlled by the relief, periodic change in the pressure conditions, the predominance of maritime air mass, the western disturbances during winters, the local mountain and valley winds.

The surrounding mountains and hills of Arunachal Pradesh, Naga and Patkoi Hills and the Plateau of Meghalaya exert significant effect on the pressure, temperature and precipitation of the valley of Brahmaputra. The northern mountain barriers not only protect the valley from the chilly cold winds of the Central Siberaria, but also obstruct the warm moist wind that blows from the southwest in summer months and causes deflection and consequent development of 'orographic low'. The varied surface configuration of the different hilly tracts thus affects the incoming winds and causes clouding and precipitation. Rain fall on the windward side and on the slope is, therefore, higher than that at the base. On the basis of temperature and precipitation a year in the Assam state is divisible into: (i) Winter season, (ii) Pre-monsoon season, (iii) Monsoon season, (iv) Season of retreating monsoon.

Cold Weather Season: The cold weather season commences at the end of November or the first weak of December and continues till late February. During the month of December a high pressure area develops over the valley. The winter season is considered to be the most pleasant and comfortable season of Assam. This season is characterised by cool weather, with occasional thundershowers and frequent morning fog. The temperature during this period remains well above 13°C except at the hill stations.

The average diurnal range never exceeds 5.5°C. The eastern districts are comparatively cooler than the western plain districts. Occasionally the southern tongue of the Tibetan high pressure extends up to the Brahmaputra valley that brings an exceptionally cold spell of short duration. The greater percentage of rain during winter is caused by the western disturbances, but the total amount of rainfall never exceeds 8 cm. In late winter, coincides with the western depression, thunderstorms may result. Fogs are very common features of winter weather in Assam. In the southern valley of eastern Assam, the fogs are much more widespread and persist for long duration. The mountain-winds sweep down the fogs from the northern valley to the south where they tend to concentrate and remain for longer periods.

Pre-monsoon Season: The Pre-monsoon season commences in the beginning of March in the state of Assam. The Pre-monsoon weather over the Brahmaputra valley is characterised by a rapid rise of temperature, the vanishing fog and occasional thundershowers. The pressure gradually becomes steep which favours the formation of thundry weather, specially in southern and northeastern Assam. The western disturbances continue to prevail in March and April and cause rainfall. The mornings are cool, pleasant and with mild winds; the afternoons are hot and irritating. This is due to the wide range of diurnal temperature.

As the season advances, the range of temperature decreases and the amount and frequency of rainfall increase. The rainfall in generally associated with thunderstorms which usually come in the afternoons. These hundred-storms are called *Nor'westers* on account of the direction from which the associated squalls usually move. In mid-April, when the western disturbances pass eastward, they induce on their front a deeper southerly moist current from the Bay of Bengal. At this stage, and even more so, when fresh northwesterly air moves down from the Upper layers, marked instability results. When these winds meet near a local low centre over the valley and incidentally the western disturbance coincides with this phenomenon, a severe thunderstorm occurs, locally Known as Bordio-chills in Assam and Kal Baiskhi in Bengal. The advance of the pre-monsoon season is marked by progressively longer rainy days, e.g. 6 days in March, 12 days in April and 14 days in May. Maximum rain occurs on, the southern slopes of the Khasi and Jaintia Hills and the upper reaches of the Brahmaputra Valley.

Season of General Rains: From June to September is the season of general rains in the state of Assam. During the season of summer monsoon the seasonal trough line that develops along the Gangetic valley also extends towards Assam. Most of the monsoon rains being along this line. When this trouph line moves northward and lies along the foot of the Himalayas, the monsoon breaks over Assam and heavy rain occurs on the southern slopes of the Himalayas.

The circulation of wind over the state is directly regulated by its orography which plays a vital role in determining weather during the monsoon season. The southerly winds hit the Khasi and Jaintia Hills and are lifted up. They consequently produce a "low" over the valley and result into heavy rainfall.

The monsoon weather in Assam is characterised by cloudy weather. Very high atmospheric humidity and weak variable surface winds. The general weather is sultry and oppressive due to high humidity, although the shooting temperature is considerably arrested by incessant rain. The rainy days are prolonged. There are about 18 to 20 days in June, July and August and about 14 days in September. In each month rain is associated with thunderstorms for about 8 to 12 days.

Season of Retreating Monsoon: The season of retreating monsoon commences in the first weak of September. By the close of September the summer monsoon winds begin to cease in Assam. In fact, this leads to the retreat of monsoon. The withdrawal of monsoon is followed progressively by fair weather and morning fogs of short duration. The temperature falls gradually, but the diurnal range of temperature increases. The diurnal range of temperature varies from 3 to 6°C in November. The southwest monsoon wind is replaced by light unsteady winds. In November the winds become northerly. These winds are fed by northwesterly winds from the Gangetic Valley and northeasterly to easterly winds in the Kachar Plain. The average rainfall during the months of retreating monsoon (October and November) does not exceed 15 cm. The stable weather of the retreating monsoon season is one of the most endurable, pleasant and delightful in the state. In general it may be said that Assam enjoys a temperate climate uniforms as compared to the rest of India. The warm weather is very moderate, and throughout the year, the nights are cool and refreshing.

5

Society

The Demography

The history of population of Assam is a record of constant impulses of immigration from the east, southeast and west directions. The alien races, ethnic groups and various religions have influenced the cultural ethos and mode of life of this region.

The state of Assam has a great diversity in its terrain, climatic conditions and resource bare. These variations have resulted into unevenness in the spatial distribution of population. In fact, over 95 per cent of the total population of Assam is concentrated in the highly fertile and productive plains of the Brahmaputra, and the remaining five per cent is sprinkled in the hilly tracts of the state.

Growth of Population

The population of Assam has grown at on stupendous rate. In 1826 when Assam came under British rule, the population of the region was only about 799,519. At that time the population of Kamrup was three lakhs, followed by Goalpara with a population of one lakh. The population of Nowgong and Darrang were around ninety thousand each. A real census operation is Assam was started in 1891 and thereafter it took place once in every ten years. Between 1891 and 1941 (pre-Independence census) the population of Assam grew at a steady growth rate. The growth rate of population has been shown in Table.

It may be seen from table that between 1891 and 1941 the grow decadal growth of population constantly remained over 11 per cent the lowest being 11.8 per cent in 1901 and the highest 18.2 per cent in 1941. The growth of population in the Assam state was affected by the various socio-economic and political factors. The 1951 census covered the plains and the autonomous hill districts of Assam. During this period in 1947 Sylhet being separated after the partition of India, the Census in 1951 showed a much reduced population because Sylhet was the most important district in Assam as regards the density of population.

Assam: Growth Trend of Population

Year	Population variation	Percentage of variation
1891	5, 478, 343	-
1901	6, 127, 411	+ 11.8
1911	7, 061, 034	+ 15.2
1921	7, 990, 775	+ 13.2
1931	9, 248, 397	+ 13.7
1941	10, 930, 388	+ 18.2

Source: Census of India, 1891-1941.

In the decade between 1941 and 1951 the population of Assam, however, increased by 19.2 per cent compared to India's 13.3 per cent. This stupendous growth in population occurred because of the inflow of refuges from East Pakistan (present-Bangladesh). During this period nearly 27 lakh migrants crossed over to Assam.

The year of 1951 has a special significance in the growth of population of Assam. Since 1951 there has been fairly high rate of growth of population, and the census of 1961 shows that the population of Assam (excluding Nagaland and NEF-A) numbers 11.87 million. In the 1951 census, the corresponding area (47.1 thousand sq mi) showed a population of 8.83 million. So during the last ten years, it has increased by more than three million, or by 34.45 per cent, the highest increase amongst the states of India. Compared to this, West Bengal showed an increase of 33 per cent, Bihar 19.8 per cent, Orissa 20 per cent, Uttar Pradesh 16.7 per cent, Maharashtra 24 per cent, Madras 12 per cent, and India as a while 21.5 per cent.

During the last eighty years from 1901 to 1981, the population of Assam has increased from 3.7 million to 19.89 million — an increase of 250 per cent, as compared to 85 per cent for India as a whole. The annual growth rate of population of Assam is thus about 3.5 per cent. This growth rate is quite alarming and demands urgent economic development, check in growth rate of population and most judicious and rational utilisation of natural and human resources.

If we analyse the causes responsible for such high increase in population in Assam, in migration turns out to be the most important factor. There have been three main streams of migration to Assam, the most important being the settlers coming from the erstwhile East Bengal (present Bangaladesh). The other two groups are the tea garden labourers and the Nepalis. The Census Report of Assam of 1911 mentioned for the first time the commencement of a voluntary stream of settlers into the Brahmaputra valley right up to Tezpur and Nowgong.

During the decade 1911 mentioned for the first time the commencement of a voluntary stream of settlers into the Brahamputra valley right up to Tezpur and Nowgong. During the decade 1911-21 the influenza epidemic retarded the growth to some extent. Yet the population continued to grow because of natural growth and migration of East Bengal settlers, tea garden labourers and the Nepalis. In the following decade the migrants consolidated their position in Goalpara District and settled in good numbers in Nowgong District and Barpeta Subdivision of Kamrup District. Only Sibsagar District escaped the in migrants.

In the following decade of 1931-41, Assam felt the effects of the world economic depression. But natural growth and migration continued to push up the population in the state. In decade 1914-51, the Bengal famine of 1943, the partition of the country in 1947 and the communal disturbances in the East Pakistan in 1950 gave a fillip to migration into Assam. The decades after independence mark a new stage of demographic development in the state. The growth rate since the beginning of the century had been steady at about 20 per cent every ten years. In the decade immediately after Independence, i.e. 1951-61 the growth rate shot-up to the unprecedented level of 35 per cent.

This was not only an all time high for Assam but also the highest among all the states for the decade. This accelerated pace continued in the last decade also with a rate of 34.7 per cent which was the fourth highest growth rate for the states of the country. As usual immigration greatly contributed to the growth of population in Assam in the decades after independence. But the natural increase in the population was also faster than before because of control of epidemics, improvement of public health and general economic development.

A brief look at the growth rates in the state of Assam, shows that the growth rate is between 16 to 20 per cent between 1901 to 1961. After 1961 the growth rate jumped to around 35 per cent which is almost unprecedented in any other state of the country.

Density of Population

The distribution of population in the state of Assam has been closely controlled by the topography, reveries, swamps, marshes and the fertility of the agricultural land. There is a marked variation in the density of population of the plain and hilly districts. Assam with lass than 4 per cent of the total area of India contained about 2.6 per cent of the country's total population. Naturally this low population and low density per sq km compared to the neighbouring states of West Bengal and Bihar received wide publicity which led to the influx of immigrants from the neighbouring states and Bangladesh.

Rural and Urban Population

The vast majority of Assam population lives in villages. There are 22,224 inhabited villages in the state. Over 80 per cent of the total population lives in villages. By a village we mean a village according to revenue records. But in some areas like the hilly regions or the forest areas of the state there are villages without revenue records. In such areas the customarily recognised villages are treated as villages. All the villages are not inhabited of the total of 23,331 villages in Assam 22,224 are inhabited and the remaining 1,107 are uninhabited. It is vividly clear that the villages in different districts are of different size. The villages can be grouped into seven groups. Thus, there is only one village in Assam with a population of ten thousand or above. The name of this village which is in Darrang District is Siparia Chapori. 29 villages with a population between 2,000 to 4,999 and 9,999. There a population between 1,000 and 1,999.

The population 5,986 villages varies between 500 and 999, and 6,744 villages' population is between 20,0499 while 5,615 villages are very small with a population of less than 200 persons. Thus most of the villages of Assam are small having a populations of less than 500 persons. In fact, in all the districts of the state the proportion of such small villages in high being 40 per cent or above. North Cachar Hills and Mikir Hills Districts show the highest percentage of such small villages, the figures being 97 per cent and 88 per cent respectively. The districts where more than half of the villages are small are Lakhimpur (69%), Goalpara (59%), and Cachar (53%). The average population of a village in 1971 was 713, which more to 751 in 1981. Kamrup with 847 persons per village (1981) on an average occupies first place followed by Nowgong and Sibsagar. The districts with the smallest average village population are Mikir Hills and North Cachar Hills.

Nearly 19 per cent of the total population of Assam was urban in 1981 (projected figures). As a matter of fact Assam is one of the least urbanised states in India having only 19 per cent of the total population as urban against 23.8 per cent for the country as a whole. The urban population in Kamrup, and Lakhimpur is however, more than the state average. Kamrup district accounts for 19 towns with an urban population of ever 4.5 Lakhs. The only city of Assam Guwahati is situated in this district. Lakhimpur District with 15 towns accounts for three lakhs urban population. Both these districts enjoy the advantage of having industries like oil, petroleum, petrochemicals fertilizers and agro based industries which have contributed to the rapid growth of urban population.

Of the total urban population 3,868,350 about 16 per cent lives in the Guwahati urban Agglomeration. The other bigger towns of Assam having a population between 50,000 and one lakh are Dibrugarh, Jorhat, Nowgong, Tinsukia, and Silchar. Rest of the towns are small and which have less than 50 thousand of the total population. There has been a nine field increase in the number of towns since the beginning of the century. The small number of 12 towns in 1901 has risen up to the figure of 92 towns. Prior to independence both the number of towns and their population size were small. The largest town had a population below 50,000. After independence, however, there was rapid change in the number and size of towns. The number of towns jumped from 25 in 1951 to 54 in 1961 and finally reached the figure of 92 in 1985.

The growth of urban population is more striking than the growth in the number of towns. The total urban population of Assam has swelled from 77 thousand in 1901 to over 17 lakhs in 1985. This means that the number of people living in towns has increased over 17 times in the last eighty years. The rapid growth in urban population after independence is due among other factors to extension of the areas of the municipalities, influx of refugees from East Bengal, economic development, increased administrative activities, increase in the number of educational institutions, establishment of industries and expansion in trade and commerce.

Population of Guwahati: Guwahati is the largest city, a hub of industrial and administrative activities Guwahati is an ancient city. Its ancient name was Pragiyotishpur. The first historical description of the town is that by Hioven Tsang who visited it about 640 AD. It is not known when the town changed its name to Guwahati but by the time it was under the Ahoms it was already known as Guwahati or Goahawtee or place dotted with arecanut trees. In the census up to 1901 Guwahati was shown as including North Gaughati also. In 1901, the population of Guwahati excluding North Guwahati was recorded as 11,661. In the first decade of the present century Guwahati increased substantially. This increase was mainly attributed to the completion of water works in 1887 and availability of wholesome drinking water and construction of railway line, linking Guwahati with the rest of the country.

Since 1901, the growth of population of Guwahati has been steady. The population increased from 11,661 to 12,481 in 1911, 16,480 in 1921; 21,797 in 1931; 29,598 in 1941, and 43,615 in 1951. The year of 1961 recorded a phenomenal spurt in the population which rose to 100,707. This gave Guwahati the status of a city for the first time in 1961. The percentage increase in population during the decade was 131 per cent. This was due to inclusion of new areas in the municipality, establishment of industries in and around Guwahati and increase in government offices and trade and commerce. The projected population of Guwahati in 1981 was 19,896,843 which recorded an increase of 33.4 per cent during the 1971-81 decade. Now Guwahati has a large urban agglomeration which besides the city of Guwahati includes Kamakhya, Pandu, New Guwahati Railway Colony, Refinery Colony, Noonmati, Dispur, Maligaon and Guwahati university complex. The population of Guwahati urban Agglomeration had a growth rate of 51 per cent during the last decade and the growth in size and population is even more striking after 1981.

Age and Sex Ratio

The sex and age composition, that is the proportion of men and women are important attributes of population. The age-sex composition of a population has great influence on the capacity for growth of population. For example, in a population that has an extra ordinarily high share of members aged over 50, would expect low birth rate and high death rate and slow growth. Similarly, a very high preponderance of one sex would tend to lead to a lowered fertility and slower growth. Such imbalances also effect the social and economic life of the population. For instance, where a war has removed a large proportion of the males, leaving large numbers of adult women with no eligible mates, normal family life is impossible for a large proportion of the adults and this leads to a good deal of social evils.

The sex-ratio in our country is measured as the number of females per 1,000 males. A high sex-ratio means an excess of females over males in a population and a low sex-ratio will indicate a shortage of female population and predominance of males. If the males and females are balanced in number the sex-ratio would be one thousand indicating that for every one thousand men there are 1,000 women. Though ideally the proportion of men and women should be balanced, in practice it is never so. There are several reasons for such inequality in proportion between the sexes.

The most important relates to the birth and death rates. It has been observed that more male babies are born than female ones; but after birth the male babies die in larger numbers than the female one. This by itself is likely to result in a balanced proportion of sexes. But in India women in their child-bearing ages die in comparatively larger numbers than men of the same age group owing to cases like frequent child-bearing, poor medical facilities, etc. The sex-ratio in Assam according to the projected figures of 901 which is less than the all India average of 936.

Population Changes

The spatial variations in the growth of population at the district level are also quite interesting. We may conclude with a brief look at the growth rates in the districts. During the first half of the last century, i.e. 1901-51, the population of Assam grew 144 per cent that is, it is more than double itself. Four Districts, namely, Nowgong, Lakhimpur, Darrang, and Kamrup experienced a higher growth rate. The highest rate was recorded in Nowgong District being 241 per cent.

This means that in half a century the population of Nowgong grew more than tripled itself. Lakhimpur is another district where the population increased three. Next comes Darrang with 175 per cent followed by Kamrup with 153 per cent. Barring North Cachar Hills which showed a slight decline in population during this period, the district with the lowest growth has been Cachar where the population increased 77 per cent. In the three decades after Independence all the Brahmaputra valley Districts with the exception of Sibsagar recorded extra ordinarily high growth rates. While Sibsagar has a growth rate of 52 per cent, in other districts it exceeds to 87 per cent. The highest growth rate rose up to 101 per cent in Goalpara District.

Social Groups

It is worthwhile to examine the proportion of different categories of workers in the rural and urban population separately. In the rural areas as to be expected, the largest proportion of workers are made up of cultivators and agricultural labour. These two categories together constitute over 73 per cent of the workers in the rural areas. Workers in Livestock, Forestry, Plantations, etc. and in other services account for 11 per cent and 8 per cent of the rural workers respectively. The remaining categories of workers represent only small proportions ranging from less than one per cent to 3 per cent of the rural workers.

The distribution of workers in the urban population is naturally more varied. As non-agricultural activity is the basic characteristic of the urban areas, the first three categories namely cultivators, agricultural labourers and workers in livestock, forestry, etc., account for only a small percentage (9%) of the total urban workers. The categories other services and trade and commerce account for the largest proportions of 28 and 27 per cent respectively of the urban workers. The category of manufacturing, processing, servicing, and repairs in household as well as non-household industries represent 16 per cent of the urban workers. Transport storage and communications also occupy an important position with 15 per cent. Mining, quarrying and construction, however, represent only small proportions ranging between one and 4 per cent.

So far as the non-workers are concerned 72 per cent of the total population of Assam are non-workers. The non-workers consist of those engaged in household duties, students, retired persons, dependents beggars, the inmates of such institutions as jails and other workers. The non-workers category also include the persons who are seeking employment.

While among the males 51 per cent are non-workers, among the females the proportion is as high as 95 per cent. Most of the women are categorised as non-workers because their main activity is household duties.

The dependents and those engaged in household duties account for the largest proportion of the total non-workers. Their proportions are 51 and 30 per cent respectively. Students form 18 per cent of the total non-working population, while the other non-workers constitute an insignificant percentage.

Social Backdrop

The migration of different human races to the ancient land of Assam began two hundreds years before the birth of Christ. The Karbis, being the descendents of Austric race, are like the Columbus of Assam. The Khasis, Jayantias, Kukies, Lusais (Mizo) are all from this race. The Kirats, being migrants from the western part of China, are from the Mongoloid race who speak Sino-Tibetan language. Bodo, Garo, Rabha, Deuries, Misings, Morans, Sutias, Dimasas and Koches (Rajbongshi), Lalung, Hajong, are also from the same race.

The assimilation started as both the races coexisted in the same geographical area. This is the background where the historic assimilation of Assamese nation-building process took place. Then the Kaibartas and Banias from Drabirian race migrated from the coast of Mediterranean came into assimilation more or less. On the other hand, the Aryans from Cocasian race migrated through the Gangetic Plain in the 1st century to the land of Pragjyotishpur. The local King amongst the Mongolian majority society rehabilitated the Aryans, being the carrier of comparatively advanced religion and language-culture. The relation and the synthesis among the different tribes, as being isolated before, were developed with the pace of the development of agriculture and communication system under the patronage of modern administration and military structure of Tai-Ahoms.

Thus Assamese became the link language amongst the peoples who speak different dialects. At the same time, a handful of rich class of businessmen and merchants developed. This brought about the development of society to a certain stage during the six hundred years of Ahom rule. On the other hand, at the Kam-peeth and Ratna-peeth a series of invasion took place under the commands of Muhammad Ghauri, Muhammad Bin Bakhtiar, Giasuddin, Nasirudin and Tughril Khan prior to the arrival of the Tais. Kamrup was still capable of keeping its sovereignty invincible. The Muslim captives of the war who were compelled to stay here after the wars have been assimilated into Assamese society. Under the leadership of Ahom administration, the sovereignty of Assam was preserved resisting the invasion of Asia-victor, the Mughals for seventeen times with the help of different tribes of Assam.

During the time of Ahom administration, the Sikh religious priest Teg Bahadur and the Muslim religious scholar Azan Fakir came to Assam and Srimanta Shankradeva, the preceptor of puritan Hinduism, was born in Assam. As the religious preceptors started the act of publicity of their religions, the language of royal house spread amongst the subjects. Again, the practice of upkeeping the history (Buranji) and the patronage from the royal house have made the language and literature richer. Again, the assimilated social life was isolated. The massive loss of life occurred and these undecided peoples' uprising caused the famine that made the total social life of Assam very weak. On the one hand the Burmese arrived accepting the call of Sarbananda Singha and on the other hand the British came in response to the invitation of Gaurinath Singha. There were enormous loss of life and property due to the invasion of these two foreign powers one after another. The Burmese occupied Assam for four years from 1822 to 1826 AD after it was invaded thrice in 1817, 1819 and 1821.

The Assamese society was in such an era of decay that all efforts, individual and collective, for the resistance against the Burmese could not produce any positive result. It was 28th February 1793, Mr. Geiger Ensaiswood and Dr. John Peter Bawdy, the emissaries of British officer Capt. Wales entered into an agreement with the Ahom Monarch Gaurinath Singha to initiate commercial activities inside Assam. The commercial activities initiated by the above British representative ran smoothly. The British Governor General Lord Amherst declared counter offensive against the "Burmese" invader who already encroached Assam and later tried to do so in the British territory. As a part of this counter offensive operation, Mr. David Scot, the British agent of North-East Frontier arrived in Cachar area of Assam and distributed pamphlets, which contained the text "we further declare that we are not led into your country by the thirst of conquest. But are forced in our difference to deprive our enemy of the means of annoying us. You may therefore rest assured that we will never consent to depart until we exclude our enemy from Assam and re-establish that country, a government adopted to your wants and calculated to promote the happiness of the people of all classes."

However, the British signed the infamous Yandaboo Treaty on 24th February 1826 with the Burmese General after defeating and chasing them away from Assam. And then, promising all kinds of happiness, prosperity and peace, above all 'to form a government of their own choice', the British occupied Assam. The refusal to fulfil the promises of David Scot led the broad Assamese people to rebel for independence under the leadership of Dhananjoy Gohain, Pioli Phukan, Gomadhar Kowar, etc. prior to the commencement of biennial anniversary of the Yandaboo Treaty. In the year 1838, the Ahom King Purandar Singha was dethroned. From that very year the whole of Assam came under the British colonisation.

The conditions required for nation building that began to conceive during the time of British rule could not be fulfilled during the Ahom monarchial period. The nation building process started among the different tribal and sectarian society of Assam. The British ruled Assam from their Bengal headquarters since 1838 to 1874. The British administration managed to complete the formation of imperialist capital by transferring the whole tea industry to the British tea planter through its conspiratory regulation. Advocating different mere commercial causes, they imported cheap labour force from Bihar, West-Bengal and Orissa, thus depriving the local workers of livelihood. The huge migration of labour from India to promote the British capital under the canopy of British administration has started to change the demography of Assam. Markets were established in favour of the needs of these migrated labour and other Indian service holders.

The Marwari and Bengali traders were provided establishment in favour of the owner of the tea plantation. All the situation vacancies for the post of clerks, writers and supervisors, etc. were filled up with Bengali outsiders that deprived the local people of these opportunities. Thus the surplus capital of tea industry and the money from the salaries of the service holders were drained out continuously. This process is still running on. This colonial exploitation prevented the free promotion of local capital and encouraged the rapid emergence of capitalists from outside. At the very outset the deceptive promises of David Scot were believed blindly by a section of Assamese bureaucrats like Maniram Dewan. And so they cooperated with the imperialist British. Later on, the exposure of the conspiracy by the British themselves caused the starting of rebellion by Maniram himself against the British in 1857. With the increase of British exploitation the people became irritated and finally they burst into rebellion.

The agitated people under the leadership and guidance of "RAIJMEL" (peoples council) turned to life and death struggle. First at Phulaguri on 17th September 1861 and later up to 1892 at Patidarrang, Nalbari, Lachima, Barama, Bajali, Khetri and Upor Barbhag; in 1893 at Rangia and the last one in 1894 in the famous Patharughat against the British imperialist to recover their sovereignty. Though these valiant struggles failed because of some limitations, the struggle under the leadership of "RAIJMEL" irrespective of different nationality, tribes and races was the harbinger of Assamese nationalism. The disposition started among the educated new middle class emerged from the foundation of old one due to the appointment of Bengali people in the post of clerks and supervisors, etc. in the tea industry and the different colonial administrative unit as grand majority.

In the mean time, in 1836 the Bengali Language was imposed in the offices and courts in Assam which caused the growth of already germinated anti-Bengali sentiment with a degree from more too absolute. Raisahab Gunaviram Barua was the founder of the Assamese middle class nationalism. The sincere effort of the educated Assamese middle class comprising Gunaviram Barua as pioneer and incessantly to Lakhiram Barua developed Assamese language and literature to modern stage. Again, it is noted that the British itself planted their colonial trickery of "Divide and Rule" to prevent the further assimilation of any nationality which was not assimilated till then with the already formed Assamese nation keeping in view to debar from a formation of likely stronger Assamese nation that was shaped within and by the British administration. In 1920, the British formed the Assam Province and imposed the "Schedule District Act" as in order to sow the seed for conflict between the hills' and the plains' people thereby rupturing the communication among the tribal and non-tribal people. If any enthusiast came in being as an opponent of British capital, he was nipped in the bud.

For example, Maniram Dewan was hanged on 26th February, 1885. The credit of Assamese new middle class was that, they have shaped the adolescent Assamese language of Arunodoy age of 1846 to a scientific mode of Jonaki age of 1889 and the Hemkosh (modern Assamese dictionary) published in 1890 which made firm the foundation of Assamese language. Moreover, after 37 years of imposing Bengali language in the place of Assamese language since 1836, the credit goes to the American missionaries like Nathan Brown, Oliver Cortrer, Miles Bronchon, Choybus Barker who have reinstated the Assamese language on 8th April 1873.

It was the British who constructed 439 miles long railway track in the first decade of twentieth century and it was the British who established the first Asian oil refinery at Digboi. In the British period, besides the waterways, the land communication also became convenient; some industries and enterprises, such as tea, coal, plywood, etc. were also founded. However, Assam has been deprived of any real benefit from these establishments till now. The degree of exploitation increased day by day as the raw materials from Assam were taken away and industries were established. On the other hand, Assam was turned into the captive market of industrial products of the colonial master and the local capital was taken away by the foreign merchants.

Social Base

The exploitation and oppression of the British administrative system produced an opportunist middle class as well as an oppressed peasantry and working class antagonistic to the British colonial administration.

The royal and the aristocrat class of pre-British period were compelled to descend to the status of general subjects after the abolition of Paik and Khel system. The class consisting the descended royal and other aristocrat persons of pre-British era, different Hindu tribes, poor high caste Hindu, lower caste Hindu and the Muslims was the majority by numbers than any other specific strata of the society. This class had initiated armed resistance against the unbearable British imperialism. These people had prepared the fertile ground for the growth of true Assamese Nationalism. As far as nationalism of a dependent nation is concerned, it clearly implies the aspiration for sovereignty, consciousness for one's national identity and above all the urge to overthrow the foreign rulers.

Hence, the real (revolutionary) Assamese nationalism was defined by the known-unknown rebellious peasantry against the nationalism of Assamese middle class which inclined to the British masters. A class of people was there with the dream of "Independent Assam". Lokeswar Barua (Jorhat), Purna Sarma (Nagaon), Ambikagiri Rai Choudhury (Barpeta) were the prominent among these nationalists.

Even during the time of second world war when Indian National Army led by Subhash Chandra Bose with the help of the Japanese army reached Manipur, Gopinath Bardoloi (prominent freedom fighter and first Chief Minister of Assam) planned to establish an independent national government in Assam, even when he was behind bar. The distinct characteristics of Assam being different from the rest of India was proved by the specific decision of 16th August 1946 which stated "the Assam Legislative Assembly comes to a consensus against the "grouping" and the elected members of the Assembly to the "Indian constituent Council" will draft an 'independent Constitution' in a separate meeting where other representatives will not be allowed to stay".

It should be mentioned that Mahatma Gandhi also encouraged Assam against the 'Grouping' with his famous speech "Assam must be totally independent and autonomously governed". And so, Mahatma Gandhi did not include Assam in his desired map of India. The cause of the omission of the name of "Assam" from the text of the National Anthem of India composed by the Nobel laureate Rabindranath Tagore had also the same cause.

Moreover, till 1921, there was no branch in Assam of the Congress Party, the Indian National Institution formed in 1885 under the patronage of the British.

The struggling leadership of Assam was allured by the resolution of forming "United Struggling Front" as per the "Lucknow Agreement" signed by Congress and Muslim League. The freedom movement of Assam joined with the freedom movement of India in 1921 only for the strategic condition to fight against the common enemy under a common anti-British United Front. The "anti-grouping" resolutions were the proof of the above fact. The conspiracy of the British to include Assam in "C" group on the time of "grouping" arrangement was aimed to compel Assam to join voluntarily with Hindustan rather than joining in the Muslim majority "C" group. The British realised that if Assam was annexed to Hindustan then it would be possible for them to keep Assam under the modified leadership of India, where already a bulk of "sterling money" had been invested in the name of tea industry.

Ethnicity

Assam has traces of at least three races: the Australoids (the first race that occupied this region), the Caucasoids (who came from the west to settle in the valley formed by the Ganges and the Brahmaputra), and the Mongoloids (who came to the northeast from South East Asia). This regular migration of different races created two distinct ethnic groups in the state. The tribals who lived in the hills and the non-tribals who generally lived in the plains. However, there is a large part of the tribal population in the plains too.

Hill Tribes

The hill and frontier tribes of Assam include the Nagas, Singphos, Daphlas, Miris, Khamtis, Mishmis and Abors, nearly all of whom, excepting the Nagas, are found near the frontiers of Lakhimpur district. The principal of these, in point of numbers, are the Nagas, who inhabit the hills and forests along the eastern and southeastern frontier of Assam. They reside partly in the British district of the Naga hills and partly in independent territory under the political control of the deputy commissioner of the adjoining districts. They cultivate rice, cotton, yams and Indian corn, and prepare salt from the brine springs in their hills.

The different tribes of Nagas are independent of and unconnected with one another, and are often at war with each other. The Singphos are another of the main population of the same race, who occupy the hilly country between the Patkai and Chindwin rivers, and are nominally subject to Burma. The Akas, Daphlas, Miris, Abors, Mishmis and Khamtis are described under separate headings. Under regulation V. of 1873, an inner line has been laid down in certain districts, up to which the protection of British authority is guaranteed, and beyond which, except by special permission, it is not lawful for British subjects to go. This inner line has been laid down in Darrang towards the Bhutias, Akas and Daphlas; in Lakhimper towards the Daphlas, Miris, Abors, Mishmis, Khamtis, Singphos and Nagas; and in Sibsagar towards the Nagas.

Castes in State

Scheduled Caste people usually live interspersed with the general population of the state in widely scattered areas. There are however, isolated pockets where these people are predominant. Nawgaon Subdivisions has the largest percentage of Scheduled Castes population, i.e. 12.3 per cent, followed by Silchar 10.1 per cent. The distribution of Scheduled Caste population shows that they are scattered throughout the state and even at the Subdivision level they do not constitute more than 12.3 per cent of the total population.

Namasudras: The Namasudras are immigrated in Assam from Uttar Pradesh. Some of them got converted into Christianity to due to disseminating treatment of Hindus. The literacy rate of Namasudras is 21.32 per cent and they are well scattered in the various Subdivisions of Assam. The occupation of these people is boating and cultivation.

Banias: The word Bania implies to business community. In Assam the Banias are the jewellers. During the British period they were all primarily engaged in making gold ornaments. But in the course of time as a result of Cold Control Act, they became handicapped and had to abandon their traditional occupation, many of them went back to their parental occupation of agriculture. The land holidays of these people were however, very tiny and small. Consequently, they became marginal farmers and agricultural labourers.

The Banias are found in all the districts and subdivisions of Assam excepting Cachar (Silchar and Karimganj). Mostly they live in clusters. Their, percentage of literacy is 38.95 which tops the literacy rate of all the Scheduled Castes of Assam. Politically they are weak having no MP or MLA since the Independence.

Hira: The Hiras owe their origin to Orissa. They are basically earthen pot makers. The Hiras differ from potters of other castes in that their women are engaged in the work and they shape their pots -by hand instead of by the aid of a wheel. They make them in four layers each of which is partially dried before the next layer is added. When the pot is complete they pile them in a heap, with grass in between to which they can set fire and thus bake the clay.

Only an insignificant percentage of Hiras is engaged in agriculture. For want of finance they cannot take to other finance also. As per the latest census reports the population of Hira community in Assam is 32,624 or 3.58 per cent of the total Scheduled Caste population. The literacy rate is around 16 per cent. Owing to poor economic condition, majority of them can not afford to educate their children and most of them assist their parents in pot making right from the childhood. With the introduction of hard-metallic utensils like aluminium and other alloys, the demand for the earthen pots is decreasing. These days the Hiras dispose off their pots in the weekly markets locally known as Hats, carrying the pots on their shoulders in Bhars.

Patnis: Patnis who were known as Patauni had different occupations like boating, boat making, basket making, trade and cultivation of crops. Now most of them are cultivators and fishing is their secondary occupation. Though well spread in the different districts of Assam, the main concentration of Patnis is in the districts of Karimganj and Silchar. The total number of Patni's population is 85,910 which accounts for 9.41 per cent of the Scheduled Caste population of Assam. The percentage of literacy of Patnis is 3-1.87 per cent. Most of them are living below the poverty line.

Sutrodhar: The Sutrodhar is the carpenter caste of the Cachar, Goalpara and Dhubri districts. Sutrodhar occupy a very low position in the society. The water touched by them is not taken by the people of Upper Castes. As per the latest Census Report the total population of Sutrodhar is 32,703 which is 3.58 per cent of the total Scheduled Caste population of Assam. Their literacy percentage is 20.26.

Malo: The Malos are said to be the Dravidian boating and fishing castes. These came in Assam from the Gangetic Delta (Sundarban). The Malos are mainly found in the Kachar District. A few families also live in Goalpara and Dhubri District. Their population as per the latest Census Report is 32,978 which is 3.61 per cent of the total Scheduled Caste population. Their literacy percentage is around 15.

Dhobi or Dhoba: Dhobis are not the original inhabitants of Assam. They immigrated in Assam from the states of Bengal, Bihar and Orissa. The Muslim washerman is usually called as *Dhobi,* while the term Dhoba is generally applied to the Hindu who follows the washerman's occupation. According to the latest census reports the population strength of Dhobis stood at 20,801 which is 2.28 per cent of the total scheduled caste population. Their literacy percentage is around 28 per cent.

Maharas: Maharas are mainly employed as zamindars peons. Their traditional occupation is Palki bearing. They are from the indigenous group of Bengal. The latest Census Report reveals that their population is 899 and their percentage is 0.09 of the total Scheduled Caste population. Their percentage of literacy is 13.79.

Dholis: The Dholis or Dholas are the drummers. They immigrated from Bengal and settled in Cachar District of Assam. Some of them are cattle keepers and cultivators. This caste is said to be very degraded one. They have no Brahmin. Its priests are chosen from amongst the members of the caste itself. According to the latest census reports there are 4,013 Dholis in Assam constituting 0.44 per cent of the total Scheduled Caste population. Their literacy rate is only 15 per cent.

Mochi: The Mochi is a leather working class and they are found mainly in Cachar. They immigrated in Assam from Bihar and Orissa. They are the offshoots of the chamar caste. Their total number is 40,774 which is 4.47 per cent of the total Scheduled Caste population. Their literacy percentage is 12.77.

Bhangi Bansfor Lalbag: Bhangis are the scavengers from outside of Assam. Most of them are employed in the municipalities and town communities. The Lalbegis follow an amalgamation of the Hindus and Muslim's beliefs, customs and traditions. It is believed that they immigrated in Assam from Northern India. According to the latest Census Report the total population of Bhangis is 7,296 which is 0.79 per cent of the total Scheduled Caste population. Their literacy percentage is only 14.48.

Bhuimali or Mali: Bhuimali or Mali are essentially dependent on gardening of flowers and sell their flowers in temples. Most of them live around the temples of Hajo Haigrib, Palasbari and other religious places. At present many of them have shifted to cereal cultivation. According to the latest census reports their total population is 22,175.

Jal Keot or Jalla Keot: Selling of fish was confined to the Kaivartas and Jal Keot in the Brahmaputra and the Surma Valleys. The Jal Keots have however started cultivation of crops also. As per the latest census reports their population in Assam is 2,537 which is 0.28 per cent of the total Scheduled Caste population.

Scheduled Caste Emancipation

For the upliftment of the Scheduled Castes in Assam the Assam Government has taken several pragmatic steps. The Special Component plan has been designed to channalise the flow of benefits and outlays from the general sector in the plan of the states for the development of Scheduled Castes in physical and financial terms. The component plans are envisaged to help the poor scheduled castes families through composite income generating programmes. In addition, it also seeks to improve the living condition of the Scheduled castes families through composite income generating programmes. In addition, it also seeks to improve the living condition of the Scheduled Castes through the provisions of drinking water supply, link roads, house sites, establishment of health centres, housing improvements, rural electrification and cottage industries.

Other Castes

Racial Properties: As discussed in' the preceeding pages, a large proportion of the population of Assam consists of tribes who originally descended from the hills in the neighbourhood such as Rabhas, Kacharies, Chutiyas, Mikirs and Lalongs.

The Ahoms, the race of the last conquerors of the valley. Though affected by many revolutions, still remain unmixed, and retain unaltered their ancient habits and institutions. They have however, adopted the customs of the Hindus and relinguished the use of beef. The people of Assam present several significant peculiarities of external form.

In complexion they are a shade or two lighter coloured than the Bengalis. The Assamese are in general short statured, robust, and active, when they choose to be so; but devoid of that grace and flexibility so peculiar to Aryans. They have flat face, with high cheek bones, presents a physiognomy resembling the Chinese. They have abundance of hair, blank, lank and coarse; but the beard is scanty, and usually plucked out, which gives the men an effeminate appearance.

Though these physical characteristics are common of the Assamese, yet there are exceptions. There are people in Assam who belong to Caucasian race, and which also include the European races. These Caucasian ethnic groups are distinguished by a peculiar delicacy, and axiality of shape, suggesting the idea of a reigned, and even effeminate people.

The women in general form a striking contrast to the men; there is a great deal more of feminine beauty in them than in commonly met with in the women of Bengal.

Different Castes: The adoption of Hindu creed led to the Assamese people into caste and subcaste groups, which form the most prominent feature in Hindu Society. Very few traces of the Varan Ashram — the four original castes (Brahmins, Kshatriyas, Vaishyas, Shudras) are met with, though the people are divided in Assam by an infinite number of distinctions.

The priesthood (Brahmins), beyond all comparison, hold the first place in point of dignity, and, clothed with the terrors of religion are regarded by classes with deep veneration.

A number of the Rarhi Brahmins of Bengal have emigrated into the Brahmaputra Valley, and to them were formerly committed the spiritual guidance of the King and the principal officers of the court. Those usually known as the Assamese Brahmins are Baidicks of the ancient Kingdom of Kamrup, and were probably introduced by Biswas Singh; but having penetrated into the Upper parts of Assam, they no longer inter-married with the families in Bengal. A large number of these are said to be learned in Hindu science. A very small number of these are Saktis; they are chiefly of the sect of Vishnu. They have a few academies, or choudharis, where the Ratnamala, Byakaran, law, and metaphysics are taught. Some few pretend to have a knowledge of astrology and magic.

The chief study, however, of spiritual guides, is Shri Bhagabut. The persons who instruct the worshipper of Vishnu; that is, most of those who have adopted the Hindu creed, are called *Mahajons* and live in Chatras. They have generally a large number of men entirely devoted to their service. Their office is hereditary in certain families. The Brahmins, who are elevated to high dignity, are said to avoid all worldly pleasures, and bind themselves by an oath of celibacy.

The elite Brahmins seem to give themselves more trouble than usual, in the instruction of their followers. They not only teach them a form of prayer, but usually assembling' forty or fifty of their scholars, they instruct them in their duty, and read some books, which are composed by their great Gurus and scholars and which seem to consist chiefly of extracts from the Bhagava, translated into the vernacular.

The chief Castes are as follows: In the District of Kamrup, at Baropeta, Pat Bousi, Biha Kuchi, Bhowanipur, Plasbari, and Shrihati. In other Districts of the Brahmaputra Plains — Annihati, Dakhynpat; Kurabasi, Gormurchotra, Dihingya, Noraya, Siliguri, Samguri, Koyamariya (Kamakhya) and Mahari.

In the district of Sadiya, the worshippers of Vishnu are not numerous enough to have procured religious guides that are of any importance. Some of the Baidiks have become barna, and in consequence, have degraded themselves in the eyes of their brethren. They instruct the impure tribes, which is considered a great degradation, to which none of the Baidiks of Bengal have submitted.

There is also a class of Brahmins, usually known as Muno Singha Brahmins. They have usually employed in low offices, totally unconnected with religion.

The Koch or Kuchis is a numerous tribe of Assam Plains. Amongst the Kuchis are the Rajbungsis. There are reasons to suppose that until very lately, the different tribes of Kamrup permitted intermarriage. Thus it must be observed, that Koch Haju, the valiant chief who is said to have expelled the Muslims from the northern parts of Rungpore, married his daughter to the Mech Herya, and from this marriage, with fabulous assistance of the god Sib (shiva), are sprung the principal chiefs of the Rajbungsis.

The Rajbungis mainly worship the god named Rishi and to his wife Jago, though some pretend to say, they worship Sib and Parboti.

Every year at the end of rainy season, a grand sacrifice to these deities is made by the whole tribe, and occasionally sacrifices are- offered in cases of distress. The blood of the sacrifice is left for the deity, while the votaries eat the meat. The people worship no images. They call on the name of their gods, and clap their hands during the ceremony of worship.

The Koch adopted a priesthood called Kolita or Kolta. These possessed some learning, and long continued to be the only spiritual guides of the Koch, and in fact in some place still retain by for the chief authority over that sect. In the historical records the people of Assam have been referred as "Assamians" and "Koltanians" — the former being the temporal lords and the latters the spiritual guides; when probably the Kolitas were for more powerful than they are at present. What tenets the Kolitas, while independent of the Brahmins possessed is difficult to say, but they were not orthodox. The power of the Kolitas received a severe blow by the introduction of the Brahmins by their Prince, whose example they were under the necessity of following, and receiving instruction from the sacred order. These persons have now entirely adopted the Hindu worship and customs, and are contented with being considered as Shudras.

The Kolitas and most of their followers, have taken the part of Krishna, and assume the title of Dhokot, what is worshippers or disciples, as being alone those who follow the true God. They have of late been very successful in converting many of the Kacharis, Mikirs, and other ignorant tribes of mountainous tracts.

The Mech is a small tribe, but appear at one time to have been a far more numerous people than they are at present. A large proportion of their number have assumed the title of Rajbungsi. It is to be presumed, that this innovation took place when Biswas King, the son of Mech's wife, became the sovereign of Kamrup, and being ashamed of his barbarous ancestors, declared that he was the son of a god.

The Nodigals or Domes is the most numerous tribe in Assam. They came from Bengal and settled in the Valley of the Brahmaputra. They seem to observe all the rules of purity, in eating and drinking, with greater strictness than even the Brahmins of Bengal. They have not only procured a Brahmin for spiritual guide, but follow the instructions of the Kolitas.

Kaiasths is another important caste of Assam. It is difficult to ascertain the number of Kaiasths in Assam, since, Kolitas lost their importance, especially in the more civilized parts, they have assumed the title of Kaiasths. They number of the pure scribes of Bengal it is presumed must be very small, and these are mostly of the division called *Uttar Rarhi*.

There are a good many Keyots also Known as Kaibartas. They are divided into several classes, the two principal are called the *Haluya Keyots* and the *Jaluya Keyots*. The occupation of the former class is cultivation of crops and they worship lord Krishna. The Jaulya Keyots are fishermen, and without having relinquished their name or profession, have in many points followed the tends of Islam, yet they keep themselves distinct as a caste, and do not mix with the Muslims.

The Sonars or goldsmiths, though probably more diffused are vary small in number.

The Haris or potters are a very small sect.

The Dhobis or Dhobas (washer man) came in Assam from Bengal the number of washermen (Dhobas) in the total population of Assam is insignificant.

The Moriyas are generally employed as braziers. They are looked upon as the people of inferior caste. They are by no means scrupulous in their food habits. They eat both beef and pork and in general very much addicted to the use of spirituous liquors. They bury their like that of Muslims.

Vocation and Life-style: In Assam there seems to have been little or no distinction of castes from profession, and each caste practised all the arts which are known in the country. They were farmers, traders, blacksmiths, goldsmiths, carpenters, extractors of oil, potters, weavers, and dyers; but they had not the art of shaving, or washing, or bleaching, or working in leather, or making sweetmeats, butter or Ghee. All these arts seem to have been unknown, and are now entirely followed by the people who entered the state of Assam from the states of Bengal, Bihar and Bangladesh, while the old arts are practised indifferently by all.

Muslims constitute a large proportion of the inhabitants of Assam. But Muslims are generally held in low estimation, like most of the Hindus, they are by no means rigidly observant of high caste principles. In fact, a far greater latitude and toleration exists among the inhabitants of Assam in general, than is usually observed in other parts of the subcontinent of India.

By the manners of a nation are understood the peculiar mode in which the ordinary business of human life is carried on. The business itself is everywhere essentially the same. In all nations men eat and drink, they meet, converse, transact business, and sport together. But the manner in which these and other things are performed, is as different as the nations are numerous into which the caste is divided.

The life style of most of the Assamese resemble to that of the Hindus. Most of them are Hindus by faith, and whose daily avocations consist so much in religious services, that the delineation of their religion is a delineation of the principal branch of their manners. Much of that gentleness and urbanity of manner which reign to a gentleness and urbanity of manner which reign to a greater or less degree in the whole intercourse of native society, and which in the superficial observer would produce a high conception of their benevolence and amiability, would, on a more minute inspection, present a much less favourable picture.

The species of polity under which the national character is formed is perhaps to a great degree the cause of this speculiarity of behaviour. When the mind is free, and may vent.

The Assamese however possess some very good qualities of character the habits of life Assamese are pre-eminently domestic. Respect for old age is carried to a great height, and when parents are no longer capable of labour, they are supported by their children, and are seldom allowed to become a burden on the public. They also have in general a very tender regard for their offspring, and are affectionate and kind to their relations. They are also hospitable to their own caste, but to no others.

Tribes of Effect

Miris: The areas in which the Miri tribe dominates are the low hills and undulating plains of Banskotta and Lakhimpur. From the foot-hills they have spread into the plains and now are well spread over the plains of Upper Assam.

The Miris have some villages on the banks of the Dihong, of which Matgong is the principal. Before the beginning of the present century their villages used to be ravaged by their formidable neighbours - the Abors. Essentially the Miris are the cultivators, especially along the banks of the Brahmaputra.

The Miris are very laborious and highly industrious people, and seem partial to living on the fringe of the forests, clearing new grounds in the forests for cultivation. Many of them are expert marksmen and have great skill in bows and arrows. The arrows are poisoned, and the poison used is so fatal, that even a scratch from them is followed with certain death. The language of the Miris is a dialect of that of the Abors.

The Miris in the plains employ themselves but they make a very large profit by bartering and selling and selling it to Assamese. They also cultivate cotton to a large extent, and engage in the manufacture of cotton rugs.

Besides agriculture the Miris in general rear a large number of pigs and poultry. The Miri tribal group that lives on the banks of Subansiri is more powerful in their traditions. Their Gam (headman) used to come down to the plains annually to receive presents from the British government. There had been intermingling of blood and the Miris are fast loosing their ethnic attributes.

Abors: The Abors and Bor-Abors occupy an extensive range of mountainous country, along the southern exposure of the Great Himalayan chain. The Abors are divided into numerous clans and each clan or village forms a democratic republic by itself, and is governed by the laws enacted by all the inhabitants in a formal meeting. This meeting is held in the morning and every male has an equal vote.

An Abor village usually consist of about one hundred houses, built near each other on a stony slope of easy ascent: the floor of each house is made of bamboos, supported on beams driven into the ground; and the space underneath is meant for cattle. In the centre of the village is the Morung — a large house which serves as a hall of audience and debate, as a place of reception for strangers, and as a house for the bachelors of the village generally, who by their laws are not entitled to aid of the community for the construction of a separate dwelling. It is a usual practice with these adults and youngmen, at the down of day, to go the round of the village, warning sleepy folks that it is time for work to commence. Their granaries are generally built apart from the village as a security against fire.

The dress of Abors consists principally of a Suria (the Assamese name of Dhoti, the common dress of the people). It is tied around the loins, and hangs down in loose strips about fifteen inches long. The rest of their dress is apparently a matter of individual taste, beads round the neck are not uncommon. Some use plain basket caps, solve have the cane caps partly covered with skins and other ornaments with stained hair. The beak of Buceroli is a favourite and striking ornament of their caps; this on the top in front, and the red chowry tail flowing down behind, gives very much the appearance of a helmet. During the winter almost every man has some article of woollen dress, varying from a rudely made blanket waistcoat to a comfortable and tolerably well-shaped cloak. All the more wealthy among them have cloak of Tibbetan woollens.

The Abors are not particular in their diet, and eat the flesh of elephant, rhinoceros, dog, buffalo, cow, and deer as well as ducks and fowls. They exhibit a marked predilection for fermented liquors, and large quantities are usually drank at their feasts. The trade of the Abors consists chiefly in Manjit, ivory, and woollens. They also bring down occasionally a few fine-woollen sheep, and white lamb skins very neatly tanned.

Some Abors have lately settled at the foot of the hills in the district of Sadiya where they cultivate fields. They keep a bow and quiver of arrows, a number of which are poisoned. They also carry light spears, or Dao (sword) of the Singhpos.

Akas and Kapachors: The Akas and Kapachors occupy the tract between the country of Bhutan and Darrang. Very little is Known about these tribes but they are warriors and ferocious people. The Akas speak a language nearly allied to that of the Abors. The food of the rich people consists of the flesh of goats, swine, and cattle and rice. They are very fond of tea and use it in large quantities. The poor people eat wheat and barley. All classes are very much addicted to the use of inebriating liquors.

The Singphos: The Singphos are by far the most powerful tribe bordering on the valley. They are also the most numerous and scattered in the northeastern districts of Assam. On the north they are bounded by the Lohit river, on the south by the Patkoi range which divide them from the Burmese.

The Singphos are divided into four class called *Shangai, Myung, Lubrung,* and *Mirip.* The language of the Singphos is a mixture of Abors, Burmese and Manipuri. They follow the tribal religion and decorate their temples with idols of different religions. They bury their deads; but the chiefs and the principal individuals are sometimes not buried for years. The reason alleged for this consummation of the funeral rites is, to allow the widely scattered relations of the deceased to have time to attend, who would not fail to take deadly offence at being deprived of an opportunity of paying reverence to the ashes of the head of their family. If the person had died a violent death, a buffalo is sacrificed as a propitiation to their deities, and the head of the animal is fixed to two crossed bamboos and placed near the grave; but if he has died in the course of nature, no sacrifice is considered necessary.

Social Problems

Polygamy: Polygamy is admitted by the laws of the tribe, and every man keeps as many wives as he chooses, free women or slaves, and treat the offsprings of both kinds without partiality.

Paddy is the dominant crop grown by Singphos. Milk is very little used by these people. They however relish rice and fish, and meat of cattle, pig, wild animals and birds.

Marriage is considered as a religious duty, so that very few that can afford it, neglect at an early age to fulfil this sacred obligation. Early marriages are common though in the lower classes many young women do not succeed in getting husbands till the age of twenty five.

Slavery: Slavery existed to a considerable extent in the past, and most of domestics, both male and female, were either slaves, or bondsmen, who for a few Rupees have been enthralled by mortgaging their bodies, and for the want of means of accumulating the original sum, increased by exorbitant usury, continued in bondage for life. The unfortunate subjects of this disgraceful system are bought and sold, and even mortgaged like any other article of property.

In the event of their death, their cruel and hard masters seize upon their descendents or their nearest relations, whom they kept in bondage and so from generation to generation. The females among them were permitted to marry, but have no right to go away with their husbands, and when they beget children, these children, became the property of their masters, and neither the parents nor other relations have any claim to them. The males also by marriage used to increase their masters stock, and render their partners slaves with themselves.

A great number of slaves were disposed of to the neighbouring states, where they are in general devoted to the most menial and degraded works. These slaves used to feel that they are the property of their masters, who have the power to do as they like with them, and it was their duty to submit to all. It was also their impression that any appeal to the public authority will not redeem them from their thraldom, which on the contrary this will only bring upon them the displeasure of their masters and their connections.

In Assam still most of the higher classes and rich people keep slaves, it being difficult to procure servants, especially of the female sex. The free men-servants Bhandaris are usually paid nominal wages, besides food. Though Bhandaris properly signifies a store keeper, but such servants are usually employed in all sorts of work.

Tribes in State

The total Scheduled Tribe population in Assam according to the latest census reports, is 26,656,000. This constitutes nearly 12.41 per cent of the total population of Assam. This is quite high compared to the all India proportion of Scheduled Tribes of 7 per cent. The total Scheduled Tribe Population of India is 84,326,000. The Scheduled tribe members of Assam constitute 5 per cent of the all India total.

The Scheduled Tribes are spread overall the districts of the state but their proportions to the total population of the respective districts vary. The hilly districts are predominantly inhabited by Scheduled Tribes.

According to the latest census reports the highest percentage of the tribal population is found in the North Cachar Hills and the Mikir Hills Districts the percentage share being 69.15 and 55.37 per cent respectively. These districts are followed by the Goalpara and

Lakhimpur which have over 13 per cent of their total population as tribal. The lowest concentration of the tribal population is in the Cachar District which has less than 1 per cent of its total population as tribal. The remaining districts situated in the Brahmaputra valley the percentage of Scheduled Tribes varies between 6 to 11 per cent. If we consider the absolute numbers, we find that over 66 per cent of the Scheduled Tribe population lives in the plains. The Bodos and Miris are some of the Plain tribes.

The members of the Scheduled Tribes like those of Scheduled Castes live mostly in the villages. The proportion of Scheduled Tribes living in Urban areas is insignificant in all the Districts of Assam.

There are 35 important Scheduled Tribes in Assam. The dominant tribes are:

Barmans in Cachar, Boro Barokkachari, Chakma, Deori, Dimasa (Kachari), Garo, Hajong, Haolai, Hammar, Hojai, Kachari including Sonwal, Kukis, Lakher, Lalung, Man, Mech, Mikir, Miri, Pawi, Rabha, Thado, Uibuh and Vaiphei.

Boro-Barokachari is the numerically strongest tribe in the state. Its numerical strength is about six lakhs. Next come Miri with population of 2.60 lakhs. Next come Miri with population of 2.60 lakhs and 2.43 lakhs respectively. Other tribes among the first eight numerically strongest tribes are Kachari including Sonowal (1.99 lakh), Mikir (1.77 lakhs), Rabha (1.39 lakhs), Lalung (0.96 lakhs).

The Scheduled castes and tribes being socially backward, it will be interesting to look into the literacy among their members and compare it with the general population.

The literacy rate of Scheduled Caste is 25.79 per cent and that of the Scheduled Tribes in 26.03 per cent as against the literacy rate of 28.72 per cent of the general population of Assam. Thus comparatively our Scheduled Caste and Scheduled Tribe population are better off than their counterparts in some other states. If a comparison is made of the literacy rates of the males and females of these communities of Assam separately it may be noticed that here also both the male and female literacy rates are quite close to the general male and female literacy rates for the state as a whole.

So far as the occupational structure of the Scheduled caste and Scheduled Tribes is concerned it differs from that of the non-Scheduled population. Out of the total of 912,639 persons belonging to Scheduled Castes 257,253 persons or 28 per cent are workers. These workers are spread over different sectors of the economy. The majority of them, i.e. 67 per cent is however, engaged in the primary occupation of agriculture. About 17,934 or 2 per cent of the workforce is engaged in forestry and plantation, while trade and commerce and other tertiary activities engage 31 per cent of the workforce.

The proportion of workers among the Scheduled Tribe population is also 28 per cent. But the proportion of workers engaged in agriculture is much higher (92%) than that of the Scheduled Caste. Other services and tertiary activities account for 7 per cent, while only one per cent is dependent on the secondary sector.

Religion

Religious Atmosphere: In considering any group of mankind, it is imperative to know its faith and religion. The knowledge of faith of the people is even more important of the areas in which Hinduism is the dominant religion.

In Assam there appears to have existed among all ancient nations some faint idea of the one God, with the primitive worship of whom one finds an extraordinary form of superstition, denominated the worship of aerial beings, under the general name of spirits, by which it was probably superseded, more particularly among a rude and barbarous people. This may easily be accounted for, from the proneness of mankind to superstitious fears respecting invisible existence.

There spirits it is reasonable to suppose, were soon after divided into two great classes — good and evil spirits. These appear to have been the first gods worshipped by the ancient inhabitants and probably continued till their conversion to the Brahminical faith. Traces of this system are however, still discoverable in the lower classes, and the mountain tribes.

Spread of Faith: On the introduction of Brahmins into, the country, followed the promulgation of Hindu faith, which, with its numerous forms and grand ceremonies, were all to attract the attention of a wild and uncivilized people. They soon imbibed the tenets of the new faith, whilst the priests acquired and maintained an authority, more exalted, more commanding and extensive, than they had been able to engross in any other part of India. Numerous temples and holy edifices soon rose into existence, more numerous than are generally met within any province of equal extent. Almost every grove and secluded valley, and wild and lofty mountain summit, had some religious or superstitious notions connected with it, and frequently presented to the eye, some picturesque shrine or antique temple. The greater number of these temples are now in ruins.

Islam cane in the Brahmaputra valley during the Medieval Period of the Indian history. The followers of Islam, as discussed under the heading of religious composition, are the second largest religious group in Assam. But these are generally held in very low estimation; like most of the Hindus they are by no means rigidly observant of high caste principles. In fact, a far greater latitude and toleration exists among the inhabitants of Assam in general, than is usually observed in other parts of India.

Christianity in Assam is for less than two hundred years. After the establishment of the British rule in India, the Christian Missionaries made a concerted efforts to convert the schedules castes and schedule tribes into Christianity. They achieved tremendous success in their missions in the areas of isolation and relative isolation. At present Christianity is the third important religion in Assam after Hinduism and Islam.

Holy Places: The Brahmin seem in general to have exhibited a remarkable taste and judgement in selecting the site of their sacred buildings. Sometimes they are situated in the midst of beautiful scenery, surrounded by woods and forests, and almost concealed from observation by thick groves, within the dark gorge of the mountain, or on its rugged summit, and at the sources of streams, where sites of seclusion, beauty, and sublimity excite alternately the fervour and the awe of superstitions devotion.

One of the most remarkable temples in Assam, is the shrine of Kamakhya, the goddess of love, situated on the summit of a hill, about three Kilometre to the west of Guwahati. This fair is one of great celebrity, and is frequented by a vast number of pilgrims from all parts of India and the neighbouring countries. It owes its celebrity to its structure nor situation, but to the image itself. Yet the site is not uninteresting, nor is devoid of beauty. To the south it is shut in by a cluster of hills, and to the north flows the sacred mighty Brahmaputra, which bathes the extreme points of the hills, within these bounds, is the sanctuary of the goddess, but her sway is not confined to these precincts. The whole of the province of Kamrup, as its name implies was in ancient times a sort of Italian grove, a privileged region for mirth, and dance and revelry, and all manner of licentiousness.

Some of the formulas used at the festival in honour of this goddess, licentious scenes. During the daily ceremonies of worship performed before the image, the spectators are very few, and these feel no interest whatever in the mummery going forward. Were it not for those who come to pay a visit of ceremony to the image, and to present their offerings, the temple would be as little crowded on festival, as on common days, but as soon as the well-known sound of the drum is heard, calling the people to the mid-night orgies. The dance and the song, whole multitudes assemble, and the crowd becomes dense.

The women employed to dance and sing on these occasions, are those consecrated to the temple, of whom it is reputed that there are no less than five hundred women. Their presence, together with their songs form the chief attractions. A song is tolerated which does not contain the most marked allusions to unchastity, while those which are so abominable, that no person could repeat them out of the temple, receive in general the loudest plaudits. All this is done in the very face of the idol, nor does the thought "Thou God seest me" ever produce the slightest pause in these midnight revels.

Haju Temple: Another temple, of less consequence than the Kamakhya is that situated at Haju, a village in the District of Kamrup, about six miles from the northern bank of the Brahmaputra.

The great object of veneration is an image called "Mahamuni" in a temple on the summit of a hill about 100 metres high from the surrounding plains. Thousands of votaries of every rank and condition are here annually congregated together, and towards this shrine a tide of costly offerings from every point of the compass is constantly setting in. It is visited not only by pilgrims of the Brahminical faith, who proceed to it from all parts of India, but Buddhists likewise contend that it was the presence of their great prophet and legislator, which conferred its holy fragrance and mysterious virtue on the spot. But whatever was the original cause of its sanctity, no orthodox Hindu now doubts the efficacy of its atmosphere in removing sin.

The pious Buddhist too, imbued with the same faith, leaves his home in the distant regions of China and Tibet, and crossing the pathless tracts of the snowy Himalayas, burdened with the load of his offences, hastens to make obeisance at the shrine of his country's deity, and departs in joy and gladness, lightened of his load.

Brahmakund: Besides the temple, another place distinguished for its peculiar sanctity, is a supposed source of Brahmaputra, or that large circular basin termed the Brahmakund. The Shashtras of Hindu religion have taught, that the performance of religious rites at this sacred place is an act of peculiar merit, productive of great spiritual benefit. Accordingly, numerous pilgrims annually resort thither. Of these, some reside there for a time in the hope of imbibing a sort of odour of sanctity, which shall shed its influence over all the actions of their remaining life. Others who have devoted the prime of their days to Mammon, retire thither when the lamp of life begins to burn low, that they may thus make sure of heaven after death.

The Assame Brahmins are Known as Baidicks of the ancient Kingdom of Kamrup. A great number of these are said to be learned in Hindu science. A very small portion are Saktis; they are chiefly the sect of Vishnu. They have a few academies or chaubaris where the Ratanmala, Byakaran (Grammar), law and metaphysics are taught. The persons who instruct the worshippers of Vishnu, that is, most of those who have adopted the Hindu creed, are called *Mahajans* and live in Chatras. They have generally a large number of men entirely devoted to their service. Their office is hereditary in certain families. The Brahmins who are elevated to this high dignity, are said to avoid all worldly pleasures, and bind themselves by an oath of celibacy.

The chief Chatras are as follows: In the District of Kamrup, at Baropeta, Pat-Bousi, Biha Kuchi, Bhowanipur, Plasbari, and Shrihati. In the rest of Assam — Annihati, Dakhynpat, Kurabasi, Gormurchotra, Dihingya, Noraya, Siliguri, Samguri, Koyarnariya, and Mahari.

There is also a class of Brahmins, usually Known as Mun Singh a Brahmins. They are Koch or Kuchis and Rajbangsis. They worship a god named Rishi and to his wife Jago. Every year at the end of the rainy season, a grand sacrifice are made in cases of distress. The blood of the sacrifice is left for the deity, while the votaries eat the meat. These people worship no images. They call on the name of their gods, and clap their hands during the ceremony of worship.

Rites and Rituals: The Assamese have two principal festivals, called Bihu. The first festival of the year is termed as the Baisak-Bihu. It is celebrated in the first three days of Baisak. On this occasion people devote the whole of the first day to mutual visits and compliments. The cause of their jubilation and rejoicing is two fold: first, that the month of Chaitro, every day of which is considered as unlucky, has expired; second, that it is succeeded by a month of which every day is a fortunate. The cows are then worshipped with great honour. They are first sprinkled with holy water or bathed in the sacred stream of the Brahmaputra. The devotees next prostrate themselves before them, their horns are painted with various colours, and their necks are decked with garlands of flowers and strings of fruits. The consecrated animals are then driven in a body through the villages, by crowds of people who make a discordant noise upon various musical instruments.

During the remainder of the day the cows are permitted to stray wherever they please, and seek a pasture in every field without restraint. On the following two days of the festival, large groups of people parade about, attended by number of dancing girls, who pause from time to time to exhibit their wanton movements, and charm the audience with their lascivious songs.

The other Bihu or festival known as the Magh Bihu, is celebrated about the end of the month of Pous or the beginning of Magh. The festival occurs after the winter harvest. It continues for two days, both of which are devoted to feasting and merriment.

Holi: The month of Phalgun (March), is of peculiar liveliness, as it ushers in the spring season. During the Phalgun (Holi) festival groups of men and children are continually patrolling the streets, throwing a crimson powder at each other, or ejecting a solution of it from syringes (Pichkaris), so that the garments and visages of all are one mass of crimson. At might fall, the last day of the festival concludes with the burning of the Holi, the Gulal (crimson powder) used at this festival, when large fires are lit into which various combustible substances are thrown, and around which groups of children are seen dancing and screaming like so many little infernals.

Durga Puja: Durga Puja is another important festival celebrated in Assam. It is celebrated in the month of Ashim (October) in honour of the ten armed goddess. It is needless to enter upon any description of this festival, since it is well-known to all who are in any degree conversant with the customs of the Hindus. Innumerable bloody sacrifices are offered at this festival, when the multitude of rich and poor, daub their bodies all over with the mud formed with the blood which has collected when the animals were slain, and dance like furies on the spot. On the last three days of the festival, dancing and singing are kept up at the house where the images of the goddess have been set up. On the afternoon of the last day, the images are brought out, placed on a stage, and carried to the river. Each idol is here placed on the centre of two canoes lashed together and filled with people, among whom are a number of dances, musicians, singers, etc. Who chant the praises of the goddess.

The river on this occasion presents a scene of peculiar animation, and the banks are crowded with spectators, rich and poor, old and young, who come from many miles round, arrayed in gayest costumes. Whilst the images are rowed up and down the stream to the melody of songs and music, the vast number of boats accompanying the procession are engaged in racing. The boats or canoes are most gaudily painted, each containing a complement of from twelve to twenty men, according to its size. The emulation of the native gentry and that of the crew, is to the greatest degree exciting and the whole scene is one that baffles description.

People following many religion and many ethnic groups of people live in the state of Assam. The majority population of Assam comprises non-tribal population mainly concentrated in the Brahmaputra and the Barak Valleys. The language spoken by them is Assamese. Among the non-tribal population the majority of them are Hindus are divided into castes and subcastes like Brahmins and Khatriyas, Vaishyas and Shudras.

Buddhists, Sikhs and Jains are scattered in various parts of Assam. Buddhists of the Khamti tribes and the Sikhs of Borkhola living in the Nagaon District follow their religion and culture in traditional way. As per 1991 Census, the total population of Assam was recorded as 2,24,14,322, in which nearly 20 per cent comprises the tribal population. The state has 16 Scheduled Castes and 23 Scheduled Tribes of which 7.40 per cent and 12.82 per cent, respectively constitute Assams's population. Apart from the major religions, the tribes follow animism, and nature worship. The Dimasas tribe of North Cachar Hills worship trees, mountains and rocks.

Researches have shown that huge number of non-tribal population of today were actually the tribes of yesterdays who adopted Hinduism and its culture which is called as *Sanskritisation* by anthropologists. The non-tribals community can be again separated on the basis of religion. After, the Hindus the Muslims are the second largest group, which is followed by the Christians, Sikhs and the Buddhists.

Theology

Religious Composition: Religion is an important social attribute. It is of particular importance in our country because we have many faiths and our civilization is closely linked to religion. It is because of this social relevance that data and information on religious composition have occupied an important position in Indian censuses.

The religious composition in Assam is somewhat different from that of the all India pattern. Hindus in Assam account for 71 per cent of the total population of the state as against the all India figure of 83 per cent. While Muslim form 24 per cent of the population Christian about 45 per cent with accounts for less than one per cent of the total population of Assam.

Buddhism, Jainism and Sikhism may be said as the insignificant religions in the state of Assam as none of them has even one per cent of the population in any of the districts. The highest percentage of Sikhism is in Lakhimpur being 0.14 per cent of the total population. The proportion of Buddhists is below one per cent in all the districts of Assam. As regards Jainism, in none of the districts the proportion exceeds 0.18 per cent. It is interesting to note that the rural and urban religious composition is different from the pattern in the general population.

In the rural part of the population the proportion of Hindus is slightly lower than the proportion for the general population. But the percentage of Muslims is slightly higher than the general figure. In the urban area, however, the proportion of Hindus goes up considerably (84%) and that of Muslims (11%) falls well below the figure for the general population. The population of Christians is also slightly lower than the general figure in the urban areas.

So far as the religious composition of the various towns is concerned, Hindus constitute the majority in all these towns. The proportions, however, vary from one town to another. The highest percentage of Hindus is found in Tezpur, Silchar, Haflong, and Diphu. The percentage of Hindus in each of these towns is over 80 per cent. In the rest of the towns the proportion varies between 73 and 87 per cent. The proportion of Muslims is the highest in Chubri where Islam accounts for 24 per cent of the total population. The second highest proportion of Muslims is in Nowgong where the figure is 21 per cent. In the remaining district headquarters of the plain's districts the proportion varies between 8 per cent and 14 per cent.

The Muslim population in the towns of the Hill districts is comparatively small, being around 5 per cent only. Christianity is common in the hill towns. The percentage of the Christians in Halflong and Diphu are 13 per cent and 5 per cent respectively. The Christians are less than two per cent in the remaining towns of the state. The followers of the other major religious like Buddhism, Jainism, and Sikhism form very small proportions in these towns. Guwahati the only city of Assam presents the following figures for the numerically important religions. Hinduism 87 per cent, Islam 10 per cent, Sikhism 1.4 per cent and Christianity only one per cent.

The scheduled caste population comprises of 16 subcastes. Among them Namasudras and Kaibortas are dominant which accounted for 32.97 and 32.31 per cent of the total scheduled caste population. Namasudra, Kaibortas and Patnies constitute 74.69 per cent of total Scheduled Caste population in Assam. The occupy a dominant position in the political field. The Scheduled Caste people in Assam are not residing in concentrated pockets. Cachar has the highest Scheduled Caste population where as Nowgaon Subdivisions tops the list Subdivision wise followed by Silchar, Karimganj, Guwahati and Nowgaon.

Family System

The joint family system appears to be traditional among both the tribal and non-tribal village communities of Assam; it is based on blood relationship. In the case of inheritance, the Dayabhaga system was followed in olden days, as at present. As long as the father lives, the sons cannot claim any share in the property. So the father is the centre of the family and he rules supreme. There are a few tribal societies which follow the matriarchal system. The Khasi is one among them. They look upon the mother as the centre of the clan. The mother's property goes to her daughters. When there is no daughter, the property goes to the youngest daughter of the mother's sister. The Garos also follow a similar system in the Garo Hills. Among the Dimasa-Kacharis the prevalent custom is that the sons inherit their father's properties and the girls inherit their mothers properties. When there is no children of their own, their relatives inherit the properties. Though Assamese women are given an honoured position, no other community in Assam follows the matrilineal inheritance system. The common paternal system governs general Assamese society.

Lifestyle

Assamese are very conventional, cordial and believe in plain living and high thinking. Education has been given priority and thus the region is hub of educational institutions like IIT Guwahati, Assam University. It is home of several ethnic communities, mainly speaking official languages like Assamese and Bodo. Bengali too is spoken in Assam especially in Barak Valley. The Assamese have got literary flair; fine literary works have developed from this region of the country. The Charyapadas is regarded as the earliest instance of literature in Assam. During 17th to 19th century, prose chronicles, namely, Buranji, were in vogue. It flourished in the courts of Ahoms. The Modern era saw the marked influences of Missionaries. The American Baptists first published Bible in Assamese in the year 1819. In the year 1836, they also formed the first printing press in Sibsagar in 1836 and local Asamiya dialect was used for the first time for writing. A monthly periodical called *Arunodoi*, and the first book on Assamese Grammar were also published during this period.

In 1867, The Missionaries printed the first Assamese-English Dictionary and M. Bronson hoarded it. Litterateurs like Jyoti Prashad Agarwal, Hem Barua and others had embellished the modern Assamese literature with their masterpieces. It is also land of renowned poets namely Anupama Basumatary, Ajit Barua, Anis-uz-Zaman. Assam too had a treasure of exquisite crafts and artefacts. It is copious in producing brass craft, metal craft, mask-making, potteries, cane and bamboo crafts, and jewelleries. The people of Assam have tried their hands in producing boats, traditional gun and gunpowder, iron utensils. Assam is known to the world for its dainty silk. The silk tinged with golden embroideries known as Muga is prominent. Others include Pat silk, which is cream-coloured meshed with silver colour. Nice woollens called *Eri* are found here. The lineage of Assam rulers had presented the region with marvellous paintings.

Costumes

Assam, the land of abundance and fruition, is addressed, as the eldest of the seven sisters, i.e. the seven states, cumulatively forming, northeast India. The Muga or the golden silk fibre of Assam constitutes the lion's share of the costumes of Assam. It is the outstandingly rich texture of Muga, which gifts Assam silk saris, their breathtaking beauty. Almost 28,000 families are engaged in silk-rearing in Assam. The exquisite designs, finely woven, on the saris cater to patterns in nature, for example the flora and the fauna. Embroideries also incorporate, acquainted and culture-related things, such as architecture and stone-sculptures on the Madan Kamdev Temple in Assam.

Nowadays, Muga artisans, indulge in experimentation. They offer contrast creations of pinkish red, or greenish blue, and other innovative as well as traditional colours of red, blue, yellow, green, against the inherent golden colour of the fabric. Bridal wears are decked with gold and silver threads, to make the bride catch a marvellous get-up on her special occasion. A Mekhla is a mix and match of Aanchal and Lungi. However, the Chadar, is adorned with spellbound weavings, integral to the weaving-ace Assamese. The Chadar is worn in a special criss-cross pleated-form, down the front side. Assamese women look marvellous in these fascinating costumes of Assam. Tribes reside amidst the lush greenery of Assam. The Bodo tribal womenfolk acknowledge Mekhla as their prevalent costume. The Dimasa tribes are renowned for their expertise in silk- culture and weaving-prowess. They are indeed the producers of Endi. A Dimasa woman covers herself in a skirt-like attire, known as the Rigu, topped by an embellished vest-like cloth, called Rijamphai.

Ceremonies and merry occasions, see the women, decorating themselves in more ornate Rijamphai, locally named as Rikhaosa. Again, like the Bodo men, a Dimasa man, wears, a Risha, which is a loin cloth of deep green colour. He puts in a vest, called *Rimsao*. He also attaches on his head, a turban woven from pure cotton or Endi. Jewellery is a fundamental aspect of costume of any place. The remarkable feature of Assamese jewellery is Khopo Phool, an earring which appears like an orchid. The outlook is like two small shoes paired together and crowned by a floral construct, which is again connected to a chain.

Traditional Costumes

Long hidden behind red tape, Assam's beauty is a fact that defies imagination. The rarest of flora and fauna, blue hills and green tea, a bustling capital and black oil, it is a beauty that soothes even as it disturbs. Arunachal Pradesh and Bhutan bound Assam in the north, Nagaland to the east, and Manipur and Mizoram to the south. In the southwest, Assam touches the borders of West Bengal and Bangladesh.

There is one ensemble that can be called the traditional costume of the Assamese women. It is known as the "mekhala and chadar". The dresses of most Assamese women, whichever tribe they may belong to, can be called variations of the mekhala and chadar. Today, India exports a wide variety of silks to western Europe and the United States, especially as exclusive furnishing fabrics. Boutiques and fashion houses, designers and interior decorators have the advantage of getting custom-woven fabrics in the designs, weaves and colours of their choice. A service that ensures an exclusive product not easily repeatable by competitors. The Tribals on the other hand have a wide variety of colourful costumes, some of which have earned International repute through the export market.

Food

Food of Assam, as of any other place, is largely influenced by its climate, soil and vegetation. This Northeastern State of India is mainly of agrarian nature. Rice is the staple diet and the common people of Assam eat it everyday. Along with rice, fish curry is very common. Other dishes include those made of lentils, vegetables, meat and some sweet dishes. The people of Assam prefer to eat non-spicy foods. Spices like cumin, coriander, mustard, ginger, garlic, fenugreek, panch foran, cardamom and some ingredients that are found in Assam only are generally used.

Traditionally, Assamese food is cooked in earthen ware. This method imparts a smell from the utensils to the food itself giving it a distinct flavour. Vegetables in sour soup are common. The Assamese have a typical habit of using all the leftover vegetables together to eat it next day with Assam slices, green chillies and mustard. This gives a variety of taste at one go and is also very appetising. Different types of herbs are also used sparingly in the cuisine of Assam giving it a characteristic aroma of its own.

Thirty-nine herbal recipes prevalent among the different tribal groups of Assam have been identified that are medicinal for the protection of liver. These are slowly gaining recognition among the urban world for its immense benefits. Sweets from Assam are mainly made from rice paste. This paste is used in various consistencies and shapes and is even mixed with additional ingredients to make the variation. A typical food of Assam may be reserved only for a certain festival or occasion and such foods have made themselves an inevitable part in the particular celebration.

Common Occupations

Profession: Out of the total population of 2,66,55,528 in Assam, 4,240,112 or 28.35 per cent are workers and the remaining 71.65 per cent are non-workers. In other words, out of every ten persons in the state only three persons produce economic goods and services while seven persons are dependent on them.

It may be noticed from Table that in each of the component areal units of Assam workers constitute less than thirty per cent excepting the North Cachar Hills and the Mikir Hills Districts in which the percentage of workers is 41.91 and 31.16 respectively.

In Assam also like all the other States of the country, workers are mostly men. In fact 49 per cent of Assam's men folk are workers. The share of women in the field of productive work is very small. Only 5 per cent of Assam's total women are workers. This however, does not mean that most of the women do not make any contribution to the economy. In fact, there are many women, particularly in the rural areas, who work in the fields or participate in household industries in addition to their household work. But such marginal contribution to work are not reflected, in these figures.

If we consider the rural and urban areas separately, it may be noticed that the proportion of workers in the urban population is slightly higher than the proportion in rural population. About 30 per cent of the urban people are workers against 28 per cent in the rural population. The same pattern of slightly higher proportion in urban areas as compared to the rural areas is visible in respect of the male population. The pattern is however, reversed for the female population which shows a smaller proportion of workers in Urban areas.

Workers and Non-Workers/District-wise

	Total Population	Percentage of workers and Non-workers	
	Total Population	*Workers*	*Non-workers*
Assam	14,957,542	28.35	71.65
Goalpara	2,225,103	26.91	73.09
Kamrup	2,854,183	26.09	73.91
Darrang	1,736,188	29.11	70.89
Nowgong	1,680,895	29.12	72.88
Sibsagar	1,837,389	28.48	71.52
Lakhimpur	2,122,719	29.08	70.92
Mikir Hills	379,310	31.16	68.84
North Cachar Hills	76,047	41.91	58.09
Cachar	1,713,318	28.77	71.23

As discussed at the outset 28 per cent of the total population of the state belongs to the workers category. The percentage of workers however, varies from district to district. The percentage of workers in highest in the North Cachar Hills being 42 per cent. In all the other districts it ranges between 23 and 32 per cent. Among the plains districts, the highest proportions of workers are found in Darrang and Lakhimpur districts (29%) and the lowest in Kamrup District (26%) and the lowest in Kamrup District (26%).

As regards male and female workers the proportions of workers among men are much higher then those among women in every district. About 49 per cent of the male population are workers for the whole state. In the plains districts the proportions vary between 46 per cent 51 per cent. In the hills districts the figure ranges between 51 per cent and 57 per cent. The proportions of workers among women, however, differ more widely. In the hill districts where shifting cultivation is the rule the womenfolk participate in cultivation in much greater measure than their counterparts in the plains districts. The proportion is in North Cachar Hills District (24%). The districts with the lowest percentage in each of these districts is below 2 per cent. Lakhimpur and Sibsagar Districts show a comparatively higher percentage of women workers (above 8%). This is perhaps due to the presence of large number of women among the tea plantation workers in these districts.

It may be seen from Table that agricultural workers predominate in the state. The cultivators alone form 57 per cent of the total working population. If we add the agricultural labourers to the cultivators the percentage of workers in agriculture rises to 66 per cent. After agriculture, the next highest proportion of workers is in livestock, forestry, fishing, hunting, plantation, orchards and allied activities (10.5%). The services rank third with a percentage of 9.8 other services include all government employees, employees of local bodies, teachers, doctors, social workers, etc. The workers in trade and commerce occupy the next highest position with 5.5 per cent. The industrial backwardness of Assam can be seen from the fact that the workers in the main industrial category account for only 4 per cent of the total workers.

Tea Gardens and Men Power

- Tea cultivation in Assam occupies about 1,657 sq km with a labour force 5.5 lakh working daily. As the labour was not available locally it, was imported from the different parts of India, mainly from Bihar, Orissa, Andhra Pradesh, Madhya Pradesh and eastern Uttar Pradesh the tea garden labourers in Assam form a separate class of population, no matter to what region, state, tribe caste and creed they belong. Many of them after fulfilment of contract with the gardens have settled permanently in Assam and have taken up agriculture as their main occupation.

  The immigration of garden labour was maximum during the period of 1911 to 1931, and attempts were made in the census reports of those periods to find out the total strength of garden labourers and their descendents. In 1921, it was estimated that the total population of tea garden labourers was 12 lakh. This number increased to 14 lakhs in 1931. There is a considerable number of agricultural population in upper Assam and Cachar who are tea garden labourers. Though this labour class is socially backward, it nevertheless include very good workers who can easily be employed in other sectors of the economy.

- The partition of the subcontinent led to large scale migration from Pakistan to India and India to Pakistan. In the late forties and early fifties a large population from East Pakistan migrated into the Brahmaputra valley.

Dependency Factors

The dependency ratio for Assam is 107 dependents per 100 of working population as against 92 for the country as a whole. In other words every 100 persons who can work and produce there is more than equal number of old persons and children who, cannot work but depend on them. Thus the working population in Assam has to carry a heavy burden. In fact the actual burden is even higher because the entire population which is capable of working do not find employment in our Assam. The very high dependency ratio in Assam is mainly due to the high proportion of young people of the age group of 0-14 in the population.

In Assam, nearly 42 per cent of the population is below 15. This high proportion of young in Assam's population is the result of high birth rate. A large number of dependents on a comparatively small number of workers as in the country as a whole is an obstacle to economic development. This is because the workforce has to spend a substantial part of their income on maintaining the aged and the children and cannot therefore save enough to invest in the development programmes of the country. Such high dependency ratio is typical in all the developing countries of the world. The age structure of the population of Assam is identical to the age pyramid of the country. There is a large base and the pyramid has a conical shape, indicating that the population of both males and females decrease with the increase in age.

Functional Elements

The rapid increase in population from 1891 to 1941 is mainly due to immigration from different sources, and since the partition of the country in 1947, the influx of Hindu displaced persons is the main source of immigration. The percentage of foreign born persons in Assam according to the census of 1911, 1921, 1931 were 12.5, 16.1, and 15.2 per cent respectively. Although afterwards they were not counted separately, it can be assumed that it would be at present as high as 25 per cent. At the same time, due to improved methods of public health. Assam has suffered comparatively less from epidemics like cholera, plague, and influenza during the period. Kalazar (black fever) was the only epidemic that ravaged Kamrup, Nowgong, and the Golaghat subdivisions of the Sibsagar District during 1911-21. So the natural growth of the local people was also appreciable.

There major sources of immigration may be classified as: (i) Tea garden labourers, (ii) East Bengal immigrants or Mymensigh, (iii) Nepali Grazers, (iv) East Bengal displaced person.

Invasion and Immigration

In fact, the invasion began sometime in 1911 and continued unabated till 1941. Goalpara District was the first target of attack, and the population of this district which increased by two per cent in 1891-1901 increased by 30 per cent in 1901-11, due to inflow of immigrants. Gradually, they began to spread to all other districts — especially to the Charlands — lands formed by the alluvial deposits of the River Brahmaputra. The most affected districts Goalpara, Kamrup, Darrang and Nowgong.

In 1931, the total number of immigrants was estimated at 575,000 and hence the impact of their inflow was clearly realised. According to the Census Report of 1931. It had but by no means improbable that in another thirty years Sibsagar District will be the only part of Assam in which the Assamese will find themselves at home. Wherever there is wasteland, thilher flock the Mymensinghis.

In fact, the way in which they have seized upon the vacant areas in the Assam valley seems almost uncanny. Without fuss, without tumalt, without undue trouble to the district revenue staff, a population which must amount to over half a million has transplanted itself from Bengal to Assam Valley during the last twenty five years." Agriculture was revolutionised and many new crops like jute and vegetables were introduced on a commercial scale by the immigrants and by clearing the marshes and jungles they helped to improve the health of the country side. The immigrants in their eagerness to graph as much land as possible, they frequently took possession of wasteland or reserves of the government. So a lot of friction and litigation mostly for land between the immigrant and local people became very common. The Assam Government could foresee it and they introduced a line system as early as 1920 and this imposed certain restrictions on settlements on certain areas.

East Bengal Immigrants

The last phase of mass migration into Assam is of a very recent origin and its causes are too well Known to be recounted here. After the creation of Pakistan, the Hindus started migrating to other parts of the Indian Union. Assam, being a state adjacent to east Bengal, naturally had to receive a large number of Hindu displaced persons from East Pakistan. The 1951 census gives the total number of refugees in Assam as 274,455 of there 272, 075 came from East Pakistan, only 647 from West Pakistan and 93,177 followed by Goalpara with 44,967 Kamrup with 42,871, Darrang with 18,833 Lakhimpur with 13,965, Sibsagar with 7,514. The number rose to 628,249 according to the Census Report of 1961. Most of the Hindu immigrants settled in urban areas and they have not taken up agriculture, forestry, and cattle keeping.

The immigrants came with new technology and attitudes. They through their hard efforts substantially transformed the agricultural landscape. In fact, they proved as the most industrious, efficient and progressive formers. Their efforts have enhanced the agricultural production in the state, by their more intensive agricultural production in the state, by their more intensive agricultural techniques and by putting more input of labour. Despite all there achievements, the state of Assam also has a limited resource base and the frontiers of arable land have almost been pushed to the limit. Bringing more area under plough in not possible without - making heavy labour and capital investments. The influx of immigration therefore, should be stopped failure to which there may be an ecological crisis in the state.

Nepali Grazers

The Nepalese also entered in large numbers in the Brahmaputra valley from the west and northwest. The period of 1911-31 was the most important for the migration of Nepali immigrants to Assam, when their total number stood at 70,244 in the census of 1921. During the next ten years this increased to 83,306 in 1931 but thereafter the flow of migration personnel after retirement have settled permanently in the urban areas of Assam, and the Census of 1951 gave the number of Nepali speaking population as nearly as 1.25 lakh. The majority of Nepali settlers are graziers by profession and have occupied the Charlands of the Brahamputra or the foot hill regions. Many of them occupy the outskirts of urban areas and supply fuel and milk to town dwellers. The main consideration of the Nepali settlers in the availability of fodder for their cattle (cows and buffaloes). Many of them are employed as porters in Shillong, Kohima and other hill stations.

The Khari, Hills, the Mizo Hills, Kamrup and Darrang are the favourite areas for settlement of the Nepali people. At the present moment the entire business of milk and milk products is in the hands of these grazers. According to the projected figures (1981) the total number of Nepali speaking people was 27,826 about 2 per cent of the total population.

Arts and Crafts

The richness of the art and handicrafts of Assam beautifully reflects the bountifulness of its culture. The craftsmen here have long perfected the art of creating wonderful objects from very ordinary products. The craftsmen make several handicrafts apart from the famous silk fabric and cane and bamboo products. Different regions of Assam are known for their different forms of art and handicrafts.

Making Idols: In Assam the fine arts have made relatively less progress. A brief account of sculpture, dance, theatre, music has been given in the following paras.

Of the arts which an early stage of society acquire the greatest excellence, the first is that of preparing brilliant trinkets for ornamenting the person. The natives cut stones and precious stones, polish them to a high degree of brilliancy and set them in gold and silver with an extraordinary neatness; and when we come to compare the extreme imperfection, the scantiness and rudeness of the tools by which the artist in general perform their task, with the simplicity of process, the neatness, and in some cases the celerity of the execution, we can not but acknowledge that the degree of delicacy which the artisans have acquired in their professions, challenges a high admiration.

The workers in gold and silver usually finish their work with a great degree of neatness, and the same may be said of workers in ivory, who have carried their art, comparatively to a high state of perfection. But of all the artists it may be said, that their style and taste are very wretched. They possess a wonderful aptitude for imitating the arts, innovations and inventions of the other Indians and Europeans as soon as the method has been pointed out to them. They are in general correct workmen, but possess merely the glimmerings of genius.

With respect to the sculpture and painting of the Assamese, hardly by any panegyrist can it be pretended that they are in a state beyond that in which they usually appear in the most early stages of society. The remains of temples and other public buildings, which are so often met within various parts of the country, testify that the Assamese had once made considerable progress in sculpture. Their productions, however, are not merely void of attraction, they are unnatural, and not infrequently offensive and disgusting.

The story of the Assamese sculpture is however, quite old. Terracotta is the medium of objects used in rituals like mother goddess figures as well as for recreation like toys of a great variety. Despite their small size stone sculpture achieves monumentalism and animals like bulls represented in the small steatite seals have a vibrant realism. A gentler style in the bull and the sympathetic treatment of animals continued throughout the Assames sculpture.

The Yakshas and the Yakshis (spirits of hills and trees) are also found in the sculpture of Assam. Scenes of revelry with the wine flowing freely are represented in sculpture. Examples of feminine apparel beings its fine adventure of ambivalence, revealing while pretending to conceal, for the Mathura nymph wears so transparent a fabric that she appears nude are also found in the Assamese sculpture. There are examples of far more sensitive in modelling and poetic in sensibility in the representations of woman in her various moods of longing, expectation, reverie in some of the sculptures. Eroticism is also found in the sculptures of Assam of the thirteenth century. In these sculptures the poetic and romantic figuration of woman are more sensitive.

Exposed to stimuli from the various parts of the country, the south east Asia and all over the would, Assamese sculptors today are experimenting in all styles, using new materials. But the most significant trend seems to be the one which seeks to recover the iconic quality, the power to stir the impulses of awe and adoration which are humanistically the most valuable strains of the Indian sculptural heredity.

Drawing Pictures: Despite great gaps in our Knowledge of continuities in history, the story of the Indian paintings in general and that of the Assamese painting in particular has to begin with the art of primitive man which has survived in rock shelters and caves in places. Stone Age paintings have been discovered in the hilly parts of the state of Assam. The primitive intellect and vision can survive for long when communities are isolated: Thus these paintings share the vivid realism of primitive art that has been discovered in many places. The silhouette effect creates a dramatic shadow play of scenes of hunt.

The paintings of Buddhism represent only the transience, of things, the pervasiveness of pain. But, though Siddhartha, it said is wished to take his infant son with him when he left the palace, he could not because the mother's hand lay protectingly over the child even in her sleep. He remembered this after his enlightenment and told all to have the same kind of protective regard for every living thing. He rejected Niruana for himself and was born again and again to help humanity in its travails, not only in many human roles, but as a deer, an elephant, a swan.

In Assam like other parts of the country, painting had come down from the extended mural surface to the miniature dimensions of the manuscript, originally on palm-leaf, later, on paper. The miniatures of Pala period Bengal (tenth and eleventh centuries) conserve the sensuous line of Ajanta. But there is a rapid decline now and line becomes brittle and angular. The lyricism of poems becomes supple, colour lustrous. The Indian as well as the Assamese miniature stabilises a fine pictorial style even before the advent of the Mughals.

The influence Bengali paintings, especially that of Rabindranath Tagore, Jamini Roy who discovered the virility of folk tradition and modulated it in many ways may also be seen in the Assamese paintings. Rabindranath Tagore who demanded for paintings music's autonomy and independence from factuality and thus gave a charter for free variations on naturalism, abstraction and expressionism also influenced the paintings of Assamese painters appreciably.

House of Antiques: The museums are repositories of cultural, historical, technical, industrial or other kinds of material for preservation against decay and for transmission to posterity as record of history. They serve as important audio-visual means of education.

The Constitution makes the states primarily responsible for the setting up and maintenance of museums. The Central Government has, however, set up a number of important museums and provides financial assistance for the development of private museums, university museums, etc. Great emphasis is laid on documentation of existing collection in the government and private museums, preservation of the Collection by using the latest scientific aids and publication of catalogues of collection. The Department of culture has set up in April 1978, an autonomous organisation Known as the National Council of Science Museum with headquarters at Calcutta to administer. The Regional Science Centre, Guwahati (under progress) has been established under this organisation. The Council and the Regional Science Centre, Guwahati also organise multifarious educational activities for children, students, teachers, housewives and unemployed youths.

Conservation: The records and manuscripts constitute an important part of the Indian cultural heritage. These are the major repository of the contribution that over predecessors made in the diverse fields 'of religion, philosophy, astronomy, literature, history, medicine and science. They constitute the primary source of reconstruction of India's past. Government has jurisdiction only over libraries established by it and institution of national importance declared so. However, it takes initiative to secure the voluntary cooperation of the State Governments and to promote a coordinated development of national state and other libraries. Unfortunately, there is no archives in the state of Assam. The manuscripts and records are however, preserved in the Central Library of the Guwahati University.

Place of Reading Books: The development of the library system is an important component of the scheme of non-formal and continuing education. Constitutionally the subject 'libraries' is included in the state list. The centre has jurisdiction only over libraries established by the government and institutions of national importance as declared by it. Although there is no Central Reference Library and the Public library in Assam, all the Universities, Engineering Colleges, Medical, Colleges and other colleges have sizeable Collection of books in their libraries.

Divisional Cultural Points: The Zonal Cultural Centres have been conceptualised with the avowed aim of projecting cultural Kinships that transcend territorial bounds. The idea is to arouse and deepen awareness of the local cultures and how these merge into zonal identities and eventually into the rich diversity of India's composite culture. Besides, these are intended to document, preserve, and to sustain the vanishing art forms and oral traditions. The involvement artists and creative people has been inbuilt in the set up through a system of autonomous governance.

Although there is no Zonal Cultural Centre in the state of Assam, the North East Zone Cultural Centre, Dimapur (Nagaland) takes care of the interest of art and artists of Assam. The participation of State in more than one zonal cultural centre according to their cultural linkages is a special feature of the composition of different Zonal Centres.

Performing Arts

Assam has rich tradition of performing arts. *Ankiya Nat* (*Onkeeya Naat*) is a traditional Vaishnav dance-drama (*bhaona*) form popular since 15th century AD. It makes use of large masks of gods, goddesses, demons and animals and in between the plays a *Sutradhar* (*Xutrodhar*) keeps on telling the story. The Bihu dance and *Hucory* performed during the *Bohag Bihu, Kushan nritra* of Rajbongshi's, *Bagurumba* and *Bordoicikhla* dance of Bodos, Mishing Bihu, *Banjar Kekan* performed during *Chomangkan* by Karbis are some of the major folk dances. Sattriya (*Xotriya*) dance related to Vaishnav tradition is a classical form of dance. Moreover, there are several other age-old dance-forms such as Barpeta's *Bhortal Nritya, Deodhoni Nritya, Oja Paali, Beula Dance, Ka Shad Inglong Kardom, Nimso Kerung*, etc. The tradition of modern moving theatres is typical of Assam with immense popularity of many large theatre groups such as Kohinoor, Apsara, Hengul, etc.

At the same time musical tradition is also rich. Folk songs and music related to Bihu and other festivals dates back to time-immemorial. *Borgeet*, the popular Vaishnav songs are written and composed in 15th century. Assam has large numbers of traditional musical instruments including several types of drums, string instruments, flutes, cymbals, pipes, etc.

The indigenous folk music has substantially influenced the growth of a modern idiom, that finds expression in the music of such artists like Bhupen Hazarika, Anima Choudhury, Nirmalendu Choudhury Utpalendu Choudhury, Luit Konwar Rudra Baruah, Parvati Prashad Baruva, Jayanta Hazarika and Khagen Mahanta among many others. Among the new generation, Zubeen Garg and Jitul Sonowal have a great fan following.

Paintings

Painting is an ancient tradition of Assam. The ancient practices can be known from the accounts of the Chinese traveller Hiuen Tsang (7th century CE). The account mentions that Bhaskaravarma, the King of Kamarupa has gifted several items to Harshavardhana, the King of Magadha including paintings and painted objects, some of which were on Assamese silk. Many of the manuscripts available from the Middle Ages bear excellent examples of traditional paintings. The most famous of such medieval works are available in the Hastividyarnava (A Treatise on Elephants), the Chitra Bhagawata and in the Gita Govinda. The medieval painters used locally manufactured painting materials such as the colours of hangool and haital. The medieval Assamese literature also refers to chitrakars and patuas. Traditional Assamese paintings have been influenced by the motifs and designs in the medieval works such as the Chitra Bhagawata.

There are several renowned contemporary painters in Assam. The Guwahati Art College in Guwahati is the only government institution for tertiary education. Moreover, there are several art societies and non-government initiatives across the state and the Guwahati Artists Guild is a front-runner organisation based in Guwahati.

Traditional Crafts

Assam has maintained a rich tradition of various traditional crafts for more than two thousand years. Presently, cane and bamboo craft, bell-metal and brass craft, silk and cotton weaving, toy and mask making, pottery and terracotta work, wood craft, jewellery-making, musical instruments making, etc. are remained as major traditions. Historically, Assam also excelled in making boats, traditional guns and gunpowder, colours and paints, articles of lac, traditional building materials, utilities from iron, etc.

Cane and bamboo craft provide the most commonly used utilities in daily life, ranging from household utilities, weaving accessories, fishing accessories, furniture, musical instruments to building construction materials. Traditional utilities and symbolic articles made from bell-metal and brass are found in every Assamese household. The Xorai and bota have been in use for centuries to offer gifts to respected persons and are two prominent symbolic elements.

Hajo and Sarthebari/Xorthebaary are the most important centres of traditional bell-metal and brass crafts. Assam is the home of several types of silks, the most prominent and prestigious being Muga, the natural golden silk is exclusive only to Assam. Apart from Muga, there are other two varieties called Pat, a creamy-bright-silver coloured silk and Eri, a variety used for manufacturing warm clothes for winter. Apart from Sualkuchi/Xualkuchi, the centre for the traditional silk industry, in almost every parts of the Brahmaputra Valley, rural households produce silk and silk garments with excellent embroidery designs. Moreover, various ethno-cultural groups in Assam make different types of cotton garments with unique embroidery designs and wonderful colour combinations.

Moreover, Assam possesses unique crafts of toy and mask making mostly concentrated in the Vaishnav Monasteries, pottery and terracotta work in lower Assam districts and wood craft, iron craft, jewellery, etc. in many places across the region.

Sculpture and Architecture

The archaic Mauryan Stupas discovered in and around Goalpara District are the earliest examples (c. 300 BC to c. 100 AD) of ancient art and architectural works. The remains discovered in Daparvatiya (*Doporboteeya*) archaeological site with a beautiful doorframe in Tezpur are identified as the best examples of artworks in ancient Assam with influence of Sarnath School of Art of the late Gupta period. Many other sites also exhibit development of local art forms with local motifs and sometimes with similarities with those in the South East Asia. There are currently more than forty discovered ancient archaeological sites across Assam with numerous sculptural and architectural remains. Moreover, there are examples of several late Middle Age art and architectural works including hundreds of sculptures and motifs along with many remaining temples, palaces and other buildings. The motifs available on the walls of the buildings such as Rang Ghar, Joydoul, etc., are remarkable examples of artworks.

Culture and Heritage

The culture of Assam is traditionally a hybrid one, developed due to cultural assimilation of different ethno-cultural groups under various politico-economic systems in different periods of pre-history and history.

Evolution

The roots of the culture go back to almost two thousand years, when the first cultural assimilation took place with Austro-Asiatic and Tibeto-Burman as the major components. With reference from the great epics Mahabharata and on the basis of the local folklore it is also hypothised that there was probably a strong kingdom of these mixed population (of Austro-Asiatic and Tibeto-Burman origin) in the era before Christ, which led to an early assimilation at a greater scale. Typical naming of the rivers and spatial distribution of related ethno-cultural groups also support that. Thereafter, western migrations such as those of various branches of Mediterraneans, Inrano-skythians and Nordics along with (or in the form of) the mixed northern Indians (the ancient cultural mix already present in northern Indian states such as Magadha) have enriched the aboriginal culture and under certain stronger politico-economic systems, Sanskritisation and Hinduisation intensified and became prominent. Such an assimilated culture, therefore, carries many elements of source cultures, of which exact roots are difficult to trace and are matter of research. However, in each of the elements of Assamese culture, i.e., language, traditional crafts, performing arts, festivity and beliefs either local elements or the local elements in a Hinduised/Sanskritised forms are always present.

It is believed that under the great dynasties of Pragjyotisha-Kamrupa (Varman Dynasty for 300 years, Xalostombho Dynasty for 200 years and the Pala Dynasty for another 200 years) during the first millennium AD, Assamese culture in its original form got developed. The records of many aspects of the language, traditional crafts (silk, lac, gold, bronze, etc.), are available in different forms. When the Tai-Shans entered the region in 1228 under the leadership of Sukaphaa to form one of the strongest politico-economic systems (Ahom Kingdom) in Assam for the next 600 years, again a new chapter of cultural assimilation was written. The original Tai-Shans assimilated with the local culture, adopted the language on one hand and on the other also influenced the mainstream culture with the elements from their own. Similarly, the Koch Kingdom in the western Assam and the medieval Kachari Kingdoms (Kocary) and Jaintia Kingdoms in the southern Assam provided stages for assimilation at different intensities and with different cultural-mix.

Vaishanav Movement, the 15th century religio-cultural movement under the leadership of great Srimanta Shankradeva (Xonkordeu) and his disciples have provided another dimension to Assamese culture. A renewed Hinduisation in local forms took place, which was initially greatly supported by the Koch and later by the Ahom Kingdoms. The resultant social institutions such as *namghar* and *sattra* (the Vaishnav Monasteries) have become part of Assamese way life. The movement contributed greatly towards language, literature and performing fine arts. It is also noticed that many a times, Vaishnav Movement attempted to introduce alien cultural attributes and modify the way of life of common people. *Brajavali* a language specially created by introducing words from other Indian languages had failed as a language but left its traces on the Assamese language. Moreover, new alien rules were also introduced changing people's food habits and other aspects of cultural life. This had a greater impact on alienation of many local ethno-cultural and political groups in the later periods.

In an historical perspective, in brief, it is not difficult to understand that on one hand, during the strong politico-economic systems under stronger dynasties, greater cultural assimilations have created common attributes of Assamese culture, while on the other during smaller politico-economic systems or during political disintegration, more localised attributes were created with spatial differentiation. Time-factor for such integrations and differentiations has also played extremely important role along with the position of individual events in the entire series of sequential events.

With a strong base of tradition and history, the modern Assamese culture is greatly influenced by various events which took place in the British Assam and in the Post-British era. The language was standardised by the American Missionaries with the form available in the Sibsagar (Xiwoxagor) District (the nerve centre of the Ahom politico-economic system). A renewed Sanskritisation was increasingly adopted for developing Assamese language and grammar. A new wave of western and northern Indian influence was apparent in the performing arts and literature.

Due to increasing efforts of standardisation in the 19th and 20th century, the localised forms present in different districts and also among the remaining source-cultures with the less-assimilated ethno-cultural groups have seen greater alienation. However, Assamese culture in its hybrid form and nature is one of the richest and is still under development.

Composition and Characteristics

Assamese culture in its true sense today is a 'cultural system' composed of different subsystems. It is more interesting to note that even many of the source-cultures of Assamese culture are still surviving either as subsystems or as sister entities. In broader sense, therefore, the Assamese cultural system incorporates its source-cultures such as Bodo (Boro) or Khasi or Mishing (Micing) but individual development of these subsystems are today becoming important. However, it is also important to keep the broader system closer to its roots.

Some of the common cultural traits available across these systems are:

- respect towards areca-nut and betel leaves;
- respect towards particular symbolic cloth types such as Gamosa, Arnai, etc.;
- respect towards traditional silk and cotton garments;
- respect towards forefathers and elderly;
- great hospitality;
- bamboo culture.

Symbolism

Symbolism is an important part of Assamese culture. Various elements are being used to represent beliefs, feelings, pride, identity, etc. Symbolism is an ancient cultural practice in Assam, which is still very important for the people. *Tamulpan*, *Xorai* and *Gamosa* are three important symbolic elements in Assamese culture.

Tamulpan (the areca nut and betel leaves) or *guapan* (gua from *kwa*) are considered as the offers of devotion, respect and friendship. It is an ancient tradition and is being followed since time-immemorial with roots in the aboriginal Austro-Asiatic culture.

Xorai being a traditional symbol of Assam is a manufactured bell-metal object and an article of great respect and is used as a container-medium while performing respectful offers. It simplistic term, it is an offering tray with a stand at the bottom. There are xorais with or without a cover on the top. Traditionally, xorais were made of bell-metal although, nowadays, they can be made from brass and/or silver. Hajo and Sarthebari are the most important centres of traditional bell-metal and brass crafts including xorais. Xorais are used as an offering tray for tamul-pan (betel nuts and betel leaves) to guests as a sign of welcome and thanks. As an offering tray for food and other items placed in front of the altar (naamghar) for blessing by the Lord. As a decorative symbol in traditional functions such as during Bihu dances. As a gift to a person of honour during felicitations.

The *Gamosa* is an article of great significance for the people of Assam. Literally translated, it means 'something to wipe the body with' (*Ga* = body, *mosa* = to wipe); interpreting the word 'gamosa' as the body-wiping towel is misleading. It is generally a white rectangular piece of cloth with primarily a red border on three sides and red woven motifs on the fourth (in addition to red, other colours are also used).

Though, it is used daily to wipe the body after a bath (an act of purification), the use is not restricted to this. It is used by the farmer as a waistcloth (*tongali*) or a loincloth (*suriya*); a Bihu dancer wraps it around the head with a fluffy knot. It is hung around the neck at the prayer hall and was thrown over the shoulder in the past to signify social status. Guests are welcomed with the offering of a *gamosa* and *tamul* (betel nut) and elders are offered *gamosas* (*bihuwaan*) during Bihu. It is used to cover the altar at the prayer hall or cover the scriptures. An object of reverence is never placed on the bare ground, but always on a *gamosa*. One can therefore, very well say, that the *gamosa* symbolises the life and culture of Assam.

The word *gamosa* is derived from the Kamrupi word *gaamasa* (*gaama+chadar*), the cloth used to cover the Bhagavad Purana at the altar.

Significantly, the *gamosa* is used equally by all irrespective of religious and ethnic backgrounds.

At par with Gamosa, there are beautifully woven symbolic clothes with attractive graphic designs being used by different cultural subsystems and ethno-cultural groups as well.

There were various other symbolic elements and designs traditionally in use, which are now only found in literature, art, sculpture, architecture, etc., or used for only religious purposes (in particular occasions only). The typical designs of *Assamese-lion, dragon, flying-lion*, etc., were used for symbolising various purposes and occasions.

Festivals

There are several important traditional festivals in Assam. Bihu is the most important and common and celebrated all over Assam. However, there are other important traditional festivals being celebrated every year for different occasions at different places. Many of these are celebrated by different ethno-cultural groups (sub and sister cultures). Few of these are:

- Me-dam-me-phi;
- Ali-aye-ligang;
- Kherai;

- Garja;

- Hapsa Hatarnai;

- Awnkham Gwrlwi Janai;

- Chojun/Swarak;

- Rongker;

- Sokk-erroi;

- Hacha-kekan; and

- Porag.

Bihu: Bihu is a series of three prominent festivals of Assam. Primarily, a festival celebrated to mark the seasons and the significant points of a cultivator's life over a yearly cycle, in recent times, the form and nature of celebration has changed with the growth of urban centres. A non-religious festival, all communities — religious or ethnic — take part in it. Three Bihus are celebrated: *rongali*, celebrated with the coming of spring and the beginning of the sowing season; *kongali*, the barren bihu when the fields are lush but the barns are empty; and the *bhogali*, the thanksgiving when the crops have been harvested and the barns are full. Rongali, kongali and bhogali bihu are also known as 'bohag bihu', 'kati bihu' and 'magh bihu', respectively. The day before the each bihu is known as 'uruka'. There are unique features of each bihu. The first day of 'rongali bihu' is called 'Goru bihu' (the bihu of the cows). On this day the cows are taken to the nearby rivers or ponds to be bathed with special care. Traditionally, cows are respected as sacred animals by the people of Assam. Bihu songs and bihu dance are associated to *rongali* bihu.

Popular Games

The amusements of the Assamese are few, and these are for the most part of innocent nature.

Children may frequently be seen playing with earthen balls, and with Kauris (small shells) which pass for money. Bigger boys are seen amusing themselves in different Kinds of inferior gaming, throwing kauris, etc. They also pass their time with Kites, leaping, wrestling, Kabaddi, in hide and seek, and the alike.

A fondness for those surprising feats of bodily agility, and dexterity which form the art of the tumbler and the juggler, as well as taste for buffooney, are occasionally indulged in, and may be considered as a part of the character of a rude people.

Story telling, which entirely harmonises with the tone of the native mind, is also a favourite diversion. The recitation of the bards, which in general consists of the wildest fictions, afford an entertainment of the same description, and to these may be added music and dancing.

Many of the native melodies possess a plaintive, touching simplicity and others on the contrary, a peculiar wild originality no less pleasing. The musical instruments are indigenous and consist of drums, of great variety of shapes and dimensions, of cymbals, tabors, horns, and trumpets, used usually during the festivals, whilst in attendance on religions ceremonies, and on occasions of great rejoicings. The violin, though indigenous and usually made of an excavated gourd, is, when played by a master hand, one of the most pleasing instruments the Assamese possess.

Game is often procurable, especially during the season of general rains, when the poors have frequent opportunities of indulging in the luxury "of a hunch of venison, or steaks of wild hog, or buffaloes" and most of the inhabitants have sense enough to enjoy them.

At present, modern games like football, cricket, Table-tennis, volleyball, basketball and athletics are quite popular in all the schools, colleges and universities of Assam.

6

Education

The Highlights

Assam has one of the most extensive networks of higher educational institutions in the entire Northeastern Region of India. The Government of Assam introduces innovative education policies to create a centre of attention for aspiring students all across the country. Assam's largest city, Guwahati is a major destination for students of the entire Northeastern Region for higher education.

Presence of institutions including the Indian Institute of Technology (Guwahati), National Institute of Technology (Silchar), Tezpur University (a Central University), Assam University (Silchar) and K. K. Handique State Open University, adds stature to the education system of Assam which already encompasses elite higher education institutions like the Guwahati University, Dibrugarh University, Assam Medical College (Dibrugarh), Guwahati Medical College, Assam Agricultural University (Jorhat), Assam Engineering College (Guwahati) and Jorhat Engineering College (Jorhat). These on the whole, make Assam the top edu-destination both at the state level and national level.

Today, the state of Assam is home to six universities, one deemed university, one institute of national importance and several reputed professional institutions. The colleges of Assam (including medical, engineering and law colleges) are affiliated to Guwahati University, Dibrugarh University, Assam University and the Assam Agricultural University. The demand of technical education in the state has been well understood by the State Government and due attention is being paid towards rapid development in this field. The institutions offering professional courses are rapidly growing along with the other institutions which mean the students of Assam will be exposed to newer areas of opportunities. Thus, the whole educational scenario of Assam is improving gradually.

There are also a large number of higher secondary schools in Assam.

The medium of instruction at the school level is generally Assamese; however, some schools also use English as their medium of study.

The Assam Government has introduced the policy of free and compulsory education for students up to the age of 14.

The state has recently made strides in setting up several high standard institutions to provide education in the field of engineering and management. Assam has an overall literacy rate of 76.3 per cent. While male literacy rate is at 71.93 per cent, the female literacy rate however is only at 56.03 per cent, a cause for concern for the State Government.

Educational Development

Like other parts of India in Assam also education has always been held in high esteem. In Assam, education had always been of a classical and spiritual nature than a practical one. The subjects taught were the Scriptures, Grammar and Philosophy. Learning among the Hindus was a monopoly of higher, especially of the Brahmins-the priestly caste. The 'Gurukula' system was maintained through the country. Under this system, schools were held in Mandirs (temples), private residences, homes of Gurus or teachers and aristocratic people and mostly under the shed of trees. Under the strict Gurukula system the Shishya (pupils) were to live with the teacher till the course of studies was completed.

Old Education

The traditional Indian education system however, got affected under the British rule. Assam came under the British rule. Assam came under the British rule in 1826. The British could establish their sway in the Northeastern Region of India because the Ahom rulers, exhausted as they were by internal dissension, failed to protect their subjects from the ravages wrought by repeated Burmese invasions.

The internal conflicts and the repeated invasions emanating from Burma destroyed the old educational institutions and the need rose to lay the beginnings of a new system of education in conformity with the requirements of the new regime. In other provinces under the British, the indigenous system of education flourished at the time of extension of British rule. Assam's educational institutions consisted in Pathshala for Hindus, Tols for Brahmins and upper class Hindu, Madrassas for Muslims, and Satras for the Vaishnavites. The anarchy of the later Ahom times and the Burmese invasions very largely destroyed this indigenous system, therefore, new institutions were required to be created under the patronage of the new regime.

Before the charter Act of 1833, there was no noticeable progress in the field of education in view of the lack of efforts to direct the educational policies of different parts of India. There was also the controversy between the orientalists and the advocates of

Anglicised education. As far as the Assam was concerned, David Scott, Agent of the Governor-General for the Eastern Frontier, favoured the encouragement of oriental learning by improving the indigenous system of education. It was his belief that an undue emphasis on English would not only wound local sentiments and exacerbate feelings but also generate misapprehension in the public mind to the disadvantage of the rulers. Scotts ideas were largely accepted by the Government of East India Company with the result that the orientalist view prevailed at the official level as a general policy. This continued from 1813 to 1834 after which changes were brought in favour of English education.

The British and Education

The Missionaries reported to their society in England, "Commerce has raised new thoughts and awakened new energies, so that hundreds, if we could skillfully teach them graits, would crowed to learn the English language. Sir John Shore, the Acting Governor-General of Bengal wanted the introduction of the English education along with a bias of Christianity in the interest of political gain. According to him. "Until our subjects there shall be animated with us by a community of religious faith, we shall never consider our dominion as secure against the effects of external attack or internal commotion." Lord Mornington; the successor of Jhon Shore, more intelligently avoided interfering with the religious practices of the Indians and that it as his duty to get the Christian Scriptures translated into languages of the East so that the natives of the country could have the advantage of getting into the touch of Christian faith.

Thus, is found that the British Education Policy in Indian was based on British political and religious interest. Lord Macaulay's view in this respect is noteworthy, "We must at present do our best to form a class who may be interpreters between us and the millions when we govern; a class of persons, Indian in blood and colour, but English in tastes, in opinions, in moral and intellect.

The British Education Policy in India as Arthur Mayhew observes, 'aimed at the production of Government officials, lawyers, doctors, and commercial clerks and, within this narrow range, they have succeeded remarkably well. Where they have failed, almost completely, is on the cultural side.

In order to meet the problems at the administrative level, Scott proposed to appoint more local people in Government service. In order to facilitate this, it was found necessary to establish schools imparting teaching in English. Scott's plan was to establish one, English school at Guwahati so that the Assamese products from the school could at least be absorbed as clerks in the administrative service. But Scott's death in 1831 led to postponement of the implementation of the scheme. One school was, however, established at Guwahati with the help of Christian Missionaries for imparting instruction through the medium of Bengali. Obviously, English education was yet to come and Assamese was relegated to the background.

The British rulers were no novices and they must share the main responsibility for the subordinate status to which Assamese was reduced. It was in 1836 that Assamese was dislodged and Bengali became the court language and medium of instruction in schools.

The need for more schools under Government auspices to provide instruction to Assamese youths was keenly felt by Captain Jenkins, the Commissioner of Assam (1934-61). He was apparently perturbed over the fact that it was the non-Assameses who virtually monopolised all the posts in Government offices. Writing to the Government of India, he expressed the view that the few Assamese in their present uneducated state do not suffice to carry on the duties' of the courts whose offices were "mostly filled by natives of Sylhet and Raiore," in, such a situation, the old families of Assam were losing their influence `in their own native province': this state of things appear to me pregnant with evil and I know no other method by which it could remedied than by the government takings some active measure to education in the province, Jenkines pleaded with the Government of India to establish schools to impart English education to the Assamese youths at each of the Sadar stations, i.e. Guwahati, Darrang, Nowgong, and Biswanath. Without waiting for the decision of the Government Commissioner Jenkins raised public donation from the inhabitants of Guwahati with a view to starting a school there.

In June 1835, the Government of India recommended the establishment of an English School at Guwahati. Towards the end of 1835, Guwahati School was started with Mr. Singer, an European as Headmaster at a monthly salary of Rs. 150. This school came under the academic care of the Calcutta University in 1858, and it could present candidates for the first time at the entrance. Examination in 1861. Anandaram Dhekial Phukan was a product of this school.

In 1835, twenty one schools including all-total were started in the District of Kamrup. Upper Assam was under the governance of Purandar Singha up to 1838. He proposed that every Kheldar must set up a school in his jurisdiction. But the British Government annexed Upper Assam in 1838 and the proposal of Purandar Singh remained unfulfilled. In Upper Assam, a Government school was started at Sibsagar towards the end of 1841, with D'Souza as Headmaster. With the introduction of the new revenue system in 1834, in the Lower Assam Division, when a right of Patta was first distributed, the necessity of having education was felt by the people. To cater to this growing demand, James Mathie, the collector of Guwahati, submitted to the government a scheme of village education. This scheme bore the generals of our primary schools of the latter period.

He proposed for the establishment of Anglo-Vernacular School at a central site in Kamrup for higher education, and for improvement of the indigenous schools with a view of imparting education in the three R's to the masses. Though eminent educationalists like Adams Elphinstone and Munro supported the proposal, yet the attitude of the East India Company Government towards mass education was indifferent. The Government's aim was to give good education to a few rather than the many, because of the fact, it wanted educated local people to run the administration smoothly. The scheme, however, received sanction at last with the provision that its continuance in future would be determined on results.

The whole education system in British India proved to be unsatisfactory. In Assam also until the middle of the last century, we had a system of education which was ricketty to the extreme. The product of the system were only copyists, clerks, accountants, petty revenue officials, tea garden Mohorrers, Pandits and Mauzadars, and services of that type. For the development of education in India the British Parliament constituted an enquiry committee.

The responsibility fell on Sir Charles Wood to formulate a policy for the development of education in India. The dispatch made by Sir Charles Wood on 19th July 1854 to the Government of India is very well known as Wood's dispatch in the History of Education in India. The dispatch "imposed on the Government of India the duty of creating a properly articulated system of education from the primary school to university." The Government of India was told that it was "peculiarly important not only to produce of higher degree of intellectual fitness, but to raise the moral character of those who partake of its advantages, and so supply you with servants to whose probity you may with increased confidence commit offices of trusts. Spread of education in India was also necessary in the material interest of England as it would enable Indians to develop their vast resources and would secure to them a larger and more certain supply of many articles necessary for the people in Britain.

The despatch emphatically declared that the people in Britain. The despatch emphatically declared that the type of education to be imparted was to the "improved arts, sciences and literature to Europe." For historical and antiquarian purposes and for the study of Hindu and Muslim laws and for the improvement of the vernaculars, the institutions of old Indian system were not regarded as completely unnecessary. English was to be the medium of higher education, but it was not to be substituted for the vernaculars.

On the basis of this famous despatch the Government of India took some import decisions for the number of schools providing English education remained comparatively poor; rather was a rapid increase in the number of Vernacular and Middle vernacular schools in the province. Up to 1874, the number of Primary Schools was 513, Middle Vernacular Schools was only six. Up to the end of the 19th century, i.e. 1919, the total number of M.V. Schools came down to 27, the number of M.E. Schools came down to 27, the number of M.E. Schools rose up to 32 and the number of High English School became 13 only. Among all these institutions, only 11 M.V. Schools, 2 M.E. Schools and 8 English Schools were run by the government.

Towards the end of the country, it was found that the urge for English education gradually became more intensive. The Upper and the middle classes considered it very much necessary in view of the fact that for want of English education the high offices in the state became a monopoly of the Europeans or of the non-Assamese. In 1892, Jorhat Saruajanik Sabha submitted a memorial to the Commissioner of Assam and urged upon the government to give employment facilities to the soil.

Anglo-vernacular Schools: Beginning: During the last century, Assam and Assamese were not viewed in respect of educational facilities with due sympathy and proper care. Due to slow and hesitant policy of the government and their negligence in eradicating the evils, the educational progress in Assam, higher education in particular, was slow, much more slow than in Bengal. The general notion prevailing at that time was, "Assamese would never improve in European languages." Though in Bengal, the government proposed to establish central Anglo-vernacular schools at the principal districts in the expectation that the scholars who there in such schools obtain an acquaintance with the literature and science of the west, will be able to improve their own language, and to instruct their countrymen in the branches of Knowledge most useful to them.

Moreover, imposition of Bengali as the medium of instruction in Assam made the progress of education much slower. On the other hand, there was no provision for giving college education to the qualified students. The Guwahati School was raised to a Collegiate School with the F.A. class of the Calcutta University in 1865. The Collegiate School also could not desirably progress due to the small number of successful candidates at the entrance test. Difficulties arising out of a foreign medium contributed enough for the failure of a large number of candidates at the entrance examination. English was introduced from the lowest classes and was also used as the medium of instruction. Moreover, mother tongue Assamese was also not recognised even as a subject, while Bengali was the vernacular taught in the schools of Assam.

Anandram Dhekial Phukan, in his Observations on the Administration of the Province of Assam, very rightly protested against the continuance of Bengali as the medium of instructions even in schools styled vernacular schools. He pointed out, "Instructions in the schools are imparted in a foreign language, viz. Bengalee, which is but imperfectly understood by the teachers themselves, not to speak of the pupils. For the development of education in Assam, Phukan advocated for rehabilitation of assamese as the medium of instruction in the lower classes, establishment of more English Schools with competent teachers in Lower and Upper Assam and for establishment of Sanskrit College in the province.

Role of Christian Missionaries

The Christian Missionaries also deserved credit for promoting the cause of educational progress in Assam. They learnt the language of the people and acquainted themselves with the traditions of local culture and habits of doing things. In a sense, they ceased to be "foreign" at least in the matter of promoting the growth of education in the place of their work. The style of work of missionaries earned for them the confidence of the people and their self-sacrificing spirit led them to traverse long distances even to normally inaccessible places for the purpose of establishing mission societies. Rev. Nothon, Brown and Rov. A.t. Cutter were the pioneers among the missionaries: they started their work of founding schools after three months of their settlement at, Sadiya in March 1839.

Their mission was to spread the message of Christianity, and education could be extended. The pioneers were joined by other of their fraternity. The drowning of Rev. Thomas while sailing by boat on route to Sadiya, the sufferings of other Missionaries due to diseases in an unhealthy and natural discomfort in a foreign land could not dampen the spirit of the missionaries. They paid especial attention to the hilly areas. By 1844, the American Baptist Mission established 14 schools at Sibsagar. Twelve schools were established by the Welsh Mission in Khasi, Garo and Naga Hills and also in Nowgong. The Missionaries work extended to the Hills and Plains alike.

The most important feature of missionary activity in the field of education was their emphasis on education through the mother tongue. In hill which education was imparted to the hillmen. In the plains, it fell to the missionaries to uphold to claim of local languages. The missionaries had methods in their work and beyond the realm of propaganda along in defence of Assamese, they did solid work to establish the rightful claim of Assamese. They prepared textbooks and books on Assamese grammar, translated the Bible into Assamese, and Bronson prepared an Anglo-Assamese Dictionary with 14,000 words. To the missionaries goes the credit of publishing the first ever magazine Assamese, namely, Aronodoi, published in 1846 from Sibsagar. Aronodoi became a powerful vehicle of the Assamese language. The missionaries also laid stress on English education so that local scholars could extend their sphere of the activities and jobs. Primary schools and English schools claimed a great deal of their attention.

The missionaries acted as pioneers in another field, namely female education. The wives of the missionaries established zanana' schools. But in Assam, they were confronted with a number of difficulties. First, local customs disfavoured the practice of school going among the married ladies, secondly, a difficulty was posed in the matter of fixing school hours for married ladies. The result was that there was very slow progress in female education. Though, the effort of the Missionaries in this regard met with failure, they deserved appreciation as the trail blazers of female education in Assam.

Colonel Ketinge, the first Chief Commissioner of Assam, favoured the abolition of collegiate section of the Guwahati School. Towards the end of the century, the demand for opening a college became stronger. Hon'ble Manik Chandra Barua, a person of high social repute, who was also a product of the Collegiate section of the Guwahati School, submitted a memorandum in March 1899, supporting very strongly the cause of establishment of a college at Guwahati. Sir Henry John Steadman Cotton, the Chief Commissioner, though favoured the idea of more residential facilities for Assame students at Calcutta, he invited public opinion and to his great surprise, representations poured in from all quarters unanimously favouring the college and not the hostel scheme at Calcutta.

Sir Cotton without the least objection accepted the people's verdict and took immediate decision to lay the foundation of the first college in Assam. At the down of the 20th century the first college, which at the public demand was named after Sir Henry Cotton, was started. The Chief Commissioner formally opened the college in person on the 27th May, 1901. The establishment of this college had contributed to a great extent for a cultural renaissance in the province of Assam. Prior to the establishment of this college, Calcutta was the controlling centre in all respects. Even the modern Assamese literature found its development in Calcutta through the Jonaki an Assamese Monthly, edited and published by the Assamese students studying in Calcutta colleges. It is to be noted that the jonaki was also shifted from Calcutta to Guwahati in the same year, the Cotton College was started.

Ethics and Education

Values are always determined by the cultural ethos of a given society Language, aesthetics, religion, science and economics, in a unified pattern determine the behaviour and culture of a given society. Language in a given society plays an important role in the formation of a society and its values. Radhakamal Mukerjee observes, "Society through the collective focus of attention and reflection, transforms man's vital urges and fundamental interests and experiences into values, virtues and ideals. Generally agrarian societies are conservative in their attitude towards their traditional way of life and values. Therefore, the people in these societies cannot accept anything new immediately. Consequently, a conflict between the old and the new is very much natural.

Assamese Society of the 19th century, therefore, was not ready to accept the new order of the administration and the incomings of education, culture, civilization and along with them social values. Education in India as already stated could not be separated from religion. In the old informal system of education in Assam, the same character prevailed.

New Schemes: Before the arrival of the British power, institutional education, in the strict sense of the term, was somewhat unfamiliar. There were, Tols, and Chatra-Sali where only the Brahmins and Kayasthas had the privilege of having traditional education. The curriculum consisted of Sanskrit grammar, lexicon, the epics, the Puranas, and other religions works. This old system of the education planted some values firmly in the minds of the people.

Through the network of the Satras and the Namghars spread all over the country, the teachings of the Vaishnava religion were imparted almost to every adult. The writings of Shankradeva and Madhavdeva and the translation of the Ramayana, the 'Mahabharata, the Puranas and other religious and semi-religions treatise `were within the reach of the people. The Vaishnava dance drama and music were practised almost in every village besides some local folk dance and songs. The Satradhikar was highly esteemed, and in most cases in a villages his verdict was regarded supreme. Moreover, there were some other religious cults and beliefs followed by cross sections of the people.

In brief, the government's active role in the field of education of Assam was initiated by the famous educational despatch of 1854. The policy of 1854 was carried forward with appropriate changes through a number of subsequent resolutions, those of 1884, 1904; and 1913. The Government did their endeavour to introduce a comprehensive educational system in Assam as in other parts of the country, starting from the Primary to the university stage.

The government encouraged all agencies to promote the expansion of education in the state. The government accepted the policy of religious neutrality but allowed the missionaries to establish and maintain schools wherever necessary by giving them grants from provincial revenues. The missionaries made valuable contribution in the expansion of education in Assam. Moreover, the local bodies were given the power to maintain and establish primary school when necessary, while at the same type private enterprise could not open schools of any type. Donations, subscriptions endowment and trusts, were also used for the establishment of schools. The policies formulated by the government were intended to promote education by all means.

The Structure: Assam worked within the framework of these policies. The local bodies in Assam proved to be the main agency of the expansion of primary education. As far as the private missionaries concerned the work of the missionaries stood out most prominently. They paid great attention to the improvement of Assamese language and literature besides establishing schools. In fact, the missionaries were the first to the demand for recognition of Assamese as the medium of instruction. Due to their innate capacity for hard work the missionaries penetrated the backward and isolated areas and generally inaccessible hilly tracts.

Motives: Progress of Primary education was however, not at the desired level. The Acts, resolutions and schemes were not implemented effectively. Consequently education and literacy spread at snail pace. The single teacher schools, untrained teachers and prevalence of general illiteracy came in the spread of primary education. The indifference of the parents, to the proper education of their children, lack of proper environment at home involvement of children in domestic work for reasons of poverty of the family, and lack of balance between the educational and economic needs of the community as a whole.

The objective of secondary education was to produce a set of men suited to running the administration at the permissible levels. There was more stress on learning of English education, but it failed to produce practical minded educated men who could utilise their knowledge and skill in different professions. Further the system was dominated by examinations, because success in matriculation examination appeared to be summum bonum of below average or in cases even average merit could not often do well in the examination.

Collegiate education in Assam was imparted up to 1930 in two colleges, the Cotton College, and the Murarichand College. Private colleges could not prosper due to lack of official interest in regard to their needs. It was the absence of good aided colleges that led to the concentration of students in the Cotton College. The Calcutta University had a very wide jurisdiction and even with the best efforts, it could not be expected to give the time and attention needed to look after the needs of Assam's growing colleges. The need arose for a separate university in Assam. The Assam University was established in 1948.

Progress in the field of technical and special education was tardy and many of the specialised institutions relating to law, medicine, and technical and industrial education did not attain maturity even by 1937.

Progress of education depends to a great extent on trained and qualified teachers. But the small percentage of trained teachers for the entire period of our survey revealed a sorry state of affairs. There was slow progress in the matter of teachers training. Many teachers were themselves responsible for their evident lack of interest in the matter, because a sizeable section of the trainees did not complete the term time in the normal schools and left them without taking any examination. But the government's responsibility was greater, for they closed down some training schools for a number of years.

The women education also could not progress satisfactorily up to the Independence of the country.

Education System

Assam is one of the Northeastern States of India with its capital at Dispur, which is a suburb of Guwahati, the largest city in the state. Assam is located south of the eastern Himalayas, and comprises of beautiful river valleys and hills. In terms of education, Assam has developed into a top educational destination at the state as well as at the national level. To enhance the status of Assam education, the State Government has introduced many innovative education policies. It's capital city; Guwahati is a key destination for higher education for students of the whole of Northeastern Region.

School Education

School education in Assam is imparted through a number of pre-primary, primary, middle, high and higher secondary schools. The Government of Assam has implemented the free and compulsory education policy for students up to the age of 14. Schools in Assam are either state run or under the management of private organisations. The syllabus at primary schools is set up the Directorate of Elementary Education, Assam. While most schools are affiliated to state boards there are several schools in the state affiliated to the Central Board of Secondary Education (CBSE).

Higher Education

Assam boasts of the most wide-ranging networks of higher educational institutions in the whole of Northeastern Region of India. Presence of institutions like the National Institute of Technology, Silchar; Indian Institute of Technology, Guwahati and Tezpur University (a Central University) and several others help to add stature to the higher education system of Assam. The state is also home to several elite higher education institutions which include:

- Assam University,
- Guwahati University,
- Dibrugarh University,
- Assam Medical College (Dibrugarh),
- Guwahati Medical College,
- Assam Agricultural University (Jorhat),
- Assam Engineering College (Guwahati),
- K.K. Handique State Open University,
- Jorhat Engineering College (Jorhat).

Medium of Instruction

The medium of instruction in Assam at the school level is usually Assamese; though there are as few schools in the state that also use English as their medium of study. The Central Board of Secondary Education (CBSE) affiliated schools in the state use English as their medium of instruction. English is also used to teach at most higher educational institutions in Assam. Please find links below to access information about schools, colleges and universities in Assam.

Significant Schools

When it comes to education in the northeastern part of India, Schools in Assam deserves a special mention. Assam has a literacy rate of 64.28 per cent and Guwahati is the major centre of learning in the region. Over the years, the State Government has taken up several measures to enhance the standard of education in Assam. It has introduced free and compulsory education for all students up to 14 years of age. In addition, the department of education has also introduced a common academic calendar and unit tests for 10th standard students.

Vigorous monitoring of the educational institutes has also ensured quality education at the school level in the state. However, the education scenario is not too good in the tribal regions where 75 per cent of the tribal women are still illiterate.

Different Kinds of Schools

The schools in Assam are either private or run by government. Most of the schools in Assam are equipped with modern infrastructure and facilities. Residential and convent schools are also there for the students to join. The schools are affiliated to either Assam Council of Secondary and Higher Secondary Education or CBSE or ICSE.

Number of Schools

The total number of schools in Assam is approximately 37,652. Most of the schools in this state are known for imparting quality education to the students.

Medium of Teaching

Most of the schools in Assam have Assamese as the medium of instruction. However, one can also come across English medium schools in the state. The public schools also use Bengali as the medium of instruction.

Drop Outs in Schools

The drop out rate among girl students at the primary level in schools is 42 per cent. It is 72 per cent and 75 per cent at the middle and high school level respectively.

Famous Schools

Some of the popular schools in Assam are DPS Digboi, Saint Mary High School, Don Bosco, Guwahati, Gurukul Grammar Senior Secondary School and Army School, Narangi, Guwahati. One can also come across several CBSE affiliated schools in the state like Kendriya Vidyalaya Nagaon, Kendriya Vidyalaya, AFS, Chabua, Kendriya Vidyalaya Hathimatha Kokrajhar, Kendriya Vidyalaya, Khanapara Kamrup, Kendriya Vidyalaya 9th Mile, Kendriya Vidyalaya, Doomdooma, Kendriya Vidyalaya Haflon and Kendriya Vidyalaya IOC, Noonmati.

Significant Colleges

Higher Education

Assam boasts of one of the most widespread network of higher education institutions in the whole of Northeastern Region of India. It has the maximum number of colleges and universities as compared to the other states in North-East Region in India. The male literacy rate in the state is higher than the literacy rate recorded amongst the female population. According to the 2001 census, the literacy in Assam was at 63.30 per cent with female literacy at 54.60 per cent and male at 71.30 per cent. The dropout rate is higher among the tribal women in the state as compared to the men. In the recent years, the state has made strides in introducing several high standard institutions to offer education various disciplines.

Courses Offered at Colleges

The colleges in Assam offer a wide range of courses in various subjects. Students can apply for specialised courses such as Bachelor of Science in Agriculture, B.Arch., B.Tech. in Biotechnology and several other degree programmes. The Government Ayurvedic College also offers courses on the age old principle of Ayurveda. These include Ayurvedacharya and Ayurved Vachaspati. Other courses offered by different colleges in Assam include LL.B., Diploma in Pharmacy, Bachelor of Veterinary Science, B.H.M.S., B.E./B.Tech. in Mechanical Engineering, Electrical Engineering, Chemical Engineering and Civil Engineering.

Affiliations

Various colleges of higher education in Assam are affiliated to top universities in the state. Most of the leading colleges in are affiliated to Guwahati University. Other universities to which the colleges of Assam are affiliated include Assam Agricultural University in Jorhat, Assam University and Dibrugarh University. Most of these affiliated universities are AICTE Approved.

Top Colleges

There are numerous leading colleges in Assam that cater to students in the state as well as other parts of the North Eastern region. Colleges under the Assam Agricultural University include B. N. College of Agriculture, Viswanatha Chariall, Sonitpur, College of Agriculture, Jorhat B, College of Home Science, AAU, Jorhat and College of Fisheries Sc, Raha. Leading engineering colleges in Assam include Jorhat Engineering College, Assam Engineering College and National Institute of Technology. Assam also has a dental college known as Regional Dental College located in Guwahati.

Some of the law colleges of Assam include Bongaigaon Law College, Dispur Law College, A. K. Chanda Law College, Barpeta Law College, DHSK Law College, Dr. R. K. Barua Law College and Jorhat Law College. Other renowned colleges in Assam include Guwahati College of Architecture and Pandu College (Department of Biotechnology).

Famous Institutions and Universities

Assam Engineering College

Assam Engineering College established in 1955 is located in Jalukbari area of Guwahati city. It is the premier technical institute of the entire North East India. It is the first under graduate engineering college in the Northeastern India and today becomes a premier technical institute of the entire country. AEC has been the hub centre of many academic and supplementary activities in Assam for almost half a century. The college is approved by the All India Council for Technical Education AICTE. The college offers Bachelor courses (BE) on the fields of Electrical engineering, Chemical Engeneering, Civil

Engeneering, Computer Sc. and Engineering., Electronics and Telecommunication Engineering., Industrial and Prod. Engineering., Instrumentation Engineering. and Mechanical Engineering. It also offers Masters courses on Computer Application (MCA), Computer Sc. and Engineering (ME), Civil Engineering (ME), Industrial and Prod. Engineering (ME). It also offers Ph.D. facility in Soil Mechanics and Hydraulics. All the courses are affliated to Guwahati University, the educational hub of the entire North-East Region.

Indian Institute of Technology Guwahati

Indian Institute of Technology Guwahati is an autonomous engineering and technology-oriented institute of higher education established by the Government of India, located in Guwahati, in the state of Assam in India. It is the sixth member of the IIT fraternity.

IITG is officially recognised as an Institute of National Importance by the Government of India. The institute consistently ranks amongst the top engineering colleges in the academic ranking of Indian colleges by various engineering education surveys like India Today, Dataquest, etc.

Jorhat Engineering College

The Jorhat Engineering College was established in 1960 by the Govt. of Assam. It is one of the premier technical colleges in the Northeastern Region. The college as well as all the courses are recognised by the All India Council for Technical Education (AICTE) and affiliated to The Dibrugarh University, Dibrugarh, Assam.

Jorhat Engineering College was set up with an intention of providing an efficient system of education and to cater to the needs of technical manpower in the Northeastern Region of the country. The college now offers four year under graduate courses in five disciplines, viz. Civil Engineering, Computer Science and Engineering, Electrical Engineering, Instrumentation Engineering and Mechanical Engineering, one three year post-graduate course in Computer Application leading to The Master of Computer Application (M.C.A.) degree, and a post-graduate degree in Production Engineering under the Mechanical Engineering Department from the session July 2004. Each department of the college has a well equipped laboratory. The well organised Workshop of the college provides exhaustive hands-on-training to the students. The college maintains a good relationship with the leading Industrial Organisations of the region by extending consultancy services and through industry-institute interaction programmes.

National Institute of Technology, Silchar

National Institute Of Technology Silchar (NIT Silchar), an Institute of National Importance under the NIT Act was established in 1967 as a Regional Engineering College (REC), Silchar. NIT Silchar is situated on the banks of river Barak. In year 2002, it was upgraded to the status of an NIT from a Regional Engineering College (REC).

In Infrastructure parameter, NIT silchar comes in 1st place among all NITs. And comes behind IIT-B and IIT-D in overall ranking in India. This is also according to DQ ratings. The institute has undergone rapid and radical transformation in its Infrastructure and Academic facilities during the last 4 years since its upgradation to NIT.

Silchar is a district headquarter of Cachar, Assam. Being a peaceful place in the North-East earned it the bon mot of "Island of Peace" from India's Prime Minister Indira Gandhi. Silchar has become a centre of Education in Assam, with one NIT, side by side with a Medical College.

Girijananda Chowdhury Institute of Management and Technology

Girijananda Chowdhury Institute of Management and Technology (commonly known as GIMT or sometimes GCIMT) is the first institute offering degree level technical course in the state of Assam in the non-government sector established by Shrimanta Shankar Academy (SSA) Society. The college is established with prior permission from the State Government and approval from the All India Council for Technical Education (AICTE), New Delhi and is affiliated to Guwahati University.

Assam Medical College

Assam Medical College was formally established on November 3, 1947 at Dibrugarh. It was, however, earlier known as Dr. John Berry White Medical School, which was established in 1902. It has the distinction of being the first medical college in the entire Northeastern Region of India. Following the establishment of 2 other medical colleges in Assam, one at Guwahati and another at Silchar, it now serves as the tertiary medical referral centre for the entire upper Assam as well as the some areas of neighbouring states, especially Arunachal Pradesh.

The college is situated at one corner of Dibrugarh and set in the midst of flowing green fields of several Tea Estates. Some buildings are modifications of the original British architecture, although several new constructions have come up recently under the joint collaboration of both the North Eastern Council and State Government to upgrade the college to a premier medical institution of Asia once again. The main charm that draws almost 150 undergraduate and 50 post-graduate students to this college every year is the campus life it has to offer. 14 hostels for the students ensure that everyone, excluding a minority of day-boarders, stay together within the lavish campus area; consequently everybody knows everybody, if only by face. The campus also contains staff quarters, meaning professors and students are always in close contact. The college boasts for some of the best teachers of the respective fields. The college is also proud to have some great principals from time to time of which one has also won the Padmashree award. Right now the college is in full gear for its preparations for the upcoming Diamond jubilee celebrations to be celebrated in November 2007.

In addition to the medical courses, also available are paramedical courses, viz. Nursing and Midwifery and Diploma in Pharmacy.

In a recent nation wide survey, the Assam Medical College and Hospital was ranked amongst the top 10 medical college in the country.

Guwahati Medical College and Hospital

Guwahati Medical College and Hospital (GMCH) is located in Guwahati, Northeastern India.

Graduate Education: Degree Awarded: M.B.B.S. Duration of the Course: Five years, which include one year internship. Major subjects: Anatomy, Physiology, Biochemistry, Pharmacology, Pathology, Microbiology, Forensic and State Medicine, Community Medicine, Medicine, Surgery (which includes Orthopedics), Paediatrics, Obstetrics and Gynaecology, Ophthalmology and Otorhinolaryngology. University of Affiliation: Guwahati University. Medical Council of India recognises M.B.B.S. Degree.

Assam University

Assam University is a teaching-cum-affiliating university. The university has nine schools which offer Social Sciences, Humanities, Languages, Life Sciences, Physical Sciences, Environmental Sciences, Information Sciences, Technology and Management Studies. There are 29 Departments under these nine schools. The five districts under the jurisdiction of Assam University have 51 Undergraduate Colleges. Drawing its faculty from many disciplines, from all over the country, the university sustains a multidisciplinary approach to higher education.

The campus, in an area of 600 acres, is situated at Dargakona, about 20 km from Silchar. The university is situated in South Assam, bordering Bangladesh, Mizoram, Manipur, Maghalaya, and Nagaland.

Guwahati University

Guwahati University, the first University of North East India, located in Jalukbari area in the western part Guwahati city, Assam, India the university was established in the year 1948. It is a four star university rating by the National Assessment and Accreditation Council. It has 183 affiliated colleges.

The university is located at Jalukbari within the Guwahati city area. The campus has got some hillock on the southern side and the mighty river Brahmaputra is flowing on the northern side of it. The campus areas has been developed to a small township, now known as 'Gopinath Bardoloi Nagar'. It has now about 5,000 population including 3,000 students residing in the hostels. Apart from the residential quarters of teachers, officers and employees of the university, there are 22 halls of residence for university students. The necessary civic amenities such as health service, water supply, street lighting, internal roads, guest house, Post and Telegraph office, a branch of State Bank of India, canteens, a market, parks, playgrounds, auditorium, indoor stadium, etc. are provided in the campus. The university is 10 km from the Borjhar International Airport on National Highway No. 37; 5 km from Kamakhya Railway Station; and 10 km from Guwahati Railway Station as well as from the Bus stop near the Cachari (D. C. court) at the heart of the Guwahati City. The capital complex of Assam at Dispur is 22 km away from the university. The university is easily accessible from the Guwahati city, and Guwahati has road, rail and air links from all parts of the Country. A large number of bus services from various parts of Assam have their station at Adabari Bus Stand which is 2 km away from the campus.

To automate the internal processes within the university, Guwahati University has chosen Kalingasoft's flagship Education ERP solution, Greycells. This implementation has resulted in the complete automation of the university's Academic, Administrative and Financial processes under a single solution. The prestigious Bholanath College of Dhubri is affiliated with this university.

Tezpur University

Tezpur University is an Indian Central University located in Tezpur in the state of Assam, India. The university campus is at Napaam about 15 km. East of Tezpur, the head quarter of Sonitpur District of Assam. Napaam is a rural area surrounded by peace loving people of diverse caste, religion and language; yet it presents the unique feature of unity in diversity. The Napaam campus of the university is in a plot of an area of 242 acres (0.98 sq km) of land.

The campus is bounded by pucca walls. Napaam is linked by a PWD road from the National Highway No. 37A at almost midpoint between Kalia-Bhomora bridge and Misson Chariali. Tezpur is linked by road and rail with the rest of the state and the country. There is also a tri-weekly flight service between Kolkata and Tezpur. The institute is situated in a scenic place called *Napaam* surrounded by greenery and with many historic as well as tourist places nearby, including Ganesh Ghat, Agnigarh, etc.

Assam Agricultural University

Assam Agricultural University (AAU) was established in 1969 under the Assam Agricultural University Act 1968 January 2, 1969. The jurisdiction of the university extends to the entire State of Assam with regard to teaching, research and extension education in the field of agriculture and allied sciences. The university has a number of campuses with its head quarter located at Borbheta at a distance of about 5 km from both bus station and railway station and 2 km from airport of the Jorhat. The city can be reached easily from Guwahati, the capital of Assam, by Air/Road/Rail. The latitude, longitude and altitude of Jorhat are 26°44′N, 94°10′E and 91 m above mean sea level respectively. The objectives of the university are:

- to make provision for imparting education to the people in agriculture and other allied branches of learning.

- to further the advancement of learning and research in agriculture and other allied sciences.

- to undertake the extension of such sciences especially to the rural people of the state.

Assam Institute of Management

Assam Institute of Management (AIM) is an Institution providing post-graduate courses in management in Assam, India.

It was established in 1988 by the Government of Assam to promote professional education in North East India. It is run as a Government of Assam Society, the chief Secretary of the State being the chairperson of the Governing Body. The institution has offered a Post-Graduate Diploma in Business Management (PGDBM) since 1994, approved by AICTE. Its courses are modelled on courses offered by the Indian Institute of Management.

Apart from PGDBM, the Institute also offers a course in Post-Graduate Diploma In Travel and Tourism Management Industry (PGDTTIM).

Jorhat College

Jorhat College (Amalgamated) is an undergraduate humanities college located in Jorhat, Assam, India. It offers two- and three-year degrees as well as vocational training.

The college was formerly two separate institutions, Jorhat College and New Jorhat College. Both formed in 1962, the former was initially a night school created to serve economically disadvantaged students, while the New Jorhat College was a day school. In 1967, the original Jorhat College began construction of its own campus. Given economic depression in the region, the two schools amalgamated in 1970 under the guidance of principal Bidyakanta Baruah. In the early 1970s, the college affiliated with Dibrugarh University. For many years the college continued offering night courses, but eventually economic difficulties forced the school to discontinue.

Institute of Hotel Management

The Institute of Hotel Management, Catering Technology and Applied Nutrition, Guwahati is an education institution for training students in hotel management, catering technology, general food management, and allied subjects, located in Guwahati, the capital of Assam, India. It was established by the Ministry of Tourism of the Government of India in 1984 as the Food Craft Institute. It was upgraded to an Institute of Hotel Management in 1995 and is affiliated with National Council for Hotel Management, Noida.

Centre for Management Studies, Dibrugarh University

The Centre for Management Studies, Dibrugarh University (CMSDU) is the easternmost Management School of India and started functioning on February 3, 2003 with the holding of classes for the first batch of Master of Business Administration (MBA) students. Since then, the centre has made tremendous strides by introducing newer programmes of study, doing consultancy work and becoming a platform for the interaction of industry and academia. The 3 – year Bachelor of Business Administration (BBA) and the 3 – year MBA (Part Time) classes started in the year 2004. 2006 saw the launch of the 1 – year PGDTM (Post-graduate Diploma in Tourism Management) Programme. There is also a Research Programme in Management.

Since its inception, CMS has left no stone unturned to provide inspiring and contemporary education, keeping in mind the corporate environment and providing its students a greater exposure towards the same. Amidst certain strains and obstacles, CMS has completed more than three years of its existence with flying colours, bringing along with it laurels and glory. Team CMS is committed to developing professionals who are committed to excellence in their personal and professional endeavours and who have the vision, courage and dedication to initiate and manage change. As part of its activities related to providing quality consultancy services to the Industry, a 'Consultancy Cell' has been made operational. Named *Parivartan*, it is striving to provide management consultancy in the fields of Marketing, Finance and Human Resource Development besides undertaking Training and Development (T&D) programmes.

Cotton College

Cotton College is a premier institution for higher education located in the heart of Guwahati, Assam, a Northeastern State of India.

Cotton College was declared open on May 27, 1901 by Sir Henry John Stedman Cotton, the then-Chief Commissioner of the erstwhile British province of Assam. The college was named after Sir Henry, as the "Cotton College", in appreciation of his genuine concern for the cause of higher education in the province. The college was started with five professors, which included Frederick William Sudmerson, the first principal of the college, and 39 students.

Cotton College was the centre of the freedom movement and the literary and cultural movements of the country to build the identity of Assam as a distinct integral component of the Nation.

From a small undergraduate college, Cotton College has now become a post-graduate institution, integrated with undergraduate education having enrolled 5,000 students and 244 teachers, among 21 undergraduate and 20 post-graduate departments in science, humanities and social science faculties.

On October 16, 1992, the college was declared as a post-graduate institution, an occasion celebrated in a solemn ceremony with Shankar Dayal Sharma, the then-President of India.

Cotton College celebrated its centennial with year-long programme from May 27, 2001 to May 26, 2002. Krishan Kant, the then-Vice President of India graced the closing ceremony.

Cotton College has produced numerous talents including politicians, authors, athletes, and artists.

Diphu Government College

Diphu Government College was established in 1964 in Diphu with the main aim of providing higher education in the backward Karbi Anglong District of Assam. Distinguished local leaders of that time like Chatrasing Teron, Chandra sing Teron, Dhaniram Rongpi, Gojendra Nath Goswami, Joysing Doloi, Sar Rongpi, P. K. Baruah were among its founders. When the academic session started from July, 1965. Prof. P. K. Bhuyan was the first Principal of the college. Thus began a new venture in the field of higher education.

In the year 1967, it was taken over by the Government of Assam and since then the college has never looked back. Within a few years the college got its own building which provides accommodation for class rooms, office room, department staff rooms, auditorium, library, etc. Besides, there are two Girls' Hostels and one Boys' hostel. There are 23 quarters for teachers and 8 quarters for non-teaching staff in addition to one full furnished official residence for Principal. Over the years, the college made much progress in infrastructural development out of grants received from several sources like UGC, KAAC, Govt. of India, Govt. of Assam and from MP LAD fund. The college has a beautiful botanical garden cum recreation park, one peace park, one state of art Auditorium with all facilities, Seminar Hall (A/C), Cultural Museum, etc.

Distance Learning

Distance Learning Courses

Assam is one of the North Eastern States of India located in south of the eastern Himalayas. There are a number of students in the state who are unable to complete or pursue their higher education through regular institutes and universities due to various reasons. The opening of various Assam distance learning institutes and colleges have provided opportunities to thousands of students who do not have access to higher education institutes in their place of residence and also to working professionals who wish to upgrade their qualifications.

Distance Learning Institutes

There are a few distance learning institutes in Assam offering degree as well as professional and vocational courses in a number of disciplines.

The leading university in Assam offering distance learning in Assam is the Post-Graduate Correspondence School (PGCS), Guwahati University. This correspondence school was established in May, 1998 with an aim to facilitate higher education for the vast number of students who could not enrol as regular students for various reasons. The school provides students an opportunity to obtain a PG degree of the Guwahati University through the mode of distance education. The degree offered by PGCS has the same standing as the regular post-graduate degree given that the syllabi for both courses are the same.

Krishna Kanta Handique Open University (KKHOU): The Krishna Kanta Handique State Open University is first of its kind in the entire North East. It was established by the Assam Legislative Assembly by an Act (XXXVII of 2005) in the year 1995. This Open University had officially started functioning since 11th December, 2006. The Krishna Kanta Handique State Open University was set up with the aim of providing higher education opportunities to a large segment of the population and also to promote Open University and distance education system in Assam.

Language and Literature

Language

Assamese

Assamiya or Assamese is the language of Assam, although English, Hindi and Bangla are also used in different walks of life in the region. Assamiya was relegated to the background for some time by the British, although consequent upon a prolonged public protest and agitation they had to withdraw their order. During the initial period of their rule, the British found that an overriding majority of the Assam natives were unlettered and only very few could use English. Resultantly with no malice towards the Assamese, the British had to immigrate thousands of literate Bengalis to run their administration. Unfortunately the British fell prey to the forceful demand of the Bengali elite that their *lingua franca*, i.e. Bangla should be made the official 'language of Assam.

The Bengalis had their vested interest but it caused a great damage to the Assamiya language and literature. Viewed minutely, one would find that the seeds of discordance between the Assamese and the Baharkatya, i.e. aliens particularly the Bengalis were sown with this unjust and unthought of action of the then British authority. Although this unjust act was reversed after some years yet the discontentment between the two communities never died out and a simmering ill-will continued unabated which burst in the form of current Assam problem. Based on the observations of those fateful years some scholars have erroneously called *Assamiya* a dialect of the Bangla.

Assamiya and Bangla, the two neighbouring languages are said to have originated from Magadhi. Thus Assamiya belongs to the Aryan groups of languages. An in-depth probe reveals that Assamiya emerged out of Sanskrit, Prakrit and Apbhramsha Magadhi. Prachya Apbharmsha was once the language of the Gauda Kingdom. Gauda (Malda of the present day) was the capital of this kingdom. This language led to the evolution of Bangla and Assamiya towards east and that of Oriya, outwards.

At a later stage Assamiya came under the impact of some other Asiatic languages. The impacts of the Burmese, Chinese and Tibetan language are indicative of the contact of Assam with these neighbouring regions. In the context of degree of impact it is probably the Burmese language (the language of Ahom people) which stands distinctly at the top. Assamiya does not have the sound of *Ch*; thus *Ch* becomes *S* and similarly *S* becomes *Kh* in Assamiya. These are the characteristics of the Ahom language. It goes to the credit of the Ahoms, who ruled for nearly seven centuries (12th century AD to 18th century AD), that instead of thrusting their own language on their subjects they accepted the native language as the official language which no doubt because of obvious reasons could not avoid the impact of the Ahom language. Words like *pung* (my), *Karen* (palace) and *pruva* (coal), etc. have come into Assamiya through Ahom language.

The Assamiya language contains some traits of Magadha and Bihari dialects. A majority of the tea garden labourers and construction workers have always immigrated from Bihar and no wonder one finds a fairly good impact of the dialects of this region on Assamiya. As would be explained in the context of the current Assam problem, one finds people of many other regions of the subcontinent settled in Assam. It is obvious that one would find the influence of languages like Marathi, Marwari, Punjabi and Nepali in Assamiya. Apart from language, even arts and crafts of Assam also carry outside impact. But it is surprisingly true that neither the language nor art and culture of Assam carry any Dravidian traces, although scholars are of the opinion that Assam was once an abode of the Dravidians also.

As far as the ancient literature of Assam is concerned, Huen-T-sang has said that scholars craving for more and advanced knowledge used to come to this part of India. The copper plates found at Vidhanpur speak amply about the ancient literary achievements of the Assam valley. After the dissolution of the Hindu Kingdom of Kamrup, it was the Kamta Kingdom centred around Guwahati that came to dominate the region during the thirteenth century. One Kamta ruler, Raja Durlabhanarayan patronised two great poets, Harihar Vipra and Hema Saraswati. They wrote Babruvahan Yudha, Lava Kusha Yudha and Prahlada Charitra. Another poet Kaviratna Saraswati wrote Jaydaratha Vadha.

In the early period of Assamiya literature Madhva Kanwali, a leading court poet of Raja Mahamanikya translated Valmiki Ramayana in Assamiya. Nonetheless, it was the saint poet Shankradeva (1449-1568) who has left an unparalleled impact on the old literature of Assam. Through his verses, preachings and practices he succeeded in bridging the gulf that separated the high and low, the haves and have-nots of different communities. Shankradeva also translated the Ramayana and Srimad Bhagvadgita in Assamiya. Bhattdeva also brought out Assamiya renderings of these two treatises. Raja Naranarayan of Cooch Behar patronised many scholars for academic pursuits in the fields of Astrology,

Astronomy, Grammar and Mathematics during the 16th century. In the following century the Ahom rulers entered the portals of Hinduism and made efforts to propagate this religion. Three Kings, viz. Rudra Singh, Shiba Singh and Rajeshwara Singh did a yeoman's service in this regard. It was during their times that Kaviraja Chakravarti translated the Brahmavairat Purana and Kalidas's Shakuntla in Assamiya. Raja Rajeshwara Singh was himself a dramatist of no mean standard. Keecha Vadha drama flowed out of his pen while he extended all help and support to Surya Kumar Buyan for the translation of Naradivya Prakasha. Kavi Shekhar Bhattacharya composed Kama Shastri in Assamiya for imparting knowledge of sex to the young Prince Charu Singh, the heir apparent after Raja Rajeshwara Singh. On the insistence and inspiration of Raja Shiba Singh and Rani Ambika Devi, Sukumara Barkaith produced a volume of Hastika Viddharnava that dealt with the taming and care of wild elephants. This title was amply illustrated. During the same period Mrigavati Charit of Ramadwija and Sant Sampradaya of Gobind Das found favour with the devout people.

In the modern age of the Assamiya literature it were the Baptist missionaries who rendered a commendable service for reviving it. In the eighteenth century AD they adopted Assamiya as a medium of their preachings. Atma Ram Sharma produced an Assamiya rendering of the New Testament which was published by the Christian Mission. The Mission also put up the first Assamiya printing press at Sibsagar and brought out a primer in Assamiya. Anand Ram Dhekyal a staunch and untiring advocate of the Assamiya brought out the first grammar of this language in 1855. The first Assamiya dictionary was brought out by Jaduram Barua. In the post-Partition period many and varied steps have been taken to propagate Assamiya language and literature. It was in the year 1960 that Assamiya was accorded the status of a regional language.

Saint Poet Shankradeva and the Assamese Culture: Sixteenth century AD is aptly called the period of religious uplift, social emancipation and general awakening of Assam. The major credit for such happy state of affairs goes to the saint poet Shankradeva. The commendable work done in the realms of religion and social order by Saint Shankradeva is similar to the one rendered by the Arya Samaj leader Swami Dayananda in Northern India in the ninteenth century AD. Looking at the works of Shankradeva, one is led to believe that this great poet was an incarnation of a great soul. It is gathered that the people of Alipukhari (the native village of the saint poet) witnessed some miracles at the time of birth of this great soul. Bells, couch shells and other musical instruments got automatically played upon. The worship lamps placed in temples, shrines and in front of deity idols got lighted automatically. The clouds started thundering in the sky.

Shankradeva was born to Kusumpar Bhuyan, a respectable and devout Kayastha of Alipukhari village. The young child lost his parents within one year of his birth. He was, nonetheless, brought up with all the care by his maternal grandmother Shrimati Khersuti Ayi. Right from his childhood Shankradeva exhibited unusual physical strength and he was rated as a first-class playmate by his friends. When he attained youth he is said to have attained physical strength and prowess of no mean order. He is believed to have caught hold an amuck bull from his horns and effectively controlled the animal. Once he is said to have chased a fleeing deer and succeeded in catching hold of the creature. He is also believed to have swam across the flooded Brahmputra many a time. His grandmother, however, was not happy with all his physical feats and she once scolded him calling a beast.

This remark pinched him and he decided then and there to receive spiritual knowledge. He joined the school run by Pandit Kandali, a great scholar of his time. Shankradeva devoted himself to studies. At the age of fifteen he composed his first verse which pleased his teacher beyond description. Shankradeva was such a laborious lad that he made maximum and fruitful use of every moment of time. Apart from pursuing his studies, he served his teacher and at times looked after the school in the capacity of a watchman. Once while attending to the latter job during day, he fall asleep. While he was asleep a huge black cobra sat near his head providing shelter to the sleeping lad by way of his hood. When Pandit Kandali saw this scene that a destroyer of life was protecting Shankradeva against sunshine, he was convinced that Shankradeva was an unusual human being gifted with spiritual and divine power. Besides getting knowledge of the Vedas and other religious titles, he learnt Yoga and music. And later on he sang his verses to the tune of musical instruments for preaching his cult.

Shankradeva led household life also. He got married at the age of twenty three. Unfortunately his spouse died shortly thereafter, after being delivered of a female child. Shankradeva then left on a 12-year pilgrimage to all the important religious places of northern India. After this long sojourn he returned to Assam and got remarried to settle down in Dhuanhat. Here he came across a brilliant youngman Madhav, whom he accepted in his fold after a rigorous test of his capabilities.

The cult and preachings preached by Shankradeva and his followers were non-traditional and also made a severe attack on the preachings of the conventionalists. The conventionalists were greatly dissatisfied and got aggrieved by Shankradeva and his men. Resultantly they approached the then Ahom ruler Chahungmung Swargadeva and urged upon him to punish the person who had hurt the customs and traditions long preserved. Shankradeva was brought as a captive to the court of the ruler.

The ruler was, nonetheless, impressed by the countenance and arguments of the young saint. He arranged a debate on the disputed issues between him and it group of traditionalist priests. These priests were no match for the scholarly spiritual leader. They could find no answer to many of his logical arguments. So pleased was the King that he honourably freed the scholarly saint and promised him all help and support in his mission. The rivals, however, were not to be cowed down. They took recourse to underhand means and intrigues to liquidate Shankradeva. With the connivance of some court officials and outlaws they disturbed and disrupted a religious meet organised by Madhav, his principal follower, and Hari, the son in law of Shankradeva. They were charged for disturbing law and order and convicted for this crime.

The royal court ordered them to be trampled by elephants. Madhav was a brahmachari (youngman given to life-long celibacy) and as per tradition could not be put to death but Hari was executed. This unfortunate but fateful event greatly distressed Shankradeva who quit the Ahom rule and went to the Kochh Kingdom. Here also he was pesterised by the traditionalists who arranged a debate with him. In this debate some traditionalists from Kashi also participated. The debate continued for two days. Finding no side losing ground the King announced that the side which succeeded in rendering an easy and comprehensible Assamiya translation of Bhagvat Puran in one night would emerge victorious. It was, however, Shankradeva who won the day. At the age of 119 one day the great saint called all his followers and devotees to a religious gathering where amidst religious chants and discourses, he is said to have given up his mortal self in 1568 AD.

The contributions of Shankradeva to the Assamiya literature, Assam's cultural and spiritual life, history and society were not only great but have so far remained unparallel. He in a way brought a silent and non-violent revolution in the Assam society. Status variations, caste-colour distinctions, communal differences and many other such evils started slowly and gradually disappearing without any mass revolt. He thus worked for the cause of socio-economic integration in this region. He himself was a poet and dramatist. He translated Ramayana and Bhagvadgita in Assamiya and wrote plays in this language. He presented such plays and it was his personal touch that appealed the masses.

The religious movement initiated by Shankradeva gave birth to a universal brotherhood. He replaced the ritual of animal as well as human sacrifice by meditation, worship, religious discourses and religious singings. He convinced the masses that through such acts the mind gets diverted from physical pleasures and is attracted to spiritual peace and social welfare. He preached against caste distinctions and also worked for a classless and egalitarian social order. He also succeeded in replacing the superstitious order by spiritual awakening. He was an exponent of the Vaishnava cult of Hinduism and his preached faith came to be known as Bhagvati in Assam. The religious singings pursued by him were called *Nam Kirtan*. The cult of Nam Kirtan became so popular that every village of Assam came to be adorned with a Nam Kirtan house where people of all ages, all stratas of society, all castes, etc. used to participate in common religious chants and the like. Plays based on such religious feelings were also exhibited in these houses.

The Nam Kirtan houses in due course of time became the nerve centres of social and religious activities of the villages. He also initiated the Satra tradition. The Satras were spiritual schools run under the care of scholarly persons, named as Gosains or Satradhikaris. Such officials were given to life-long celibacy. The institutions also worked as havens of art, music and crafts. By this time the Assam society had come to be divided on the basis of classes, castes and communities and such developments had started adversely affecting the sociocultural spectrum of Assam. The faith propagated by Shankradeva was intercaste in nature, international in spirit and democratic in content. In nut shell it may be said that this widely-travelled as well as well-read spiritual giant and a social stalwart contributed a lot to the sociocultural life of Assam. The revival of his teachings in a meaningful way is surely to put an and to the social, political and economic ills of the present-day Assam.

Literature

The Tongue: The language of the state of Assam is called *Asamiya*, *Assamese* in English. Assamese should not however, be taken as a Tibet-Burman language. It is a full-fledged modern Indo-Aryan language both in respect of grammatical structure and vocables.

Like Bengali and Oriya, Assamese also originated from the Prachya Apabhramsa.

The antiquity of the Assamese language goes back to the seventh century of the Christian Era. During the first half of the seventh century AD on the invitation of Bhaskaravarman, King of Kamrupa (earlier name of Assam), the Chinese pilgrim, Hiuen Tsang visited the province. In course of his reference to various aspects of the Kingdom of Kamarupa he spoke of its language as 'slightly differing' from that of mid India. From this account of Hiuen Tsang, it can be known that by the seventh century the Indo-Aryan language had penetrated into Assam and that this Aryan language spoken in the province differed to a certain extent from the Magadhi dialects then current in mid India. The earlier specimens of the Assamese language are discoverable in the place names and proper names occurring in the old inscriptions.

Other specimens of language of its formative period are noticeable in the songs and aphorisms composed by the Tantric Buddhist Acharyas between the eight and the twelfth centuries AD and commonly known as Charyas. Bengali scholars consider these Charyas to be the specimens of early Bengali. But on examination it appears that their language represents the latest phase of the Magadhi Apabharamsa, and as such it presumes to a considerable extent the earliest forms of the eastern new Indo-Aryan language namely Bengali; Assamese and Oriya. Dr. Banikanta Kakati has ably shown how certain phonological and morphological peculiarities registered in these songs have come down in unbroken continuity to modern Assamese.

Geographically, Assam is located in the midst of speakers of Austric and Tibeto-Chinese language. It is therefore, natural that these languages would greatly influence the phonological and morphological traits of Assamese. Dr. Kakati traced Austric influences in Assamese to three languages, namely, Khasi, Kolarian, and Malyan. He states, further, that Austrict elements constitute an essential substratum of Assamese vocabulary. The vocables that are regarded in Assamese as indigenous have mostly been taken over from the Austric speakers. The slang words denoting sex-life and sex-organs, the terms that denote closest family relationship according to varied grades of life and the names of various descriptions of animals seem to go back to Austric source.

So too, do the names of places such as Kamrupa, Kamakhya, Pragjyotisa, Tezpur, etc. Austric endings are easily recognised in the names of villages; the most distinctive are — to (Chamata) and — tul (Dharamtul). Of the other languages, the Bodo or Kachari and the Ahom contributed a large number of vocables. The Bodo speakers and the Ahoms both ruled over Assam at different historical periods and this led largely to the influences on the Assamese. Assamese have received from these languages a large number of words relating to the names of places, rivers, hills and objects of nature, of all the new Indo-Aryan languages; Assamese has had most contact with these languages.

It should however, be noted that the extent of non-Aryan influences does not appear to be so great as to change the entire Aryan structure of the language. This seems, as pointed out by Dr. Kakati due to two outstanding historical facts. Assam always lay on the highway for emigrants for all parts of India to the Far East, and this kept Assam in constant contact with the rest of Aryan-speaking India, and checked non-Aryan tendencies from making any radical changes in the structure of Assamese. Then there was the rise of standard literature in the early part of the fourteenth century that exercised a stabilising influence upon the speech and resisted the in-roads of non-Aryan idioms to a considerable extent.

Vocabulary in Assamese is largely derived from Sanskrit, its morphological structure is also based on Sanskrit grammar. In spoken dialect, however, the original Sanskrit word is sparingly used, and they are mostly replaced by Tadbhava or Ardhatatsama words. For instead of Satya, Shloka, Svada, an Assamese villager will say Salt, Solok, Svad. The derived words often betray a good deal of semantic variations. For Gar from Sanskrit Ganda in Assamese means Rhino; xah from Sasya means Kernel of a fruit, Yatra from Yantra (apparatus) means a spinning wheel, Chereki from Chakra (wheel) means an apparatus for winding yarn.

Inclusion of Indo-Aryan Languages: Assamese is all along a borrowing language and as such it has been borrowing a great number of words from other new Indo-Aryan languages also. Homely Assamese words, often with slight alterations in meaning, show parallel equivalents in Oriya, Bengali, Bihari, Urdu, Hindustani and other western languages. These might have descended as observed by Dr. Kakati from common sources, and in some cases might also have been due to migration and interprovincial contacts. Certain Assamese words have parallel formation in western languages like Marathi and Gujrati, which the other modern north Indian languages do not seem to possess. For example, Beji (needle) Barangani (subscription), Khabani (scraper), Tangaran (edition of a book), and so on and so forth.

Assamese has also received the Persian and Arabic words, chiefly the administrative terms and legal phraseology. English words in recent years are making a heavy inroad into Assamese. The intrusions of Persian, Arabic and English words lead to the formation of hybrids. We have such hybrid compounds as *Lebera-hata* (left-handed), *Kaladila* (flower of banana tree), *Head-Pandit* (Head-Master), etc. Generally Assamese endings are added to foreign forms; but certain words are created with foreign affixes also as in *Nalicha* (tube of Hooka), *Bagicha* (garden), *Bajikar* (Magician), *Daktarakhana Manjadar* (Revenue Collector of a Manza), *Rangin* (colourful), etc.

All these have led to the development of an enormous vocabulary. A large number of synonyms from various languages contributed towards creation of another noteworthy feature in the vocals of Assamese. In Assamese different words are used with reference to the same relation according as he or she senior or junior in age to the person with whom relationship is indicated. Thus, the elder brother is Mai; the younger brother is Bhai, the younger sister is Bhani, elder sister's husband is Bhinihi, younger sister's husband is Bainai, etc. In these words used to denote a senior or junior, one is often of non-Aryan origin and the other Aryan:, e.g. Kakai as non-Aryan, and Bhai Aryan.

The nouns of relationship led to the origin of another strange morphological phenomenon. Assamese shows a trait of affixing personal endings to nouns of relationship on the model of verbs. In this respect Assamese seems to stand out alone amongst all new Indo-Aryan languages. Words of relationship take on different personal affixes according as the relationship indicated is with the first or the second or the third person.

In the case of the second person, the rank of person also is taken into consideration, for example, "my father" is Mor Bopai; "your father" is Tomar Bapera (honorific), or Tor Bapera (inferior), etc. Dr. Kakati, therefore, observes that other morphological phenomena may be shared in one or another respect by other new Indo-Aryan languages also, but this peculiarity marks out a form as distinctly Assamese. Assamese also stands isolated in the Eastern group or new Indo-Aryan languages in prefixing the negative as an integral part of the conjugated verb root as in Nejao (Na Jao = not going), Nakaro (Na Karo = not doing), etc.

Due to race mixture original Indo Aryan sounds in Assamese have undergone various transformations. The old Indo-Aryan cerebrals and dentals have been changed to aleolors; the three sibilants have lost their original character and developed peculiar sound traits. The process of spontaneous nasalisation, an active phenomenon in non-Aryan languages, greatly operates in the Assamese sound system. Other special phonological peculiarities of the language are less use of conjunct consonants, preponderance of vowel-sounds, and abundant use of fondling endings. Original conjoint consonants are generally multilated by insertion of vowel sounds.

As the language does not possess very many hard words to express strong likes and dislikes, its speakers have consequently resorted to intonation in expressing such emotions.

All these traits turned the language no doubt vigourless and forceless, but on the other hand they brought in politeness and a soft musical quality. In adding politeness to the language, the Vaishnavite religion has had no small influence. The Vaishnavite scriptures had been studied by the writers in all periods of our literacy history and a great many Vaishnavite phrases and terminology have been coined in the vocabulary of Assamese.

Evaluation

Literature Under Vaishnavite Influence (AD 300 to 1600): Apart from folk-songs which, psychology should precede any account of all literature but which being always found in a comparatively modern linguistic garb cannot be placed early, the earliest recorded specimens of Assamese literature have to be traced to about the end of the thirteenth century AD. These specimens are religious or rather derived from Sanskrit Puranas and foreshadow the trend of literature for several centuries.

Starting Time: Hem Saraswati's Prahlad Charit, based on an episode from the Bamana Purana, is taken to be the first work in the language. The language of the Kavya is Sanskritic Assamese, dignified, but not difficult, and the versification is competent, suggesting a tradition behind. A more voluminous work of Hem Saraswati titled Haragauri-Samvada containing about 900 verses has recently been discovered. The book in Pada metre describes the stories of Hiranyakashipu's death, burning down of Kamadeva at Shiva's wrath and birth of Kartikeya. Another contemporary of this writer is Harihar Vipra who wrote Vabruvahanar Yudha and Lavakusha Yudha.

The theme of Vabruvahanar Yudha is derived from the Mahabharata but the descriptions and dramatic situations owe a great deal to the fertility of the poet. The story has special interest for Assamese as the scene is laid in Manipur where the sacrificial horse of Yudhisthira comes, followed by Arjun. The horse is secured by Vabruvahan, the King of Manipur. Learning from his mother Chitrangada that Arjun is his father he makes advances to the latter. But Arjun disclaims any relationship with Chitrangada and casts aspersions on her virtue. This inflames Vabruvahan and the war which ensues is bitter and prolonged. Arjun loses his life, to be revived by Krishna who reminds him that he had indeed married Chitrangada on a former occasion when he was sojourning in Manipur. Arjun returns with the homage of his son as well as the horse.

Hem Saraswati and Harihar Vipra both record that they were patronised by King Durlabhanarayan, a potentate who ruled in western Assam including parts of Cooch Behar, now West Bengal, during the latter part of the thirteenth century AD Rudra Kandali, another poet of the period, makes mention of King Tamraddhwaj, probably belonging to the 14th century AD Rudra Kandali translated an episode from the 'Dronaparva' of the Mahabharata relating to the powers of Satyaki, son of Shiva of the Yadu race. Kaviratna Saraswati was probably their contemporary. He wrote Jayadratha Vadha from the "Dronaparva" of the Mahabharata.

In about fourteenth century the cultural centre of the land seems to have moved eastward, to the court of the Kachari King Mahamanikya who patronised the chief poet of the time, Madhav Kandali. Shankaradeva, the leading Vaishnavite writer of the fifteenth century, refers to Madhav Kandali as "that preceding poet who did not make blunders." It is indeed a high compliment paid by one poet to another.

Madhava Kandali translated the Ramayana into Assamese, as he records, at the request of King Mahamanikya, a convert to Hinduism, it may be noted. Of all the early Assamese writers Madhav Kandali is distinguished by the attitude — he brought to bear upon his work. He was conscious that his work was meant for the people.

The poet wrote in a language which bears traces of Assamese in its formative stage, interspersed with popular usage and references to customs and rituals obtaining at the time. Because he wrote unhampered by the prestige of the Sanskrit language he could be true to himself and he rendered the Ramayana tale elaborating it when it was necessary and condensing it when he felt it needed condensation, and further inferring the narration with a poetic flavour all his own. Simplicity of the narration — occasionally taking on a lyrical fervour, as when Hanuman's journey to Lanka is described — and the self confidence of the poet make of Madhav Kandali's Ramayana a landmark in early Assamese literature. The book was influential later on and regarded as a standard to which all other writings of the later poets were to conform. Two cantos of it which got lost during some political turmoil were, however, rendered from the Sanskrit by the neo-Vaishnavite saints Shankradev and Madhavdeva towards the end of the fifteenth century AD.

In another of Madhava Kandal's works, Devajit, there is a foreshadowing of the neo-Vaishnavite movement which was to come a century later, for in this poem the poet established the superiority of Krishna as an incarnation of Vishnu overall other gods.

Though Madhav Kandali endeavoured to write in the "idiom of the people" there were other poets who became popular by then songs which described episodes from the Puranas. Of these Durgabar, Pitambar and Markar probably flourished in the century following that of Madhav Kandali. Durgabar's Giti-Ramayna, Pitambar's Usha-Parinaya, the marriage of Usha with Aniruddha, and Mankar's Behula Lakmindar, around the theme of Behula's revitalisation of her dead husband — both supposed to have belonged to Assam, are all in songs prefixed with names of their melodies. These are dominated by the erotic sentiments and are popular even now. That they were not looked on with an eye of the toleration by the neo-Vaishnavite movement is seen in the stormy that Shankradeva on one occasion snubbed a follower of his reciting from Usha-Parinaya.

These earlier works in the language were derived from the Sanskrit Puranas and the writers themselves were more or less versed in the classical language, but they were not weighed down by any religious zeal and could not indeed by realistic in a relative sense. The metre used was mainly the rhymed complete and the figures of speech were derived from the Sanskrit, though in the metaphors things in existence were not ignored. The poets were to a certain extent conventional, in the matter of folk poets. When the primary purpose in narration the folk poet cannot stress over much on his diction; he must have certain expressions and turns of speech ready to hand, otherwise he cannot maintain the continuity of his late. These early poets were not as much individualised as modern writers. The conventionality would be seen in the crop of poets which comes in the wake of the neo-Vaishnavite movement at the turn of the fifteenth century AD.

The Ahom invaders from across the Patkai Range had entered the land early in the thirteenth century AD and the three centuries that followed saw their expansion and consolidation. It took the Ahom some time to get accustomed to the culture and religion of the land and, therefore, central and western Assam were probably better placed for cultural activity than farther east. In the sixteenth century King Naranarayn of Cooch Behar, an enlighted ruler, attracted to his court much of the literacy and academic activity of the time.

Later Time: The new Vaishnavite movement, in the late fifteenth century AD, gave an impetus to the vernacular literature as to artistic activity in general. Shankradeva, born in 1449 at Bardowa in the Nowgong District, led the new movement. He and his chief apostle Madhavdeva were powerful writers and could inspire others. Secondly, the importation of fresh ideas from other parts of India as from Sanskrit sources brought about an enrichment of the outlook of the writers.

Growth of Literature: Shankradeva lived for 119 years and his long life in a way spans the new artistic activities of the fifteenth and sixteenth centuries. He was well educated in the classical lore of the time and had developed spiritual carvings which got a stimulus when he lost his wife and daughter in the prime of life. He left home and roamed about for twelve years in Puri, Banaras, and other religious centres both of the Northern and the Southern India, and probably came in contact with Kabir and Vishnupuri Sannyasi. When he returned home he again entered domestic life, but took upon himself seriously the mission of propagating the Bhagavata religion, known in Assam as the Ekasaraniya, as it insisted on surrender to the one.

He took to writing poems and songs and plays as a means of drawing the people to his way of thinking. In a way, he combined in his personality the various strands of the artistic revival which ran parallel to the course of the new faith. Besides, being a poet and playwright he was a musician, actor and painter of note.

The first play that he put over in Chihna-Yatra, not extent, but of his biographies record, he painted scenes to represent the seven Vaikunthas, carved marks and trained the actors for the staging of the play. It is probable that the play was not written at all but was a series of pictures of the Jama-Patrika type which were explained by actors in different roles. His other plays were Rukmini-haram, Kalidaman, Rasa-Krida, Patni-

Prasada, Parijata-Harana, Ramavijay, etc., all of Puranic episode. All are in a Brijbuli-leavened Assamese prose, and in one act, interspersed with songs. He is thus the first north-Indian to use vernacular prose in plays. Because they are in one act they are known as Ankiyanat; the term Anka in later times often connoting a play. The plays are distinctly musical and poetic. Another feature of them is the Sutradhar who not only conducts the show but stays on the stage to explain every stage of the play. As their purpose is religious there is not much scope for characterisation in the plays but they are relieved by a variety of moods — love, adoration, sense of frustration, pathos, violence and humour.

Shankradeva tapped the Vaishnavite Purana for material to be transmuted into the forms suitable to his creative personality. Besides, translating in active and easy verse most of the Bhagavta Purana he made an attempt to put certain Puranic episodes into a form of suitable for recitation. The result was the poems found in the anthology Kirtan. The date of composition of the Kirtan is not known. Some biographers say that Shankradeva did not write the book during one particular period, and that the composition was spread over several years. From the methodical arrangement of the chapters, it may be that though the book was written at different periods, the entire work however was planned and it was certainly not a work of his early years. Furthermore, the Kirtan is not a single poem but a selective collection of twenty-six poems comprising about 2,261 completes in diverse metres.

These poems were written by two of his disciples Ananta Kandali and Sridhar Kandali and were incorporated in anthology at the desire of the authors. The very name Kirtan is suggestive of the fact that the poems were recited in religious services. Each poem bears a Ghosa, refrain. More serious attempts by the poet in the Kavya form are seen in Rukamini-haran and Harischandra Upkahyana, the former noted for its poetic flavour, sweetness of language and ethos of Assamese social life, and the latter for an able handling of an intensely human theme. It is recorded that Shankradeva's disciples secured larger alms if they recited from Harishchandra Upakalyana.

Poetry and Fiction: Shankradeva's literary activities cannot be summed up without any reference to his lieutenant the celebrate Madhavdeva (1489-1596). Madhavdeva cooperated with his master in composing religious songs. The poetic Bargit which he and his master composed are set to classic Ragas. There Bargits resemble very much the Dohas of Kabir and Bhajans of Meera, Madhavdeva further added to Kirtan with his thousand Ghosa hymns (Known as Hazari-Ghosa are Nam-Ghosa) and the combined Kirtan Ghosa come to be accepted as the Bible of Assamese Vaishnavites. Its verses are found on the lips of even the illiterate villagers. The Nam Ghosa or Hajari Ghosa contains a large number of hymns on repentance and entreaty, self instruction, and self, reproach. In each of then the lyric cry is predominant and passionate.

The last few section of the book serve as a literary, consisting of an enumeration of names, praises, and laudatory epithets of Krishna. Profundity of thought, unity of outlook and music of expression make the Nam Ghosa a foremost work of art. At his master's request Madhavdeva translated Bishnupuri Sannyasi's Bhakti-Ratnavali, a textbook of the Bhakti cult. He also made a metrical rendering of a Sanskrit anthology titled Namamalika, which extols the merits of the holy name. While Sankradev rewrote the first canto of Madhav Kandali's Ramayana he added the last canto. In this rewriting probably the older Ramayana was retouched to suit the Vaishnavites. He wrote a fine kavya Rajasuya Yajna on the episode of the Rajasuya sacrifice of the Pandvas as in the Mahabharata.

The kavya is full of battle scenes, and shows traces of Magha's influence. Madhavdeva was drawn to the conception of child Krishna and in his plays like Bhumi-Letowa and Piparaguchawa, Krishna's childhood is attractively portrayed. He was an able writer and musician and his work evinces the sincerity of his personality. The history of Assamese drama and music will be incomplete if interest in the spectacular art and the Bargit songs are not taken into account. The three topics that form the main there of Madhavdeva's Bargits are — this enviable human life as affording the fullest scope for spiritual realisation, its uncertain nature and fitful progress through this illusive world, where Hari Bhakti above is the guiding star. Some of his Bargits, however, depict the childhood of Krishna the cowherd.

The example of these two masters was taken up by writers who moved in their orbit. The Koch King Narayana at Shankradeva's suggestion "sent cartloads of manuscripts" to Ramsaraswati that he might translate the Mahabharata.

This immense work was done into Assamese mostly by Ramsaraswati, the rest being by others. Ramsaraswati had a rich imagination and he freely introduced into translation episodes and images not found in the original. His Vanaparva (in about 25,000 completes), is a storehouse of adventure and romance, all in a vivid and write style.

Ananta Kandali's Saharsa-nama found a place in Kirtana. He is well-known for his Kavya Kumar Harana, around the theme of Usha and Aniruddha. Probably some of his major Kavyas have been lost. He collaborated with Shankradeva in rendering Bhagvata Purana into Assamese. He made an abridge edition of the Ramayana.

One of the writers, Sridhar Kandali, took the bogey — the Ear — eater from the nursery and wove around it the metaphysical topic of Krishna's incarnation; but the poem Kankhowa became so popular that it came to be used as lullaby.

Another major writer of the time is Bhattadev (1558-1638), an outstanding scholar and the father of Assamese prose. He also took the task of translating in prose the Bhagavata, "so that women and Shudras (inferior castes) all can group the work." The second work that he undertook was that of the Gita. The language of Bhattadev is dignified, but expository, and a little burdened with Sanskrit Syntax. Assamese prose was still at a formative stage and the writer did not have any model before him. Bhattadev's work in really significant as not only making a beginning but as having covered a considerable distance in the formation of a new genre. He further compiled three manuals on the Bhakti cult.

There were several other scholars who assisted Shankradeva to produce Bhagvata Purana in Assamese verse. Other writers who undertook the translation of different sections of the Bhagvata were Ananta Kandali, Keshavacharan, Gopalacharan, Kalapachandra, Vishnu Bharti, Ratnakar Mishra, Shri Chandra Deva, Aniruddha Kaysha and Hari of the other writers who worked at that time, the most significant are those who started the vogue of the Charit Puthi, biographies of the Vaishnavite masters who had just passed away.

Most of the biographies are in verse, often pretty detailed, and conserve a living tradition. Perhaps the biography of Shankradeva and Madhavdeva written by Madhavdeva's nephew, Ramcharan Thakar is the most detailed. Ramcharan Thakar is also the another of a play Kansa-vadh. Other early biographers are Bhusan Diviji Vaiknuthanath Diviji, and Ramanand Diviji, who wrote an important biography of Shankradeva and another of Gopaldev. These early biographies also contain pictures of contemporary religious life, record of customs and manners current at the time, and accounts of religious institutions.

The Vaishnavite age saw the production of non-religious works also, like Bakul Kayastha's Kitabat Manjari, on Mathematics, the translation of Lilavati and of Chanakya's aphorism. It was an age when Sanskrit scholarship was its highest in the land. Purushottam Thakur's Ratanmala Vyakarna is still used as a text, book. There were beside compilations of a religious character, like Bhattadev's Bhakti Viveka Ratna, works on astrology and Smriti. A few Sanskrit plays have also been found but these probably belong to a later period. It is true that the bulk of the literature of this period is made up of translations, adaptations, and compilations and in the main it was religious.

But it should not be forgotten that it was the Vaishnava writers who set the example of appealing to the popular intellect, with the result that Assamese literature, even' now, is markedly simple in its expression and not weighed down with an ornamented and heavy style. Further, Vaishnavite writers took cognizance of the lore of the people and idiomatic expression, and proverbs as well as folktales, if not folk songs as such, came to be absorbed into the corpus of the literature. On the other hand the popular songs associated with the spring festival (Biha) or with marriage come to take on sublime or gentle character by incorporating religious sentiments as well as the themes of Rama and Sita, Krishna and Rukmini, Hara and Gauri.

Support for Literature: From the 17th century AD onwards the court of the Ahom Kings in Sibsagar District become a centre of cultural activities. The Ahom Kings patronised greatly the development of art, architecture, literature, music and painting. They introduced Assamese in state papers, files and documents, and this very much widened the scope of the language. Assamese prose become the vehicle of expression in diplomatic letters, state records, and grants and the medium of the law courts. Under the Kings patronage many Sanskrit books other than religious were translated into prose. These books relate to medicine, astronomy, rules of Arithmetic, Grammar, dancing, architecture, road and building constructions. The result was that prose explained in different directions, developing different techniques and forms and getting enriched in its vocabulary.

But the greatest development in Assamese prose of the period in found in the Buranjis, the Chronicles of the Ahom court. The Buranjis were compiled under the orders of Kings and of the high dignitaries of the state, for they along could grant access to state documents on which the chronicles had invariably to be based. These documents were principally the periodic reports transmitted to the court by military commanders and frontier governors, diplomatic epistles sent to and received from foreign rulers and allies, judicial and revenue papers submitted to the Kings and allies, judicial and revenue papers submitted to the Kings and ministers for their final orders and the day to day annals of the court which incorporated all the transactions done, important utterances made, and significant occurrences reported by reliable earwitness.

These Buranjis were at first written in Ahom, the language of the rulers. Later, however, they came to be compiled in Assamese language. The Buranjis constitute an unprecedented and glorious chapter in Assamese literature. It will not be an exaggeration to remark that it is through these Buranjis that modern Assamese prose emerged.

The Ahom Kings on their conversion to Hinduism took lively interest in popularising Hindu religious ideas and beliefs. To that and they promised poets either to translate Shastras from the Sanskrit or to compose Kavyas from materials adopted from the religious texts. Kavi Raj Chakravarty, who was a poet of the court of King Shiva Simha (AD 1714 -44) made a partial rendering of the Brahmavaivarata Purana under the orders of the King. Under the joint inspiration of Shiva Simha and Ugra Simha of the King. Under the joint inspiration of Shiva Simha and Ugra Simha of the Ahom dynasty, Kavi Chandra Divija composed the Assamese version of Dharma Purana.

In the seventeenth century AD the literary activity set on foot by Vaishnavite master tended to lose its religious and further to break out into various secular channels. The romantic element in Ramsaraswati is carried on in a work like Ram Diviji's Mrigavati Charita, an attractive romance which narrates the love of a Prince for a Princess. A later romance of this popular type is Adrista Purana by Shiva Sharma which narrates how the servant of a Prince makes an attempt to foil the love of a Prince which describes the discomfiture of Yama who has brought a mortal to his Kingdom that his wife may see him. It is amusing to note that the man shakes his Rattan at Yama, sits at the latter's throne and gathers round himself" the blind, the hump backed and the cripple", declaring it as their government from onwards. The 18th century work Siai Gosain by Kaviraj Misra describes how a human baby was adopted by foxes. It is inspired by folklore.

One of the foremost poets of the Ahom period was Kaviraj Chakravarty who during the reign of King Rudra Simha (1696-1714) translated Jaydeva's Gita Govinda and wrote the Shakuntala of Kalidas in a Kavya form.

During this period Raghunath Mahanta brought out a prose version of the Ramayana. His Katha Ramayana is not literal translation of Sanskrit epic. The Adi, Ayodhya, Aranya, Kiskindha cannot have been abridged. The theme has been handed in a dramatic manner. The influence of Ankiya Nats is especially to be noticed in the language of Katha Ramayana. The same author has to his credit. The metrical compositions Satrunjaya and Adhut Ramayana. In Satrunjaya the poet describes the various exploits and expeditions led by Bali the King of the monkeys.

The work done under the patronage of the Ahom court was of a diverse character, and had further a predominantly secular tone. Erotic and 'panegorical vensas, drama and music produced even by non-Vaishnavite writers for entertainment of reigning Kings and their consorts, greatly liberalised the literary tradition issuing out of the neo-Vaishnavite renaissance. This was a flowering time for songs of diverse kinds.

There were also books on the science of elephantology, dance, medicine and magical practices. The book on elephantology is illuminated with pictures in three colours, red, blue and yellow-ochre. The Vaishnavite monasteries founded by Madhavdeva and others have maintained a vital tradition of the dance.

The literature of this period, though developing in many directions, lost much of the intensity of religious fervour of the preceding period. The shaping influence of the monastic and religious elements also gradually become less and less powerful in the face of a growing sense of objective conditions. But the verse models, in Payar, Tripadi, etc., as well as the use of effects of the Vaishnavite tradition were also not effected.

New Literature: The last three quarters of the eighteenth country and the first half of the nineteenth were on the whole a dull period for the Assamese people. Culturally, the neo-Vaishnavite influence was on the wane, Sanskrit scholarship was at the low ebb, and the tradition of indigenous learning was on its last leg. The gloomy picture was framed by an uninspiring political situation. Civil dissensions, the Burmese invasions, wide use of opium — all these had tended to disorganise social and political life, and when the British took over charge of Assam (1938) they found a people who were proud but disillusioned. Psychologically the atmosphere was ready for the absorption of new ideas but then at this moment a fresh misfortune overtook the Assamese. It was the imposition of Bengali language on the schools and courts. Consequently, the British had to import Bengali assistants and these were later instrumental in persuading the English officers that Bengali was the main language while Assamese was but a patois with no literature. The Bengali language remained officially for some forty years (1836-73) but the bogey of the Bengali textbook did not disappear till the first decade of the present century.

The same year the Assamese thus lost its rightful place in the scheme of things two remarkable members of the American Baptist Mission, the Rev. Nathan Brown and O. T. Cutter, set foot on Assamese soil. Among other things a printing press was part of their missionary equipment. Designing to hand out the message of Christ in the language of the people the missionaries set about learning it and within three months of their arrival produced the first Assamese Primer for use in the schools which they began establishing in Assam.

In 1846, the American missionaries founded a monthly magazine. Orunodai Sambad Patra, at Sibsagar. The magazine provided literature on various literary, historical scientific and religious themes. The magazine utilised illustrations adapted from the Illustrated London News, the blacks being locally produced. The missionaries wrote a prose homely and naive, simple in sentence structure and reminding one of the manner of the Buranjis, but with an amusing disregard for the Sanskritic spelling of the language.

The missionaries realised that the imposition of Bengali in Assam was of a great injustice and one of them, A. H. Danforth, wrote in 1853: "We might as well think of creating a love of knowledge in the mind of stupid English boy by attempting to teach him French before he know anything of the rudiments of English. To my mind, this feature of the educational policy pursued in Assam is not only absurd, but destructive of highest motives of education, and must necessarily cripple the advancement of the schools, as well as separate them from the sympathies of the people."

The efforts of missionaries bore fruit and Assamese was resorted to its rightful status in 1873. Moreover, the missionaries were active in bringing and translation from English. The first Assamese novel Kaminikanta was written. This was the story of conversion to Christianity of a young Hindu and glorification of Christian faith.

The history of modern Assamese literature could be woven around the there of the effort of the missionaries and Assamese intellectuals to reinstate the local language in the rightful place and the had realisation by the more advanced of the loss of independence and the consequent social and economic deterioration into which the land was passing. One of the most brilliant and outstanding young men of the time, Anandram Dhekial Phukan, a contemporary of Raja Ram Mohan Roy exhorted his countrymen to be national minded unlighted and shake off their torpor. He felt that his countrymen should be as industrious and enlightened as the English. These systems of national consciousness secured literary expression in the lyrics and essays of poet-patriot Kamalakanta Bhattacharya.

The patriotic note had a fuller and more varied expression in the hands of certain writers who bridged the last and the present country. But this early national consciousness was not at all barren from the stand point of literary creation. In fact, the later writers only followed the path laid by such persons as Hemachandra Barua, and Gunabhiram Barua. Hemachandra Barua (1836-96), wrote a neat play Kaniya Kirtana to show how the use of opium was devitalising the landed gentry, while in a novelette Bahire Rangchang Bhitare Kowabhaturi (All is not gold that Glitters) he made an attempt to expose the hypocrisy of the typical religious pontiff of Assamese Society. This compiler of the best Assamese Dictionary (Hemkosh) and a grammar was a master of prose and his mock serious style in the novelette was later imitated by a more powerful writer Lakshminath Bezbarua. Gunabhiram Barua (1837-94) wrote a pleasant and informative biography of Dhekial Pukhan (1880) and a systematic and robber history of Assam (Purani Asam Buranji).

The mid-nineteenth century prose was fairly mature, for the Assamese writers had mostly followed the spoken language and besides had the model of Buranjis. The tendency of the writers wag to free themselves from the Sanskritic vocabulary as well as Sanskrit ornamentation. In poetry this early period was rather initiative, the poets were either continuing the tradition of making an attempt to imitate from Bengali or English.

The literature came into its own in the hands of the trio: Chandra Kumar Agarwal, Lakshaminath Bezbarua and Hemchandra Goswami. While studying in Calcutta these three friends founded in 1899 the monthly *jonaki* (Glow-worm) and this magazine ushered in some of the notes which had characterised the English Romantic Movement — concern with love and mystical sympathy for nature. These writers not only composed tender lyrics, inspiring patriotic verses, vigorous descriptive poems, essays, touching on a variety of subjects — literary, social and religious, and short stories plays and novels, but also took interest in such activities as historical research and the collection of folk songs, and folktales.

The Second World War which made itself felt by about 1942 came as a dark storm-cloud threatening the normal activity of the people. Literacy expression tended to get stifled; publication of books, became difficult, the magazines became irregular; many writers found the social and economic atmosphere uncertain and uncongenial for creative work. It was, further, a period of ideological turmoil for younger writers and some of those who probably did not produce much though promising considerably, made themselves felt before long and seem to give a lead to those older writers who had not been able to decide which way to go — to go the way of the art of the leisured class or to follow in the van of changing world.

Writers and Playwrights: The war years and especially the August movement of 1942, led to national consciousness which was also felt in the modern literature of Assam and which occasionally had tended to ring out in a cry of the oppressed in general, became less sentimental and indeed underwent a transformation in the face of the sterner realities, storming the consciousness of sensitive persons. Most of the poems in the anthology Adhunik Assamiya Kavita (1946) record on the part of younger writers an awareness of capitalist exploitation, class conflict and the need for a quick change in the order of things.

In fiction, the last few years have seem a revitalising of the novel. A better understanding of life, a deeper awareness of character, and the courage narrative recounted. Instead of wearing the narrative around unconvincing flat idealistic characters, the writer is making attempt to produce men and women who react to ideas, a fact which lends the novel a philosophical significance. The short story, like the new poetry, has suffered a little in respect of form. The range of subject matter is varied, and humbler people have drawn the attention of writers, still somehow the genre does not seem to be as full-blooded as before the war. Abdul Malik wrote Parasmani (1946) a leading short story in Asamiya.

In the drama, a revitalisation has taken place as in the novel. The tendency has been towards the social play, as in the work of Pravin Phukan. The Assamese stage is not professional, hence in the town there is not much demand for good plays, the cinema is making a greater claim on the interest of the educated.

In recent years several publishing firms, mostly at Guwahati, have shown considerable initiative in bringing out a fair number of books on a variety of subjects, though, as elsewhere, books mostly published belong to the fiction class. A few of the outstanding novels published since 1958 are of the 'regional' type. Rasna Barua's *Seuji Patra Kahini* (the story of Green Leaves), analysing the growing up of a village boy, is set in the background of a tea garden, with its natural beauty, the song full life of garden labourers and the queer doings of the planters — all a new rather romantic world for a lad who is simple in make up but observant. Abdul Malik's *Surujmukhir Swapna* (The dream of the Sunflower) is recreation of a chapter in the life of an isolated Muslim village.

On a large canvas is Birendranath Bhattacharya's Iyaruingam based on a study of Tangkhul Naga life. The story, rather complex, begins with the retreat of the Japanese and the cross currents of views, social and political that swirl about in warn-torn Naga Hills. Assamese novelists have considerably widened range of their subject matter and their outlook is no larger romantic. Novels dealing with the life of army men or problems of patriotic resistance are Phani Sarma's *Banariya Phul* (Wild Flower), B. Bhattacharya's *Sataghni* (the Weapon which Kills a Hundred). To come to the short story, a few of the outstanding names us this field are Mahim Bora, Bhaben Saikia, Suren Medhi and Anil Roy Choudhury.

Drama is not as flourishing as fiction in spite to annual dramatic competition. The most outstanding play to be published just after Independence was Jyotiprasad Agarwal's Labhita. The action of the play is set in the political background of the war years. Agarwal's Rupalim, posthumously published, is set in a tribal background and evidences the playwright's idealistic concern for beauty and harmony in life. The younger generation went for newer ideas and fresher techniques in playwrights. Arun Sarma's Jinti is romantic play, set in a tribal background and somewhat like Agarwal's Rupalim.

In poetry, them Barua and Navakanta Barua are leading names, but the problem is that it is after difficult to make out what they write about! There is hardly any coherence in the bundles of disjointed images that go under the name of verse in them Barua's Balichanda (Mica).

Among older poets, Ambikagiri Roychoudhury, who died only a few years ago, cried out till the end against weakness in man and corruption in national life in bold sinuous verses.

It is not possible to write in detail about the other productions in Assamese literature. In biography and autobiography two of the most striking names are Harakanta Barua Sadaramin's belatedly published Atmajivani and Benudhar Sarma's Congressar Kachiyali Rodat (in the early sunshine of the Congress).

Foreign travel has produced books like Prasannachandra Goswamis Baidesika, Barua's Sagar Dekhisa, Birinehikumar Barua's Professor Baruar Chithi. There are travelogues on the USSR, Britain, Afghanistan, Nepal and other countries as well. These travelogues partly serve as children's reading, which is not very adequate in the language. Crime fiction by writers like Premnarayn Dutt and Rangman do not escape the notice of Children. Some of the outstanding and at the same time readable scholarly works in literary criticism are Umakanta Sarma's Kavyabhumi on the theory of Poetry.

Manoranjan Shastri's Vaisnav Darsanar Ruprekha on the Vaisnavism of Assam, Jogeswar Sharma's Kalidas of Tapasya, S. Barua's Natak Aru Abhinay Prasanga on the drama. Some of the stimulating prose of recent years, by writer's such as Nagen Hazarika, Bhaben Barua, S. Barman, have appeared in Magazines. Assamese magazines are not doing too well, being neither very regular nor long lived, but a quarterly like Natun Prithvi, leftist in trend, and Sanglap, appearing twice a year, have been able to maintain a high standard of writing. A magazine like *Bismay* (wonder) flourishes by supplying popular reading material. *Rahimala* (the Juicy one), published occasionally specialise in humour and satire (1972).

In brief Assamese is fairly rich in short story, personal essay, biography and other forms of modern prose. Both in poetry and prose, a Marxian emphasis is evidenced the forties and fifties of the present century. Western literature has considerably influenced the contemporary Assamese writings.

At the end of 1988 there were three dailies and twenty eight weeklies published and printed in Assamese language mainly from the city of Guwahati.

8

Economy

Economic Development

Tea Industry: Historically, the development of tea in Assam is mainly due to the zeal and enthusiasm of the British. It may, however, be noted that the ownership has gradually passed into Indian hands. In 1954 out of the total of 384.8 thousand acres under tea plantation in Assam, the European gardens accounted for 299.5 thousand acres producing 294.9 million lb and the Indian owned 85.3 thousand acres with 58.1 million lb. The size of the European gardens was much bigger, the average being 580 acres, while the Indian gardens were smaller (342 acres). Out of 786 tea gardens in 1954, 173 were below the size of 100 acres.

European gardens were better managed with better amenities for the employees, and their product always fetched a higher price because of the better quality of tea produced.

Assam tea is noted for its colour and flavour and so is in great demand in the world market. Nearly half of the total capital invested in the tea industry in the whole of India was invested in Assam alone, and of the amount invested in Assam nearly. 76 per cent was in sterling capital, about 13 per cent non-Indian Rupee capital and only 11 per cent in Indian about 13 per cent non-Indian Rupee Capital and only 11 per cent in Indian Rupee Capital. Now the situation has changed and most of the estates belong to Indians and there is 95 per cent investment of Indian Rupees in the gardens.

The major concentration of the tea industry in Assam lies in The Districts of Lakhimpur and Sibsagar. There are 236 and 264 tea gardens in Lakhimpur and Sibsagar Districts respectively. The per unit production of tea is also higher in these two districts of Assam. The District of Cachar has low yield per acre and the quality of tea is also inferior in this district. In all there are 115 tea gardens in Cachar District.

Tea industry contributes a great deal of income to the Central Government through taxes, such as excise duty, export duty and less under the Tea Act. The total collection from these sources was 98 crores (1985), besides another sum of Rs. 75 crores was realised as income tax and super tax from the plantations. The Government of Assam also realised Rs. 150 crore annually as agricultural income tax. It also derived a share of the income tax and export duty collected by the centre. Tea gives direct employment to about 8 per cent of the total population and 12 to 15 per cent of the population is dependent on it for its livelihood.

The tea industry of Assam is now confronted with enormous difficulties and problems such as increasing cost of production, decline in quality and competition from other growing areas in the world market. The difficulty of transport from the gardens to Calcutta since partition of the subcontinent has also added to the trouble of this industry. Smaller and uneconomic gardens in Cachar have already underlined the difficulties. Another major problem faced by all plantations in the problem of the old age of the crops. Plants more than forty years of age will yield less and the quality shall be inferior, but to replace than with new crops will breed quite a big investment.

Trade and Business

The State of Assam is essentially an agrarian State and has enormous forest, water, soil and petroleum wealth. Most of the total population is dependent on cultivation of crops, forests, sericulture, and petrochemical industries. There are numerous agro based and forest based industries in the rural and urban areas of the state. Consequently, the state exports a large variety of agro-based, forest based and petro-chemical products. It imports, assorted machines, salts, electric and electronic goods.

Tea, Silk, ivory, jute and jute products, rice, wax, black pepper; long pepper, manjit (Indian madder), aotenga (fruit of the dellenia speciosa), beetlenuts, ratans, decoration pieces, petroleum and petroleum products, ceremics, decoration pieces, bamboo artifacts, toys, tiles, cement, tannery, joinery products, paper, pulp, timber, cinnamon, species, proclaim plywood, Agarbathis, edible oil, ginger, bananas and pine apples are exported to the neighbouring states as well as to the world market.

The principle commodities which the state imports include machinery, iron and steel goods, electric and electronic goods, chemical elements and compounds, non-ferrous metals, vehicles, motor parts, oil seeds, sugar, salt, dyestuff, coal-tar, and woollen goods.

It may be seen from the articles of import and export that the people of the state export agricultural and forest based products and import from the neighbouring states machinery, salt, chemical and electric goods. A series of measures have been put into operation which cover finance for export, assistance and incentives, transport facilities training, market research and rationalisation of institutional arrangements and technical services. Despite many incentives the process of export is slow and most of the goods are exported as raw materials. A rational policy is to be followed to enhance the export of processed goods from the state of Assam.

Transport and Communications: Development of cheap and efficient means of transport and communications is the prerequisite for the speedy and balanced economic growth. Various modes of transport provide the infrastructure for the development of the primary, secondary and tertiary sectors. Without the development of infrastructural facilities the natural endowments of a region cannot be utilised optimally and judiciously. The development of transport system, however, largely depends on the physical, historical, sociocultural, economic and political factors.

Transport involves movements of goods, persons, letter, newspapers, as well as the non-physical transfer of information by phone, radio, telex, wireless, etc. In other words, transport and communications involve the transfer of people, commodities and information over space. This transfer takes place along a line of communication between two places.

Transportation has always been an important activity of man from antiquity. It is both a result and cause of an advancing society. In modern times, development of transport system has reflected the rate of advance of a country. The potential of a country and its transportation is determined largely by the topographic features, mountains, terrain, nature of rocks, swamps, deserts, thick forest, sand dunes and prevailing temperature and climatic conditions.

Such topographic features stretching across mainlines of trade and travel serve as barriers to land surface transportation. Moreover, sociocultural, political and economic factors also exert great influence in the development of nation's transportation. In fact, the commercial and industrial growth stimulates invention and innovation in agriculture, mining and manufacturing which tend to increase demand for transportation. Good means of transportation and communications are thus necessary both in war and peace for the very existence of a nation.

Big Problems: The State of Assam has both the plain and mountainous topography. Development of roads and railways in the mountainous tracts is not only a stupendous task, it may be uneconomic and difficult to explain.

Poor accessibility and difficulties of transport have been a major hindrance to rapid economic development of Assam. This has however, been, realised by both the State and Central Governments and considerable efforts have been made in the Five Year Plans to improve the situation. The remoteness of the state from the centre and its geographical location are the main reasons why its economic development including transport has failed to keep pace with the tempo of progress in the rest of India. Difficulty of terrain, a large number of rivers, shortage of labour and imbalance between, export and import are some of the major barriers to the speedy improvement of the transport system. But recently two reasons, one, the prospect of rapid industrialisation and, two, the strategic location of Assam, are likely to dictate a more accelerated rate of development in the transport system of Assam.

There is no denying the fact that whatever development in transport took place before the Independence, it was all due to tea, forest and oil. In the early period of British rule, a good overland communication system was not considered feasible due to sparse population, uneven topography and backward economy, but with development of tea, coal and petroleum industry in Upper Assam, the necessity of speedier and more efficient method of transport was keenly felt and steps were taken to connect the centres of these industries with consumption centres. Development of the transport system in the Hills was considered unnecessary during the early British Period in order to avoid any contact between the people of the Hills and the plains. The existing transport system of Assam has been discussed in the following paras.

Travel by Road: The density of roads in Assam is less as compared to the Sutlej Ganga Plains. Road development in Assam has special difficulties owing to the existence of numerous ranges of hills of varying heights, rivers and streams which often change their courses, requiring considerable extent of bridging and circuiting of roads in hilly tracts the state has been crisscrossed by the river Brahmaputra and its tributaries at numerous places. Consequently, the construction and efficiency of the road system needs many bridges or the maintenance of ferry services at many points. At the same time, for the excellence of waterways, the people were less dependent on road transport in Assam than in other parts of India.

Due to heavy rains and floods from May to October, roads construction and their maintenance is almost impossible which demand huge sums of money, good building material and efficient and energetic labour. As a result of these physio-socio-economic conditions up to 1903-04 there were only 230 km of metalled roads in the whole state, about 6,400 km suitable for bullock-carts and about 5,680 km of bride. Motor transport in the state was insignificant till about the thirties of the present century.

Serious road construction work however, began only after the constitution of Road Board in Assam in 1927. Progress was very slow and in 1929 there were 904 km of metalled road, and 6,979 km of earth roads in the state including Sylhet. During that period roads were classified into three, categories: (a) metalled roads, (b) gravelled roads, and (c) unsurfaced roads. The Board of Roads also recommended that the construction of Bridges over a 91 metre (300 feet) span should be financed by a separate loan for the purpose. In 1929-30 another additional central duty was imposed on motor spirit (12 paise per gallon) to raise funds for improving roads in the state. Nearly 20 per cent of the fund was kept for all India projects, and the rest was given to the various states for approved works on the basis of consumption of motor spirit. From 1929-30 to 1937-38, Assam received Rs. 21.8 lakhs from the Central Fund and Rs. 36.9 lakhs from the Reserve Fund. So with these funds, the Public Works Department (PWD) started construction on roads in right earnest, and improved those already constructed.

The Shillong Sylhet Road through the Khasi Hills was started. In 1937-38, another extension programme of road construction (at a total cost of Rs. 107 lakhs) was separated by the Road Board. The funds for this project were to come from the Central Road Board Fund of the Indian Government. But the state communication Board selected only eleven projects at an estimated cost of Rs. 25 lakhs. Twelve more projects costing Rs. 7.5 lakhs were added to this programme in 1938-39.

When the War came nearer to Assam in 1941, defence requirements stimulated the improvement of road transport in the state in the following ways:

- The South Trunk Road from Goalpara to Saikhowaghat was considerably widened and improved. Jogighopa on the north bank of the Brahmaputra opposite to Goalpara was linked by a good road with Siliguri, the nearest broad-gauge railhead. The main purpose of this road was to carry the traffic of Assam as far as possible, releasing the Railways mainly for defence purposes.

- The Dimapur-Kohima-Manipur Road was extended to Tamu in Burma via Pallel and Moreh.

- The Makum Lekhapani Road (connecting the famous still well Road in Burma) was also improved by the Defence Department. The volume of heavy traffic over these roads was so great that it was impossible for the local PWD to maintain these roads. Besides, roads not needed for the army were neglected and they deteriorated greatly.

The Nagpur Congress in 1943, estimated that Assam required at lest 21,700 km of roads. Accordingly vigorous road development programme was prepared under the Post-War Development Programme. It could not be executed due to shortage of funds until the of the First Five Year Plan.

After 1947, the Inter-State Trunk Highways were termed as National Highways and they came under the responsibility of the Central Government and on their behalf the local PWD executed the actual work.

At the time of Independence, Assam had only 4,167 km of motorable roads including the National Highways of which 3,264 km were in the Plains. As Sylhet became a part of Pakistan, Cachar lost her road communication with Shillong, so very hurriedly a jeepable road was constructed from Shillong to Silchar via Jowai and Hawai and Haflong. To remove the isolation of the' Garo Hills as a result of partition, another road known as the Medhipara-Phulbari Tura Road was constructed.

Assam's road programme under the first plan included the construction and improvement of 2,197 km of roads and 10 major bridges of up to a length of 4,300 km at an estimated cost of Rs. 4.23 crores. Owing to delay in finalisation of the plan, approximately 50 per cent of roads and no major bridges could be completed. The road construction in the hills was very slow and during this plan about 480 km of road in the hills and about 128 km in the tribal areas in the plains were completed. In the Second and Third Five Year Plans, more importance was given to road development. The Chinese aggression in 1962 also exposed our weakness in this regard. So emphasis was laid on the improvement of transport, as a result of which the road position improved substantially. The total mileage in Assam increased from 19,156 km (11,972 miles) in 1950-51 to 29,198 km (18,448 miles) in 1960-61.

On the other hand, the length of motorable roads increased over the same period from 10,972 km (7,230 miles) to 16,415 km (10,260 miles) against the target of 21,243 km (13,402 miles) of motorable roads for Assam envisaged in the Nagpur Plan formulated in 1943. Subsequently, the 20 Year All India Road Development Plan envisaged (35,200 km) 22,000 miles of motorable roads in Assam to be achieved by 1981, and the state Road Development Programmes in the Plans were formulated keeping these broad objectives in view.

A significant feature of the metalled roads of Assam is that all the important roads run parallel to the Brahmaputra river, and there are very few roads coming from the north and the south to the National Highways.

The main National Highways of Assam are:

- From Goalpara to Saikhowaghat connecting Guwahati, Nowgong, Jorhat and Dibrugarh.
- The Guwahati-Shillong-Tambali Road.
- The Dimpur Kohima-Manipur-Moreh Road.
- The Shillong-Jowai-Passi-Badarpur Road. This route is considered to be of particular importance to provide a link with Tripura and the Cachar and Karimaganj Districts of Assam.
- The Guwahati-North Salmara-Bsirhat-Siliguri Road is the most important road from the point of interstate road transport. It gives Assam a direct connection with the rest of the country.
- The Guwahati-Chariali-Tezpur-North Lakhimpur Road (formerly known as the North Trunk Road).

The construction of rail-cum road bridges over the Brahmaputra has brought a tremendous change in the roadways of Assam. Some of the important rivers like the Burhi, the Dihang, the Ranganadi, and the Burhi which the North Trunk Road crosses have also been recently bridged.

During the Third Five Year Plan the Central Government gave top priority to road development in the border areas of Assam. An alignment parallel — and close to the northern boundary of India, running through the state of Assam, West Bengal, Bihar and Uttar Pradesh for about 1,600 km by the Government of India for improvement as a double-lane road and styled as 'Lateral Road from Bareilly to Amingaon has been constructed. About 128 km of this road fall within the state of Assam from the left bank of the Sankosh to the right bank of the Ai, and the remaining portion from the Ai river to Amingaon merges with the national highway no. 31.

The total length of roads in the state was 34,000 km which includes 2,038 km of National Highways. The construction of 160 km of barbed wire fencing and 27 km of the border road along the Indo-Bangladesh International have been completed.

Road transport in Assam plays a very important role in the transport system of the state. Both the public and the private and sectors are important participants in this field. There has been considerable expansion in the number of motor vehicles in the state especially during the last two decades.

In the public sector, there are two road transport organisations, viz.:

• The State Transport of the Government of Assam.

• The Central Road Transport Organisation.

The former plies vehicles exclusively within the state, while the latter operates over Assam, West Bengal and Bihar. The State Transport Organisation of Assam functions as a purely departmental enterprise of the State Government. It was started in the year 1948 on the route Guwahati-Nowagong, a distance of 120 km or (75 miles). On an average, the State Transport carries 68,900 passengers and 10,000 quintals of goods everyday.

Network of Railways: The first railway line known as Dibru Sadiya Railway covering a distance of 126 km (78 miles) from Dibrugarh to Jaipur was opened for traffic in 1882. The main purpose of this railway was to carry tea and coal from interior areas of the Dibrugarh Subdivision to the river port of the same name for export to Calcutta via the Brahmaputra.

Another small railway system — known as the jorhat Provincial Railway — in the Jorhat Subdivision connecting tea growing centres like Titabar and Mariani with the river port of Kokilamukh was constructed in 1885. The route was only 48 km in length. In the same year the Tezpur Balipara Railway — about 32 km, connecting the tea-growing region of the Darrang District with Tezpur was also opened. This was a narrow gauge (2 feet 6 inches) system. Initially, such railway routes remained isolated from one another, and simply carried local products, mostly tea, to the river port, on the Brahmaputra for export to Calcutta. When the Assam Bengal Railway Company was formed in 1892, it was decided to connect Assam with the rest of India by railways. The Surma Valley received the first attention and, in 1896, a railway line from Chandura (Bengal) to Badarpur (Cachar), a distance of 184 km, was constructed. The Guwahati Jamunamukh section of the Assam Bengal Railway was opened in 1897, but the earthquake of that year greatly damaged the route.

The Lumding Badarpur section — better known as the Hill Section — was completed in 1903. This route, which is 185 km long, is an engineering marvel-as the route had to pass through as many as 37 tunnels (aggregating 4,791 metres in length) in the hills which were constructed by the Cornish Miners of England. By 1904, Dibrugarh was connected by train with Chittagong, and this helped immensely in the growth of the tea industry in Upper Assam and the Barak Valley.

The Eastern Bengal Railway was constructed in order to connect Dhubri with Calcutta in 1902. The railway mileage increased from 183 km in 1891 to 1141 km in 1904. Then the Dhubri-Amingaon route was extended in 1909-1910. In the following year, another extension to Tangla from Rangia in the Kamrup District was undertaken. This was ultimately extended to Balipara in Darrang in 1932-33.

Now the length of railway tract in Assam is 2,391.76 km comprising 1,061.29 km under broad gauge and 1,330.47 km under metre-gauge lines. The extension of broad-gauge line from Guwahati to Dibrugarh has been completed and the Naranarayana Setu, the third bridge over the Brahmaputra at Jogighopa-Panchratna was opened in 1998.

The construction of the Chaparmukh-Silighat line (80 km) and the Katakhal-Lalbazar in Cachar (37 km) was undertaken, and the two were opened for traffic in 1920 and 1924, respectively. By 1929, the Furkating in Badulipara-Jorhat, the Kamingong Longai Valley and the Shaistagong Habiganj route of the Assam Bengal Railway had been opened for traffic.

The Simaluguri-Naginimara extension was also completed during this period. In all before the outbreak of the Second World War in 1939, there were about 2,040 km of railways in Assam. The development of railways war very rapid till about 1933, but during the Second World War, the expansion programme came to a stand-still.

The Assam Bengal Railway operating in East Bengal and the Surma Valley up to Lumding in Assam and the Eastern Bengal Railway operating from Parbatipur to the Brahmaputra Valley were amalgamated in 1942 and were named as the Bengal Assam Railway with headquarters in Calcutta for better coordination. During the War, the Railways in Assam were used to their maximum, reducing key locking at stations and improving supervision.

The capacity was increased to 8,975 tons per day in March 1945 from 2,400 tons in January 1944. But before rehabilitation of the war damaged and worn out railway system could be undertaken, Assam had to face a serious dislocation in her communications as a result of participation in 1947. Assam lost her direct contact with the rest of India and, having no port in its territory, faced a serious problem in exporting its raw materials. By December 1949, all routes from Assam to the rest of India via East Pakistan were completely stopped. To restore direct communication the Government of India issued order to construct a new route — known as the link route — at a cost of Rs. 8.9 crores in January 1948. Three major gaps in the existing railways had to be filled up to establish a connection with the railways of Assam.

These gaps were to connect: (a) Kishenganj with Bagrota, (b) Madarihat with Hashimara, and Alipur Duar with Fakiragram. This link route is 229 km long but the bridging of the turbulent rivers just after their emergence from the Himalayas was a baffling problem in the initial period. The new route was opened in 1950 for traffic, but was beset by innumerable problems, especially the floods during the summer monsoon months.

To manage all the railways inside Assam, a new railway system — known as the Assam Railway with headquarters at Pandu was set up in 1947. With the regrouping of the Railways into a zonal system, the Assam Railway was merged into the Northeastern Zone with Gorakhpur as Headquarters in 1952. This arrangement having found inconvenient was annulled and in 1958 a new zone known as the North Eastern Frontier Railway was created to managed all the routes east of Katihar (Bihar), with the Headquarters of North Eastern Frontier Railway located at Pandu.

Meanwhile the Government of India could realise the strategic importance of the state of Assam in the northeast corner, and tried to improve its transport facility-both by road and railway. Among the noteworthy development in recent times in railway transport, the following projects are also important:

- The Saraighat rail-cum-road bridge over the Brahmaputra established a direct connection between the north and the south bank of the river.

- The construction of a broad gauge line from Siliguri to Jogighopa to increase transport capacity. Jogighopa has become now the most important inland port in Assam.

- Tripura, so long isolated, has been connected with Assam by opening a new railway between Kalkalighat and Dharmanagar in Tripura, a distance of about 35 km.

- The north bank route from Rangapara has been extended to Silapathar via North Lakhimpur and a further extension of this line to Murkongselek is in progress.

The railway track between New Bogaigaon and Guwahati which was only a metre gauge up to 1983 has been converted into broad gauge.

This connected Guwahati and Dispur with Delhi and Calcutta by direct trains and now Super fast trains like Tinsukia Mail, Kamrup Express and connecting Guwahati with the capital of the country (New Delhi) and the seaport of Calcutta respectively.

Travel by Sea: The Brahmaputra River with its tributaries served the purpose of the main line of transport and communications for a long time, and it is only because of this facility that the tea industry started in its valley even half a century before the long distance railway was started in the northeastern parts of India. A regular steamer service was operated from Calcutta to Dibrugarh by the Joint Steamer Companies through the Brahmaputra.

Tea, jute, timber and other bulky products were exported by this route. After the creation of Pakistan movement of goods by the Brahmaputra received a serious set-back since the lower portion of the river beyond Dhubri fell in Pakistan. Even then the volume of cargo between Assam and Calcutta both ways handled by steamer service, was about ten lakh tonnes a year. But with the Indo-Pak conflict in September 1965, the river route was closed indefinitely for transporting tea and jute from the state, and it was only through an effective coordination between, rail road and river transport along the Bongaigaon-jogighopa axis, that the flow of goods to and from Assam continued unabated in spite of a sudden closure of the direct through the Brahmaputra.

The internal waterways of Assam are estimated at over 9,600 kilometres. Approximately 1,600 km are navigable by steamer and large country — boat and the rest by smaller boat. The Brahmaputra with her important tributaries like the Subansiri, the Dihang, the Buri-Dihang and the Disang in their lower reaches is always navigable. After the earthquake of 1950, the steamers could not go up to Dibrugarh, and the service had to be terminated at Disangmukh 74 km (46 miles) downstream, because the bed of the river had become raised.

Dhubri, Pandu, Guwahati, Neamati, Tezpur, and Disangmukh are prominent ports on the river. In would be quite apparent that the inland waterways of Assam cater largely to intrastate traffic and that the local traffic is proportionately less.

There are many ferry crossings at different places along the Brahmaputra. These services are operated by the PWD or by private parties which have obtained permits to run such services by paying an annual fee fixed at public auctions to the government.

Inland waterways have certain advantages over other forms of transport. Most of the tea and jute produced in Assam must go to Calcutta for internal distribution and export overseas. Due to limitations of capacity, the railways cannot handle this trade, and it used to take more time due to change of Ganges, especially at the New-Bogaigaon Railway station. Water transport is quicker than rail and the tea-ware houses in Calcutta are so located that they can be used with ease in conjunction with water transport.

The Course of Brahmaputra is not maintained properly, and the terminal facilities are very poor. The Joint Steamer Companies are responsible for the conservancy of the river, and they do it with a subsidy from the state which they consider to be inadequate.

During the period of various plan efforts have been made to formulate concrete proposals for the development of inland waterways and the centre provided funds for: (i) loan assistance to the joint Steamer Companies; (ii) purchase of launches and dredgers for Brahmaputra; and (iii) improvement of foreshores at Guwahati.

In the state sector, a Directorate of Inland Water Transport was set up to look after problems arising in connection with inland water transport. In addition, a number of river surveys were completed among which special mention might be made in respect of a reconnaissance survey of the Dhales Wari river flowing from the Mizo District to Cachar and also a survey of the Kushiara river in the Karimganj Subdivision for construction of a lock at Nathiakhal.

Since the Indo-Pak conflict in September 1965, Assam has to face serious transport difficulties especially in transporting bulk tea, jute and timber. Arrangements were being made to run internal river services within Indian territory based on two rail heads — the broad gauge from Calcutta to Jogighopa and the metre gauge from Barauni to Dhubri. The Government of India has sanctioned the construction of a major inland port with all modern facilities at Jogighopa on the bank of the Brahmaputra. In the meantime the Guwahati port constructed at Pandu has also been improved to receive and berth steamers for loading and unloading for onward despatch to Calcutta.

The Brahmaputra, which is Assam's arterial waterway, is proposed to be declared a national waterway. The Central Government and the Inland Transport Department have already completed a detailed hydrographic survey of the river and prepared a report on the problem of conservancy.

Travel by Air: The Second War Period may be said as the period of rapid airways development. In fact, during the Second World War, several air strips were constructed in Assam for military operation. After the War was over, these temporary air bases were handed over for use of civilians and as such with little improvement Assam is fortunate enough to have many airfields operated by the Indian Airlines and the Rajdoot Service. The inter-State air services are of special importance to this state in view of the road and rail transport difficulties.

Air transport is relatively independent of physical barriers such as mountains, deserts, rugged terrain, landslides and floods. It is used for cargo either when speed is essential, as in the case of perishable goods, urgently required medical or food supplies or high value luxury goods. One specialised role played by air craft is in the relief of major disaster when land transport would be usable to reach. In the case of wars, earthquakes, floods, etc. medical supplies, food, and rescue personnel can be quickly airlifted to affected areas.

The major airports and air-fields of Assam now in regular use are Borjhar (Guwahati), Salani (Tejpur), Rowrayah (Jorhat), Mohanbari (Dibrugarh), Lila-Bari (North Lakhimpur) and Kumbhirgram (Silchar).

Air borne traffic from Delhi, Calcutta, Patna and other big cities of the country is considerable. There is a direct Airbus service from Delhi to Guwahati. It is interesting to note that the traffic is heavier from Calcutta to Assam then from Assam to Calcutta. Again during the busy tea season, when large quantities of tea are flown from various places in Assam to Calcutta, return cargo from Calcutta becomes a problem to the carrier and they book at most any traffic at low rates. There are several private companies to handle this air traffic with chartered planes from the Indian Airlines.

With the introduction of Boeing and Airbuses, the flying time is now considerably reduced between Guwahati and Delhi and Guwahati and Calcutta. The major Cities of Assam are connected with the big cities of the country which have helped in the amalgamation of various cultures, existing in the various parts of the country.

Each new development in transportation and communication has brought distant parts of the country closer and Assam is no more an area of isolation. In Assam for a long period, transportation was by inland waterways and road all these modes were slow and painful. The movement of goods was then difficult and expensive. But now fast trains and air-services are available.

A major significance of the modern mean of communications in that they enable areas to specialise in production and to exchange their products for other goods in which other area of the country/world specialise. This geographical division of labour permits large scale production and sale of crops, minerals, lumber and manufactured products at much lower costs than would be possible if every family or every physical or biological region tried to be self-sufficient. By bringing together the diverse rural and urban landscapes and ecosystems, the transport system make a whole nation and Assam including its neighbouring states are amalgamating with the rest of the country at a faster pace.

Business and Industry

Industrial Units

Of agriculture-based industries, tea occupies an important place. A good share of the economy of the state has increasingly been contributed by the tea industry. Assam leads the country's tea producing states, both in terms of quantity and labour force. Tea gardens in the state occupy an area of about 2.25 lakh hectare. Assam contributes about 15 per cent of the world's entire tea production and Guwahati Tea Auction Centre has now become the biggest tea auction centre in the world for CTC tea. According to latest figures, Assam had the highest tea output in the country in 1987 producing 54.7 per cent of the entire tea output. In terms of quantity, Assam produced about 379.9 million kg of tea in 1990. Exploration, exploitation and refining of petroleum form bulk of the rest of the industries in the state. Cottage industries include handloom, sericulture, cane and bamboo articles, carpentry, brass and metal crafts. An export-oriented handloom project has been established at Sualkuchi to exploit the potentiality of Eli and Muga silk textiles.

Industrialisation is the cornerstone of economic growth. It is the desired goal of all relatively underdeveloped and backward areas. In our country, the programme of industrialisation was launched vigorously from the Second Five Year Plan onwards. Industrialisation is indispensable for overall economic growth, the absorb the surplus labour from over saturated agriculture and to open up additional employment avenues. It is a recognised fact that the economy of Assam is industrially backward.

The industrial development of this state is mainly handicapped by its isolation and relative isolation from the rest of the country, a poor accessibility and transport system, a very small local market, and lack of sufficient capital and skilled labour. As a result, Assam has very few industries of significance, other than the production of tea, wood and refining of oil.

Of agriculture based industries, tea occupies an important place. There are six industrial growth centres in the state and two such centres are being set up at Balipura and Matia. Presently four oil refineries have been working in the state including the one at Digboi. Construction of the Export Promotion Industrial Park (EPIP) at Amingaon near Guwahati is nearing completion. A Software Technology Park will be constructed at Borjhar near Guwahati. A Central Institute for Plastic Engineering Technology (CIPET) has been established at Amingaon near Guwahati.

Assam has always enjoyed the highest reputation for her arts and crafts, associated with her cottage industries. Cottage industries include handloom, sericulture, can and bamboo articles, carpentry, brass and bell-metal crafts. Assam produces varieties of silk, Endi, Muga, Tassar, etc. Muga silk is produced only in Assam in the world.

Most of the large and medium industries belong to Plywood, and Roller Flour Mills located mainly in Dibrugarh and Kamarupa Districts and owned by the private sector.

Small Factories

In Assam, there are only 34 small scale industrial units functioning as ancillary units. Of the 34 units; only three units have been declared officially by the Hindustan Fertilizer Corporation as its ancillaries, while the others are supplying their products to some other large scale units. In addition, another 25 units promoted by the Assam State Electricity Board are under consideration for declaration as ancillaries. Though there is vast scope for development of ancillaries, its progress so far has not been satisfactory. Some of the important industries of Assam are as under.

Natural Wealth

The state of Assam is well endowed with the enormous natural resources. It has a colourful history, a distinct geographical personality, variegated natural landscape, diverse ethnic stocks and delicate strategic location in the subcontinent of India. The people live in various stages of economic, social and political development.

From the economic point of view the state of Assam is underdeveloped. There is misuse and under use of many of the natural resources. The resource potential in fact has not been utilised at the optimal level. Consequently, most of the people, especially the landless labourers, marginal farmers, tea-estate workers, tribals and rural folks are living below the poverty line, and a substantial percentage, i.e. 35 per cent are close to the poverty line. The per capita income in the state is only Rs. 2,475 as against Rs. 3,184 for the country as a whole.

In general the standard of living of over 80 per cent of the total population is poor. Most of them are under fed and the malnutrition and under nutrition may be seen both in the rural and the urban areas. Apart from food, the clothing and shelter aspects are also not at a desirable level. The people have generally thatched huts and Kutcha houses as shelters and even the towns and urban places do not have the impressive modern structures. The low rate of literacy, the poor standard of food and low standard of life reveals the economic scenario of the state in which the population is living at a low level of subsistence.

The growth of agriculture, the main occupation of the people, has not yet been able to keep pace with the increase in population. During the last two decades, while the population of the state has been increased by more than 38 per cent, the food production has gone up by only about 15 per cent. The industrial development of the state of Assam lags far behind, compared to the rich potentialities of the local resources. The Tertiary sector is also inadequately developed. As a result of underdevelopment developed. As a result of underdevelopment and rapid increase in population there is unemployment in the state which has acquired a serious dimension and resulting into social tension and political unrest in the state in general and among the youths in particular.

In Assam the percentage of agricultural labourers is comparatively high. The percentage of agricultural labourers in this state is about 10 per cent. Though the percentage (9.98%) is low in comparison to the national percentage (26.35), the figure of Assam is not a small. Keeping this high proportion of agricultural labourers, it is high time for the planners for creating alternate employment opportunities so that the man power may be utilised judiciously in future.

Types of Land

The land not available for cultivation may be divided into two sub categories because of the distinctly different uses:

- Area under non-agricultural uses which generally comprises rural settlements, metalled and unmetalled roads, railways, embankments, canals, tanks, cemetery and crematory grounds, camping, thrashing grounds and shooting grounds. About 10.90 per cent of the total reporting area of Assam is under these uses.

- The area not available for cultivation also includes the barren land and pastures. About 19.84 per cent of the reporting area of Assam is barren and useless from the agricultural point of view. This figure is very close to the national average (20.23%) of wasteland. High concentration of barren land lies in the Mikir Hills where it is 68.22 per cent of the reporting area of the district. This high percentage is owing to barren rocks resulted from jhuming (shifting cultivation) and steep slopes on which the soil erosion is quite conspicuous.

Other uncultivated land excluding fallow land includes pasture, other grazing grounds, miscellaneous tree-crops, groves and culturable waste. The permanent pastures and other grazing lands cover all grazing lands. The common land in the village and grazing land within the forest areas are included under this head. The miscellaneous tree crops and groves are grown in the areas, not included in the net area sown.

The land under thatching grasses, bamboo, bushes and other groves, trees for fuel, etc. which are not included under orchards are placed under this category. The culturable waste includes lands available for cultivation whether or to taken up for cultivation or abandoned after a few years, for one reason or the other. Such lands may be covered with shrubs and jungles which are not put to any use. It is a sort of residual class which includes all uncultivable lands not accounted for any other class.

Land under permanent pastures and other grazing land is only 2.38 per cent of the total reporting area. The maximum percentage (7%) of permanent pasture and other grazing land lies in Nalbari, Barpeta (Kamarupa District), and Marigaon (Nowgong District) Tehsils. In other Tehsils this percentage varies between 4 to 6.

The land under tree crops, groves, etc. is also found in all the Subdivisions of the state. The share of this category of land varies between 1.30 in Tinsukia to 7.11 per cent in Guwahati Subdivision.

In Assam, 1.86 per cent of the total reporting area is culturable waste. There is however, unequal distribution of culturable waste. The highest percentage of culturable waste is found in Marigaon Subdivision of Nowgong. In most of the Subdivisions the proportion of culturable waste is 0.50 per cent.

The fallowland other than the current fallow comprises of all lands which were taken up for cultivation, but are temporarily out of cultivation for a period of not less than one year and not more than five years. Assam has only, 1.62 per cent of the area under fallowland which is well below the national average of 2.84 per cent.

Net area sown represents the actual physical area under crops and orchards. It may be referred as net cropped area also. Only 33.1 per cent of the total reporting area of Assam is sown as against 47 per cent for the country as a whole. In Dhubri and Nalbari Subdivisions the percentage of net sown area is around 70 per cent. In Mikir Hills, Silchar, North Lakhimpur, Dhemaji Subdivisions the proportion of net sown area is less than one third of the total reporting area. Only 6.5 per cent of the net cropped area is double cropped or sown more than in a year.

Dealing with Land Tenancy

The present land tenancy in Assam is a legacy of the colonial system of the British rulers. The traditional occupance and land tenancy of land was significantly transformed after the annexation of the province by the Britons in 1826. The British administration gradually introduced the present land settlement and land revenue system into the plains of Brahmaputra. At the beginning of British rule in Assam, Goalpara, Kamrup and Sylhet Districts formed a part of Bengal Presidency and when the permanent settlement was introduced in Bengal, these two districts came under the new system of tenancy. The Permanent Settlement, therefore, became prevalent in Goalpara District and the Karimaganj Subdivision of the present Cachar District.

The land tenancy system in the plain districts varies from that of the hill areas. In the hill districts, there is no land revenue system at all. People in such tracts do not hold any permanent interest in land because of the jhuming (shifting cultivation). In lieu of the land revenue they pay a house or hearth tax to the village head. The management of the Jhum land is carried on by the village councils locally called as *Khanja*. Prior to the legislation in the fifties excepting the areas under permanent settlement, the general character of land settlement in the Assam plains was Ryotwari. The principle Ryotwari settlement is that the government deals directly with the actual occupant and his separate holding. In principle, it is quite sound but in practice, it does not mean that the government has direct contact with the actual tiller of the soil. In fact it was not possible by a foreign government to establish direct contacts with the tillers because of the socio-political factors.

Tenancy rights in Assam are governed by the Goalpara Tenancy Act of 1929, the Sylhet Tenancy Act of 1936 and the Assam Temporarily Settled District Tenancy Act of 1937. The effect of all these acts (together with amendments of 1948, 1953, 1956) have been to confer important rights in the tenants over the land which they occupy. At present the following main types of tenancy are recognised in different parts of the plain districts of Assam:

- Privileged Raiyats.
- Occupancy Raiyats.
- Non-occupancy Raiyats.
- Under Raiyats.

A Raiyat means a person who has acquired a right to hold land from a landlord for the purpose of cultivating it. A Raiyat may acquire his interest from a proprietor a permanent tenure holder or a settlement holder. A 'under Raiyat' is a person holding land under a Raiyat, but does not include a tenant holding under any person who holds land on condition of rendering service. A 'privileged Raiyat' is a tenant who holds land at the rates of rent not exceeding the land revenue rates payable to the government. An occupancy Raiyat is a tenant having the right of occupancy. A non-occupant Raiyat has no such right.

Raiyats with Advantages

The state of privileged Raiyats is attained when a tenant has been in continuous occupation of the land for not less than twenty years or either (a) a rate of rent not excluding the land revenue rate in addition to the service rendered by him, or (b) On payment of Bhog (Bhog means articles of food required by custom to be offered to a deity).

The tenants in the Lakhiraj estate are usually privileged Raiyats of transfer or subletting of the land on which he has got possession. The occupancy right can be acquired if a Raiyat has been in Continuous occupation of the land for twelve years. In the Karimaganj Subdivision of Cachar District and in Goalpara District on occupancy Raiyat can transfer of sublet his rights without the consent of the landlord, but the written consent of the landlord is necessary in Ryotwari areas both for transfer and subletting. Both the privileged Raiyat and the occupancy Raiyat can use the land, excepting the trees standing before the common of the tenancy as they like. The occupancy Raiyat is to pay a fair and equitable rent, which is slightly higher than the actual land revenue rate payable to the government. He cannot be ejected on the ground of non-payment of rent, but the land he occupies may be sold in execution of a decree for the arrears of rent and the rent shall be the first charge on the sale proceeds. Both privileged and the occupancy Raiyats can be ejected by a decree of a court when they render the land unfit.

Raiyat and Non-occupancy

A non-occupancy Raiyat is to pay the agreed by both' the landlord and the tenant. Without a written agreement his rent cannot be enhanced and after one enhancement it remains in force for at least five years. He can be ejected from the land by a decree of a court of law, when he refuses to agree to a fair and equitable enhancement of rent. A non-occupancy Raiyat cannot transfer his interest or sublet his estate without the written consent of the landlord.

An Under-Raiyat usually pays a higher rate of rent than the Raiyat under whom he holds the land. The right of the under Raiyat is heritable only for the unexpired period of lease. An ordinary under Raiyat holding land under a privileged Raiyat can transfer his holdings to his cosharer or heir. He has no right of subletting. The non-occupancy tenant can be ejected. A tenant may the rent in cash or in Kind. The privileged and occupancy tenants are generally cash tenants and their burden of rent is not much higher than usual land revenue rates payable to the government. But as has been, the tenancy in Kind in fairly common in many parts of the state.

A share tenant, normally pays half of the total output to landlord, the tenant himself bearing the operational expenses of cultivation. Besides the share rent, a fixed rent in kind which is fixed quantity of crop, irrespectives of the output is also prevalent in many parts of Assam.

This fixed rent in kind is usually much higher than the rent in cash, though it may be lower than the share rent. These crop tenants whether they pay in cash or in kind cannot be described as tenants in the proper sense of the term as they do not possess any right over the land, they cultivate on behalf of the owners.

The term of their tenancy and the right of the land they cultivate are insecure and very limited. After independence in 1948, the Government of Assam enacted the Assam Adihar Protection and Regulation Act to safeguard the interest of the share of crop tenants. The Act was however, implemented only after 1957. Land reform measures from early sixties were directed towards: (i) abolition of intermediaries, (ii) tenancy reforms, (iii) ceiling on land holdings, (iv) consolidation of holdings, and (v) distribution of land among the landless labour.

"The Assam temporarily settled areas Tenancy Act 1971" was enacted. The new Act has given adequate security to tenants, who can become owners of the land for three years. The maximum rent has-been fixed at three times.

The land revenue in case of cash rent and not exceeding to one fifth of the produce of the principal crop grown in a year in case of rent in kind.

Amount of Holdings

The size of operational holdings has a direct bearing on the agricultural typology and the production per unit area. The number of operational holdings has been given in the Table.

Assam: Number of Holdings (operated) and their Area by Size of Holdings

Size of Holdings	No. of Holdings in lakhs	Area in lakh acres
Below 1 acre	2.27	1.27
	(15.50)	(2.2)
1 - 2.49	3.76	6.27
	(25.6)	(10.7)
2.50 - 4.99	4.87	17.77
	(33.10)	(30.40)
5.99 - 9.90	2.95	20.11
	(20.1)	(34.44)
10.00 -14.99	0.59	7.28
	(4.00)	(12.40)
15.00 - 24.99	0.79	3.57
	(1.30)	(6.10)
25 acres and above	0.36	2.25
	(0.40)	(3.80)
Total	14.69	58.52
	(100.00)	(100.00)

(Figures in brackets indicate percentage of total)

It may be noted from Table that most of the holdings in Assam are small and uneconomic. From a survey, conducted by the Department of Economics and Statistics, it has been estimated that the total operated area of 58.5 lakh acres in Assam is distributed.

The size and distribution of holdings of less than 5 acres constituted 74.2 per cent of the total number of holdings though they represent only 43.3 per cent of total area. There holdings are uneconomic. The holdings of a size of 5 acres to 14.99 acres constitute 24.1 per cent of the total number of holding and account for 46.3 per cent of the total operated area.

The Assam Fixation of Ceiling Land Holding Act 1956 was enacted to fix the ceiling at 150 Bighas (20.25 acres) for all kinds of land irrespective of family size or soil or irrigation facilities. This could be enlarged by another 30 Bighas (4.05 hectares) for permanent orchards. Subsequently, the ceiling was reduced to 75 Bighas (10.12 hectares) in 1970 and then to 50 Bighas (6.7 hectares) in 1973. With the operation, of ceiling laws 4.87 lakh Bighas (66 thousand hectares) of surplus land have been vested in the government. It is reported that up to June 1986 about 5.4 lakh Bighas of surplus land has been distributed among 127,505 landless families besides providing house sites to 8,250 homeless families on the basis of status of the tenants.

The Agricultural census 1970-71 on the basis of status of the tenants classified the operational holdings into three groups: (i) wholly owned, (ii) wholly rented, and (iii) partly owned and partly rented. The proportion of the various categories have been given in Table.

An examination of Table shows in the small size of holdings about 78 per cent are wholly owned, about 18 per cent are wholly rented and only 4.16 per cent are partly rented and partly owned. The large operational holding farmers, i.e. 20 acres and above give about 20 to 30 per cent of their holdings on rent. It reveals the fact the large farmers have land in excess which is managed with the help tenant farmers. The very small and inviable holdings are also rented out by the marginal farmers as they do not provide subsistence and employment to the farmers. There is therefore an urgent need to implement the Land Ceiling Act in the state of Assam more effectively operating 17.93 per cent of the area were partly owned and partly rented. The proportion of the holdings entirely owned in higher in the lower size (below 5 hectares). But in the higher sized holdings (above 20 hectares) there is a large proportion of the holdings which was entirely rented. In Assam, the land leased out by the land holders of operational holdings is of the following two types:

- land owned and rented by private owners, and
- land owned by the government but occupied without settlement.

The number and proportion of the small sized of holdings is on the increasing side. For example, about 52 per cent of the total holdings were below one hectare in 1971-72 which rose to 64 per cent in 1986-87. The land ceiling Act has not brought significant change in the various categories of land holders. In fact, the large fixed farmers know the evasive tactics and they do not surrender their surplus land to the government for redistribution to the landless workers and people.

Assam: Proportion of Holdings according to the Status of the Tenants

Size of holding	wholly owned holding	wholly rented holding	Partly owned and partly rented
Below 1 acre	77.85	17.99	4.16
1 -10 acres	70.39	9.06	20.55
10 - 20 acres	61.20	7.45	30.93
20 - 30 acres	61.69	19.05	19.06
30 - 40 acres	61.68	22.00	16.02
40 - 50 acres	54.55	32.95	12.50
Above 50 acres	70.61	9.31	20.08

Agriculture Sector

Agriculture covers slightly less than two-third of labour force, i.e., about 63 per cent of the state's working force are engaged in agriculture and allied activities. Principal food crop is rice. Cash crops are jute, tea, cotton, oilseeds, sugarcane, potato, etc. Major horticulture items are orange and other citrus fruits, banana, pineapple, arecanut, coconut, guava, mango, jackfruit, etc., which are grown on a smaller scale. The state has a gross scrapped area of about 35 lakh hectare, more than 79 per cent accounting for foodgrain crops. Paddy along covers about 26 lakh hectare. During 1992-93, the state has achieved a production of 25.93 lakh tonnes of foodgrains and 10.02 lakh tonnes of sugarcane. Area under forest, categorised as reserved forests covers 17.581 sq km or roughly 22.41 per cent of the total area of the state. Unclassed forests cover 10.064 sq km.

Various Types of Farming

The agricultural systems in Assam vary from the most primitive (shifting cultivation) to the highly mechanised plantation. In between these two extremes is the subsistence and intensive subsistence (paddy dominated) agricultural systems.

Jhuming (Shifting Cultivation): Shifting cultivation or Jhuming is a very primitive technique of land utilisation for the cultivation of crops. It is mainly practised by the tribals in the hilly and forested areas of Assam, especially in the districts of Karbi-Anglong (Mikir) and North Cachar. The actual acreage under Jhuming is difficult to ascertain as it fluctuates from year to year. The main characteristics of the shifting cultivation are: (i) shifting of fields, (ii) use of fire for clearing the forest and its undergrowth, (iii) keeping the land fallow for the regeneration of forests, (iv) use of human labour as the main source of energy and input, (v) non-employment of draught animals, and (vi) use of rudimentary tools and implements.

The loss of fertility of the soil is very rapid on the slopes of the hills. Consequently, the Jhumias abandon the field after one or two years. The Jhuming is creating many ecological problems in the hills of the state and therefore needs to be converted into sedimentary agriculture.

Intensive Subsistence Agriculture: Settled cultivation in Assam is of intensive subsistence type in which Crops grown are consumed by the growers. The farmers of the Brahmaputra valley from Goalpara to Dibrugarh practice intensive subsistence agriculture. It is also extensive practised in the North Cachar and Cachar Districts. The chief implements used in this system are the wooden ploughs drawn by a pair of bullocks or a single buffalo. Besides plough Moi (harrow), Binda (spike-tooth-harrow), clod breakers (Dolimari), Khurpi (hand-weeder), Kodali (spades) and hoes are the main tools of the subsistence farmers. Modern equipments like tractors, power-tillers, mechanical weeders, sprayers have not made much headway, though they have appeared on the scene in the area.

Plantation Agriculture: The plantation agriculture is practised mainly in the tropical and subtropical areas to grow perennial cash crops. It is a specialised commercial cultivation on large scale estates. It represents the development of agricultural resources of tropical and subtropical countries in accordance with the methods of secondary occupation. It is a large scale enterprise in agriculture.

Plantation involves the existence of a regular workforce under the control of a more or less elaborate management and frequently a considerable capital outlay, although some of the plantation crops except tea and rubber are also grown in small holdings. The farming in plantation is carried on with specialised and wherever possible with the application of machinery fertilizers, weedicides, insecticides and pesticides. It aims at high yields, high quality production and a large output, most of which is exported.

Tea is the only plantation crop in the state of crop. Assam produces more than half of the tea produced in the country. At present the area under tea is about 1.92 lakhs hectares which produces nearly 2.69 lakh tonnes of tea annually. The number of tea gardens in Assam is 757 and the average size of a tea estate garden is nearly 250 hectares. The main concentration of plantation agriculture lies in Dhemaji, Lakhimpur, Sibsagar, Cachar, Naogons, Goalpara, and Kamrup Districts. From the agricultural point of view, kamrup is the most important district in quantity and variety. Sibsagar comes next to it.

Agricultural Crops

Assam is essentially an agrarian state. The overwhelming importance of agriculture in the economy of the state may be appreciated from the fact that over 80 per cent of its total population is directly or indirectly dependent on agriculture. Only one fifth of the total population is urban and the remaining four-fifth is residing in rural areas. The main occupation of the, rural population is agriculture, forestry and fishery.

The density of population in Assam State is however, relatively low being around 110 persons per sq km consequently, Assam has been regarded as a state whose potential resources are in excess of its needs, and which therefore relief to some of the more thickly populated states of India.

It has, in fact, received a large number of emigrants from different sources and her population has increased from 37 lakhs in 1901 to 2,66,38,407 in 2001. In spite of this, Assam is the only state in which it is Known for certain that there is scope for extension of cultivation and which can therefore support a large agricultural population.

Assam: Percentage of Area under Various Uses

Use of Land	Percentage of Land
1. Forest	25.42
2. Land put to non-agricultural uses	10.90
3. Barren	19.84
4. Permanent Pastures	2.38
5. Land under trees and groves	3.79
6. Culturable waste	1.86
7. Fallow	1.62
8. Current fallow	1.42
9. Net area sown	39.40
10. Area sown more than once	10.58

An examination of Table shows that 25.4 per cent of the total area of Assam is under forest which is higher to that of the national average (21%). The Subdivision of Kokarajhar with 54.4 per cent of the total area under forest has the maximum area under forests in the state. Contrary to this the Subdivisions of Nalbari and Mangaldoi have less than 10 per cent of their total area under forest. In the remaining Subdivisions the forest area percentage varies between 26 to 54. The spatial distribution of forests shows that the concentration of forests is highly uneven in the state of Assam.

Different Crops

The crop season in Assam can be divided into three periods:

- The Aman or Cold weather crop season (November and December).
- The Rabi Crop Season.
- The Kharif Crop Season.

The Aman or Cold Weather Crops mainly consist of Aman rice. It is sown in the months of September and October at the advent of late monsoon. Sugarcane is another crop harvested during this period. The total area devoted to Aman rice is only about 15 per cent of the gross cropped area.

The rabi crops are those sown in November and reaped in early summer (February and March). Rabi crops in Assam include rice, pulses, wheat, barley, mustard, oilseeds, tobacco and vegetables. Though rabi crops total production is less than that of the kharif season, they include a number of cash crops. After 1965 the High Yielding Varieties of wheat have been diffused in the Brahmaputra valley. The HYV of wheat are performing quite encouragingly and more and more farmers are going for the adoption of new varieties of wheat.

Kharif crops are those which are sown during the summer months March to July and harvested from August to October. The dominant Crops of kharif season are rice, jute, pulses and vegetables. The distributional patterns of kharif crops are closely controlled by the prevailing weather conditions, especially temperature and precipitation, and the topographic and pedological conditions. About 70 per cent of the total cropped area during the kharif season is devoted to rice in the plains of Assam while about 20 per cent is given to Jute. The cultivation of jute is however more dominant in the lower valley of the Brahmaputra.

The success and yield per unit area of crops in Assam largely depends on two factors: (a) the general slope and level of the land, (b) the land being flooded by rains. Thus transplanted paddy can be grown on land which is neither too high to retain moisture, nor too low to be inundated by the early rains.

On a still higher level, where water drains off quickly Ahu or Aus (broadcast rice) is sown. A crop of plush or sugarcane can be grown on high land. Bao paddy or long-stand deep water paddy is grown in those areas which go under water in early rains and remain submerged until the water subsides in September. For the purpose of cultivation, the plain districts of the Brahmaputra Valley can be divided into four groups according to the level of the land.

- The first is the Chapari or lowland near the river which is heavily flooded during the rains. These lands produced a good Ahu crop in summer and mustard and rice in winter.

- Behind the Chapari comes a belt of lowlying region in which Bao or summer rice is grown. The water drains of slowly from this belt and the land remains too damp for winter crops.

- The level of the country then rises above the reach of the ordinary flood and Soli rice becomes the chief crop. This is a broad belt containing most of the permanent cultivation and majority of the agricultural population.

- Beyond this tract comes a submontane area where the level rises higher and higher and the fields are often irrigated from hill streams.

These four topographical belts are, however, not found equally in all parts of the valley. For example the District of Darrang has no Bao land.

Sibsagar and Lakhimpur districts are also poor in this belt. The chapari is found generally on both sides of the Brahmaputra river, but in Kamrup and Goalpara, the margin of cultivation often comes down to the river bank.

Crop of Kharif

The season of Kharif Crops Corresponds with the commencement of summer monsoon which actually prevails in Assam from mid-May to October. The crops which require more heat and moisture are grown in kharif season. This is the only season when extensive cultivation of crops adapted to warm environment may be cultivated. In the kharif season more than 92 per cent of the net cropped area and 78 per cent of the total cropped area is sown and devoted mainly to kharif cereals. About 6.7 per cent of the net cropped area is devoted to jute, sugarcane, fodder, vegetables. Rice, maize, small-millets and pulses are the other principal cereals of this region.

Rice: Rice is the most important food crop in Assam, occupying nearly two-third of the total cropped area. Winter rice, known as Sali or Aman, is the most important variety and Autumn or Ahu or Aus is the next. A third crop of minor importance, known as spring rice or Boro, is sown between Sali and Ahu and harvested in February and March.

The different districts and Subdivisions have a large number of local varieties of each of these three principal rice crops.

The statistics shows that in ten out of the twenty two subdivisions of Assam, between 70 to 80 per cent of the net cropped area is devoted to rice.

The subdivisions in which rice is the dominating and single most important crop are Dhemaji, Jorhat, Marigoon, Ganhati, Goalpara, Silchar, Hailakandi, Dhubri, Karbi-Anglong and North Cachar Hills. Excepting the North Cachar Hills and Karbi-Anglong Subdivisions, rest of the areal units fall within the plains of the Brahmaputra.

The subdivisions of Golaghat (57.65%) in Sibsagar District, however, has less area under rice. In Sibsagar tea is an important cash crop owing to which less area is available for the sowing of paddy and other crops.

In three subdivisions, namely, Kokrajhar, Nalbari, and Karimganj; more than 80 per cent of the net cropped area is under paddy crop. In the remaining subdivisions rice occupies 60 to 70 per cent of the net sown area.

Assam: Acreage under Rice in Different Seasons

Subdivision	Autumn Rice	Winter Rice	Summer Rice
Silchar	15.78	61.06	3.91
Karimganj	24.25	68.12	8.66
Hailakandi	16.10	55.47	2.33
Cachar	18.53	68.17	5.11
Goalpara	24.95	47.10	2.43
Dhubri	38.95	34.12	1.37
Kokrajhar	29.31	58.12	0.15
Goalpara	31.77	45.87	1.26
Guwahati	22.52	48.87	2.15
Nalbari	33.92	48.66	0.70
Barpeta	30.01	36.26	0.29
Kamrup	28.85	44.06	0.11
Tezpur	11.58	5. 51	0.28
Mangaldoi	24.62	38.70	0.13
Darrang	19.28	44.84	0.19
Nowgong	13.53	53.75	2.47
Mariagaon	17.99	58.18	6.60
Nowgong	14.76	54.42	3.61
Sibsagar	1.78	68.00	0.01
Jorhat	14.03	58.88	0.01
Golaghat	5.03	52.62	- -
Sibsagar	1.78	73.30	0.03
N. Lakhimpur	12.69	56.03	0.05
Dhemaji	13.25	59.04	0.11
Lakhimpur	12.92	56.20	0.10
Dibrugarh I	9.01	61.81	- -
Tinsukia	13.51	52.78	- -
Dibrugarh II	10.93	57.96	- -

Source: Department of Economics and Statistics.

Jute: Next to rice, jute is the main crop in the Brahmaputra valley of Assam. Its successful cultivation needs highly fertile alluvial soil, heavy rains, high relative humidity, high temperatures and cheap manual labour. It is sown in February and March and harvested in June and July. After sowing at least one hoeing is necessary to remove the weeds growth and loose the soil to increase the aeration.

In Assam generally two varieties of jute are grown. These varieties are known as capsularies and outliers. Capsularies variety is grown in both the well-drained high levelled and the damp low-lying areas. It however, thrives well in lowlands in which water can remain standing for a longer period. Olitories jute is a more sensitive crop which is cultivated only in the well-drained high lands. Just before harvest jute crop required sufficient quantity of water and, therefore, it is sown in the early parts of summer and harvested in June-July after the onset of summer monsoon.

Jute cultivation is not a very old phenomenon in the agricultural mosaic of Assam. It has been especially diffused by the Bengalis who arrived here from East Pakistan (Bangladesh). The hard working Bengali farmers are innovative and they started its cultivation in Assam, especially after the partition of the subcontinent.

The spatiatial distribution of jute shows that the Lower Brahmaputra Valley is the main area of its concentration. Consequently, Goalpara, Kamrup, Darrang and Nowgong are the leading producing districts of jute.

Since jute and Aus rice can be grown on the same land in the Brahmaputra valley, there is always a competition for areal strength in these two crops. So when the price of jute seems to improve, the cultivators bring more land under jute and reverse in the case when the market shows a downward trend due to some other economic factors. Since partition jute cultivation has been extended in every growing region due to higher prices in the market and the government propaganda under a 'Grow More Jute' programme to make India self-sufficient in respect of this crop.

As stated at the outset, the principal factors controlling jute cultivation are the prevalence of fairly high temperature, abundant rainfall including its timely arrival and even distribution, light silt renewed soils and sufficient clear water for retting. Rainfall both in amount and time of occurrence largely determines the success or failure of the crop. It is a typical rainy season crop, and a hot and humid climate is favourable to its growth. But excessive rainfall saturating the soil with moisture delays sowing as well as its after treatment.

The growing season extends from February to September and harvesting starts from June. The period of early sowing and early growth synchronises with the outburst of the Norwester and the mature crops faces the monsoon. The temperature of all jute growing areas in Assam hardly exceeds 38°C during the growing season and rarely falls below 18°C. Relative humidity is generally high and varies from 65 to 95 per cent.

Jute plants thrive well in light fertile soil and does not grow well in stiff red clay. This is the main reason for jute cultivation being confined to the new alluvium of the lower Brahmaputra Valley, particularly the districts of Goalpara, kamrup, Nowgong and Darrang. The Charland on the bank of the river or recently reclaimed wasteland produce the major share. Places like Dihing in Nowgong, Kharupatia in Darrang, Tarabari in

Kamrup, Goalpara and Bilasipara in Goalpara District, all situated on the banks of Brahmaputra are famous for jute cultivation and its trade. The Marigaon Subdivision with 10 per cent of its net cropped area has the largest concentration of jute, followed by Nowgong Subdivision in which jute occupies about 6.5 per cent of the net sown area. Most of the jute produced in Assam is sent to Calcutta.

Sugarcane: Sugarcane is another important kharif crop of Assam. It occupies about 4,800 hectares (1985-86) or about 1.80 per cent of the net cropped area. Sugarcane is grown in the well-drained soils. Before the sowing of sugarcane, land is ploughed repeatedly and the field is manured properly. Sowing of Sugarcane commences in March when the Temperature of the day is around 25°C. In March and April the crop is irrigated if rains do not occur. The Subdivisions of Nowgong, Karimganj, Golaghat and Tinsukia have over 2 per cent of their net cropped area under sugarcane. Nowgong Subdivision with 6 per cent of the sown area is the leading producer of sugarcane in Assam. It is harvested from November to April and mostly crushed locally for the preparation of Gur (unrefined-sugar).

Maize: Maize is an important coarse cereal crop grown in Assam. It is consumed as a food by the poor people and serves as a green fodder to livestock in the summer season. It is generally grown under rain-fed conditions in elevated well-drained lands.

Maize is generally sown after the first shower of monsoon in the first part of June. The crop matures in August and September. A long break in rainfall or heavy down pours leading to floods affect the crops adversely. Though and insignificant area is given to maize, its cultivation is carried on in all the Subdivisions of Assam. The Subdivision of Tinsukia with over 6 per cent area under maize is the largest producer of maize.

Urad (Black-gram) mesta, and cotton are the other crops in the kharif season, but their total area is less than one per cent of the net cropped area.

Tea: The cultivation of tea in Assam was started as early as 1835 near the confluence of the Brahmaputra and the Kundil rivers under the initiative of the British Government. Before that Mr. C. Bruce, brother of Mr. R. Bruce, the discoverer of tea in 1823 was appointed as the Superintendent of the Government Tea Forest. It was however, not the intention of the government to carry on tea trade, but as soon as experimental cultivation proved successful, it was decided to handover the trade to private enterprise. The first garden did not prove successful owing to faulty location of site, and the plants were removed to Joypur, where a new garden was established. In 1837, Mr. Bruce manufactured tea with imported Chinese labour and 46 boxes of tea for export to England from Calcutta. Due to defects in packing, very little of this tea reached London market in good condition, but it was reported there to be of high quality.

Subsequently, the Assam Tea Company took charge of the government plantation in 1840, and this can be regarded as the real start of tea cultivation in Assam. The first factory was established in Dibrugarh and fed by both planted and wild leaves. During the initial period, the company was far from prosperous as it had to overcome innumerable adds but gradually it began to improve and by 1859 it had 4,000 acres under tea cultivation and an out turn of 760,000 lb of tea. In 1854, new gardens were opened in Darrang and Kanrup and in the following year it was discovered that wild tea grew also in Cachar.

During the next ten years, capital flowed to the tea industry from all quarters. Land was racklessly taken up to be sold to speculators in England at extravagant sums and tea-growing for a time fell into the hands of stockbrokers and bubble companies. Many high Government Officials resigned their jobs to start tea plantation. The crash came in 1866 and for the next few years it was in a state of great depression. About 1869, matters began to improve and during the next 30 years, there was great development in tea industry.

The diffusion, spread and successful progress of tea cultivation in Assam is entirely due to the enthusiastic interest of the British capital and organisation and the cheap labour availability from the neighbouring states of Assam. In order to encourage the taking up of land for tea plantation, very favourable terms have at different times been sanctioned by the government to private companies.

There are but a few agricultural crops which are grown for leaf production and fewer still which are dependent upon a systematic - and regular collection of leaves throughout the growing period. Organised tea industry depends on a regular supply of young new shoots having a desirable character of flavour, aroma, and briskness.

Most of the tea in the Assam valley is grown between the Brahmaputra and the Naga Hills in Upper Assam. The two Districts of Lakhimpur and Sibsagar located here have more than 200,000 acres of area under tea plantations. The District of Lakhimpur, growing the finest tea in the North East India, is steadily extending eastward from Doom Dooma and a new subregion in the Khamti area is being gradually developed.

Whilst the bulk of the soil in the Lakhimpur District extends from the river to the hills in a belt about 30 miles wide in Sibsagar, most of the gardens are confined to the area between the National Highway No. 37 and the hills. The Golaghat Subdivision is partly situated in a bay between the Mikir Hills and Nagaland, shut off from much of the monsoon rain. This is a sun-baked thatch ridden area which combined with the stiff nature of the soil does not provide a congenial condition for the best tea growth, although the quality of the tea raised is much above the average.

To the west of the Mikir Hills is the Nowgong District which contains a small tea-growing area. To the north of the Brahmaputra is the Darrang District in which about 60,000 acres of land are put under tea. Much of the tea is put on the red banks well away from the hills, although some very recent alluvium deposits are also brought under its plantation.

In Cachar, the tea consists mostly of long narrow valleys running to the Barak. The valleys are formed by ranges of low hills usually bamboo-clad, which are thrown off from the main ranges. Innumerable hillocks or Tillas are dotted over the valleys and these together with flats between them carry tea. Unfortunately, many tea plantations in the Cachar District have now become uneconomic and pose a great problem to the state.

The number of tea gardens, area and production of tea in the various districts of Assam have been given in Table.

Assam-Districtwise Number of Tea Gardens, Area and Production.

District	No. of Tea Gardens	Area in hectares	Production in '000 kg.
Darrang	97	26,58	29,429
Goalpara	10	1,658	1,596
Kamrup	15	2,116	1,483
Lakhimpur	229	50,520	71,921
Nowgong	23	5,578	5,478
Sibsagar	258	46,807	47,355
Cachar	114	29,928	16,747
Assam	746	163,28'	173,900

An examination of Table shows that there are 746 tea gardens in Assam out of which 258 or 34.58 per cent in Sibsagar and 229 or 30 per cent are in Lakhimpur district. Cachar and Darrang districts have 114 and 97 tea gardens respectively. Nowgong district has 23 tea gardens while there are 15 tea gardens in Kamrup district and only 10 in Goalpara district. The production of tea is dependent on the areal strengths of tea acreage in the respective districts. Sibsagar district which has 46,807 hectares under tea produces about 47,355 thousand kg annually. The next district in area and production being Lakhimpur which has 50,520 hectares under tea and produces 71,921 thousand kg of tea annually. In Cachar the total acreage under tea is 29,928 but it produces only 16,747 thousand kg of tea annually.

Thus the production per unit area in Cachar District is comparatively low. The shares of Nowgong, Kamrup and Goalpara is relatively insignificant while Darrag District has 26,583 hectares under tea producing 29,429 thousand kg of tea annually. Taking as whole the average yield per unit area is highest in Lakhimpur district in which each hectare produces 1,423.6 kg per annum.

Tea is usually propagated by seed although cultings are also successful in many cases. In Assam infilling is now done from cultings taken from the bushes on the same plot. The success of propagation depends on the time when the cultings are taken. Generally culting and propagation are done from April to June. The plants are raised from seeds of cross-fertilized tea pushes that reach a height 4.5-6 metres (15-50 ft). The quality of tea differs with different fats and it is desirable to use one type for the same plantation.

On gentle slopes and flat lands, tea seedlings are planted at a distance of 1.5 metres apart either in a line at 90° or 60° to the base line, the two systems — being known as square and triangular plantings. On steep slopes they are planted in lines following the contour. They are planted in holders dug in places marked by stakes with large lumps of necessary earth round their roots at the age of six months to two years. Shade trees are planted nearly 15 metres (about fifty feet) apart in the field.

Pruning is necessary to induce a vigorous vegetative growth as it ensures a continuous supply of tea flushes for tea manufacture, and keeps the tea bush at such height that it can be plucked by hand. The first pruning is done when the plants are two to five years old, during the slow-growing period when the food reserves are at the minimum. In Assam this is done annually or biannually. The intervals become longer on higher elevations. Heavy pruning is resorted to when the bushes have become too high for plucking and light pruning when a part of the plant is affected by disease.

Harvesting of Tea

Tea-harvesting consists in collecting the newly-grown vegetative shoots composed of the terminal buds and two or three leaves immediately below it, together with the intervening stalk. It is considered to be full when two leaves and a bud are plucked, anything less is considered to be fine plucking and when more than two leaves are taken, it is known as coarse plucking. The quality of tea is dependent on the nature of plucking. To enable the bush to keep on producing a succession of new shoots, it is necessary to leave some active new leaves so that the plants may synthesise the substance necessary far developing it.

New shoots Known as 'flushes' develop from the axil of the leaves left after plucking, and the second and subsequent flushes are often plucked so as to leave no more than a small undeveloped one Known as "Jhanam" near the base of the shoots. New shoots develop quickly, and the bushes need to be plucked at short intervals of seven to ten days. In Assam, depending on the supply of moisture, tea bushes give five to seven flushes in a season and the average interval is only seven days. Plucking commences in April or May just after the beginning of the rainy season. Plucking is done mostly by hand and hence requires a large number of labourers.

Process of Productions

The state of Assam is well-known for its black tea. About 98 per cent of the total production consists of black-tea. It involves four different operations, i.e. (a) Whithering, (b) Rolling, (c) Fermenting, and (d) Drying.

Whithering: Whithering means the drying of fresh green leaves by placing them thinly and evenly on racks or shelves protected from weather to a state when it contains only about 40 per cent of water. This takes about 16 to 18 hours.

Rolling: After whithering the next stage in the processing is that of rolling of leaves. The withered leaves are passed through rollers when it is twisted so as to damage the individual leaf cells and to extract the sap, which is smeared on the surface of the rolled mass.

Fermenting: The rolled leaves are spread out on a cement floor to a thickness of 2.5 to 10 cm (1 inch to inches) according to season, weather and condition of the leaves and allowed to ferment for two to six hours. During this process, the colour changes from green to a bright reddish coppery colour. This is to be carried on in conditioned rooms in an atmosphere of high humidity and low temperature.

Drying: Drying is a continuous process and usually, carried out in automatic machines. The fermented leaf is brought into intimated contact with a current of hot air at not less than 54.4°C (130°F) and later during its passage through the drier, the leaf encounters hot air the temperature of which is 88°C to 93°C (190°F to 200°F). The time for drying varies between 30 and 40 minutes. The product contains 3 to 4 per cent moisture. It is then cleaned and sorted out into various commercial grades.

Blending: Tea as manufactured in the factory does not reach the consumer directly. Tea from different estates has different characteristics and the tea from the same garden varies in quality from season to season. To turn out a product of uniform quality in respect of flavour and colour, the tea of various places is blended together so that consumer can get a uniform product in each packet. Blending is essentially an art and demands skill and experience of a high grade.

The tea product in Assam is exported to Calcutta by road, rail and waterway. The tea industry occupies a prominent place in the economy of Assam. It contributes in all about 21 per cent of the state's income apportioned at 12 per cent from the tea plantations and 8 per cent from the tea industry as such.

The crop of the garden consists of plants of a very heterogeneous nature and therefore it is of prime importance to the industry that attempts should be made to evolve a genetically pure basic type of a homogeneous character suited to different sets of conditions. Breeding should also be done to improve strains; reliance, should not be placed on vegetative propagation alone, as is the case at present.

The tea industry of Assam faces certain serious problems. The tea gardens in Cachar District (37 in number, occupying about 10,000 acres and producing 3.3 million lb. annually) have now proved to be unviable and uneconomic. The causes of the economic weakness of tea gardens are both technical and economic. The technical causes are related to plantation as well as to manufacture. The main drawbacks are a high percentage of vacancy, old age of bushes and an unscientific technique of cultivation. The out-dated machinery and inefficient handling also damage the processing of tea. Many of the gardens are in debt, so paucity of capital, inefficient management, transport difficulties, price fluctuations and labour unrest constitute some of the economic causes.

Crop of Rabi

The season of Rabi Crops correspond to winter months, i.e. from October to March. In the rabi season only those crops are sown which germinate in cool weather and moderate moisture in the soil. Consequently, rabi crops are sown from October to December but the seeds do not sprout for about six to eight days. During the period of winter months when the temperatures are low, the crops show a stunted growth. In February and March the weather of spring months bring in a new flush after the winter slumber from which the plants rise to resume their suspended growth. Because of these the rabi crops have a longer life span and harvest in about 120 to 150 days.

In the agricultural year of 1985-86, in the rabi season about 11.42 per cent of the net cropped area was devoted to rabi crops. Out of the net sown area 53 per cent was devoted to cereals (rice and wheat) and the remaining 47 per cent was given to oilseeds pulses (lentil) vegetables and fodder.

Wheat: Cultivation of wheat in the Brahmaputra valley is a new phenomenon. Its cultivation has especially been diffused after the Green Revolution (1965) in which the High Yielding varieties of wheat were successfully adopted in India. Its acreage is steadily increasing. Wheat is generally grown in loan, sand-loom and clay loam in the riverine tracts of the state. The available data and information medicate that wheat in Assam is grown in only those fields in which controlled irrigation is available. It is sown in November and harvested in March and April.

In 1985-86, wheat covered an area of about 65,000 hectares, constituting about 18 per cent of the net cropped area of the rabi season. The highest concentration of wheat occurs in Goalpara Subdivision in which about 6 per cent of the net sown area in rabi is devoted to wheat. It is followed by Marigaon (4.25%), Dhubri (3.7%), which it occupied about 2 per cent in each Subdivision of Guwahati, Nalbari, Barpeta, Barpeta, Tezpur and Naogong. As the provisions of controlled irrigation are being developed in Assam, the area under wheat is also increasing.

Mustard and Rapeseed: Mustard and rapeseed are the main sources of oil and fat in Assam. These oil-seeds occupy about 168,000 hectares (1985-86) or about 7 per cent of the net sown area during the rabi season. Rapeseeds and mustard are grown in Assam throughout the riverine belts. It grows well in flood prone lowlying areas with alluvium soils which are less acidic. The Crop is sown in October and harvested in February. In fields in which one irrigation is provided give better returns. Mustard and rapeseeds are grown in all the subdivisions of Assam. For example in Lakhimpur and Tinsukia subdivisions it occupied about 12 and 10 per cent of the net cropped area. In each of Kokrajhar, Marigaon and Naogong subdivisions it got about 7 per cent of the copped area. In Jorhat, Mangoldoi and Nalbari its percentage share was over 6 per cent in each subdivision. Its cultivation is however insignificant in the District of Silchar.

Rice: In Assam rice is also grown during the rabi season. The rice sown in rabi season is locally Known as Boro. It is grown in marshy land. In winter rice crop is repeatedly irrigated as winter is the period of scanty rains. For Bord rice, seeds are grown in nurseries in the months of November and December and the seedlings are transplanted in the irrigated and well puddled fields in the months of December and January.

The Boro rice is an important cereal crop in Karimganj, Marrigaon, and Silchar Subdivisions. In Karimganj it occupies about 9 per cent of the net cropped area and in Mrigaon 6 per cent, while in Silchar it occupies about 4 per cent of the rabi cropped area. In rest of the Subdivisions its percentage share in the sown area is below 2 per cent.

Potatoes: Potato is an important crop grown in the rabi season. It is cultivated in all the districts of the state, though the hectarage it occupies is not very significant. The jute fields and Ahu paddy fields which are less suitable for Sali rice are often devoted to potatoes. Potato crop is planted in the month of October and harvested from February to March. The Subdivisions of Tinsukia, North Lakhimpur, Jorhat, Tezpur, Mongoldoi, Nalbari, Dhubri, Haila Kundi are the leading growers of potatoes in Assam.

The Livestocks: Assam has a large population of livestock but their breeds and quality are inferior. The cattle in the state are small in size, poor in health and not strong enough either to draw heavier types of improved ploughs or to draught heavy loaded carts. The number of cattle per acre in Assam is which is the highest in the country. The average yield of milk is also very low, being only 140 litres per cow and 315 litres per buffalo per year, while for all India it is 413 litres and 1100 litres, respectively. The per capita availability of milk per day is 1.2 oz as against the requirements of 10 oz according to approved nutritional standards. The contribution of state income from the animal husbandry sector is only about 4 per cent as against 7 per cent for the country as a whole. The number of livestock and poultry and their products in the state of Assam have been shown in Table.

It may be seem that there is a steady increase in the number of cattle, buffaloes, goats and poultry. There is however not much change in the number of sheep, horses and ponies. The wet climate of Assam especially during the summer monsoons is not conducive for sheep. The horses and ponies are not very useful even as the draught animals.

The poor productivity of cattle is largely due to malnutrition, diseases and inferior breeds. Professional grazers are mostly from Nepal and they like to settle on the outskirts of towns and cities where fodder is available. But unfortunately the damp and humid climate of the state is not conducive to better growth of fodder. Again, the poor size of the cattle in Assam is due to inadequate mineral contents, especially calcium and phosphate in the soil. The fodder grown cannot have these two minerals as they are being constantly washed away from the soil by torrential rains of the summer monsoons.

Due to excessive heat and drought in summer (April-May), precarious fodder conditions prevail in the plains of Assam and during floods the animals get nothing to eat as store-up reserves get washed away and movement of fodder is often impossible due to disruption of transport.

Assam-The Number of Livestock and Poultry and their Products

		1951	1961	1971	1981
1.	Catty	4145	64,88	8110	9894
		(578)	(546)	(405)	(494)
2.	Buffaloes	475	583	699	834
		(53)	(49)	(35)	(42)
3.	Sheep	33	54	55	58
4.	Goats	917	1886	2430	3255
5.	Horses and Ponies	16	17	17	18
6.	Poultry	6569	9907	10,260	11525
		(734)	(834)	(514)	(576)
	Total	6878	9479	11256	14001
		(773)	(798)	(562)	(700)

The figures in the brackets indicate the number per 1000 persons.

(Latest Figures Available)

Cattle in Assam do not come under any recognised breeds. Schemes are already under way to upgrade the indigenous cattle with improved breeds through the Key-village scheme, artificial insemination drives, and castration of old bulls. The Upper Shillong Cattle Farm was opened in 1897-98, and the Khanpara farm near Guwahati in 1926 to look into these problems. But progress in this respect is very slow.

Livestock, especially cattle, suffer from a heavy incidence of disease such as liver flukes, bovine pleuro, penumonia, hump sore, etc. The number of hospitals for supply of vaccines and medicines to fight against these epidemics is not adequate. Stall-feeding of dry grasses in Assam is generally not practised. The animals are allowed to graze in the fields. But the constant dereservation of the grazing reserves located in the vicinity of the villages has posed a big problem to the professional grazers. Therefore the Nepal; people keep their animals in the interior of the forest far away from the consuming centres of their products.

Irrigation: In the modern agriculture and especially for the High Yielding Varieties of wheat and rice, a controlled irrigation is a must for getting better agricultural returns.

In fact, the supply of an adequate quantity of water during the growth, development and flowering periods is one of the surest means of ensuring a higher return from arable land on a permanent basis.

In the past, in Assam, the rainfall was plentiful and its distribution was so uniform that the problem of irrigation did not draw adequate attention of the pest administrators of the state. However, some areas were irrigated by the Kacharis, Mech and other tribal people who lived on the high grassy plains at the foot hills of the lower Himalayas.

The villages joined hands to construct small channels, sometimes of considerable length, and through them provided water of the hill-streams to higher fields. In 1929-30, there was only 5.5 lakh acres of land under irrigation, mostly from private sources. Ten years later the situation was no better only 6.5 lakh acres of land were irrigated, but in 1949-50 irrigated areas increased to 13.2 lakh acres, just double the figure of 1939-40. It became possible due to the keen interest taken by the government by starting the "Grow More Food Campaign."

As a part of this scheme, steps have been taken not only for supplying water to deficient areas, but also to drain out excess water in those areas which are periodically submerged. The irrigation activities of the state are now classified as follows:

Major Schemes

The major irrigation projects are executed by the Public works Department of the State Government. The Public Works Department has taken many such schemes, out of which the following are the most notable:

The Jarhuna Irrigation scheme in the Nowgong District is the first big venture in the irrigation sector of the state. The detailed estimate and plan including the water requirements were prepared by the central Water and Power Commission of the Government of India, and the execution part was left to the local Public Works Department. All these projects are to be completed by 1969-70 and they should bring 88,000 acres of new land under agriculture. The main barrage of the Jamuna Scheme is at Bakaliaghat on the river Jamuna in the Mikir Hills. It contains seven spillways of 6.15 metres (20 feet) width. The total length of the canal system in Mikir Hills and Nowgong district will be 164 km (102 miles).

Mora-Dhansiri in Sibsagar District Sukla, Lanka and Patradisha in Cachar District are the other important Major Irrigation Projects of Assam.

Minor Schemes

The Minor Irrigation Projects are the most popular schemes of the Agricultural Department of Assam. They got increasing popularity during the last two decades. The main types of works undertaken under the Minor Irrigation Projects in the Brahmaputra Valley were as under:

- Bund or drainage channels for irrigating new land and for providing better facilities for land already under cultivation;

- Bund or drainage system to draw out excess water from the field especially from the water logged areas or protecting the field from flood damage, or for storing water;

- Silt channels for encouraging silt deposits on low-lying land to raise them and to make them suitable for cultivation;

- Combined silt and drainage for areas which require both silt deposits and drainage; and

- Sluice gate for controlling the water level in the field.

Assam: Irrigation Projects

	Project	District	Irrigation Potentiality	Cost in Rs. Lakhs
1.	Jamuna	Nowgong	64,000	168.00
2.	Lanka	Cachar	3,000	5.00
3.	Mora-Dhansiri	Sibsagar	9,000	20.E
4.	Sukla	Cachar	3,000	6.00
5.	Patradisha	Cachar	9,000	19.00
	Total		**88,000**	**218.00**

System of Power Pump

The development of power pump irrigation is very essential for extending areas under Boro paddy in the flood affected and low-lying areas of the state. The necessity for such schemes arises from the fact that there are some parts of the state which are subject to annual floods where scarcity of water makes the growing of winter crops vulnerable.

As a result of introduction of these irrigation schemes, both major and minor, the area under irrigation in the state has gone up 1,982,000 acres or nearly 27 per cent of the net sown area.

Lakhimpur and Kamrup are the two districts where irrigation is not widespread. With the completion of the Jamuna Irrigation Scheme, Nowgong District which is now considered to be the driest part of Assam will be substantially benefited by irrigation.

The Kacharis along the northern frontier in Chatgari and Chutia and about the Bhutan Duwars exhibit great skill in the art of irrigation. They are in the habit of irrigating their rice fields from the small streams which intersect these districts. The irrigation water adds to the fertility of their fields.

A land reclamation scheme was launched at Kaki in the Naogong District, and another at Subhankhata in the Kamrup District to reclaim over 12,000 and 3,160 acres of land respectively.

Agriculture in Assam suffers most from the inadequacy of drainage. Those waters which traverse the valley, and are the chief source of its fertility, often over spread the country in a manner extremely destructive. There are in many parts extensive swamps and morasses that act in a still more prejudicial degree; for while during the rains they inundate the adjacent country, at the beginning of the dry season, when acted upon by the heat of the sun, the vegetable matter with which they are usually covered begins to decay, and they form the hot-beds of disease and malaria. In some places these fens are drained in the course of the extension of cultivation, and when once brought under culture, they may be considered as permanently reclaimed. After reclamation they give good agricultural returns.

There is no general system of embankments in lower Assam, though partial embankments to guard against the inundations of particular streams at particular places are not uncommon. These are most frequently meet with on either bank of the Kullung, though there can be no doubt, much valuable land is now covered by reeds, or abandoned owing to the periodic floods, might be recovered by adopting a general system of Bunds. But in Upper Assam, almost every stream was anciently Bunded and the recovery of these embankments is now a great source of solicitude to the administrators and authorities.

Inundations are no doubt are very useful to some tracts which are so elevated that the inundation spreads over them gradually. But on the whole the Bunds would be far more advantageous to the people than abandoning the lands to nature and the gradual operation of sitting. Whenever the inundations move more violently, they never have the effect of raising the loan, and leaving a sandy deposit. In some places, especially in the vicinity of great rivers; where the inundations move slowly, and by depositing a fine soil tend gradually to raise the level, yet the operation is so exceedingly slow that ages may pass away before the land will be culturable, while in the mean time, the understrained currents are often making particular sets, and in one season destroy the work of years. Where embankments raised, these lands might be rendered abundantly productive, and being liable to the effects of currents across their surface, would be permanently protected.

Tea Gardens

Tea is the leading and most efficiently organised industry of Assam. In 1985, there were about 6.8 lakhs people dependent on tea industry. The land suitable for tea is not suitable for the cultivation of rice and the greater part of it would have been covered by dense forest if it had not been cleared by planters. These gardens provide an in falling source of employment for local cultivators who for any reason a may wish to work for hire. The literate classes have obtained numerous clerical and subordinate jobs in the gardens, since labourers are mostly imported from outside.

The tea industry has given a great impetus to trade and improved the means of Communications by road and railway. In fact, the entire prosperity of the Lakhimpur and Sibsagar Districts, with subsequent discovery of oil and coal, is more or less due to the extension of tea cultivation. Upper Assam and Cachar Districts are served by better roadways than kamrup and Goalpara only because the latter areas have not much of tea cultivation. To encourage tea plantation in the state, the government also made a liberal provision to settle the wasteland with the planters. The Tocklai Experimental Station, established in 1911, under the auspices of the Indian Tea Association, has been helping the industry by carrying on research practically in every branch of tea cultivation. This is the only major tea research centre in the world.

Sericulture

Sericulture is another important primary activity of the people of Assam. Of the plants usually employed by the Assamese for rearing the silk warm on, Tetranthera quadriflora, Roxb (Addakuri).

Although the Muga Moth (Saturnia) can be reared in houses, it is fed, and thrives best in the open air. The worms fed on Roxb and Tetranthera quadriflora. But the tree is used only when under four years of age. It is a small ramous tree, and generally sprouts -up where forests have been cleared for cultivation of rice. The worms that are fed on this tree on the first year of its appearance above the ground, produce the best silk; on the second year, the silk is inferior both in quality and quantity; and on the third year it degenerates so much as to be little, if at all, superior to the common Muga. The leaves are lanceolate, smooth on both sides, and glaucous underneath; from four to six inches long, by one or two broad.

Tetranthera-lancifolia, Roxb (Sun) is found principally in the forests on the plains, and about villages, where the plantations of it are quite extensive. It yields three crops of leaves during a year. The silk produced by it is of light fawn colour, and esteemed next to the Mazankuri.

Tetranthera-macrophylla, Roxb (Sanabu) is common in most of the forests of Assam, and is also found in the vicinity of village settlements. It attains its full growth in six years. It is a very famous, evergreen tree of about five metres in height. The silk produced by the worms of this tree is considered as inferior in quality.

Michela-pulnensis (Champa) is another tree on which silk worms are reared. The silk worms fed on Champa is called *Champa Putrya Munga*. The silk obtained from Champa is also considered to be quite superior.

Tetranthera Diglotti (Diglutti) is a tree of small size. The silk obtained from the warms of this tree is quite good in quality. Silk worms are also reared on Kantuloa, Patti-Shunda (Laurus Obtusifolia), Eri-gach. The silk worms thrive best, and produce most when only fed on the Eri tree. It is the only plant which is cultivated purposely for it. The worms can also be reared on the Hindu Ghass and the Mikerdal, but they do not thrive well on them; many die even after having begun the cocoons, and those which survive, give poor yields. Muga is the especial silk obtained in Assam. The Muga silk, a texture peculiar to the country, affords the dress, which above all others is considered rich and valuable. It was the prescribed attire of all the high officers of government and is still worn by every one who makes any pretensions to opulence.

The silks of Assam dominated by the natives the Eria and the Muga are respectively produce of Phalaena-Cynthia and Saturnia. As stated in the preceeding paras the former is reared entirely within doors and is fed principally on the leaves of the Ricinus-communis. The duration of its life varies according to seasons; in summer it is shorter and the produce both greater and better. During this season from its birth to the time it begins its cocoon, 20 to 24 days expire; in fifteen more Moth is produced, the eggs are laid in three days, and in five days they are hatched, making the total duration of a breed forty-three days. In winter it lives nearly two months; the number of breeds in the year are reckoned at seven.

For the purpose of breeding, the natives select cocoons from those which begin to be formed in the largest numbers on the same day; those that contain males are distinguished by a more pointed end. On the second or third day after the cocoons have begun to be formed, they are put in a closed basket, and hung up in the house, out of reach of rats or insects. Twenty four hours after the Moths have been produced the females (Known only by the larger body) are tied to long reeds or canes, from twenty to twenty-five to each and these are hung up in the house.

The eggs that have been laid during the first three days are alone kept, they are tied in a piece of cloth, and suspended to the roof till a few begin to hatch; these eggs are white, and about the size of a turnip seed. When a few of the worms are hatched, the cloths are put on small bamboo platters hung up in the house, and here they are fed with tender leaves. After the second moulting they are removed to feed on bunches of leaves suspended a little above the ground and upon the ground a mail is laid to receive them when they fall. When they have ceased feeding, they are placed in baskets filled with dry leaves, amongst which they form their cocoons.

The cocoons are next put over a slow fire in a solution of potash, whereby the drawing of the silk is rendered easy. They are then removed, and the water gently squeezed out. This done, they are taken one by one, and the silk placed within the thumb of the left hand, whist the right is employed in drawing out the silk. Any inequalities that might exist are reduced by rubbing them down between the thumb and finger, this made is also adopted for joining on new cocoons. The thread is allowed to accumulate in small quantities of about a quarter of a kg. These are afterwards exposed to the sun, or near a fire till dry, when they are wound up into skins, and the silk is then ready for the weaver.

The Muga Moth (Saturnia), is usually reared on trees in the open air, and the tending of the worms is attended with much care. There are generally five breads of Muga worms in the year, distinguished by the natives according to the month in which they generally occur.

- Jaruwa in January and February.
- Jaituwa in May and June.
- Aharuwa in June and July.
- Bhodia in August and September.
- Kholia in October and November.

The Jaruwa and Kholia obtained in January and February, and in October and November respectively are the best crops in quality and quality. The Aharuwa and Bhodia are the inferior crops in quality and production.

The cocoons are put into a closed basket suspended from the roof, the day after they are hatched the female Moths are taken out and tied to small wisps of thatching grass, taking always from that part of the house immediately over the hearth, its darkened colour being thought more acceptable to the Moth. These wisps are then hung on a string tied across the house, to protect them from rats and lizards. They are taken out morning and evening and exposed to the days of the sun. The eggs laid during the first three days are the only ones considered worth keeping.

Ten days after the laying of the eggs, when a few of them are hatched, the wisps of straw to which the Moths had been fastened are hung to the trees on which it is intended the caterpillars should feed, and these soon find their way to the leaves. Care must be taken that there be no ants about the trees for their bite usually proves fatal to the worms in their early stages. Previous to placing the worms on the trees, the natives generally rub the trunk with molasses, and tie fish and other things to it to attract the ants, when accumulated in great numbers they destroy them with fire. The ground about the trees must also be kept free from underwood, which renders it easier to find the worms should they happen to fall off.

To prevent the worms coming to the ground, fresh planting leaves are tied round the trunk over the slippery surface which they cannot crawl. During the day the worms require to be constantly watched, crows and other birds being so fond of them, that they lie in wait for them in the neighbouring trees. Bats, owls, and rats are very destructive at nights. A number of Caterpillars are also destroyed in the more advanced stages by the stings of wasps, and by the ichneumon insects, which deposits its eggs in their body.

The worms thrive best in dry weather, but a very hot sunny day proves fatal to many at the time of moulting. At these periods rain is considered very favourable, thunderstorms do not injure them as they do the mulberry worm. Continual heavy rains are hurtful by throwing them off the trees; showers, however, heavy, cause no great damage. The worms generally taking shelters under the leaves with perfect safety. The worms during their moulting remain on the branches, but when about beginning to spin, they come down the trunk, and the planting leaves preventing their going further down, they are then collected in baskets, which are afterwards put under branches of dry leaves suspended from the roof of the house, they crawl up into these and there form their cocoons.

The total duration of a breed varies from sixty to seventy days. This period is divisible into 20 days for moulting, 10 days from fourth moulting to beginning of cocoons, 20 days in the cocoon, six days as a moth, and about ten days in the hatching of the eggs (total 66 days).

The chrysalis not being easily killed by exposure to the sun, a number of cocoons are placed on bamboo stages, and covered with leaves, time helps to kill them. The cocoons are then boiled for about an hour in a solution of potash, when they are taken out and laid in folds of cloth, hence they are taken as required. The floss is removed with the hand and the cocoons are thrown into hot water.

The instrument used for winding off the silk is the coarsest imaginable. "A thick bamboo, about three feet long, is split into two, and the pieces driven equally into the ground two feet apart; over the interior projection of one of the knots is laid a stick to which is fixed, a little on one side a round piece of plank, about a foot in diameter, the rotary motion is given by jerking this axle, on which the thread rolls itself, in front of the vessel holding the cocoons; a stick is placed horizontally for the thread to travel upon."

Two persons are employed, one attends the cocoons, the other jerks the axle with the right hand, and with the same hand directs the thread up the left forearm, so that it is twisted in coming down again towards the hand, the left hand directs the thread over the axle, fifty cocoons is the smallest number they can wind off in one thread, though twenty is the usual number.

This is no doubt to be attributed to the coarseness of the instrument used. When nearly 250 grams of the silk has accumulated on the axle, it is dried in the sun, and made into skerins. Fifty thousand cocoons are obtained from an acre of Muga trees. These cocoons produce about 5 kg of silk which is considered to be quite profitable.

From Muga silk, Suria, Ditto (Sair Cloths), Melka (Petticoats), Rahia (Scarfs), Gamsha (turbans), Jotha Borkapur (made of floss of cocoons and worn as covering during winter). The Eira silk is used for the manufacture of Borkapur, Meklas, Rhia and Gamsha (used by the people of lower income group).

Raising Fish

Fish constitute an important ingredient of the diet of Assamese. Fishing is a pursuit carried on by the natives with examplary labour and skill. During the rainy months when the rivers are inundated, fish are very scarce, but as the inundation subsides, and when the fish are confined within narrow bounds. These fish are captured by various simple means which the natives employ. The most simple method when a pond, ditch, or marsh has become nearly dry, and the fish of a large space have been collected into a small pool, is to divide it by dams of mud and then having thrown the water from each successively to catch the fish as they are left dry.

A few simple traps are frequently used. One is a basket, with a hole in the bottom called Polo. In shallow water the fisher puts the mouth of the basket on the mud, and then passing his arm through a hole in the bottom, gropes for the fish. Another Jokai is a attached a bamboo shaft which serves as a handle. The fisher places the bottom flat on the mud, treads among the weeds before the opening and thus drives the fish into the trap, then suddenly raising the handle, he brings the opening above the surface of the water. Three methods can be practised only in very muddy places, covered with aquatic plants and are commonly employed by the poor classes to catch fish for their own use.

Nets are used only by the professional fisherman. The most simple net in the country is the Dainijal which is stretched between two bamboos that meet behind at an acute angle, where it is held by the fisherman. The net is of triangular form, so as to apply to the bamboos, but is much bagged behind. The fisherman walking up to the middle in water, pushes the points of the bamboo along the bottom for a little way, and then raises then up to secure whatever fish may have come into his net. The length of the bamboos used for these nets, varies from four to five metres.

A net of the same form, but enlarged so as to have bamboos about nineteen cubits long is frequently used in canoes. Two men manage the canoe which is kept broadside on the stream while a third lowers the points of the bamboos which are fixed at right angles to the gunwale, and then occasionally raises them to secure the fish.

The same kind of net locally called as *Jaujal* is fixed on the steep side of some river and is raised by a complicated machinery of the bamboos. A frame of four strong bamboos supports the net which is placed with its descending edge towards the river. This frame also supports two slopping bamboos on which a man walks, who has one end of a long rope round his middle, while the other end passes over a bamboo, and raises the net when the man walks down and lowers it into the water when he walks of the slopping bamboos. Two men are employed to use this net.

The fishermen also use another kind of net somewhat of a similar type and which would appear better fitted for the large machine already described. This net is locally called as *Parangani*. It is of a square form, a good deal bagged in the centre. Its angles are fastened to the ends of two bamboo bars that cross each other at right angles in the centre which is suspended from the end of a bamboo lever, the other end of which rests against the bank where the fisher sits. He lowers and raises his bet by means of a rope that is fastened to the far end of the lever. This net is used chiefly by poor farmers and labourers.

In the Brahmaputra and other big rivers and lakes, the casting net is used by the fishermen. The casting nets are of various sizes and are commonly thrown from the shoulder either from the shore or from a boat. In these nets the mesh is usually small, and the sinkers are often merely earthen rings baked by the potters, but iron rings are also used for the purpose. Fishermen also use reins of different names and sizes.

Power and Water

Strategy so far adopted for irrigation development in the state was to mainly provide supplemental irrigation for kharif crops and also pre-kharif and rabi. The state has of late been ravaged by successive floods almost every year causing extensive damage to the kharif which is the main crop. A total of 4,54,426 hectare of irrigation potential have been created so far. Two major, five medium and 1,278 minor irrigation schemes have been completed in 1992-93. The total installed capacity of power generation in Assam is 514.4 mw. Up to 1992-93, 21,481 villages of the state were electrified. An ambitious gas cracker project and a few more thermal power plants are going to be set up in Assam by utilising the abundant natural gas available in the state.

Transportation

Roads: National highways are of 2,253 km and State highways 1,898 km PWD and other roads constitute a total length of 22,272 km. Assam State Transport Corporation (ASTC) operates nearly 6,00 different services covering a total length of over 1.16 lakh km. Private transport operators handle both passengers and goods traffic inside the state and at interstate levels as well.

Railways: Railway link connecting Assam with the rest of India was established in 1950. At present, the length of the railway track in Assam is 2482.59 km comprising both metre gauge and broad gauge lines. The extension of broad-gauge line from Guwahati to Dibrugarh has been completed and the Naranarayana Setu, the third bridge over the Brahmputra at Jogighopa Pancharatra was opened in 1998. The extension of broad-gauge line from Guwahati to Dibrugarh has been completed and the Naranarayana Setu, the third bridge over the Brahmaputra at Jogighopa Pancharatna was opened in 1998. There are a number of long distance passenger trains connecting Guwahati with the rest of the country.

Aviation: There are six civil airports in the state operating regular air services. These are Borjhar (Guwahati), Salonibari (Tezpur), Mohanbari (Dibrugarh), Lilabari (Lakhimpur), Kumbhigram (Silchar) and Rowriah (Jorhat).

Festivals: Assam has an exclusive range of colourful festivals. Bihu is the chief festival celebrated on three occasions. Rangali Bihu or Bohag Bihu marks the advent of the cropping season and ushers in the new year, Bhogali Bihu of the harvest festival and Kangali or Kati Bihu of lean period.

Bihus are popular agricultural festivals. Vaishnavites observe birth and death anniversaries of prominent Vaishnava saints through day-long singing of hymns and staging of bhaonas (theatrical performances in traditional style). Ambubachi in Sakta shrines and Sivaratri in Siva temples are observed by most people.

Sivaratri mela at Umananda and other places in Siva temples, Askastami mela, Rash mela, Parasuram mela, Ambubachi mela, Durga Puja are the other religious festivals. Population of Assam is a mosaic of different tribes like Bodo Kacharis, Rabhas, Karbi, Mishing, Deuri, Chutias, Dimasas, Hmars, Lalungs, etc. They have their own festivals. Some of them are: Bathow, Kheraipuja, Rajni Gobra, Ali-ai-Ligang, Po-rag Bahagiya Visu, Baiskhu, etc.

9

Polity

Importance of the State

Foundation and Development

The word Assam is derived from Sanskrit Asom meaning peerless, judged by her exquisite natural beauty, cultural richness and human wealth. Assam has a rich legacy of culture and civilization behind her. Being the homeland of different races of men: Austric, Mongolian, Dravidian and Aryan that came to dwell in her hills and valleys at different times, since remote antiquity, she has developed a composite culture of variegated colour.

Assam during the epic period was known as Pragjyotisha and later as Kamarupa: Naraka's son Bhagadutta took part in Kurukshetra war. The earliest epigraphic reference to the Kingdom of Kamarupa is found in Allahabad pillar inscription of Samudragupta. Kamarupa is mentioned as a Pratyanta or frontier state outside the Gupta Empire but with friendly and subordinate relation to it. Hiuen Tsang, Chinese scholar pilgrim who visited Kamarupa in about 743 AD on an invitation of its monarch Kumar Bhaskar Varman, left a record of the Kingdom he called *Kamolupa*. Kamarupa also figured in the writings of Arab historian Alberuni in the 11th century. Thus since the epic period down to the 12th century AD, the eastern frontier kingdom was known throughout Arya Varta both as Pragjyotisha and Kamarupa and Kings called themselves 'Lord of Pragjyotisha.' Advent of the Ahoms across eastern hills in 1228 AD was the turning point in Assam history. They ruled Assam up to 1826. Burmese entered through eastern borders and overran the territory at a time when court intrigues and dissensions were sapping the vitality of the Ahom royalty. The British appeared on the scene and by the Treaty of Yandabu in 1826, Burmese ceded Assam to the British.

Political System

In Assam the legislature consists of only one house — the Legislative Assembly. The system of government in the state of Assam closely resembles that of the union. The executive consists of the Governor and Council of Ministers with the Chief Minister as its head. The Governor of the State is appointed by the President of India for a term of five years and holds office during his pleasure.

The Council of Ministers, with the Chief Minister at the head aids and advises the Governor in the exercise of his functions except in so far as he is by or under the Constitution required to exercise his functions or any of them in his discretion.

The Chief Minister is appointed by the Governor, who also appoints other Ministers on the advice of the Chief Minister. The Council of Ministers is collectively responsible to the Legislative Assembly of the state.

Formation of State

Bill for Reorganisation: The Constitution (Twenty-second Amendment) Bill, 1968, has a definite purpose; the purpose is to reorganise the present State of Assam. The political contents of the Bill are too vivid and too evident.

This Bill somehow or other does not reflect the spirit of the declaration made on September 11, 1968 by the Home Minister. But, at the same time, there is the political aspect of the problem. If this Bill to reorganise the state of Assam is accepted, there would be a process of disintegration in the country. The seeds of disintegration are inherent in the very body of this Bill.

This matter was raised before the States Reorganisation Commission also. The Commission rejected this idea altogether because the Commission knew the psychology of the people, of some of these people, to have a separate State so that they may rule to their own advantage. Therefore, the Commission rejected that idea of a separate State in Assam as not feasible and it put down its heavy foot on the dismemberment of Uttar Pradesh also. We must not forget the basic fact that Assam is a border State and it is of strategic importance. We must not also forget the fact that after the armed aggression by China in 1962 and by Pakistan in 1965 — and because these armed aggressions failed — these two countries are now interested in sabotaging the life in Assam by encouraging the fissiparous tendencies within the state and also by encouraging the Naga and Mizo hostiles with arms and ammunition.

Governance of the State

The State of Manipur was given the status of 'C' category in 1950 as provided in the First Schedule of the Indian Constitution. In 1971, the Parliament enacted the Northeastern Areas (Reorganisation) Act which went into effect in 1972. This resulted into the creation of three new States, i.e. Manipur, Meghalaya and Tripura and the two Union Territories of Mizoram and Arunachal Pradesh.

The Indian Constitution is federal in structure with strong unitary features. It defines and demarcates the areas and jurisdiction of the Union and its component units. In our federal system the Central Government is the dominant partner enjoying various types of powers, over-riding in nature, over the states including the power to issue directives and to ensure their implementation. Above all, Part XVIII of the Constitution on Emergency. Provisions confers upon the Central Government the power virtually to convert the Union into a unitary state.

Yet the states occupy a vital role in the governmental system in the country. The vigour and competence with which the State Governments function are of crucial importance for the efficiency and effectiveness of administration in the country. The responsibility for the execution of planned programmes rests mainly with the states and most subjects, which constitute the ingredients of development administration, are within their exclusive jurisdiction.

In addition, even in the execution of the Union Government's projects and programmes the states are involved at several points. State Governments also act in many cases as agents of the Union Government assisting the latter in the discharge of its functions. Again, it is only at the state level that people's participation in government and administration can become a reality and it is with this end in view that the Constitution has provided for a system of local self government (Article 40). It follows therefore, that the state hold the Key to the nation's progress on economic and social fronts, in other words, to the realisation of socialist State.

The states, however, vary considerably, in terms of their size, population, resources — physical, economic and manpower — in terms both of quantity and quality, political, social and cultural development and quality of their administrative machinery. This constitutes a major difficulty in a description of the state administrative system.

The State administration may be described under the following sections:

- Headquarters organisation-secretariat, and executive agencies.
- Territorial divisions and district administration.
- Special agencies such as state Public Service Commission.
- State Service and their training.
- Statutory autonomous bodies and public corporation.
- Local Self-government.

The system of government in the state closely resembles that of the Union. The executive authority of the state is vested formally in the Governor, corresponding to the

President of the Union, while the real executive authority in the states lies in the Chief Minister Corresponding to the Prime Minister of India. The State has a Council of Ministers, a State legislature, a High Court. It has been truly said that the State Government is a miniature model of the Union Government within its own jurisdiction.

The State executive consists if the Governor and the Council of Ministers with the Chief Minister at its head. The executive power of the state is vested in the Governor and all executive actions of the government of the state are formally taken in his name. The Governor has to act on the advice of the Council of Ministers, except is so far as he is required under the Constitution to exercise his powers in his discretion. Such powers, as specifically stated in the Constitution, relate to certain matters concerning the administration of the Tribal areas including that of Manipur.

As in the case of all the other States of the country, the Chief Minister is appointed by the Governor, who also appoints the ministers on his advice. The Council of Ministers is collectively responsible to the legislative assembly of the state. The position of the Chief Minister is unique. He is incomparably the first and the pre-eminent in the Council of Ministers. In fact, he constitutes the linchpin of the ministerial organisation. He is the power, to guide, direct, control and coordinate the activities of other Ministers and to discipline them when occasion arises. He combines in himself the four roles of the leader of the party in power, the leader of the House with some exceptions, the leader of the government, and the political head of the services. The discharge of his multifarious functions together with the fact that the task and responsibilities of government have immeasurably increased throw up to Chief Minister a variety of complex and important work which must be disposed of expeditiously.

Duties of the Governor

Every bill shall be submitted to the Governor. In giving his assent, the Governor shall act on the advice of the Chief Minister of Assam who will consult the Tribal Ministers of his Council of Ministers as well as the Chief Executive Councillor of the autonomous areas concerned.

In the matter of an appeal affecting minority interests, the Governor will be the appellate authority.

In appointing the ministers from the hill areas the Chief Minister will consult the members of the Assam Legislative Assembly representing the hill areas as well as the Chief Executive Councillors as a matter of convention.

Mehta Committee Suggestions: The assessment of the Mehta Committee recommendations indicate that it favours the balanced solution; while conceding the maximum possible autonomy to the hill areas, it has not opposed the autonomous statehood. The Assam Chief Minister Mr. Bimla Prashad Chaliha along with the state Congress Party supported the Mehta Committee recommendations and pressed for its earliest implementation. However, the APHLC rejected the Mehta Committee recommendations as it is contrary to their demand of separate Hill State. The APHLC insists on 13 January, 1967 statement of the Union Home Ministry, which has been opposed by Assam Chief Minister and his Government. The Chief Minister has warned that the division of the state would not be accepted in any circumstances. The autonomous hill state will divide the frontier state.

Though Mehta Committee recommendations were welcomed by the Assam Government as a solution, the Central Government hesitates to implement it due to the opposition from the APHLC. The Union Cabinet is also divided over the issue. The Prime Minister's statement at Guwahati on 28 December, 1967 that "Mehta Plan cannot provide solution to hills problems", confirmed the view of the Central Government that it was not willing to accept the Mehta Committee recommendations. The Prime Minister said: "If anybody does not want to live with Assam would it be proper to keep them in Assam against their wishes?" There was a great resentment against the Prime Minister's remark. The Executive Committee of the Assam Pradesh Congress was of the unanimous view that a solution should be found on the basis of Mehta Committee recommendations. Mr. B. C. Bhagwati, Pradesh Congress President said that Prime Minister's statement at Guwahati on 28 December, 1967 has created a great resentment not only in the Congress Party but also among the general public of the state.

A state-wide resentment was displayed on 13 January, 1968, the Ist anniversary of the Union Home Ministry's announcement on 13 January, 1967 that the state of Assam would be reorganised on the basis of a federal plan with two or more units independent of each other. While it was "the Assam unity day", the effigies of some of the Union Ministers were burnt in the public meeting in protest against her (Prime Minister's) statement at Guwahati on 28 December, 1967. At Guwahati the processionists carried placards bearing "Down with Federal Plan", "No more vivisection of Assam", "Lachit Sena Zindabad", "Youths of Assam will not tolerate the Prime Minister's prejudicial views", etc. The strike was observed also in the other parts of the state such as Jorhat, Nalbare, etc. The Indian Youth Congress also opposed the federal plan for Assam.

In a resolution in January 1968 at Hyderabad the IYC adopted a resolution which said: "The National Council viewed with grave concern the recent political development in Assam, as it is a state having a strategic position from the point of defence and unity of the country. It felt that the unity and solidarity of the people of Assam is the necessity of the time and any encouraging or fissiparous tendencies will certainly threaten the integrity of the nation. Unfortunately, a section of the opportunists is trying to divide the state into small independent units which will ultimately destroy the unity of the people of Assam.

The incidents of the 26 January, 1968 has raised the serious question whether unity will be preserved in Assam. The burning of the National Flag, the slogan of "Assam for

Assamese", the destruction of much public and private property is a great challenge to the unity of Assam and the country as a whole. The reasons for not implementing the Mehta Committee recommendations are not known. The APHLC is insisting that the Prime Minister should fulfil her promise which she gave to hill area people on 28 December, 1967 at Guwahati. Later on when there was great resentment in Assam over the Prime Minister's statement at Guwahati on 28 December, 1967, she modified her statement by saying that what she meant was that final decision has not been taken on Assam Reorganisation.

The 13 January, 1967, statement of the Union Home Ministry was also responsible for making the problem more vexed. The APHLC wants no less than a separate Hill State, which is completely unacceptable to the Assam Government.

Role of September Decision

The Central Government took the final decision on Assam reorganisation as the Home Minister had assured in the Parliament that the final decision would be taken on 12 September, 1968. According to the new decision the Union Government has decided to constitute an autonomous hill state within the state of Assam. It will consist of Garo, and Jowari (Jaintia) hill districts, in the first instance. Law and order will remain with the parent state. There was a mixed reaction over the Central Government's decision on Assam Reorganisation. Jan Sangh Chief A. B. Vajpayee commented: "Disintegration of Assam has begun with the centre's decision. Fissiparous forces were bound to gain strength in the region". Describing the government step as *"ad hoc"*, Mr. Vajpayee said that the Centre could have undertaken reorganisation of the entire east zone keeping in view the democratic aspirations of the people and the security of the region.

Mr. Hem Barua, MP (PSP) said that the Centre's decision to carve out an autonomous Hill State in Assam "can be experimented with as a measure of concerted living and harmonious relations between the different sections of the people of Assam". He said that "seeds of disintegration are inherent" in the proposal which according to him, was compromise arrangement. Mr. K. C. Barua, President of the "All-Assam Committee to oppose Disintegration of Assam" which spearheaded last year's movement against federal proposal said: "Though I am not happy with the proposal, it should be given fair trial. In Guwahati the Centre's decision evoked a favourable reaction among political parties in the valley district. They considered the proposal as a modification of the Mehta Committee recommendations and took it to mean final rejection of the idea of complete separation of hill areas.

The All Party Hill Leaders' Conference announced on 15 October at Tura its acceptance of the Centre's proposals for an autonomous area within the state of Assam, comprising the Garo and Khasi Hills. Shillong will continue to be the Capital of Assam. It will also be the headquarters of the substate for the time being. Meghalaya (the abode of clouds) has been used in some official documents for the new substate. The APHLC decided to give a fair trial to the proposal and claimed that this policy was in consonance with the consensus at public meetings held since 20 September in the two districts in this connection. The resolution of acceptance, emphasised, however that while trying out the proposals the APHLC would continue its efforts for a completely separate hill district of Assam. The Conference also appointed a Committee to convey to the Government of India what it called the shortcomings and anomalies of the present proposals.

The direct action movement for the formation of a separate state will continue to be in abeyance although volunteers would still be trained and organised for such a movement. The proposals, which have been accepted by the APHLC have also received support from all other political parties in the plains, except the SSP which have five members in the Assam Assembly. The two hill districts — the Garo and the United Khasi and Jaintia Hills — will be a substate within Assam with their own Legislature and Ministers.

Execution of the Plan

The Lok Sabha passed the Constitution (22nd Amendment) Bill on April 15, 1969, to pave the way for the reorganisation of Assam with the creation of an autonomous hill state. (When the Bill becomes law, with the approval of the state as required, it is hoped that the government will bring forth another bill to embody the decision on the reorganisation of Assam).

Though the Assam reorganisation plan is being implemented, and though the APHLC has accepted it in order to give it a fair trial, it is doubtful if the step would prove a harbinger of regional peace and would be conducive to national integration. Rather the probability is that the step would encourage other regions in India to make similar demands. Though the Home Minister Mr. Chavan, assured the House that "We do not want to have a large number of smaller states" because that would be the beginning of disintegration, some of the supporters for the Bill made it clear that they wanted to follow the precedent elsewhere also. For example, Prof. N. G. Ranga spoke of Telengana, while Prof. Hiren Mukherjee spoke approvingly of an autonomous Gorkha-speaking substate of Darjeeling in West Bengal.

The Assam precedent would give an impetus to movements for an "autonomous Jharkhand in Bihar," an "autonomous Telengana and an autonomous Rayalaseema in Andhra," an "autonomous Saurashtra in Gujarat," an "autonomous Vidharbha in Maharashtra," an "autonomous Darjeeling in West Bengal," and in that way would open the floodgate of disintegration. Shri Barua pointed out that within weeks of the announcement by the Home Minister about the reorganisation of Assam in January, 1967, Nepalese settlers in Shillong were driven out and their houses were burnt.

The States Reorganisation Commission knew the psychology of some people to rule States to their own advantage and at the cost of other people, and had rejected such demands. In the case of Assam, moreover, the real aim of the APHLC seems to be to achieve an autonomous substate in the first instance and then a sovereign state outside India. It is necessary that such type of tinkering with the territories of India should be put a halt to.

Secretary's Responsibilities

The three essential components of the State Government are the Minister, the Secretary, and the executive head. The most important function of the Minister is to decide the policy, of the Secretary to provide the material on which to reach such decisions and to oversee the implementation of such decisions and of the executive head to carry the decision into effect. The first two functionaries, i.e. the Minister and the Secretary are served by the secretariat organisation, which is nothing but a conglomeration of a number of administrative departments. Significantly, the secretariat works as a single unit with collective responsibility as in the case of the Council of Ministers. Secretaries, thus, are Secretaries to the State Government and not to any individual Minister.

Thus, the state level administration and management functions are entrusted to two agencies, viz., the secretariat and heads of executive departments. The secretariat's primary responsibility is to assist the Ministers, while the primary duty of the heads of executive departments is the, implementation of the decisions of the government through the field agencies under their control. The head of the secretariat in every state is the Chief Secretary. He is always in charge of the General Administration Department, which forms part of the portfolio of the Chief Minister himself. But his control extends to other departments of the secretariat as well.

Departments of Implementation

The work relating to the initiation and formulation of policies of the government requires decentralisation of executive direction and the establishment of field agencies. For the most part of the substantive work handled by the state secretariat, therefore, there exist executive departments, varying in size and powers, which are responsible for providing executive direction required in the implementation of policy laid down by the administrative departments to which they are attached. These executive departments serve as repository of technical opinion and advise the secretariat departments on technical aspects of questions dealt with by them. Below then are found field agencies or establishments responsible for detailed execution of the policies and programme laid down above. Powers of the head of a department, both administrative and financial, are defined in financial rules, the civil service rules, the budget manual and other codes.

After becoming a full-fledged state, there has taken place a large extension and addition in the departments, partly due to the breaking up of large departments and partly due to creation of new ones. The Table gives the names of departments along with the designation of their heads.

The above table shows clearly that there is no common nomenclature for all the executive agencies nor a common designation for their heads. It is true that in theory the departments are free in their internal working and for this purpose adequate administrative and financial authority is vested in them, but as subordinate agencies they have to submit periodic or and *ad hoc* report on their activities to their superiors.

Various Executive Agencies

	Executive Agency	Designation of Head
1.	Accounts and Treasuries	Director of Accounts and Treasuries Directorate.
2.	Agriculture Department	Director of Agriculture.
3.	Animal husbandry Department	Director of animal husbandry.
4.	Archives and Historical Documents Department	Director of Archives and Historical Documents.
5.	Ayurved Directorate	Directorate of Ayurved.
6.	Buildings and Communication Dept. (Executive)	Chief Engineer (Buildings and Communication.
7.	Charity Department	Charity Commissioner.
8.	Cooperative Department	Registrar of Cooperative Societies.
9.	Dairy Development Department	Dairy Development Commissioner
10.	Education/Public Instruction Directorate/Department	Director of Education/Public Instruction.
11.	Employment Directorate	Director of Employment.
12.	Excise Department	Director of Excise/Excise Commissioner.
13.	Fisheries Department	Director of Fisheries
14.	Food and Civil Supplies Department	Director of Food and Civil Supplies/Supply Commissioner
15.	Forest Department	Chief Conservator of Forests.
16.	Geology and Mining Directorate	Director of Geology and Mining.
17.	Government Printing and Stationery	Director of Govt. Printing and Stationery.
18.	Housing Department	Housing Commissioner.
19.	Industries Directorate	Directorate of Industries.
20.	Information and Publicity	Director of Information and Publicity.
21.	Irrigation and Power Dept.	Chief Engineer (Irrigation).
22.	Jail Department	Inspector-General of Prison.
23.	Judicial Department	Advocate/General/Registrar, High Court.
24.	Land Records office	Director of Land Records.
25.	Language Directorate	Director of Languages
26.	Labour Department	Labour Commissioner
27.	Medical Services Dept. General	Director of Medical Services/ Surgeon
28.	Motor Vehicle & Transport Dept.	Director of Transport.
29.	Planning and Development Department	Development Commissioner.
30.	Police Department	Inspector General of Police.
31.	Public Health Department	Director of Public Health.
32.	Registration Department	Registrar/Registrar General.
33.	Sales Tax Department	Sales Tax Commissioner.
34.	Settlement officer	Settlement Commissioner.
35.	Social and Harijan Welfare Directorate	Directorate of Social and Harijan welfare.
36.	Technical Education Department	Director of Technical Education.
37.	Tourism Directorate	Director of Tourism.
38.	Town Planning Department	Director Town Planning.

Urban Governance

In Assam all the three types of urban local bodies exist. There is only one Municipal Corporation Guwahati, the capital city which has a separate Act, i.e., the Guwahati Municipal Corporation Act, 1969. The other two types, i.e., Nagar Panchayats or Town Committees and the Municipal Boards are governed by the Assam Municipal Act, 1956.

Town Committee

The State Government by notification declares the specified transitional area, a notified area, to be termed as 'Small Town'. For each of such notified areas a Town Committee is formed. It consists of such number of members as may be fixed by the State Government from time to time.

In notified areas the State Government may impose any tax which could have been imposed therein, if such areas were a municipality; apply or adopt for the assessment and recovery of any tax; arrange for the due expenditure of the proceeds of taxes and of other funds; and extend provisions of the Municipal Act subject to certain restrictions and modifications as the State Government may think fit.

Constitution of Municipal Board: Each municipality has a body of commissioners designated as Municipal Board. It consists of:

- *Elected Commissioners:* Not less than ten but not more than 30;
- *Appointed Members:* The State Government may appoint persons having special knowledge or experience in Municipal Administration;
- *Ex-Officio Members:* (a) MPs and MLAs, (b) Chairman of Wards Committee. The Appointed Members have the right to attend and speak at all meetings but do not have the right to vote.

Reservation: In every municipality seats are reserved:

- for the Scheduled Castes and Scheduled Tribes in proportion of their population to the total population;
- one-third of the seats to the women belonging to the Scheduled Castes and Scheduled Tribes;
- one-third of seats for the women.

Eligibility for Election

A person is not eligible for election as Commissioner if such person is not entitled to vote at the election of Commissioners, or has been adjudged by a competent court to be of unsound mind or an uncertified bankrupt or an undischarged insolvent or has, during the four years immediately preceding the election, been convicted of an offence or imprisonment for an offence involving moral turpitude or served any portion of a sentence or has been ordered by court to furnish security for good behaviour or has been declared by notification to be disqualified for employment in the public service or during the four years immediately preceding the election been debarred from practising as a legal practitioner or is a salaried servant of Government or is an employee of any Local Authority or is in arrear for more than three months, on the date of submission of nomination paper, of any dues to the municipality, or he is so disqualified for the purposes of elections to the State Legislature.

Resignation and Removal of Commissioners: A Commissioner may resign by writing under his hand addressed to the Chairman and thereupon he is deemed to have vacated the office. The Chairman forthwith informs the Deputy Commissioner or the Subdivisional Officer of the resignation and also informs the next meeting of the Municipal Board or Town Committee.

The State Government may remove any elected Commissioner on the following grounds: misconduct in the discharge of his duties, if removal is recommended by a resolution of the Board passed at a special meeting and supported by votes of not less than two-thirds of the whole number of Commissioners or if he ceases to reside within the municipality continuously for a period of twelve months or if he refuses to act or becomes incapable of acting as a Commissioner or if he has been declared by the State Government by notification to have violated his oath or affirmation to allegiance or if without an excuse, sufficient in the opinion of the State Government, he absents himself from four consecutive meetings of the Board or if, being a legal practitioner, he appears against the Board before any court in his professional capacity in any case instituted by or against the Board or if the becomes disabled in view of other qualifications or if he knowingly acquires or continues to hold without the permission in writing of the State Government, directly or indirectly, or by a partner, any share or interest in any contract, or employment with, by or on behalf of the Board or if he is in arrears of any kind of dues to the municipality after a bill or a notice has been duly served upon him. The State Government may, after consultation with the Board remove any Commissioner if his continuance is dangerous to the public peace or order or likely to bring the administration of Board into contempt. However, no Commissioner can be removed unless he has been given an opportunity of showing cause against the order of removal. Such a removed person is not eligible for election or re-election without the consent of the State Government.

The Commissioners

A Commissioner becomes disqualified to continue in office if he, without the written permission of the State Government, Directly or indirectly, has any share or interest in any contract, lease, sale or purchase of land or any agreement, or holds office of profit under it.

A Commissioner cannot vote on any matter affecting his own conduct or pecuniary interest or on any question which regards exclusively the assessment of himself or the valuation of any property in respect of which he is directly or indirectly interested or of any property of or for which he is a manager or agent for his liability to any tax.

Chairman and Vice-Chairman: At the first meeting of the Board, called at the instance of the Deputy Commissioner or the Subdivisional Officer, the Commissioners elect one from amongst themselves for the post of Chairman. The election is subject to the approval of the State Government. The Commissioners at the same meeting or at a subsequent meeting, elect one of them as Vice-Chairman.

The first meeting is held on the date fixed by the Deputy Commissioner or the Subdivisional Officer. Whenever he considers necessary, he may vary the date. The date fixed for the meeting is notified in the Official Gazette, at least 15 clear days before the meeting. The Deputy Commissioner or the Subdivisional Officer sends copies of the notification fixing the date to the members at least seven days before meeting is held. The Magistrate appoints a member of the Board to preside at the meeting.

The President first makes the oath or affirmation himself and then administers the oath to the other members present whether there is quorum or not. In case of quorum the meeting proceeds to elect or requests the State Government to appoint a Chairman. If the quorum is not present or if the first meeting proves infructuous, the meeting stands adjourned to some future date to be appointed by the Magistrate, who causes at least three days notice of the adjourned meeting to be given to the members. The members present at the adjourned meeting form a quorum whatever may be their number and be competent to elect a Chairman.

Any member may nominate any member before the noon of the day preceding the date fixed for the meeting. The President reads out to the Board the names of the members who have been duly nominated together with those of their proposers and seconders. The election is held by Board. Where more than two candidates have been nominated and at the first ballot no candidate obtains more votes than the aggregate votes obtained by the other candidates, the candidate who has obtained the smallest number of votes is excluded and balloting is proceeded until one candidate obtains more votes than the remaining candidate or, than the aggregate votes of the remaining candidates. Where at any ballot, any of three or more candidates obtain equal votes and one of them has to be excluded, the determination of the candidate to be excluded is made by drawing of lots.

If the Commissioners fail to elect a Chairman or a Vice-Chairman, the State Government appoints by name one of the Commissioners to be Chairman or Vice Chairman or directs the Deputy Commissioner or the Subdivisional Officer to fix another date for the purpose of elections. In that case, the government may appoint a government official to be Chairman or Vice-Chairman.

Whenever the offices of both the Chairman and the Vice-Chairman are vacant in any Board, the State Government can appoint any one from amongst the Commissioners, as the Chairman to hold office, as such temporarily, till a Chairman is elected. Every Chairman and every Vice-Chairman holds office from the date of his election to the date of election of the Chairman after the next general election.

The Board at a meeting, may grant leave of absence to its Chairman or Vice-Chairman, for a period not exceeding three months in any one year. If a Chairman or Vice-Chairman overstays his leave beyond three months, he is deemed to have vacated his office and the acting person continues to act for him till the vacancy is filled up by a fresh election at the next meeting of the Board.

For filling of casual vacancy in the office of the Chairman and Vice-Chairman, in case of vacancy in the office of the Chairman, the Vice-Chairman, and in the case of vacancy in the office of Vice-Chairman, the Chairman can call a meeting to complete the election within 45 days of the occurrence of the vacancy. If the Chairman or the Vice-Chairman fails to call the meeting, the Deputy Commissioner or the Subdivisional Officer can call the meeting.

A meeting for election of the Chairman is presided over by the Vice-Chairman, unless he is himself a candidate for election or for other reasons intimates to the Deputy Commissioner or the Subdivisional Officer in writing about his inability to preside. In such an event, any Commissioner who is not a candidate for the office of the Chairman may be nominated by the Deputy Commissioner or the Subdivisional Officer to preside over.

Resignation and Removal of Chairman and Vice-Chairman : An elected Chairman may resign by laying notice in writing of his intention to do so before the Board at a meeting with intimation to the District Magistrate and the Commissioner of the Division. He ceases to hold office on laying such notice.

A Vice-Chairman may resign by writing under his hand addressed to the Chairman and thereupon he deems to have vacated the office. The Chairman forthwith informs the Deputy Commissioner or the Subdivisional Officer of the resignation and also informs the next meeting of the Board or Committee.

The State Government after giving an opportunity to explain may remove the Chairman or Vice-Chairman from his office if he is persistently omitting or refusing to carry out or disobeying the provisions or lawful orders or he becomes incapable of so acting or is declared insolvent or is convicted for any offence involving moral turpitude.

Powers of Chairman: For the transaction of business the Chairman exercises all the powers vested by the Act in the Board. He may in cases of emergency direct the execution of any work or doing of any act and the immediate execution or doing of any work, which is necessary for the service or safety of the public, and may direct that the expense incurred, be paid from the municipal fund. He forthwith reports the action taken and the reasons therefore to the Board at next meeting.

The Chairman may delegate to the Vice-Chairman all or any of the duties and powers and may at any time withdraw or modify it. During the vacancy in the office of Vice-Chairman or in the absence of Vice-Chairman on leave or otherwise, the Chairman may, by an order in writing, delegate any of his functions to any Commissioner till the Vice-Chairman resumes office or a new Vice-Chairman is elected or appointed. Every such order is communicated to the Municipal Board at the next meeting.

Duties of Vice-Chairman: The Vice-Chairman performs any of the duties and exercises any of the powers of the Chairman during a vacancy in the office of the Chairman or temporary absence of the Chairman. He performs any duty and exercises any powers delegated to him.

Allowances: The Chairman and Vice-Chairman may, if Board thinks fit, receive conveyance allowances out of the municipal fund. Such allowances are subject to the approval of the State Government. The Commissioners are not paid from municipal fund any salary or remuneration but may be allowed travelling allowance when admissible.

Election Petition

The validity of an election can be questioned by an unsuccessful candidate or person qualified to vote at the election at any time within 21 days after the date of declaration of the result of election. Such an election petition is filed before the District Judge of the district within which the election has been or should have been held.

The petitioner is required to deposit one hundred rupees in Court as security for the costs. The Deputy Commissioner or the Subdivisional Officer may also be authorised by the State Government to receive election petition on behalf of the District Judge for transmission to him.

The District Judge or any judicial officer subordinate to him and not below the rank of Subordinate Judge may, after holding enquiry pass an order confirming or amending the declared result or setting the election aside.

An appeal lies to the District Judge from any decision or order of a Subordinate Judge. A decision or order of the District Judge is final. If the Judge sets aside an election he may declare any person by whom a corrupt practice has been committed, to be disqualified from being a candidate for election for a period not exceeding five years from the date of decision, and the Judge's decision is final.

Committees: The Board at a meeting may appoint committees to assist it in the discharge of any specific duties or class of duties devolving upon it. It may delegate to any such committee all or any of its powers, or withdraw all, or any of such powers necessary for the purpose of rendering assistance. Each committee consists of Commissioners and of residents with special qualifications appointed by the Board at its meeting. The number of Commissioners is not less than two-thirds of the whole number of members of the committee. All questions connected with the removal or resignation of Commissioners from committee are settled by the Board at a meeting. The proceedings of committee are subject to confirmation by the Board at a meeting.

Joint Committee: Any Municipal Board may join with other Local Authorities or with any cantonment authority or with more than one such authorities. A joint committee consists of not more than two Commissioners/members from each of such bodies.

Conduct of Business: The Commissioners meet for the transaction of business at their office, at least once in every month and as often as a meeting is called by the Chairman or in his absence by the Vice-Chairman. If there be no business to be laid before the Commissioners at any monthly meeting, the Chairman instead of calling the meeting gives notice of the fact to each Commissioner, three days before the date which is appointed for the monthly meeting. The Chairman or in his absence the Vice-Chairman may call a special meeting whenever he thinks fit and can call one on a requisition signed by not less than three of the Commissioners. If the Chairman or the Vice-Chairman fails to call a special meeting within twenty days after a requisition is made, the meeting may be called by the persons who signed the requisition.

The Chairman or in his absence the Vice-Chairman presides at every meeting. In the absence of both, the Commissioners choose one of them to preside. A member duly elected at the meeting presides, if the resolution relates to the simultaneous removal of both the Chairman and the Vice-Chairman. All questions at a meeting are determined by a majority of votes of the Commissioners present. In the case of equality of votes, on any question other than the election of the Chairman or the Vice-Chairman, the President has a second vote. In the case of equality of votes in the election of Chairman, Vice-Chairman or President, the determination is made by the drawal of lots.

Minutes of the proceedings of all meetings are entered into a book and are signed by the President of the meeting. It is published in prescribed manner and is open to the inspection of the tax-payers at all reasonable times and without charge. A copy of the minutes is forthwith forwarded by the Board to the Deputy Commissioner and the Commissioner of the Division and another copy is submitted to the State Government. The minutes are laid before the next meeting for confirmation and are also signed by the President if the same are correctly entered.

Quorum: No business is transacted at any meeting unless it has been called by the Chairman or Vice-Chairman or by persons signing a requisition, nor unless a quorum is present.

In the case of disposal of subjects relating to scale of establishment and salaries, the framing of by-laws, the annual budget estimates, the appointment or fixing of the pay or allowance of a paid Secretary, Engineer, Water Works Superintendent, Health Officer, Assessor or Executive Officer, imposition of taxes, fees and tolls, the election of Chairman or Vice-Chairman, the raising of loan, the subject of a meeting specially convened the quorum should be one-half of the total number of Commissioners. For all other business, the quorum should be one-third of the total Commissioners.

If at any meeting, the quorum is not present, the meeting is adjourned to some future day appointed by the President and three days notice is given. The Commissioners present at adjourned meeting for transaction of business other than specifically mentioned earlier, form the quorum, whatever their number may be.

Establishment: The Board determines and appoints the establishment employed by it and fixes the salaries and allowances to such establishment. The Chairman makes all appointments if the monthly salary of the office does not carry more than fifty rupees or a salary rising by periodical increments to more than fifty rupees. The Chairman may remove such persons for efficiency, negligence of duty or misconduct. The appointment of any officer whose pay is wholly or partly conducted by the State Government cannot be created or abolished without the sanction of the State Government. Every nomination or dismissal from any such appointment is subject to confirmation by State Government.

In case of disciplinary action, every employee has the right of appeal to the Board, from the orders of the Chairman or the Vice-Chairman. In case of orders involving dismissal or removal of officers not liable to be dismissed or removed by the Chairman or Vice-Chairman, an appeal to the Local Self-government Department may be filed.

The Board at a special meeting by a resolution supported by two-thirds of the Commissioners present, makes regulations in respect of officers and employees on its staff for fixing the amount and nature of the security to be furnished, regulating the grant of leave, leave allowances and other allowances and regulating conduct and generally laying down conditions of service.

The State Government may require the board to appoint such Health Officers, Sanitary Inspectors, other public health establishments and Water Works Superintendent as it considers necessary or to employ such officers of Government as Health Officers, Sanitary Inspectors and Water Works Superintendent.

A Board may appoint an Executive Officer with the approval of the State Government. The State, Government may, if it finds that any particular Board should have an Executive Officer and the said Board does not make such an appointment, appoint any person as such officer, in respect of that particular Board. In either case, the salary of the officer and other charges are charged on Municipal Fund unless the State Government agrees to bear the same or any portion thereof.

The State Government can make rules regarding the appointment, salaries, conditions of service, powers, duties and functions of the Executive Officer and other relevant matters connected therewith and also providing that no disciplinary action can be taken against the Executive Officer, except with the approval of the State Government.

Budget: The Board has to pass the annual budget estimates for the next financial year before the end of the year. When the Board fails to pass the budget due to causes beyond its control, the Director of Municipal Administration may, on application by the Board, give such extension of time as he may deem necessary to pass the budget. The budget passed in the meeting of the Board has to be approved by the Director of Municipal Administration before 31st March of the preceding year.

Contracts: The Board may enter into and perform any contract necessary for it. Every contract made by or on behalf of the Board in respect of any sum exceeding Rs. 500 is sanctioned by the Board at a meeting and be in writing and signed by at least two of the members, one of whom should be the Chairman or the Vice-Chairman and is sealed with the common seal of the Board. Unless so executed a contract is not binding on the Board.

Municipal Fund: Each Board has a Municipal Fund vested in it. The balance standing at the credit, all sums received by or on behalf of the Board, all sums received as loan raised by the Board and such sums as the State Government may sanction as grants-in-aid are placed to its credit. The Board sets apart and applies annually out of Municipal Fund, firstly the charges of its own establishment and secondly, payment of loan and interest, thirdly, the liabilities and obligations arising from the trust legally imposed upon or accepted by the Board and fourthly, the expenses on paupers, lunatics and lepers who are inhabitants of the municipalities and are sent to public asylums. The Municipal Fund may be applied for other services and provisions within the municipality and with the sanction of the Director of Municipal Administration outside the municipality.

Without the prior sanction of the State Government the municipal fund can not be spent for contesting the case filed against the Chairman, Vice-Chairman, Commissioner or any other person in authority. All orders for payment of money from the Municipal Fund for a sum not above Rs. 5,000 are signed by the Chairman or a Vice-Chairman. All other orders for larger sums are signed by both the Chairman and Vice-Chairman or by one of them and another Commissioner of the Board.

Municipal Property: All public roads including the soil, pavements, stones and other materials thereof, and all drains, bridges, trees, erection, materials, implements; all public streams, channels, water-courses, springs, tanks, reservoirs, cisterns, wells, aquaducts, conduits, tunnels, pipes, pumps and other water-works; all public sewers and drains, and all works, materials and things appertaining thereto; all sewage, rubbish and offensive matter collected by the Board from roads, latrines, sewers, cesspools and other places; all public lamps, lampposts and apparatus connected therewith or appertaining thereto, all public gates, markets, slaughter houses and public buildings which have been constructed or are maintained out of the Municipal Fund; and all land or other property transferred to the Board or acquired by gift, purchase or otherwise vest in the Board and be under its direction, management and control.

Municipal Taxation: The municipality may impose within limits the following taxes, fees and tolls, or any of them:

- a tax on holdings assessed on their annual value, payable by the owners;
- a water tax payable by the owner or occupier on the annual value of buildings;
- a lighting tax, payable by the owner or occupier, on the annual value of holdings;
- a latrine tax, payable by the owner or occupier, on the annual value of holdings;
- a drainage tax, payable by the owner, where a system of drainage has been introduced;
- a tax on private markets payable by the owner;
- licence fee on carts, carriages and animals used for riding or burden;
- a fee on the registration of dogs and cattle;

- a fee on boats moored within the municipality;
- tolls on bridges;
- a betterment fee on holding in any area of which value has been increased due to improvement schemes completed at Board's cost;
- fees for setting up and maintenance of fire brigade;
- fees for conducting, at the cost of the Board, any scheme of social service for the improvement of public health;
- license fee on boats;
- with the sanction of the State Government any other tax, tolls, rate or fee.

The taxes on holdings and private markets cannot be imposed in respect of the same premises. All municipal taxes in respect of Government holdings are payable by the government themselves and not by occupiers. A rebate of not less than Rupees fifty per annum of the latrine tax on a holding is allowed if the holding is provided with sanitary type latrines and does not contain any service latrine.

Annual Value: The assessor after making necessary enquiries determines the valuation of all holdings and enters the same in the valuation list. For preparing the list, the assessor by notice requires the owners/occupiers of all holdings to furnish him within fifteen days, with returns of the rent of annual value and a description of the holdings. The assessor at any time between sunrise and sunset may enter, inspect and measure any holding. Whoever refuses or fails to furnish return or knowingly furnishes a false or incorrect return or description is liable to a fine not exceeding twenty rupees and to further fine not exceeding five rupees for each day during which he omits to furnish a true and correct return. A person obstructing, hindering or preventing the assessor appointed by the Board from entering or inspecting or measuring any holdings is liable to a fine not exceeding Rs. 200.

In the case of a holding with a building used or occupied for the residence by the owner himself, the annual value is lessened by 25 per cent. In case of Government buildings the annual value is deemed to be an amount which may be equal to but not exceeding six per cent of the cost of erection of the building, in addition to a reasonable ground rent of the land comprised in the holding.

A person dissatisfied with the amount assessed upon him or with the valuation or assessment, may apply to the Board to review the amount of assessment of valuation or to exempt him from the assessment of tax. Every such application is heard and determined by a committee of not more than five members or by an officer not below such rank as the State Government determines. Services of such an officer is obtained by the Board and to whom the Board at a meeting delegates the powers and functions of the committee in this behalf.

The Chairman or Vice-Chairman is one of the members of the committee and other members are appointed from among the members by the Board at a meeting. However, no member takes part in hearing or determining an application from the ward in which he resides or the ward he represents. An application cannot be heard or determined by the committee unless at least three members including the Chairman or the Vice-Chairman are present.

The committee records in brief the reasons for its actions. The decision of the committee or of a majority of the members; or of the officer of Government, is final. An application received after the expiration of one month from the date of publication of the notice relating to the list or after the expiry of fifteen days from the date of service of first notice of demand for payment, is not entertained.

Recovery of Taxes: If any tax payable by owner remains unpaid after the notice has been duly served, and owner is not a resident within the municipality or his place of abode is not known, the amount is recovered from the occupier. Within three months after a tax is due, a notice of demand duly signed by the Chairman, Vice-Chairman or an officer duly authorised, is served upon the concerned person. If any person fails within fifteen days of the notice, either to pay the tax or give sufficient reasons for not paying the amount, the arrear with costs is collected by attachment or sale of any movable property of the defaulter within six months. A penalty at the rate of 3-1/8 per cent is charged on the arrears with effect from the sixteenth day following the date of service of notice.

Powers and Functions: The Board has mandatory as well as discretionary functions to perform.

Mandatory Functions: The Board is Bilged:

- to establish, maintain and manage cattle pounds;
- to regulate line of buildings on public roads and drains;
- to prohibit erection or alteration of building without sanction;
- to permit construction of latrines and urinals which are to be properly enclosed;
- to provide for the removal of sewage, rubbish and offensive matters;
- to cause its local area to be inspected frequently to ascertain what nuisances exist calling for abatement and to serve notice to remove the same;
- to regulate the establishment of factories, workshops, offensive trades, etc.;
- to permit cinemas, dramatic performances, circuses, etc.;
- to prohibit private kilns;
- to undertake public health works and to formulate and execute schemes to eradicate mosquitoes and to prevent their breeding;

- to provide for the registration of births and deaths;
- to provide or arrange for the provision of a sufficient supply of drinking water for inhabitants and for other domestic or non-domestic purposes;
- to provide and maintain a sufficient and satisfactory system of public drains.

Discretionary Functions and Powers: The Board may:

- close a public road for repairs;
- prohibit use of public road by class of animals or vehicles;
- require repair of roads and drains and to declare such roads and drains public;
- remove obstructions or encroachments in or on public roads;
- require cleansing or lime washing of buildings;
- require fencing of building in dangerous state;
- require owners to pull down ruins;
- provide for drinking water, bathing places, etc.;
- require owners to improve bad drainage;
- require owners to clear noxious vegetation;
- require unwholesome tanks or private premises to be cleansed or drained;
- prohibit excavations;
- provide and maintain in sufficient number and in proper situation public latrines and urinals;
- inspect latrines, privies, cesspools, urinals;
- require owner or occupier to repair latrine;
- alter any latrine made contrary to orders;
- prohibit use of unlicensed markets;
- order the use of slaughter houses and the carrying on of dangerous and offensive trades to be discontinued;
- establish and maintain fire brigades;
- provide places to be used as burial or burning grounds;
- grant licenses for the sale at burning grounds of fuel and other articles used for cremation of dead bodies;
- prohibit the keeping of the brothels and the residence of a public prostitute;
- establish, maintain and manage of any school other than basic schools;

- establish and maintain dispensaries, hospitals, chest clinics, asylums and places for the reception of sick or destitutes or contribute towards the cost of the establishment and maintenance of such institutions;
- establish and maintain maternity homes and child welfare centres.

Control on Public Health

The Director of Health Services recommends for adoption by the Municipal Boards, such measures as are necessary for improving the public health administration or for safeguarding the public health. The District or the Subdivisional Medical Officer of Health regularly but not less than twice a year inspects the different areas and sends reports to the Municipal Boards and to the Director of Health Services. The Board considers the notes at its meeting and submits a report of the action taken or proposed to be taken to the State Government through the Director of Health Services. The Assistant Director of Public Health also makes inspections and submits reports.

Rules and By-laws: The State Government may make rules for the purposes of carrying out the provisions of the Act. All rules are subject to the condition of previous publication. The Board at a meeting specially convened for the purpose may frame by-laws. The Commissioners of a municipality wholly or in part situated in a hilly tract may at meeting make additional by-laws for regulating or prohibiting the cutting or destroying of trees or shrub, or the making of excavations or removal of oil or quarrying. The power of framing by-laws by the Board is subject to the previous publication. No such by-law come into force until it has been confirmed by the State Government and published thereafter. The State Government may cancel their confirmation and thereupon the by-laws cease to have effect. The Board, at a special meeting convened for the purpose, may make subsidiary rules as to business and affairs. These subsidiary rules are subject to the sanction of the State Government and thereafter its publication brings them in force.

Political Parties

Political parties play a significant role in the elections under the parliamentary system. However, there is no law at present regarding the formation and functioning of political parties in India. The fundamental right to form association which is guaranteed by article 19 of the Constitution remains unfettered although under clause (4) of the article it is open to Parliament to make a law imposing reasonable restrictions on the exercise of the right in the interest of sovereignty and integrity of India of public order or morality. The Representative of the People Acts also do not refer to political parties even from an electoral point of view except in regard to one or two ancillary matters. It therefore, becomes necessary for the Election Commission to evolve a procedure by which it could "recognise" political parties for the limited purpose of regulating the allotment of exclusive election symbols to those which were so "recognised." According to Election Commission's order (1968):

"A political party shall be treated as a recognised political party in a state, and only if either the conditions specified, fulfilled by that party and not otherwise, that is to say:

- That such party:
  - has been engaged in political activity for a continuous period of five years; and
  - has, at the general election in that state to the House of the People or as the case may be, to the legislative assembly, for the time being in existence and functioning, returned either (i) at least one member to the House of the People for every twenty five members of that house or any fraction of that number elected from that state; or (ii) at least one member of the legislative assembly of that state for every thirty members of that assembly or any fraction of that number.

- That the total number of valid votes polled by all the contesting candidates set up by such party at the general election in the state to the House of the People, or as the case may be to the legislative assembly, for the time being in existence and functioning excluding the valid votes polled by all the contesting candidates in a constituency as has not been elected and has not polled at least one-twelfth of the total number of valid votes polled by all the contesting candidates in that constituency is not less than four per cent of the total number of valid votes polled by all the contesting candidates at such general election in the state (including the valid votes of those contesting candidate who have forfeited their deposits)."

In the state of Assam, following are the National and Regional Political Parties at present.

Major Parties

- Communist Party of India.
- Communist Party of India (Marxist).
- Indian National Congress.
- Bhartiya Janta Party.
- Janta Dal.

Small Parties

- Plains Tribal, Council of Assam.
- Asom Gana Parishad.
- United Minorities Front, Assam.

10

Tourism

- -

The State of Assam is well endowed with aesthetic scenery and offers enough sights for the national and international tourists. Its mighty rivers, evergreen forests, invigorating climate, religious places, national parks and cultural milieu are unparalleled in the country.

The Valley of Brahmaputra-river was once littered with a plethora of temples, brick-built as well as stone built as the existing ruins scattered all over the state. Most of these temples belong to the 13th century. The existing temples belong to the posterior to this dividing line. The climatic conditions of the Brahmaputra Valley, which is extremely humid and the perennial flood, frequent earthquakes and heavy rainfall are responsible for the destruction of the pre-thirteenth century temples.

The temples of the medieval period constructed with the patronage of the Koch, the Ahom and the Kachari Royal dynasties are the places of interest for the pilgrims and international tourists. Some of the important religious places which the places of interest have been described in the following paras.

General Aspects

Assam dominated by the mighty Brahmaputra River, is renowned for its tea, rich flora and fauna, the world famous one horned rhinoceros and other rare species of wildlife on the verge of extinction. It has mild winters and warm summers. Summer is from March to June and monsoon from July to August. November to February is winter. Best season to visit Assam is February to May.

Assam has drawn people from diverse cultures and races in different points of time. The main tourist attraction is the Kaziranga National Park, home of India's rare one-horned rhinoceros. The city of Guwahati is another place in the state which has in its vicinity numerous ancient Hindu temples and is reputed as an ideal place to explore the whole Northeastern Region. The capital Dispur is very near to Guwahati. Other tourist destinations in the state are Hajo, Digboi, Manas, Jorhat, Tezpur, Sibsagar, Dibrugarh, etc.

Tourist Attractions

Guwahati derives its name from two words, *guwa* (meaning betel nut) and *hati* (little market). It is customary for anyone on his first visit to this city to visit the Kamakhya Temple, dedicated to the Mother Goddess. The importance of the temple is second only to the mighty Brahmaputra, the river with an undeniable presence in the town. In the centre of the city, with the magnificent backdrop of the Brahmaputra and atop Sukleshwar Hill stands the Janardan Temple. West of Chitrachal Hill is the unique temple of Navagraha dedicated to the nine planets. Once a renowned seat of astronomy and astrology, it is possibly the reason for Guwahati's earlier name of Pragjyotishpur. The Assam State Zoo is not very far from the heart of the city. The undulating topography and the three-side open enclosures make the zoo almost like a natural habitat for the animals. Guwahati has several museums, repositories of the state's ancient culture and tradition. The Assam State Museum is the largest amongst them and has sections on epigraphy, sculpture, natural history, crafts, ethnography, and arms.

The mighty Ahoms reigned supreme for 600 years at Sibsagar, at a distance of 369 km from Guwahati, where the ruins of their temples and palaces still exist. Resurrected by the Archaeological Survey of India, these ruins provide an interesting insight into the past glory and splendour of Assam.

Kaziranga National Park, situated at a distance of 217 km from Guwahati, is one of the most picturesque wildlife parks in India. The natural habitat of the one-horned rhino, Kaziranga lies on the southern banks of the Brahmaputra River, North-East of the capital city. Originally established as a game reserve in 1908, which included specific portions of Assam's Sibsagar District, Kaziranga was declared a sanctuary in 1940 to counter excessive poaching. The park's original inhabitants — the rhino and the elephant being the most noticeable — now thrive in a serene environment to the sheer delight of nature lovers. Viewing wildlife at Kaziranga Park because of its vast open spaces, the presence of the mighty Brahmaputra, and adjoining Mikir hills makes a trip to Kaziranga a complete 'jungle' adventure.

Manas National Park (176 km from Guwahati), situated amidst the gentle slopes of the Himalayas, is the only tiger reserve of its kind in the entire region. The park covers a large part of Barpeta District in Assam and extend to the Royal Manas National Park in Bhutan. Apart from the growing population of tigers, Manas is also home to the rare golden langur, the hispid hare, the pigmy hog, the one-horned rhinoceros, and at least twenty other species of animals and birds that are listed as highly endangered. Manas derives its name from the Goddess Manasa. The forest stretches beyond Indian territory to the Himalayan Kingdom of Bhutan, with the crystal waters of the Manas River demarcating the international border.

Pabitora, a small wildlife sanctuary, 60 km from Guwahati is also worth a visit. Rhino and various species of deer abound here. Hajo, 32 km west of Guwahati, is a sacred place for Hindus, Muslims, and Buddhists. The town also boasts the Hayagriva Madhav Temple, accessible via a long stone stairway. At the foot of the stairway is a large pond inhabited by one of Hajo's oldest residents: a giant turtle. Hajo is also renowned for its bell-metalwork.

Tourist Points

Important places of tourist interest in and around Guwahati are Kamakhya temple, Umananda (Peacock Island), Navagraha (Temple of nine planets), Basistha Ashram, Gandhi Mandap, State zoo, State museum, Sukresewar temple, Geeta Mandir, Madan Kamdev temple and Saraighat Bridge. In rest of the state-Kaziranga National Park (famous for one-horned rhino), means (tiger project), Sibsagar (Shiva temple), Tezpur (scenic beauty), Bhalukpung (angling), Haflong (health resort) with nearby Jatinga Hills, Majali (largest river island in the world), Chandubi Lake (Picnic spot), Hajo (meeting of Buddhism, Hinduism and Islam), Batadrava (with place of great Vaishnav Saint Sancardev) and Sualkuchi (famous for silk industry) are worth visiting.

Tea Tourism

Tea, the miracle drink originated in China and was declared a health drink 5,000 years back, by Chinese Emperor, Chen Nungmore. While boiling water below a Tea tree, a leaf fell into his pot and the King found the drink refreshing. Chinese believe it to be Divine Healer.

Tea has been known to the tribes of Assam for a long time, who are of the oriental stock and took Tea as a health drink. Local Tribal Singpho chief, Bisa Gaum helped C A Bruce in 1823, to discover Assam variety of Tea Plant 'Camelia Sinesis Var Assamica'.

The discovery of Tea and its commercial production changed Assam's economy. Vast wild forest lands were transformed into beautiful smiling Tea Gardens, along the Brahmaputra and Barak valleys.

Today, Assam produces 400 million kg of Tea, per year. Tea is an integral part of the hospitable Assamese people. They start their day with a cup of the brew and end it with one in the evening. Guests are welcomed by offering a cup of tea. The traditional way to taste the brew is in Bell Matel Bowl called "Banbati"

Most of Assams Tea Gardens are located in the Upper Assam and Southern Barak Valley Region. One can enjoy the silence of tea plantation, a sight for sore eyes. With acres of Lush greenery, a drive through the Tea Estates is also a unmatched experience.

The Heritage Tea Bungalows of Assam are century old Tea executives houses. Still retaining its ancient glory and portraying tales of opulent lifestyle of the Tea Executives.

Early in the morning you can gain a mind cooling experience while walking through the greens of tea plantation, which a concrete world can not offer. Meet tea garden manager to know, to ask and to see anything related to tea plantation. You can visit tea workers Basti to admire their simple style of living and to get to the rhythm of their 'Jhumur' dance. Toklai Tea Research Station is the place to head incase you want to know or do your own research on Tea. The place is near the city of Jorhat, Tea Capital of Assam.

The Leaves For Long Lasting Freshness

What better way to start your day than sipping on a hot cup of Assam tea, freshly picked right from your backyard. Don't bother to think, there are none. It is a black tea named after the region it is produced in. Assam tea is famous for its briskness, malty flavour, and strong colour. Assam tea are not confined to Indian subcontinent but are exported to all parts of the world as breakfast tea. In Assam, tea is generally produced in the low lying areas unlike Darjeeling and Nilgiris which are grown at higher altitudes. Today, Assam produces more than half of the tea produced in India which is sold through the auction centre in Guwahati. Around 400 million kg of tea comes from Assam tea gardens. Most of the tea gardens are situated in Jorhat which is called the 'Tea Capital of The World'.

The Start of Tea

People of Bodo Tribe are known to have brought tea into Assam. But they produced for themselves and hardly took it outside Assam. The plant was then discovered by Robert Bruce in 1823. After his death, his brother sent the seeds to British Government in Calcutta. They learned the method of tea production from china and employed it in Assam. They brought many workers from Bihar and Orissa who permanently settled here and came to be known as Assamese. For better results, local variety was crossed with Chinese tea plant to give rise to the present Assam tea.

Tea Gardens

Forest have been cleared to give way for some breathtaking tea gardens to come up. There are more than 850 tea estates and more than 2,500 tea gardens in Assam that cover thousands of acres of land. For their scenic beauty, calm and peaceful environment, tea gardens have become a great tourist attraction in Assam. While exploring Assam, many times you will cross though tea gardens sprawling for miles on both sides of the road. You can stop at one of these places and get a glimpse of life in tea gardens. You will see workers watering the plants and picking tea leaves from them. Workers picking leaves, have a huge basket on their back, in which they put all the leaves collected.

Wildlife Tourism

Nature has ungrudgingly blessed Assam with an abundance of scenic grandeur. A wealth of rarest and near-extinct species of wildlife are found in Assam, which includes

Golden Langur, Hoolock Gibbon, Pygmy Hog, Hispid Hare, White-Winged Woodduck, Tiger, Clouded Leopard, Swamp Deer, Gangetic Dolphins, etc. Moreover, During season flock of resident and migratory birds make Assam their natural habitats.

There are many wildlife sanctuaries and National Parks in Assam that make this state a unique habitat for the wild beasts. Among the well known are Kaziranga National Park (famous for sheltering the rare one horned rhino), Manas National Park (famous for the largest tiger reserve and a World Heritage Site), Orang National Park (a mini Kaziranga), Sonai Rupai Wildlife Sanctuary, Pabha or Milroy Sanctuary, Dibru-Saikhowa National Park (a biosphere reserve), Laokhowa Wildlife Sanctuary, Pobitora Wildlife Sanctuary, Namber Wildlife Sanctuary, Pani Dihing Wildlife Sanctuary, Barandi Game Reserve.

Kaziranga National Park

The first and the oldest National Park in Assam situated in Golaghat District, is a World Heritage site. Spread over an area of 430 sq km, Kaziranga National Park is the natural home of the one-horned Indian rhinoceros and a number of other exotic animals like Asian Elephant, Indian bison, Swamp Deer, Samber, Hog Deer, Sloth Bear, Tiger, Leopard cat, Jungle cat, Hog badger, Capped Langur, Hollock gibbons and numerous bird species.

Kaziranga is 217 km from Guwahati and 96 km from Jorhat by road. The nearest airport is Rowriah (Jorhat). Tourists can either fly to Jorhat or can go by surface to Kaziranga from Guwahati. Best season to visit is from November to April.

Dibru-Saikhowa National Park

The Dibru-Saikhowa National Park lies in Dibrugarh and Tinsukia District. It is 13 km from Tinsukia Town, which is 483 km from Guwahati. It covers an area of about 340 sq km. Of seven parts in the park one part is wetland and the rest are mainly glass land and dense forest.

The main attractions of Dibru-Saikhowa National Park are the semi-wild horse (Feral) and the white-Winged wood duck. Other animals are Leopard, Clouded Leopard, Elephant, Sambar, Slow Lories, Asiatic Buffaloes, Capped Langur, Gangetic Dolphin, Indian Wild Dog, etc. More than 250 varieties of local and migratory birds are also found here.

Orang (Rajiv Gandhi) National Park

Covering an area of 78.81 sq km Orang National Park is a miniature Kaziranga. It is situated in the north bank of river Brahmaputra. Sixty per cent of the sanctuary is grassland. The animals to be seen in this park are the great Indian one-horned Rhinoceros, Elephant, Tiger, Sambar, Barking Deer, Pangolin, Hog Deer, Civet cat, Otters, and Wild Boar, etc. Various species of birds including Pelican, Cormorant, Graylag Goose, Large whistling Teal, Great Adjutant stork, King fisher, King vulture have also found this park as their ideal habitat.

Manas National Park

Manas is a magnificent National Parks well known for Tigers. It is situated on the bank of the river Manas at the foothills of the Himalayas. It is also a World heritage site. Besides Tiger you can also see Rhino, Elephants, Wild buffalo, Langoor, deer and hundreds of other species of animals and birds in this park.

Manas is 176 km from Guwahati by road. The nearest airport is Lokapriya Gopinath Bordoloi International Airport at Guwahati. The nearest railhead is Barpeta Road Station that is 40 km away from Manas. Season to visit is from November to April.

Pobitora Wildlife Sanctuary

Pobitora Wildlife Sanctuary is major wildlife stock, situated in Morigaon district of Assam, the Northeastern State of India. Covering an area of 38.8 sq km, the Pobitora Wildlife Sanctuary is about 50 km from Guwahati, situated on the border of Nagaon and Kamrup District. Pobitora is mainly famous for its great Indian one horned Rhinoceros. Besides Rhinoceros the other animals are Asiatic Buffalo, Leopard, Wild bear, civet cat, etc. Assam Pobitora Wildlife Sanctuary is also home to more than 2,000 migratory birds and various reptiles.

Places of Interest

Umananda Hills

Situated in the midst of the Brahmaputra and just north of the D.C.'s office are three islets known as Karmanasa, Urvasi, and Umananda respectively. The only perennial communication to these islets is by boat.

All of the three islets bear archaeological evidences. A number of myths have been woven around them, thereby indicating their importance and antiquity. However, of these three islets, only, the Umananda is important as a centre of pilgrimage to the Hindus. The Urvasi islet, which contain bare traces of old temples and rock - cut images of the 10th/11th century AD, remains completely submerged in the turbulent Brahmaputra during monsoon. The hillock over which the temples of Umananda stand is mentioned in old records as the Bhasmachala and the British called it is Peacock Island. There are in all three temples on top of this hillock, of which two are situated within a massive boundary wall and the third one just outside the entrance to the enclosed area. The temples are respectively known as the Umananda, the Chandra Sekhra and the Haragauri, and all of them belong to the late medieval period.

Umananda is one of the finest spots of natural beauty and is considered one of the five great Panchatirthas around Guwahati. The Sivaratri, along with its fair, is the greatest festival of this place which attracts a huge crowd every year. Tezpur, the headquarters of the Sonitpur district, is reputed to be one of the earliest historical cities of the Brahmaputra valley. It is just on the north bank of the Brahmaputra and is about 180 kilometres east of Guwahati.

Tezpur is identified with Somitpur of the Epic fame. It is connected with the Naraka-Bana episode, which is indicative of struggle between the Sivas and-the Saktas. Certain places in and around the town carry legends pertaining to the love affair of Usha and Aniruddha (the nephew of Shri Krishna) which culminated in a battle between Bana, the Saivite King and Shrikrishna, resulting in the former's discomfiture and the union of the two lovers.

The undulating topography of Tezpur, criss-crossed with the dead courses of the turbulent Bharali, makes it one of the finest towns of the Brahmaputra Valley Interwoven with legends and virtually littered all over with remains of structural ruins of a glorious past, it still continues to attract people. Every temple or shrine in and around this ancient township, though is still thoroughly renovated and mutilated, has a link with the past history, however inflated and incredible it may appear, mixed as it is with myths and legend. The Bhairavi temple is situated on the eastern outskirt of the town and is very near to the Barnuni-pahar ruins. It occupies a small hill lying at the Confluence of the Brahmaputra and the old course of the Bharali. The site, because of its higher elevation, dominates a wide area around it and across the Brahmaputra.

The temple attracts a good number of daily visitors who hold it in high esteem as a Sakti Peetha. During the days of the Durga Puja every year, it witnesses a rush of tourists and visitors. The head of the first goat sacrificed on this occasions is ceremoniously thrown into the Brahmaputra, the nearest course of which to the Bhairavi hills is considered as the river Bharali itself because of its close connection with the Bhairavi legend, though in fact the real tributary flows now into the Brahmaputra, few kilometres east of the site. It is interesting to note that human sacrifice was once in vogue in this temple.

Sibsagar Shrine

Sandwiched between the two old Ahom capitals of Gargaon and Rangpur, 15 km away respectively, the modern town of Sibsagar and its periphery contain the most important groups of temples built by the Ahom royal dynasty, as well as secular buildings. During the British rule, the township constituted the administrative headquarters of the Sibsagar district. It is about 350 km east of Guwahati and is linked by State Transport and Private Bus Service with their day and night services.

Of the two erstwhile capitals of the Ahom period, the fortified capital-city of Gargaon contains a four storeyed Ahom palace, a spacious gable roofed magazine-house and evidence of some other buildings. Rangpur on the other hand contains a large brick-built four-storeyed palace known as Talatal-Ghar with a small domical temple a top, a big gable roofed magazine house and a few temples around. About a kilometre south of the Talatal-

Ghar is a very big tank, Jaisagar by name, On the north and west bank of which stand three major brick-built temples, the most famous of which is the Jai Dol or Shri Kesavarai Dol.

The town of Sibsagar has grown up with a very large 18th century tank as its nucleus, also known as Sibsagar. On the south bank of this tank stands a temple complex consisting of three structures (Sivadol, Visnudol, and Devide), brick ramparts with archways (now destroyed) and a long flight of steps.

Siva Dol

This is the tallest old structure in Assam now in existence. It is about 40 metres in height and consists of four axial chambers, such as the Garbhagriha, the Antarala, and two Mandaps, the last one being reconstructed in modern times. The Sivaratri is the biggest festival celebrated with fanfare in this temple when a huge crowd assembles and a big fair is held. The deity inside is a Svayambltu Siva Linga shaped out of a natural rock. There are Devi Dol, Visnu Dol, Jaisagar, Jai Dol, Durga Temple (Sibsagar), which are visited by thousands of pilgrimages and tourists.

Besides the temples, Vaishnavite shrines started by Shankardeva and his disciples in the 16th century onwards are numerous and unique feature of the religious life of the Assamese. These shrines called Satras (monasteries) are each in the charge of a gosain (preceptor). The four most important Satras are Auniati, Dakhinpat, Kuruabahi, and Garamur, situated in the island formed by the Brahmaputra and the Lohit called *Majuli*. Moreover, the most striking monument to the genius of Shankaradeva and his chief disciple Mahadeva is the Kirtanghar at Barpeta in Kamrup District which was the centre of their activity for many years. Spectacular and colourful boat races are held there every year on the anniversaries of the two saints.

Oldest Masjid

Panbari on the National Highway and about thirteen Kilometres east of Gaurivur in the Dhubri District, has the pride and privilege of holding the earliest extant Masjid of the state. The credit of its erection is given to Hussain Shah (AD 1493-1519), the Governor of Bengal, who after his annexation of Kochbehar and Western Assam, established his headquarters at Lalmati or Rangamati for the local people.

Gurudwara at Dhubri

Among the Gurdwaras of the state, the one at the southeast corner of Dhubri is known for its antiquity. Guru Teg Bahadur, the 9th Guru of the Sikhs, came with a Sikh regiment that constituted a component of the Imperial Mughal Army invading Assam under the overall command of the Mughal General, Raja Ram Singha during Emperor Aurungzeb's time. It is said that while encamping at Dhubri, the Sikh Guru was much fascinated by the scenic beauty of the area and desired to build a Gurudwara there. He directed every soul of his community to deposit a lump of earth each on the spot of his choice, which, on elating compliance, resulted in a mound, upon which the Gurudwara was erected. The birth and death anniversaries of Guru Nanak and his successors are celebrated here annually with due solemnity and ceremony.

National Park at Kaziranga

Situated in the Upper Assam Kaziranga is one of the most famous national parks of India. It is the home of the largest of all living species of the rhinoceros, the Rhinoceros Unicorn is, which was at one time on the verge of extinction. The number believed to have survived was put to about a dozen in the beginning of the century. Adoption of measures for protection and the conversion of the Kaziranga Forests into the National Park (the natural home, of the species) in the beginning of this century have yielded satisfactory results, the present number of the species being estimated at about 500. Poaching, however, continues, not because the animal's meat is delicious, but because its horn is believed to have powerful aphrodisiac properties. Kaziranga and other national parks and forests of Assam are full of herds of wild animals. Herds of elephants are common sight in Assam. Large numbers have been caught and trained to perform more or less, such tasks as are performed by jeeps in other parts of the country.

In these parks and forest are also found the Gaur or Indian bison. It is a huge animal, the larger, ones attaining the height of over six feet. Although the species is to be found in some other parts of India also, it is here that it reaches the fullest development. With its massive head and splendid curved horns, the Gaur is a picture of beauty and strength. Every year tourists visit the national parks and sanctuaries in all seasons in thousands of number. The forests of Assam abound in various kinds of monkeys, large and small animals, viz. tigers (same as the Royal Bengal), leopards, black panthers, golden cats, hundreds of species of birds and reptiles, especially crocodiles. This diversity of wildlife attracts tourists in Assam in large number.

Both for viewing and photographing the wildlife the most suitable places are the four wild-life sanctuaries-Kaziranga, Manas, Sonia-Rupa and Pabha. Assam offers great opportunities to the big game hunter as well as the small Shikaris. The marshy spots are good for bird-shooting. Many of the rivers provide excellent fishing. The months of January to March sanctuary is an angler's paradise. Other suitable spots are the Sankosh and Ai rivers in the Goalpara District and the Bharali river in the Darrang District.

In Assam tourism which is only of recent origin is constrained by the geological, and wet-weather conditions, especially during the summer season (May to October) in which heavy rains occur in the region. For the promotion of tourism the Government of India has approved the following two travel circuits in the state: (i) Guwahati-Kaziranga-Sibsagar travel circuit, and (ii) Guwahati-Manas travel circuit.

The State Government has also submitted a proposal for additional circuits: (i) Guwahati-Bhairabkunda Orang Bhaluking-Tezpur, (ii) Guwahati-Diphu-Haflong-Silchar. These circuits may be linked with Arunachal, Meghalaya, Manipur and Mizoram and will thus help the integrated development of tourism in the North-East Region of India.

The important places of tourist interest are Kamakhya Temple. Umananda (the Peacock Island), Basisthasram, Nabagarh Temple, Kaziranga National Park, Manas Tiger Project, Sibsagar, Haflong, Tezpur, Bhalukpong, Majuli (largest river island of the world), Batadrava (birth place of Shri Shankar Dev), Chandubo Lake, Hajo (meeting of three religions — Buddhism, Islam and Hinduism), Poamecca, and Sualkuchi.

The State of Assam has airports at Guwahati, Tezpur, Jorhat, North Lakhimpur, Silchar, Dibrugarh, and Lilabari, Vayudoot airlinks Dibrugarh, Guwahati, Jorhat, Lilabari, Silchar, and Tezpur with the rest of India.

Navagraha Devalaya Shrine

This temple of the nine planets stands on the Chitrachala hill on the north of the city. It is connected by a hilly road and is only a ten minutes' ride by motor vehicle from the heart of the city.

It is believed that from time immemorial astronomy was practised in Assam and Navagrha was its nerve centre. The word Pragjyotishapur, the ancient name of the city of Guwahati, bears testimony to this, the word meaning either 'City of Eastern Astronomy' or 'City of Ancient Astronomy.

The city contains its Garbhagriha, curiously, nine Siva Lingas representing the nine planets of the Hindu myth. The well-planned arrangement of the Lingas within the stone-pitched cella reminds one of its great antiquity. The temple is still held in high esteem by the Hindus who visit the temple all the year round to perform Graha-Puja. As can be surmised, the tradition of astrological studies in all its aspects is still a living on its premises, the making of horoscopes being one of these. The daily worship of the temple is run hereditarily by a class of astrologers. A yajna is performed in the precinct of the temple each year covering several days when a big crowd assembles here to witness it.

Kurma-Janardhana Shrine

Aswaklanta is a small hill perching on the north bank of the Brahmaputra. This area contains two brick temples of the medieval period known as Kurma-Janardhana and Anantasayi Visnu, both of which appear to have been built over the ruins of two earlier stone temples. Janmastami and Deul Utsava (Faguwa — the festival of colours) are the most important annual festivals of this place. On the occasion of Asoka-astami, this place witnesses a heavy rush of visitors and devotees for taking holy both in the Brahmaputra, as also for performing the annual Sraddha ceremony of their departed relation. On certain other occasions, such as Surya Grahana (Solar eclipse), Chamdra Grahana (Lunar eclipse), people assemble in crowds here for a holy dip (Snana).

Manikarneswar Shrine

Manikarneswar is the Northern most part of the city of Guwahati. As a place of pilgrimage, Manikarneswar appears to be one of the most important centres since the medieval period. It contained at stone temple of the early period over which the present dilapidated brick temple was constructed during the late medieval period. It happens to be the only twelve sided extent temple of the state. It is a Shiva Temple with a sunken Garbhagriha.

The location of the temple an the highest spot of the range of the hills has made the temple a rare spot of natural beauty from where a view of several temples in and around Guwahati including the scenic beauty of the Brahmaputra and a view of the city of Guwahati, can be enjoyed. The temple at present has lost its past popularity. The Siva-Ratri is the only great festival of the year here.

Kamakhya Shrine

Kamakhya is a temple town atop a 180 metre high hill known as the Nilanchala and is situated on the western part of the Greater Guwahati. It is connected with the foothills by three paths of yore from south, west and north respectively, the last one being partly contiguous to the river Brahmaputra. About 30 years back, a motorable road about five kilometres long had been constructed to reach the top from the foothills. Both bus and taxi service are available from the foothill to the top where the principal temple complex is located.

An interesting legend has been woven around the establishment of the Kamakhya Temple.

It is said that Naraka of Mithila captured this region from the Kiratas and took charge of the Kamakhya temple. The legend further has it that Naraka before long grew so bold as to ask for the hand of the Devi, to which the goddess consented on condition that he build road from the foothills to the top in one night, together with a temple and a tank. Naraka did his best and almost succeeded when the goddess, apprehensive of him inpending success, persuaded a cock to give his morning call, thereby indicating the break of dawn. The road or pathway on the which this legend centre still exists and is locally known as Kukura-Kata-Bat (Cock to cut road).

The Puranic records mention it as one of the fifty-one Pithas established over the discarded limbs of Sati, the spouse of Siva. It is considered the greatest centre of Shakti worship in Northeastern India. The Kamakhya temple and its neighbourhood record the earliest archaeological evidences of the state. The Umachala Rock Inscription on the eastern slope of the Nilachala hill dates back to the fifth century AD and is the earliest historical record discovered so far in the Brahmaputra Valley. Certain decorative carvings found in the precincts of the Kamakhya temple go back to the time of the Imperial Guptas.

Dirgheswari Shrine

It is in the eastern extreme of North Guwahati and is situated in a secluded place on a hill known in old records as the Sita Parvat, overlooking the Brahmaputra river. It can be approached by road. The name Dirgheswari has been derived from the long range of hills, of which only the eastern tip is occupied by the temple in question.

Thus the Devi is the goddess of Dirgha range of hills. Almost the entire portion of the hill in and around the temple is rocky. The brick built temple now in existence goes back to the time of the late medieval ruler Siva Singha (AD 1714-44). But evidences show that it contained another temple of an earlier period, over which the present temple was built.

The eastern and the southern slopes of the hill bear rock-cut sculptures and traces of temple foundation hew-out in rock, which go back to 10th century AD. The area of the temple being projected portion of a lengthy range of hills into the Brahmaputra, it dominates a natural view which covers a vast area of the Brahmaputra, including the Umananda group of islands, Manikar-newara temple, Sukreswara Temple, Kamakhya atop the Nilachala, etc.

The Dirgheswari is a Shakti Pith and is supposed to have housed one of eight yoginis accompanying Kamakhya Devi. Traditionally it is visited by the ardent followers. Now more tourists have started visiting this temple.

Bibliography

Abani, Kar, K. Bimal: *Geography of Assam,* Rajesh Publications, New Delhi, 2001.

Antrobus, H.A.: *A History of Assam Company,* Edinbrough, 1975.

Arun Chandan: *Political History of Assam,* Publication Board Assam, Guwahati, 1999.

Atulchandra Hazarika: *Kamarupa-Ratnamala,* Kamarupa Sahitya Parishada, Guwahati, 1973.

Banikanta Kakati: *Aspects of Early Assamese Literature,* Gauhati University, Gauhati, 1959.

Barpujari, H. K.: *Assam in the Days of the Company,* North Eastern Hill University Publications, Shillong, 1996.

Barua, B.K.: *Assamese, Indian Literature,* Prabhat Prakashan, Delhi, 1988.

Barua, H.N.: *Asamya Viyakaran,* Sibsagar, Meerut, 1873.

————: *Reflection on Assam-cum-Pakistan,* Calcutta, 1944.

Baruah, Sanjib: *India against itself: Assam and the Politics of Nationality,* Oxford University Press, New Delhi, 1999.

Bezbaroa, D.: *Asamya Bhasa aur Sahitya Buranji,* Jorhat, 1933.

Bhagabati, K. Abani and Kar, K. Bimal: *Geography of Assam,* Rajesh Publications, New Delhi, 2001.

Bhan, Susheela: *Impact of Ethnic Violence on Youth: A Study of Tribal-Nontribal Violence in Kokrajhar, Assam,* Shipra Publications, New Delhi, 1999.

Bhattacharyya, Hiranya Kumar: *The Silent Invasion: Assam Versus Infiltration,* Delhi: Spectrum Publications, Guwahati, 2001.

Bhuyan, A.C.: *Political History of Assam* Gauhati, 1980.

Bhuyan, Arun Chandan and De, Sibopada: *Political History of Assam,* Publication Board Assam, Guwahati, 1999.

Bimala Kanta Barua: *Ahom Lexicons,* Department of Historical and Antiquarian Studies in Assam, Gauhati, 1964.

Birendra Kumar Bhattacharyya: *b1924: Humour & Satire in Assamese Literature,* Sterling, New Delhi, 1982.

Birendranath Datta and Dilip Kumar Kalia: *Ciphum-Gumgam: Asamar Bhaiyamar Janajatiya Goshthisamuhar Git Pad,* Loka-sahityar Rahaghara Grantharaji, Granthapith, Guwahati, 1986.

Birinchi Kumar Barua: *A Cultural History of Assam,* Lawyer's Book Stall, Gauhati, 1969.

Bisweswar Hazarika: *Assamese Language,* Joya Prakashan, 1985.

Bordoloi, B. N. Thakur, G. C. and Sharmah, Saikia, M. C.: *Tribes of Assam Part- I,* Tribal Research Institute, Guwahati, 1987.

Bordoloi, B. N.: *The Dimasa Kacharis of Assam,* Tribal Research Institute, Assam, 1984.

Borpuzari, H.K.: *Assam: In the Days of Company,* Gauhati, 1964.

Bronson, Miles: *A Dictionary in Assamese and English,* American Baptist Mission Press, Sibsagar, 1867.

Brownrigg, H.S.: *Routes in Nepal, Bhutan, Sikkim, Tibet, Burma and between Assam and Burma,* Calcutta, 1878.

Buddhindranath Bhattacharyya: *1865-1945: The Pronouncing Anglo-Assamese Dictionary,* Lawyer's Book Stall, Gauhati, 1964.

Cantlie, Audrey: *Census of India 1961,* Manager of Publications, New Delhi, 1990.

Chatterjee, S.K.: *The Place of Assam in the History and Civilization of India,* Gauhati, 1955.

Dandinath Kalita: *1890-1955: Asam-sandhya,* Nalbari, 1975.

Das, Amiya Kumar: *Assam's Agony: A Socio-Economic and Political Analysis,* Lancers Publishers, New Delhi, 1982.

Das, H.P.: *Geography of Assam,* N.B.T., New Delhi, 1970.

Das, Kalyan: *Labour Contracts and Work Agreements in Tea Plantations of Assam,* V. V. Giri National Labour Institute, Noida, 2002.

Das, S. K.: *Spotlight on Assam,* Premier Book Service, Chanderpur, 1989.

Datta, P.S.: *Autonomy Movements in Assam,* Omsons Publications, New Delhi, 1993.

Dayarama Uwari: *Bodo Language Through English and Assamese,* Uwari, Gauhati, 1980.

Debi Prasanna Pattanayak: *A Controlled Historical Reconstruction of Oriya, Assamese, Bengali and Hindi,* University Microfilms, Ann Arbor, 1965.

Deka, Kanak Sen: *Assam's Crisis Myth and Reality,* Mittal Publications, New Delhi, 1993.

Dimbeswar Bora: *b1942: Nacaghara,* Granthalaya, Nagaon, Assam, 1980.

Dutta, Ajit Kumar: *Maniram Dewan and the Contemporary Assamese Society,* Published by the Author, Guwahati, 1990.

Dutta, K.N.: *Landmarks of the Freedom Struggle in Assam,* Gauhati, 1958.

Dutta, P.N. Baruah: *An Intensive Course in Assamese,* Central Institute of Indian Languages, Mysore, 1980.

E.N.: *All-India Centre,* by the International Book House, Bombay, 1941.

Gait, Edward: *A History of Assam,* Lawyers' Book Stall, Guwahati, 1925.

Ganggopadhyay, D. K.: *Revenue Administration in Assam,* Revenue Department, Government of Assam, Assam, 1990.

_____: *Revenue Administration in Assam,* Revenue Department, Government of Assam, Assam, 1990.

Ghose, Sumita: *Sanjoy's Assam: Diaries and Writings of Sanjoy Ghose,* Penguin Books, New Delhi, 1998.

Gohain, Hiren: *Assam: A Burning Question,* Spectrum Publications, Guwahati, 1985.

Gohain, U. N.: *Assam Under the Ahoms,* Spectrum Publications, Guwahati, 1942.

Gokhale, Nitin A.: *The Hot Brew: The Assam Tea Industry's most Turbulent Decade,* Spectrum Publications, Delhi, 1998.

Golap Chandra Barua: *Ahom-Assamese-English Dictionary,* Published under the Authority of the Assam Administration, Printed at the Baptist Mission Press, Calcutta, 1920.

Golockchandra Goswami: *An Introduction to Assamese Phonology,* Deccan College Postgraduate and Research Institute, Poona, 1966.

Gopalkrishnan, R.: *Research Priorities in North-East India: With Special Reference to Assam,* Regency Publication, New Delhi, 2001.

Goswani, H.: *Asamiya Bhasa,* Jorhat, 1972.

Guha, Amalendu: *Freedom Struggle and Electoral Politics in Assam, 1826-1947,* Sumit Pub., New Delhi, 1977.

Hamilton, F.: *An Account of Assam,* Gauhati, 1963.

Harichandra Bhattacharyya: *b1908: Origin and Development of the Assamese Drama and the Stage,* Barua Agency, Gauhati, 1964.

Hem Barua: *Assamese Literature,* National Book Trust, New Delhi, 1965.

Hunter, W. W.: *A Statistical Account of Assam,* Spectrum Publications, Guwahati, 1879.

Hussain, M.: *The Assam Movement: Class, Ideology and Identity,* Manak Publications Pvt. LTD. New Delhi, 1993.

Jacob, M.C.: *Forest Resources of Assam*, Shillong, 1940.

Jatindra Mohan Bhattacharjee: *b1908: Asamiya Puthira Talika Samanwaya*, Esiyatika Sosaiti, Calcutta, 1989.

Jatindranath Duwara: *Kabi Aru Kabi-Pratibha*, Students Emporium, Dibrugarh, 1988.

Jayakanta Gandhiya: *b1944: Huncari, Mukali Bihu, aru Bihunac*, Banalata, Dibrugarh, 1988.

Jnanadabhiram Borooah: *Folk Tales of Assam*, The Timber and Stores Agency, Howrah, 1916.

Jones T.: *Bengal (India) Correspondence Relating to Vernacular*, Returns Relating to Native Printing Presses and Publications, Calcutta, 1855.

Kakati, B.K.: *Assam, its Formation and Development*, Gauhati, 1938.

Kaliram Medhi: *Asamiya Byakarana aru Bhashatattwa*, Asama Prakasana Parishada, Guwahati, 1978.

——————: *Studies in the Vaisnava Literature & Culture of Assam*, Asom Sahitya Sabha, Jorhat, 1978.

Kalita: *1890-1955, Assamese: Poet and Dramatist*, Comprises Contributed Articles, 1990.

Kay S.P.: *An English-Mikir Vocabulary*, Printed at the Assam Secretariat Printing Office, Shillong, 1904.

Kesab Mahanta: *Asamiya Ramayani Sahitya*, Published by Bapacandra Mahanta and Kesada Mahanta, Jorhat, 1984.

Lahiri, R.M.: *An Annexation of Assam*, Calcutta, 1975.

Lakshminath Bezbarua: *1868-1938: Asamiya Bhasha Aru Sahitya*, ILRC, 1968.

Lila Gogoi: *The Buranjis, Historical Literature of Assam*, Omsons Publications, New Delhi, 1986.

Mahendra Bara: *The Evolution of the Assamese Script*, Asam Sahitya Sabha, Jorhat, 1981.

Mahendranath Dube: *b1942: Purvottara Bharatiya Bhashaom ke Sarvanama*, Sakti Prakasana, Varanasi, 1980.

Misra, Udayon: *The Periphery Strikes Back: Challenges to the Nation-State in Assam and Nagaalnd*, Indian Institute of Advanced Study, Shimla, 2000.

Moore, P. H.: *Twenty Years in Assam*, Omsons Publications, New Delhi, 1901.

Mukunda Madhava Sharma: *Assamese for All*, Asam Sahitya Sabha, Jorhat, 1963.

Murthy, T.S.: *Assamese: the Difficult Years*, New Delhi, 1983.

Nagen Saikiya: *Background of Modern Assamese Literature*, Omsons Publications, New Delhi, 1988.

Nakul Chandra Bhuyan: *1895-1968: Galpar Sarai,* Jorhat, 1962.

Naren Kalita: *A Descriptive Catalogue of Manuscripts Preserved at The Library of the Srimanta Sankaradeva Research Institute, Batadrava,* Srimanta Sankaradeva Research Institute Library, Batadrava, 1990.

Nirmal Probha Bardoloi: *Assamese Short Stories: An Anthology,* Vikash, New Delhi, 1982.

Padmeswar Gogoi: *b1907: Asamat Pracalita Pauranik Akhyanasamuhar Mul-Bicar,* Gogoi, Guwahati, 1971.

Paresh Chandra Deva Sarma: *Assamese Tutor,* Lawyer's Book Stall, Gauhati, 1962.

Parikshit Hazarika: *Asamiya Prawandha-Manjari,* Pancawatana Pharmma, Hauli, 1964.

Philip Richard Thornhagh Gurdon: *Some Assamese Proverbs,* The Assam Secretariat Printing Office, Shillong, 1896.

Pona Mahanta: *b1943: Western Influence on Modern Assamese Drama,* Mittal Publications, India, 1985.

Prabhat Chandra Sabhapandit: *Sociological Study of the Post-War Assamese Novel,* Omsons Publication, Guwahati, 1988.

Prafulla Chandra Barua: *Assamese Proverbs,* Lawyer's Book Stall, Gauhati, 1962.

Pranaw Jyoti Deka: *b1940: Jyoti Dwibhashik Abhidhan,* Pranawajyoti Deka, Guwahati, 1990.

Praphulladatta Goswami: *b1919: Ballads and Tales of Assam,* Gauhati University, Assam, 1960.

Purneswar Nath: *Dandinatha Kalita, Kriti aru Krititwa,* Tezpur Sahitya Sabha, Tezpur, 1990.

Rafiabadi, H. N.: *Assam From Agitation to Accord,* Genuine Publications & Media Pvt Ltd, New Delhi, 1988.

Rajendra Nath Hazarika: *Sahityalekha,* Published by Hazarika, Guwahati, 1975.

Ramacandra Bora: *b1923: Loka-Sahitya,* Lokayata Sodha Samsthana, Jodhapura, 1969.

Ratnakanta Barkakati: *1897-1962: Ratnakanta Barakakatir Gadya-Sambhar,* Lawyer's Book Stall, Guwahati, 1977.

Ratneswar Mahanta: *1864-1893: Ratneswara Mahanta Racanawali,* Asam Prakasan Parishad, Guwahati, 1977.

Robinson, W.: *A Descriptive Account of Assam,* Sanskaran Prakshan Delhi, 1975.

Saikia, M. C.: *Tribes of Assam,* Tribal Research Institute, Guwahati, 1987.

Saikia, Mrinal Kr.: *Assam Towards Islamisation,* Guwahati: 1995.

Sailen Bharali: *Adhunik Asamiya Sahitya,* New Book Stall, Guwahati, 1976.

Sanjayya: *Assam: A Crisis of Identity,* Spectrum Publications, Guwahati, 1980.

Sarma, B.: *Asamya Bhasa Sahityalai*, Missionary Sakalar Dan, Jorhat, 1982.

Satyendranath Sarma: *Assamese Literature*, Harrassowitz, Wiesbaden, 1976.

Shastri P.N.: *The Writers Workshop Handbook of Assamese Literature*, Writers Workshop, Calcutta, 1972.

Sidney Endle: *1840?-1907: Outline of the Kachari (Baro) Language as Spoken in District Darrang, Assam*, Printed at the Assam Secretariat Press, Shillong, 1884.

Singh, K. S.: *People of India: Assam*, Seagull Books, Calcutta, 2003.

Smith, W. C.: *The Ao Naga Tribe of Assam*, Mittal Publications, New Delhi, 2002.

Sukumar Barkath: *Hastibidyarnnara Sarasamgraha (English & Assamese)*, Publication Board, Assam, 1976.

Suryya Kumar Bhuyan: *Studies in the Literature of Assam*, Lawyer's Book Stall, Guwahati, 1962.

Sword, V.H.: *Baptist in Assam: a Century of Missionary Service*, Chicago, 1936.

Tarunram Phukan: *1877-1939: Tarunarama Phukana Racanawali*, Asam Prakasan Parishada, Guwahati, 1977.

Thakur, G. C.: *Tribes of Assam*, Tribal Research Institute, Guwahati, 1988.

Tilottoma: *Literature and Society in Assam*, Omsons Publications, Guwahati, 1987.

Trivedi, V. R.: *Important Events of Assam*, Omsons Publications, New Delhi, 1997.

Upendranath Goswami: *A Study on Kamrupi*, Dept. of Historical Antiquarian Studies, Government of Assam, Gauhati, 1970.

Wac, S.R.: *A Glimpse of Assam*, 1884.

William Barclay Brown: *An Outline Grammar of the Deori Chutiya, Language Spoken in Upper Assam with an Introduction, Illustrative Sentences and Short Vocabulary*, Printed at the Assam Secretariat Printing Office, Shillong, 1895.

Zehol, Lucy: *Tribes of Assam, Assam Institute of Research for Tribals and Scheduled Castes*, Guwahati, 1991.

Index

❑❑❑

www.ingramcontent.com/pod-product-compliance
Lightning Source LLC
Chambersburg PA
CBHW080759300326
41914CB00055B/949